A COMPANION TO THE
BRITISH COUNTRYSIDE

Foreword by Tony Soper

COLOUR LIBRARY BOOKS

CLB 1939
This edition published 1988 by Colour Library Books Ltd,
86 Epsom Road, Guildford, Surrey.
Original material © 1986–87, Marshall Cavendish Limited
This arrangement © 1988 Marshall Cavendish Limited
Prepared by Marshall Cavendish Books Limited
58 Old Compton Street, London W1V 5PA.

ISBN 0-86283-552-6

Phototypeset by Bookworm Typesetting, Manchester,
England

Printed and bound in Spain.

FOREWORD

I like to think that the British countryside starts right outside the kitchen window, and that it stretches without interruption all the way to the wild wood and the storm-wracked coast. And that's not too fanciful a notion, wherever you live, for the biological corridor carries life to every part of the land. I know that our countryside faces attacks on a wide front which threaten to change it for the worse, and there are any number of books, to say nothing of television programmes, which seek to expose the problems and redress the balance. But here is a book which sets out resolutely to look on the good side and to celebrate the astonishing variety of plants and animals which share our islands, and which, to its great credit, allows no truck with the contention that townies and countrymen are two different life forms. For it is abundantly true that bugs and birds, mammals and reptiles all find sympathetic havens in the vegetation and surroundings of built-up areas, as well as farmland and wilderness.

Gardens are good examples of potential wildlife habitats right on our doorsteps; good value because they provide a meeting-place for thrushes and blue-tits, hedgehogs and foxes, butterflies and moths. And the more native plants including standard trees as well as the mischievously-named 'weeds' there are, the greater the abundance of all kinds of life. As every bird-table enthusiast knows, there's a good deal of enjoyment to be had from managing your gardening in such a way that you can influence the visitors. Brazil nuts encourage nuthatches, suet is irresistible to great spotted woodpeckers. Great tits take to nestboxes like ducks to duckponds, and so on.

For those of us who like to revel in the companionship of these wild neighbours, this book satisfies a real need. For it breaks our surroundings down into comprehensible sections which lead gradually to our understanding of the whole. Britain is a small island surrounded by a lot of even smaller ones. But it offers splendid variety. You never need to travel far from home to explore all the different kinds of countryside displayed in this book. And you don't need to travel at all to enjoy the countryside around your own dwelling, even if it only runs to a windowbox and a peanut dispenser. Any opportunity to learn about the relationships between ourselves and the creatures which share our home range – including of course our own families – gives, I believe, an intense pleasure.

Tony Soper

CONTENTS

Introduction

Page 7

INTRODUCTION

Ecology, in the broadest sense, is about how living things relate to each other and their surroundings. Plants and animals, of course, never exist in isolation. They are linked in a vast network, a web which both connects all species and allows each individual a particular place of its own – a home. But as we speak of a home as being more than just bricks and mortar, so too the term wildlife habitat – the home of wild plants and creatures – includes the species themselves, just as much as their geographical setting.

With this in mind *A Companion to the British Countryside* explores habitats by observing how species live alongside each other and how they live as communities, typically based in certain places: they range, in our selection, from a mountain stream to a bleak heather moor, and from a town wasteland to a suburban garden. The book is arranged with the habitats grouped into four main sections – Towns and Villages, Lowland Britain, Upland Britain, and The Coast and Open Sea – to show where, characteristically, these habitats can be found in reality.

The sections are, however, by no means exclusive. Nature knows no hard and fast boundaries and certain habitats are not especially constrained by altitude, or indeed, by being either near, or remote from, the human-built environment. For instance our high, dense hedgerow packed with plant and animal species appears in the lowland section, because the lowlands are where such hedges typically can be found. But certain habitats are not so easily defined. Oak and beech woods commonly grow in the lowlands, as depicted here, but they can also arise in quite, high, hilly, regions. And conifer plantations, of course, are ubiquitous. They appear in many parts of the British isles, and their position in this book merely indicates their predominant location in the countryside.

On a smaller scale, many plants and animals do not confine their appearances to the habitats in which they find themselves in this Companion. Observers may find that the beetles and crickets seen At the Side of the Road, are also thriving at the bottom of the garden, and that, growing against all odds on the exposed, blustery habitat of a coastal headland, there are bluebells, and primroses – flowers more usually associated with the milder, protected environment of inland woods and copses.

In celebrating the immense variety of these islands this book would not be complete without a look at some very rare and some extremely common species or habitats. Our broad view of Britain therefore includes rare flora and fauna, such as corncockles and snow buntings surviving in small pockets of the countryside, and also many of the well-known species which share those habitats most frequented by people, whether it is the centre of town, the local canal, or one of our popular and well-visited commons.

Tony Soper who introduces this book is a broadcaster and author well-known for his work with the BBC's Natural History Unit. He has been involved with numerous wildlife television programmes, most recently the conservation series *Nature* on BBC2. He wrote the book called *Discovering Animals*.

CONTRIBUTORS TO THIS BOOK

Juliet Bailey, formerly publicity officer for The Wildfowl Trust in Slimbridge, works for the Farming and Wildlife Advisory Group encouraging farmers to practise agriculture which is compatible with wildlife.

Theresa Brendell formerly worked on a range of wildlife species at the Natural History Museum, and is now a freelance botanical writer with a special interest in plants of waterlogged soils.

Tony Hare is a naturalist, writer and film-maker, who has written about numerous ecological topics, including the wildlife of London's East End.

Rob Hume edits *Bird Life* for the Young Ornithologists' Club of the RSPB, and is a writer, artist and lecturer who has conducted surveys of birds, plants, and butterflies in Wales.

Geoffrey Young is an author and journalist who specialises in rural topics. He was a founder of the WATCH Trust for Environmental Education and is a Fellow of the Royal Society of Arts.

TOWNS AND VILLAGES

Few parts of Britain have remained untouched by the relentless advance of human activities, and over the centuries many of the natural habitats of Britain's wildlife have shrunk dramatically or disappeared altogether. Where once vast forests of oak and beech stood, now farms and fields and cities and villages sprawl and spread. Where once little was heard but the plaintive cry of the curlew across the marshes, now throbs the steady pulse of industry. And the myriad rivers and streams that once flowed clear and free down to the sea are in many places contained as canals, at the worst polluted, and unfit for animal and plant life.

Yet nature is remarkably resilient and adaptable, and as we have altered the face of the landscape, so all kinds of plants and wild creatures have changed their habits or found new niches to replace those that have gone. Some species have indeed been lost forever, but many have survived and prospered in the new habitats. Even in the midst of the largest cities and industrial complexes, nature has often gained some kind of foothold and if, like four out of every five Britons you live in town, the chances are you can find wildlife, as rich and fascinating as anywhere in the country, right on your doorstep.

Gardens were once attached to the great houses only, but from the 1840s onwards, many suburban houses were built which had their own plot of land, private havens from the noise and dirt of the city. Now many millions of people have their own garden, albeit small, and in this overcrowded and intensely cultivated country, suburban gardens offer a potentially massive refuge for the wildlife whose habitats are disappearing in the countryside.

Even the land that man has abandoned may be quickly colonized by nature. Wastelands are often among the few places in cities where wildlife can flourish. As our spendthrift society changes and moves on, vast areas of wasteland are left in its wake. Almost one twentieth of Britain's land surface is now derelict – there are over 250,000 acres of neglected land in our towns and cities alone, ranging from old rubbish tips to vast ruins, the aftermath of once

bustling factories. Here, amidst the debris, all kinds of creatures and plants, driven from their natural habitat, may find a home.

Right in the heart of the busiest cities, it is possible to see a surprisingly diverse range of wildlife. Towns have expanded rapidly in the last 200 years, and city centres seem to have become increasingly barren as vast, inhospitable blocks of concrete and glass replace the old buildings of brick and stone, with their ledges and crevices which can accommodate birds, small mammals and many insect species. But even the most desolate urban jungle often includes a small park where wildlife can thrive.

Our society has become so heavily oriented towards town life that many people's only experience of the countryside is driving between towns. Yet though major roads and motorways seem as much a blight on the landscape as any artificially created feature, the roadside is often richer in wildlife than the cultivated fields beyond. Unlike farmland, the roadside verge may be left completely undisturbed and untrodden, and many species can find a home there.

The countryside has been altered by our activities almost as much as places which have been overtaken by urban development, although the effects are more subtle. Yet the village, too, makes a fascinating and varied wildlife habitat in its own right, and the nearby common, though often thought of merely as a place for walks at the weekend, is a valuable wildlife refuge. There are over 1½ million acres of common land in England and Wales, encompassing all types of scenery from open moorland to mature woodland.

River and wetland habitats are especially fragile and have suffered considerably from agricultural and industrial developments. Yet here again nature has proved remarkably adaptable, and as their natural habitats have shrunk or disappeared, many species have found new homes in alternative places, such as canals and reservoirs.

Indeed, wherever human activity has made its mark on the landscape, nature too has been at work, and if you look closely you can find natural activity in even the most artificial of environments.

IN THE GARDEN

With its mix of lawn, flowers, shrubs and vegetables the familiar suburban garden provides niches for many insects, birds and mammals, and, if there's a pond, frogs and perhaps newts and a grass snake.

The midsummer lawn underfoot is a flower garden in miniature. Daisies, dandelions, buttonweed, hop trefoil and birdsfoot trefoil decorate it, growing flat enough to escape the blades of the mower. A female wolf spider scurries by, dragging her round, silken sac of eggs, and a little black and white zebra spider jumps jerkily through the grass. Where a corner of lawn has been left uncut, violet-blue self-heal and yellow hawksbeard mingle with the froth of grass flowers, and a wall butterfly pauses to lay eggs, one here, one there, on the grass blades.

In the shade of the peonies a harassed-looking male blackbird stuffs a beakful of caterpillars into the yellow gape of one of his spotty, stump-tailed youngsters sheltering from the glare of a July afternoon. It is his second brood of the year, for there is plenty of food available in gardens, particularly insects. Birds and insects do especially well in suburban gardens, for they are surprisingly rich for wildlife habitats. Indeed, blackbirds – though originally woodland birds – now breed with greater success and in larger numbers in gardens than they do in their natural woodland home.

Seething activity around an eruption of soil on the crazy paving heralds the skyward drift of winged black ants on their nuptial flight. Starlings and sparrows clumsily catch a few before they rise very far, but most drift up to where swifts arc through the blue sky collecting insects and gossamer spiders which float on the breeze.

BUSY BEES

A leaf-cutter bee, superficially like a honey bee, chews neat circles from the rose leaves to line the brood cells it has burrowed beneath seed tray compost in the greenhouse. Earlier in the year, the garden was alive with mining and other solitary bees, quartering the lawn and the bare soil of the vegetable bed. They excavate burrows with entrances like miniature volcanoes, or feed busily at the gooseberry flowers: interestingly, the success of the gooseberry crop reveals the value of their pollinating activities.

FROGS SPAWNING
Due to the loss of village and farmland ponds, garden ponds have become a major refuge for frogs. Even if not introduced, frogs will usually soon colonize a new pond and will return year after year to mate and lay their spawn. Spawning takes place between January and March. Surviving froglets take to land in early summer.

WILDLIFE IN THE SUBURBAN GARDEN

The various corners of the garden – some actively cultivated others nicely neglected – form mini-habitats, each encouraging different species. Among rotten logs are found invertebrates and fungi. Cabbage white caterpillars and slugs eat their fill on the vegetable patch. The hedge of native shrubs holds breeding birds, such as the chaffinch. Ants burrowing beneath the dry-stone path will be eaten by the hedgehog. On the neglected lawn fairy ring toadstools expand their ring outwards year by year. In the pond are spawning frogs while close by among the tea roses, spiders feed on ladybirds that feed on greenfly.

KEY TO THE SPECIES

1 Apple tree	13 Honeysuckle	25 Ladybird larva
2 Collared dove	14 Privet	26 Marigolds
3 House martins	15 Holly	27 Common frog
4 Cat	16 Rotten logs	28 Frogspawn
5 House sparrows	17 Ink cap	29 Shade plants
6 Chaffinch	18 Small tortoiseshell	30 Dandelion
7 Song thrush	19 Hawthorn	31 Snail
8 Peacock	20 Garden spider	32 7-spot ladybird
9 Ivy	21 Wasps on apples	33 Greenfly
10 Buddleia	22 Starlings	34 Earthworm
11 Tall weeds	23 Fairy ring	35 Common toad
12 Cabbage whites	24 Hedgehog	36 Ants

11

cabbage aphids, are the flattened, slug-like larvae of the same species of hoverfly. These larvae feed on aphids, sucking them dry. On the beans, the blackfly are being hunted down by bright ladybirds and their agile, splay-legged, black larvae.

The cabbages are inter-planted with marigolds, asters and dwarf convolvulus to attract hoverflies which, after a meal of pollen, will lay their eggs among the clusters of aphids. Ground cover of oxalis, chickweed and ivy-leaved speedwell provides a daytime retreat for invertebrates. Here lurk carabid beetles, sinuous-bodied staphylinid beetles, centipedes and spiders which, by night, will climb the cabbages and beans to hunt for caterpillars and other insect prey. A flash of yellow is a brief glimpse of a yellow underwing moth, which scuttles to safety once its wings are closed. Weeding is sure to disturb the plump green or brown caterpillars of the angle shades moth, for they feed on the leaves of many different weeds and cultivated plants. The moth, camouflaged by jagged buff and moss-green wings, is less often seen.

A plump, mushroom-pink collared dove

For a brief spell we can sit back and watch — but not for long, for it is gardening as such that provides food and living space for a multitude of different animals. The gardener, constantly working and watering the soil, crowds together a bewildering variety of native and exotic plants. Weeds move in naturally and a close-packed, three-dimensional mosaic of different kinds of habitats, some sunny, some shady, is created.

AQUATIC GRASS SNAKE *(above) The grass snake swims readily and is well camouflaged amid pondweed.*

WASPS' PAPER NEST *(right) Common wasps often fix their intricate nest to roof timbers. To build it they make paper by rasping and chewing wood shavings from shingles or fence posts.*

INSECTS AMONG THE PLANTS

In the herbaceous border, bumblebees zoom ponderously between the hollyhocks, their hind legs bulging like yellow pantaloons with rounded masses of pollen. Hoverflies — some banded with black and yellow, others small and dark, a few furry as bumblebees — hang motionless in the air on shimmering wings, then dart away to collect pollen from poppies or sip nectar from marigolds. Gaudy peacock butterflies, tortoiseshells and, perhaps, a red admiral or a painted lady uncoil their long tongues to suck the rich fruity nectar of the buddleia flowers. In autumn, the herbaceous border will attract seed-eating birds. Linnets will come to Michaelmas daisies, greenfinches to sage, and goldfinches to sway on the tall teasels.

Beyond, in the vegetable patch, is more activity. Cabbage white butterflies, attracted by the characteristic scent of cabbage leaves, alight to lay their eggs: the small white lays single eggs, while the large white deposits batches. Small, fidgety, parasitic wasps search for soft-bodied insects in which to lay their eggs. A long-legged spider with a pale, globular body has spanned a cabbage leaf with a frail web in which an intricately banded hoverfly struggles. Elsewhere on the plant, among mealy masses of

LAWN FLOWERS
(left) Wild flowers in the lawn are every bit as beautiful as their cultivated cousins. Growing here are buttercups, daisies and speedwells. Their strategies to cope with the lawn mower differ: the speedwell, for instance, creeps between the grass stems, while the daisy has a low rosette of leaves.

croons plaintively from its perch high on the chimney pot. These companionable little doves, originally from northern India, first arrived in Britain in 1955, but have been so successful that they are now one of the most characteristic birds of well-wooded suburbia. Like the larger, more ungainly woodpigeons, they find safe nesting sites in tall evergreens.

Earlier in the year, in spring, greenfinches, dunnocks and song thrushes nested in the dense tangle of mock orange. Blue tits and great tits made good use of nesting-boxes, a diminutive male wren constructed a disproportionately large, moss-covered nest between a thorny rose stem and the fence, and a robin appropriated an abandoned flowerpot. Many of these birds survived the frosts of winter by visiting the bird-table for peanuts and suet, and the robin is a constant companion to the gardener, confidently taking worms unearthed by the spade.

After a rain shower, a night-time patrol with a torch reveals just how many earthworms have been working the soil. At every few paces is a long, fat worm, its hind end anchored in its burrow, ready, at the lightest footfall, to slither out of sight. Garden snails and slugs,

which shelter by day in moist crevices, are now at large, laying their mucus trails across the path.

As the summer's day draws to a close, tiny pipistrelle bats leave their roosts beneath the eaves to hawk for insects. A frog crouches like a statue beside the pond, and a newly-metamorphosed froglet clambers out of the water, where sinuous little newts, still with feathery gills on their necks, glide through the pondweed. A hedgehog trundles out of the shrubbery to take advantage of a saucerful of milk, a bright-eyed wood mouse cautiously peeps from its hole beneath the shed, and the neighbourhood foxes watch attentively in the failing light as their venturesome cubs frolic on the lawn.

FOX AT HOME
(left) Once regarded as a shy creature, haunting only farm-land and spinneys, the fox has taken to suburban gardens with surprising ease. Free from disturbance by gamekeeper, poultry-man or the hunt, foxes not only forage in gardens but also rest up during the day in a patch of shrubbery, or sunbathe, perhaps, on a shed roof. Lucky households may have a fox's earth at the bottom of the garden and may enjoy the pre-breakfast sight of cubs gambolling on the lawn from summer through to autumn.

FEEDING TOGETHER
(above) Feeding here are – clockwise from the top – a robin, song thrush, greenfinch, blackbirds and song thrushes, and a great tit. The garden bird table – this one appears to be cat-proofed – is often neutral territory where birds of the same and different species can feed together on a variety of foods. In a hard winter, especially, it is common ground for all.

HEDGEHOGS SUPPING
(centre) An adult and juvenile feed on bread soaked in milk. If food is put out hedgehogs may regularly turn up for an evening meal.

NURSERY WEB SPIDER
(below) In midsummer the female slings her egg sac in a net of silk among vegetation. She mounts guard, waiting for the spiderlings to hatch.

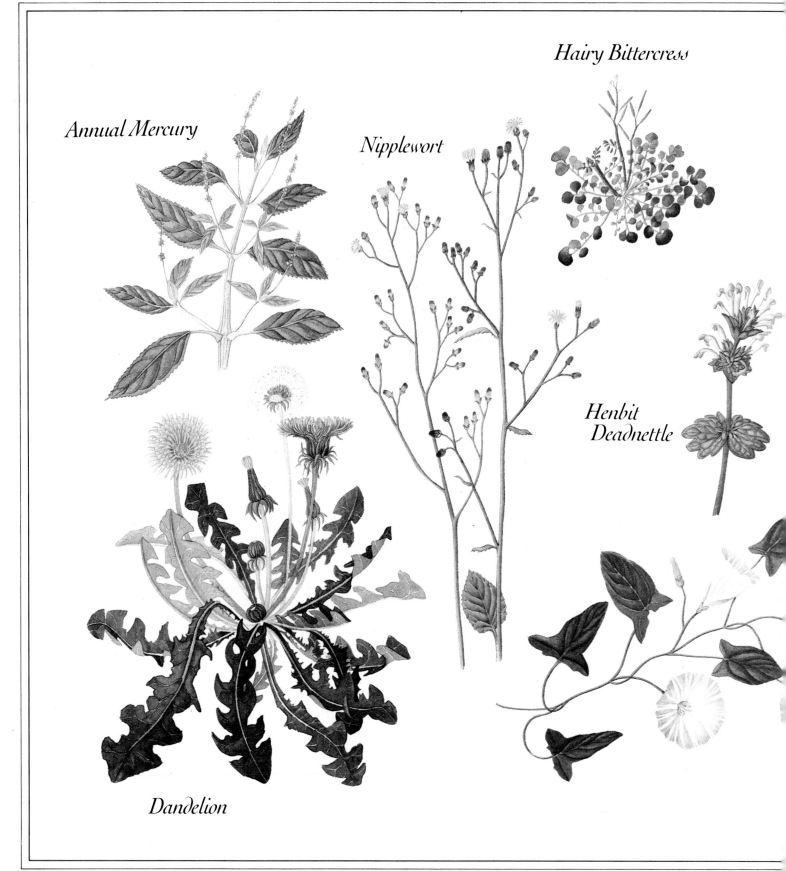

Hairy Bittercress

Annual Mercury

Nipplewort

Henbit
Deadnettle

Dandelion

DANDELION *(Taraxacum officinale)* Familiar golden heads are scattered over grasslands and waysides April-May, followed by the 'clocks' of seeds. Rosettes of deep-lobed leaves are stalkless; smooth hollow flowerstems reach 12″ (30cm) and contain bitter, white juice.

ANNUAL MERCURY *(Mercurialis annua)* This introduced plant is a weed of gardens in the South and East. 4-20″ (10-50cm), it has branched stems and toothed leaves. Male and female flowers occur on separate plants July to September, with bristly fruits in leaf axils.

NIPPLEWORT *(Lapsana communis)* An 8-35″ (20-90cm) stiff annual, the loose array of small flowerheads is borne on wiry, branched stems July-September. Basal leaves have odd-sized, toothed lobes, stem leaves are undivided and lance-shaped. Common on waste and cultivated land.

HAIRY BITTERCRESS *(Cardamine hirsuta)* Common on open, dry ground and walls, this 2-12″ (5-30cm) hairy annual has leaves divided into 3-7 pairs of round leaflets. Upright stems are topped with small, white flowers April-September, followed by long, beaded capsules.

Sun Spurge

Field Bindweed

Smooth Sowthistle

HENBIT DEAD NETTLE (*Lamium amplexicaule*) Common on light, dry soil in England, rare elsewhere, this softly hairy 2-10″ (5-25cm) annual has erect stems, branched at the base. Rounded lower leaves are stalked and leafy whorls support clusters of flowers, April-August.

FIELD BINDWEED (*Convolvulus arvensis*) Deeply growing roots make this weed very hard to eradicate. The 8-30″ (20-75cm) stem creeps and twines up other plants. Arrow-like leaves are borne singly on slender stalks and thin-petalled, scented flowers open June to September.

SUN SPURGE (*Euphorbia helioscopia*) A prolific, poisonous annual weed to 20″ (50cm), thriving on the rich soil and open aspect of flowerbeds. It has stalkless, finely toothed leaves and a head of yellow-green flowers May-October. Smooth capsules 'pop', shooting out seeds.

SMOOTH SOWTHISTLE (*Sonchus oleraceus*) A spineless, stout plant common on cultivated and waste land. Flowers open June-August at tops of hollow, branched 8-60″ (20-150cm) stems. The hairy seeds are dispersed by wind. Lower leaves stalked, upper ones clasp the stem.

15

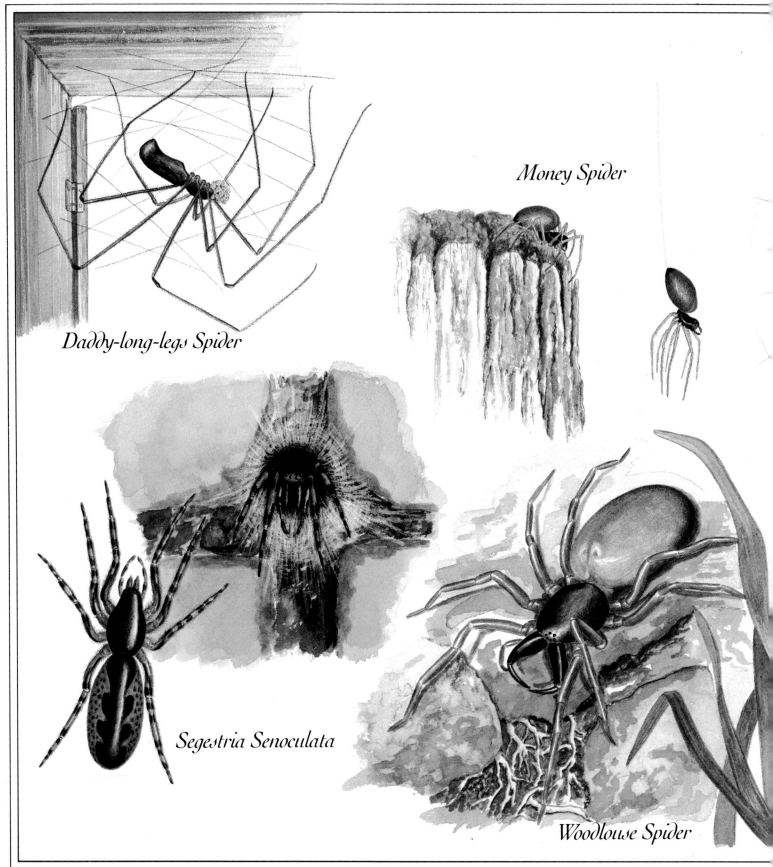

Daddy-long-legs Spider

Money Spider

Segestria Senoculata

Woodlouse Spider

DADDY-LONG-LEGS SPIDER *(Pholcus phalangioides)* Very long thin legs identify this ½″ (12mm) tube-bodied spider. Common in the South, sheltering inside buildings, it spins a tangled web. Long-living females hold the flimsy egg sac in their jaws until the eggs hatch.

SEGESTRIA SENOCULATA Both sexes of this elongated spider are about ½″ (12mm). Common and widespread, it is often found on garden walls in spring. A tubular web is built in crevices; radiating threads trip insects which the fast-moving spider drags into its lair.

MONEY SPIDER *(Ostearius melanopygius)* This minute spider with its black-tipped abdomen is remarkably widespread – living almost anywhere. It is usually encountered spring-autumn, whilst 'ballooning' through the air on the end of a silk thread.

WOODLOUSE SPIDER *(Dysdera crocata)* This shiny ½″ (12mm) spider has large fangs which are able to penetrate the tough 'shell' of woodlice. It can be found all year beneath logs and stones but is only active at night. The female guards her egg sac in a silk lair.

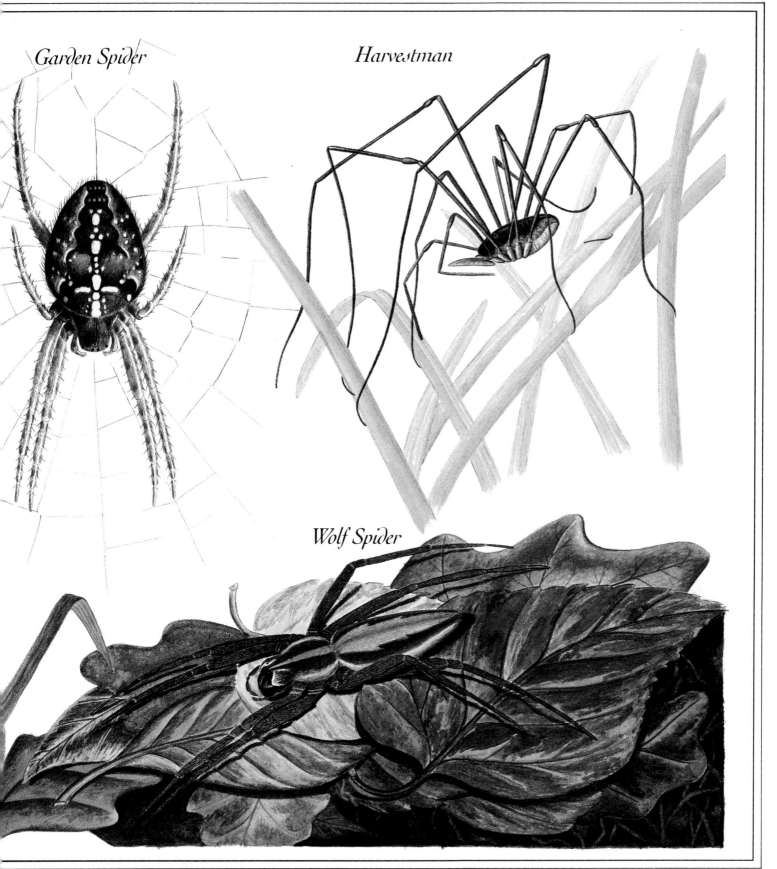

Garden Spider

Harvestman

Wolf Spider

GARDEN SPIDER (*Araneus diadematus*) The ½″ (12mm) female has a broad abdomen with a white 'cross'. Common and widespread, she is seen late summer-autumn in the centre of a large, sticky orb web. Concealed egg sacs are guarded until frost kills her. Males are smaller.

WOLF SPIDER (*Pisauria mirabilis*) This fast-moving ¾″ (19mm) spider is often seen on bare earth or paths in early summer. Courting males present females with a silk-wrapped fly. She holds her large egg sac, spinning a 'nursery tent' when young are about to hatch.

HARVESTMAN (*Phalangium opilio*) Not a true spider, this arachnid is common throughout Britain in late summer. It does not spin a web, and has a mixed diet. If attacked, the long legs are shed and do not re-grow. Females at ½″ (12mm) are bigger than males.

WASTELAND

Pockets of derelict land, both in town and country, are rapidly colonized by plants, some of them exotic, and soon swarm with many colourful insects which prove an irresistible attraction to birds.

Forgotten wasteland in the commercial heartland of large cities is often a haven for wildlife. Buddleia thickets grow as densely as in their native China, festooned with the exotic, white trumpet flowers of great bindweed. Paving-stones are pushed aside by the rampant growth of the tall red stems of Japanese knotweed, which tower over a colourful assembly of other garden escapes – lupins, marigolds, goldenrod and Michaelmas daisies.

The abundance of flowers, in particular buddleia, attracts a fluttering medley of butterflies intent on refuelling with nectar. Some, such as the small tortoiseshell, peacock and cabbage whites, are familiar as town butterflies. But there are many others more characteristic of the countryside, among them meadow browns and gatekeepers, commas and painted ladies, skippers, blues and small coppers and even, in a good year for migration, clouded yellows.

Not all the exotic plants are welcome invaders. The vigorously growing Japanese knotweed, for instance, soon ousts native plants and dominates the flora. It is almost impossible to eradicate by mechanical means as it shoots again from stem and root fragments.

Despite the foreign invaders, many native plants successfully colonize wasteland, producing a lush under-storey of grasses and wild flowers. Hairy bittercress and cheerful, golden dandelions mingle with mugwort and the sickly-smelling, maroon flowers of hedge woundwort.

NEW PLANTS AND THEIR INSECTS

One of the most abundant and attractive flowers of wasteland is rosebay willowherb, with its delicate spires of pinky-mauve flowers. A century ago, rosebay was an uncommon plant. It was, however, able to exploit the vacant spaces on bombed sites after World War 2, and is now one of the most abundant plants of newly disturbed ground.

Beneath rosebay willowherb plants, you can often find the impressive green or velvety-brown caterpillars of elephant hawk-moths. Tiny caterpillars rest on the underside of the leaves, but the older, larger ones spend the day on the ground, climbing the plant at night to munch its leaves. Conspicuous when fully grown, they are more than 8cm long, with a horn on the rear end and two pairs of dramatic eye-markings towards the front. The beautiful bright pink and moss-green adult moth is less often seen, flying only at night.

Oxford ragwort with its yellow, daisy-like flowers is a familiar plant with an unusual history. At the end of the 18th century it was collected from the slopes of Mount Etna and introduced to the Botanic Garden at Oxford. From there it spread along the network of railways, finding a hospitable roothold in the clinker of the tracks.

Feeding on the leaves of both Oxford and common ragwort are the conspicuous, tiger-striped caterpillars of the cinnabar moth. The moth, which flies by day, is sharply coloured red and black. Both the moth and its caterpillars taste unpleasant, and their bright colours act as

BURGEONING BORAGE
This rubbish tip has proved a fertile site for quick-growing borage, one of many garden escapes with a liking for waste ground. Introduced from southern Europe, borage has long been grown for its medicinal and herbal properties. The leaves may be eaten in salads or used to flavour long, cool drinks, but the plant's most attractive features are its beautiful flowers.

WILDLIFE ON THE CITY WASTELAND

Deserted land or buildings are soon taken over by nature. Mosses carpet concrete floors, providing a base for other plants to grow; strong-rooted plants such as dandelion exploit cracks in tarmac, breaking up the surface, and buddleia grows readily on brick walls. The plants that move into the site draw insects, which in turn attract birds. The pied wagtail soon finds a hole for its nest with a plentiful supply of insects for the chicks. Woody shrubs provide nest sites for song thrush and collared dove, and the leaves of willow are food for the puss moth caterpillar. At the top of the pyramid is the feral cat, hunting birds and mammals and scavenging among refuse dumped on the site.

KEY TO THE SPECIES

1 Song thrush
2 Collared doves
3 Elder
4 Rosebay willowherb
5 Willow
6 Buddleia
7 Great bindweed
8 Michaelmas daisy
9 Giant hogweed
10 House sparrow
11 Spurge
12 Dandelion

13 Feral cat
14 Hedge mustard
15 Nettles
16 Bramble
17 Small tortoiseshell
18 Dock
19 Groundsel
20 Elephant hawk-moth
21 Common blue
22 Common field grasshopper
23 Ragwort

24 Thorn-apple
25 Brown rat
26 Creeping thistle
27 Pied wagtail
28 Shepherd's purse
29 Moss
30 Woodlice
31 Cinnabar moth
32 Puss moth caterpillar

COMMON EARWIG
(left) These familiar insects give many people the shudders. They actually have no predilection for human ears but do like a tight crevice in which to spend the day. The female (shown here) is unusual in caring for her young after they hatch. The male can be distinguished by his more bowed forceps. These are used not only in attack and defence but also for folding the fan-like wings which are neatly stored under small wing-cases.

a warning to birds and other predators which quickly learn to recognize and avoid them.

A patch of nettles in a sunny spot provides a living space and food for a variety of butterflies and moths. Silken webs shelter clusters of tiny, black caterpillars of small tortoiseshell and peacock butterflies. Dispersed over the larger leaves are the spiny, older larvae: those of the tortoiseshell have a yellow stripe. There may also be caterpillars of red admirals, commas and painted ladies, although the latter are more often found on thistles.

On a nettle stem, a hairy 'woolly bear' caterpillar may be seen moving with vigorous undulations. It will hibernate while still quite small and, in the following year, complete its growth and development into the showy scarlet, chocolate-brown and white garden tiger moth.

WASTELAND ANIMALS

A rustle among a heap of discarded cardboard boxes and plastic bags betrays a larger animal. Something thin and sinewy, half glimpsed, turns out to be the long tail of a large, bold, brown rat. They thrive as scavengers on man's refuse, varying their diet with green plants and with stored food raided from warehouses.

Suddenly the plump brown rat scampers into an abandoned pipe, as a lean feral tomcat, bearing the scars of many battles, stalks confidently over to the heap of rubbish. It is probably one of a colony, an active hunter, and father of many kittens.

Overhead the sickle-shaped silhouettes of swifts wheel screaming through the air, collecting the vast numbers of insects needed to sustain

themselves and their young. They are nesting in the ventilation shafts of nearby factories and tower blocks, and remain airborne all the time they are away from the nest.

The 'cliffs' provided by tall buildings offer nesting sites for many birds. Chattering starlings, – which strip the wasteland elders of their black berries – commandeer holes in the masonry. High on a ledge is a bright-eyed kestrel, a hovering hunter of the open spaces.

The bombed sites of London were also colonized by black redstarts, one of Britain's rarest breeding birds. They did particularly well on these large, undisturbed areas, although as the sites have been redeveloped, they have again moved away from central London.

Insect-eating birds, like black redstarts and swifts, find an abundance of food in and over the lush vegetation of wasteland sites. Shiny bluebottles and grey fleshflies buzz around in the sun, laying their eggs in organic refuse. Yellow and black hoverflies hang apparently motionless in the air above flowers, or alight to lay their eggs among clusters of aphids. Their eggs will hatch into slug-like green or brown larvae which glide between the aphids, every so often seizing one, draining it dry and discarding an empty skin.

Winged aphids leave the plants and drift up into the air, caught on the lightest breeze. Small

GIANT HOGWEED
(above) Growing to a height of 16' (5m), this plant is a true giant among flowers. Avoid touching it, as its juices sensitize the skin to sunlight and can cause severe blisters.

PUSS MOTH CATERPILLARS
(right) Astride a poplar twig, these two caterpillars almost produce a mirror image. If threatened they take on a fiercer aspect, spitting their stomach contents and a stream of formic acid at their attacker.

BLACK REDSTART
The female (shown below) builds the feather-lined nest and incubates the eggs, but both sexes feed the chicks. Two broods are often raised before the birds migrate south in September.

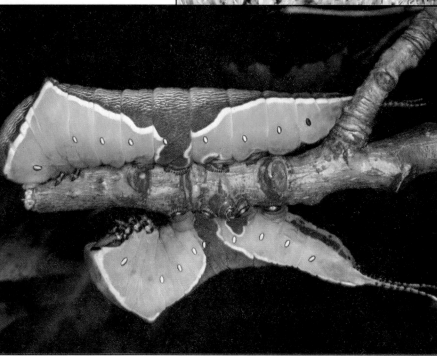

GARDEN SLUG CRAWLING THROUGH MOSS
Much loathed by the gardener, this species is widespread in both town and country, feeding chiefly on plants.

BEAUTY AMONG THE BED SPRINGS
(below left) Growing between a slag heap and the rusting remains of a mattress are nettles, thistles, dock, poppies, groundsel, ragwort, foxgloves and grasses.

grasshoppers chirrup among tall grasses, mining bees dig in sandy soil, and froghoppers crouch on stems, jumping away when disturbed.

Many different sorts of plants bear blobs of cuckoo-spit; this is formed by the green nymphs of froghoppers or meadow spittlebugs. The nymphs suck watery sap from the phloem, the food-transporting tissue of plants. They use nutrients in the sap but excrete most of the water. Air is bubbled into the excreted water, forming foamy cuckoo-spit, which protects the nymph from drying out and also hides it from predators.

IMPROVING SITES FOR WILDLIFE

In several cities, wasteland sites are now managed by urban wildlife groups which enhance and develop them as habitats for wildlife. Wasteland in the countryside, often around industrial sites, is also being sensitively managed.

In Lancashire, for instance, tips of power station ash have spontaneously developed a thriving limestone flora, including nine species of orchids. As plant succession occurs, however, shade develops and the soil becomes more fertile and acidic, pushing out the limestone flora. Ironically, the most straightforward way of maintaining the orchids is to go on tipping more and more lime-rich waste on the sites.

Wall Barley

Common Toadflax

Black Horehound

Hedge Mustard

BLACK HOREHOUND (*Ballota nigra*) This rough, hairy strong-smelling perennial has stout square stems up to 39″ (100cm). The leaves are blunt-toothed and tight whorls of funnel-like flowers open June to October. Common on wasteland and by hedges in England and Wales.

WALL BARLEY (*Hordeum murinum*) A common annual grass found on disturbed soils around buildings. It grows in loose light green clumps 2-24″ (6-60cm) and flowers from May to August and its flowered spikelets are often found clinging to clothes and animal fur.

HEDGE MUSTARD (*Sisymbrium officinale*) Growing by roads and waste places in town and country, this 12-35″ (30-90cm) annual is common, throughout England and Wales. It flowers June-July and these are followed by thin pods. Leaves are hairy and deeply lobed.

COMMON TOADFLAX (*Linaria vulgaris*) Reaching 31″ (80cm) the upright stems of this perennial bear numerous blue-green linear leaves and spikes of up to 20 snapdragon-like flowers. Found frequently on dry chalky or sandy banks. Rare in north Scotland and Ireland.

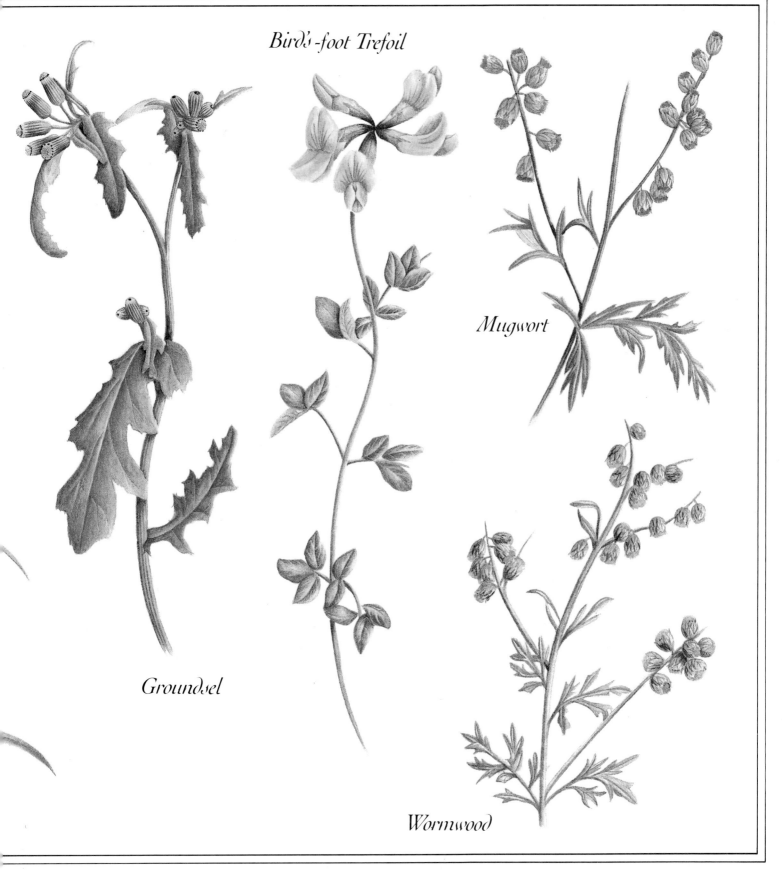

Bird's-foot Trefoil

Mugwort

Groundsel

Wormwood

GROUNDSEL *(Senecio vulgaris)* This small 3-18″ (8-45cm) annual flourishes on neglected land and is also a common weed of gardens and farms throughout Britain. Leaves are divided into blunt lobes. The narrow cylindrical flowerheads can be seen throughout the year.

BIRD'S-FOOT TREFOIL *(Lotus corniculatus)* Widespread throughout Britain among short grass on well drained soils, this is a sprawling perennial 4-16″ (10-40cm). Leaves have 5 oval leaflets. Clusters of 5-8 flowers open June-August, with long, 'bird's-foot' seedpods.

MUGWORT *(Artemisia vulgaris)* Clumps of this 24-48″ (60-120cm) perennial are a common sight along verges, banks and on waste ground. Distinctive narrowly-divided leaves are dark above, cottony white below. Branched spires of dense reddish flowerheads appear July-September.

WORMWOOD *(Artemisia absinthium)* A shrubby perennial up to 35″ (90cm), locally common on waste ground and waysides of England and Wales, especially coastal regions. It has aromatic leaves, with hairy strap segments. Tiny flowerheads appear June to August.

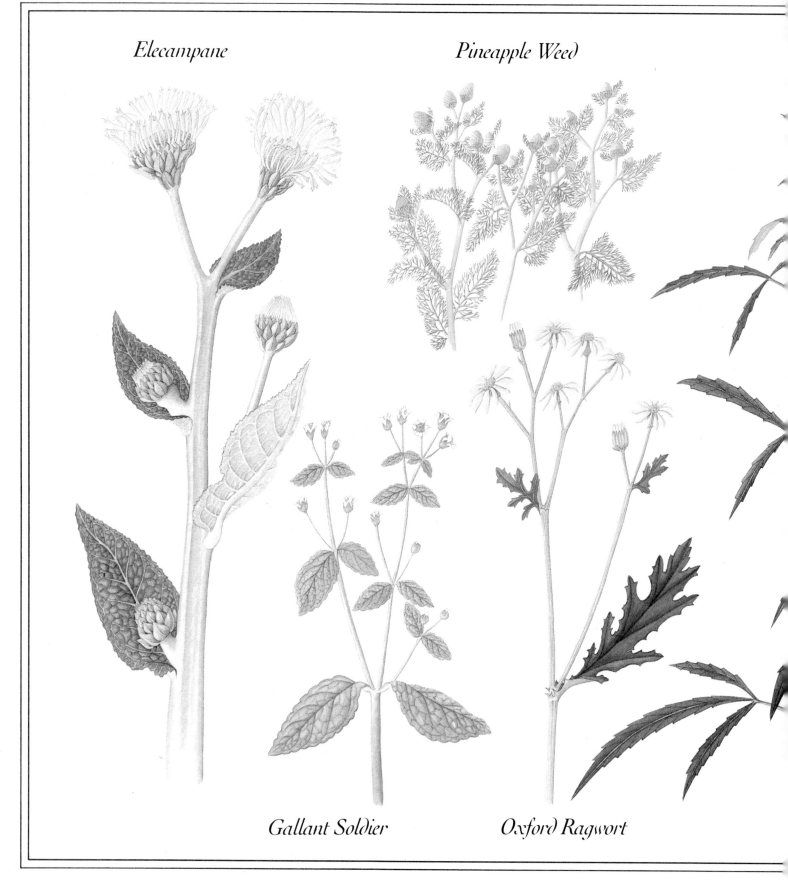

Elecampane

Pineapple Weed

Gallant Soldier

Oxford Ragwort

ELECAMPANE *(Inula helenium)* A perennial native to West Asia, once prized for its medicinal qualities. It is now an uncommon, though widespread, plant of old meadows and wasteland. Leaves are finely toothed, cottony white below. 3″ (8cm) flowerheads open July-August.

GALLANT SOLDIER *(Galinsoga parviflora)* Now a common weed throughout Britain, this South American annual escaped from the Royal Botanic Gardens, Kew, in the 1860s. 4-30″ (10-75cm) tall, it has oval stalked leaves and tiny flowers which appear from May-October.

PINEAPPLE WEED *(Chamomilla suaveolens)* Probably originating from Asia, this aromatic 2-12″ (5-30cm) annual is now a common weed of well-trodden tracks and arable waste ground. Domed flower-heads can be seen June-July. Divided leaves have fine, linear segments.

OXFORD RAGWORT *(Senecio squalidus)* A bushy Sicilian plant, now found on wasteland and derelict sites over most of England – though scarce in the North. 8-12″ (20-30cm) tall, branched stems have deeply lobed, ragged leaves and daisy-like flowers from May-December.

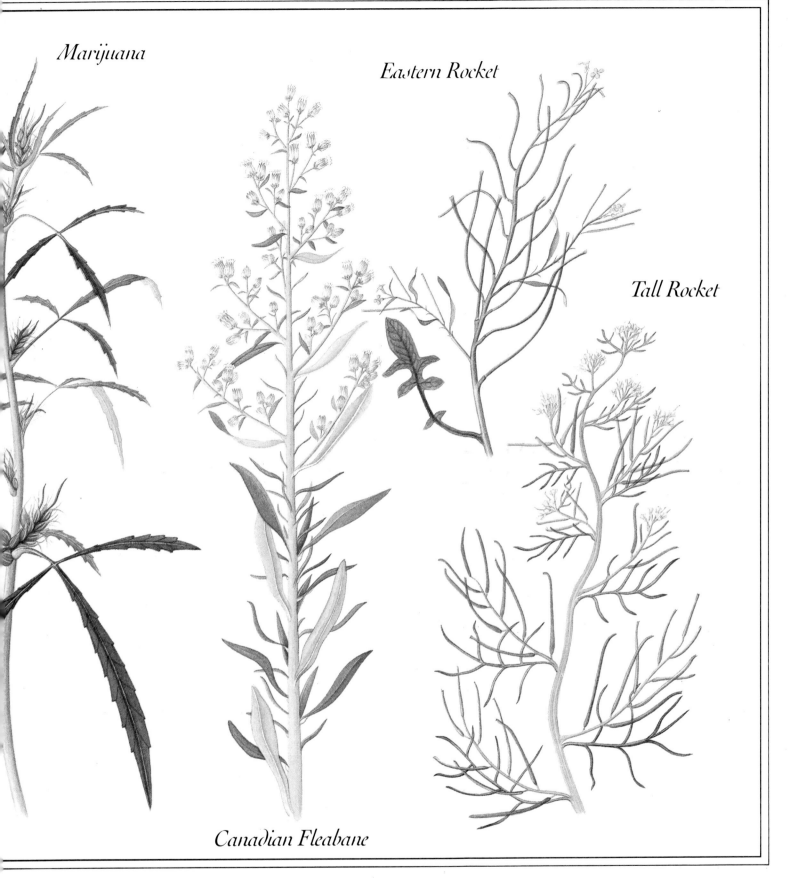

Marijuana

Eastern Rocket

Tall Rocket

Canadian Fleabane

MARIJUANA *(Cannabis sativa)* Once grown for hemp, the seeds were also put into mixes fed to poultry and cage birds. It is now a rare weed of waste tips, seldom more than 39″ (1m) tall. Leaves have toothed radiating lobes – three on female plants, five on males.

CANADIAN FLEABANE *(Conyza canadensis)* An alien from North America this 3-39″ (8-100cm) annual spreads by means of hairy seeds colonizing dry waysides of England and Wales. Leaves are linear and small, pale flowers appear August and September.

EASTERN ROCKET *(Sisymbrium orientale)* This hairy blue-green, 10-35″ (25-90cm), annual has lobed leaves and very long, stem-like 2″ (5cm) pods, hairy when young. Found on waste ground in the South, it flowers May-October. Native to southern Europe, and north Africa.

TALL ROCKET *(Sisymbrium altissimum)* An 8-39″ (20-100cm) tall annual, the lower leaves are deeply split into pairs of narrow, toothed lobes sprinkled with bristly hairs. Native to eastern Europe, it has only become common here since the 1950s. Flowers May-October.

Plate 5.

Large White Plume Moth

Garden Tiger Moth

Common Earwig

Female

Male

LARGE WHITE PLUME MOTH
(Pterophorus pentadactyla) This
striking 1″ (25mm) moth has deeply
divided feathery wings and unusually
long and slender legs. It can be seen
during the summer months displaying
a characteristic 'floating flight'. The
caterpillars feed on bindweed.

COMMON EARWIG *(Forficula
auricularia)* Armed with powerful
pincers – curved in males, straight
in females – this nocturnal
scavenger feeds on plants and
insects. Eggs are laid in the soil and
tended by the female. ¾″ (20mm)
adults have wings but seldom fly.

GARDEN TIGER MOTH *(Arctia
caja)* A large 3″ (75mm), nocturnal
moth appearing in July-August. The
black furry caterpillars or 'woolly
bears' feed on many garden plants.
The brilliant adult coloration
is defensive and when threatened
they can exude a yellow fluid.

Magpie Moth

Sheerness Scorpion

Violet Ground Beetle

MAGPIE MOTH *(Abraxas grossulariata)* This 1¾″ (45mm) vari-coloured moth hatches from a black and yellow pupa to fly both day and night during July and August. Eggs laid on leaves hatch after ten days. The caterpillars eat many plants but favour currant bushes.

SHEERNESS SCORPION *(Euscorpius flavicaudis)* Found locally in Kent, this small, 1½″ (40mm) scorpion is nocturnal, but hunts occasionally by day. Live young are born and stay on the mother's back until their first moult. Their sting is harmless to man.

VIOLET GROUND BEETLE *(Carabus violaceus)* Both adults and larvae of this nocturnal flightless beetle are carnivorous—the 1″ (25mm) adults have large powerful jaws. The larvae develop in soil and leaf litter and the adults emerge in autumn, but remain inactive until spring.

TOWNLIFE

Attracted by warmth, food and the lack of predators, wildlife can be abundant in towns and may include bustling park-lake wildfowl, squadrons of roosting starlings and enterprising foxes.

A pheasant in London's Strand. Woodcocks in the City. Skylarks and bramblings on the Embankment and a buzzard over Paddington station. Unusual perhaps, but not that uncommon. Unexpected birds like these frequently turn up in London as well as Britain's other major cities. Migrating warblers – blackcap, garden warbler, whitethroat, chiff-chaff and others – pass through Regent's Park every year, and wheatears turn up in spring and autumn on the grassy slopes of Primrose Hill.

Heron, magpie, jay, blackcap, great spotted woodpecker, goldcrest and coal tit are among the 40 or so bird species which breed in central London. In smaller cities, where the countryside is less far from the centre, farmland birds, such as rooks, may nest high above the traffic.

The brick, concrete and tarmac of the city centre may seem an unlikely habitat for wildlife but even here plants take root where they can. Oxford ragwort may sprout from the pavement cracks, rosebay willowherb quickly colonizes the tops of walls, while buddleia (much loved by butterflies) favours crumbling brickwork. A dripping drainpipe will soon be surrounded by mosses and ferns growing on the damp wall.

Even the busiest city has quiet corners where wildlife can flourish. Basement areas, vacant sites, derelict buildings and town squares all attract a fascinating diversity of insects, spiders, plants, birds and mammals. Shopkeepers and restaurateurs fight a continual battle against the more unlovable species – black and brown rats, house mice, cockroaches, wasps and flies.

The most readily seen birds—house sparrows, starlings and feral pigeons — all nest in town buildings and the young of feral pigeons (the multi-coloured street pigeons) can be found at almost any time of year.

BREATHING SPACES

The city's green lungs are the parks. Though often too neatly clipped and well managed to attract a wide variety of species, each usually has its unkempt corners. Apart from the daisies of the lawns, red dead-nettle may grow on the edges of the shrubbery, ground ivy may sneak into the flower beds and black-berried deadly nightshade may loom majestically behind the compost heap, alongside scarlet pimpernel, lilac-flowered mallow and scented cow parsley.

Even in summer, black-headed gulls are often seen in the park, jostling for breadcrumbs with other birds, and, in their off duty moments, adding white wigs to the statuary. Herring gulls have nested in London's parks, and kittiwakes – essentially sea cliff nesters – now nest inland on Newcastle's riverfront warehouses.

Birds are very adaptable. Winter-visiting redwings and the locally nesting blackbirds will both feed on exotic figs beneath an ornamental park tree. Sparrows hop inside the engines of parked cars to take flies off the radiator and pigeons scavenge on London's tube trains.

Scything through the sky, above the church spires and past the tower blocks, the kestrel is becoming a more familiar sight, feeding on house sparrows, mice and voles.

At night, the quavering *who-who-wh-whooo* of the tawny owl often echoes over the quiet

DUSTBIN DINER
(left) Urban foxes tend to be scavengers rather than hunters and dustbins provide a ready source of food. Foxes have developed a taste for fast food and may be seen at bus stops devouring discarded chicken bones or fish and chips.

streets. These woodland birds have adapted well to towns, nesting in old trees in squares, parks and churchyards.

As the air in the inner cities has become cleaner in recent years, due to smokeless zones and other anti-pollution measures, the number of airborne insects has increased dramatically so that swifts and house martins are once again nesting near the city centre. Both birds feed exclusively on insects which they scoop up

TOWN PARK WILDLIFE
Swifts, nesting under the eaves, catch insects in flight; bats hawk moths at night; and the robin, pied wagtail and starling seek out ground invertebrates, as does the nocturnal hedgehog. Tortoiseshells and silver Y moths home in on flowers while hawk-moth caterpillars feed on lime and privet.

KEY TO THE SPECIES
1 Kestrel
2 London plane
3 Lime tree
4 Swifts
5 Bat
6 Lime hawk-moth
7 Silver Y moth
8 Tortoiseshell
9 Tufted duck
10 Mallard
11 Starlings
12 Black redstart
13 Shaggy ink cap
14 Hoverflies
15 Hedgehog
16 Robin
17 Pied wagtail
18 Moth caterpillar
19 Feral pigeons
20 House sparrow

NESTING THRUSH
(below) Like the robin, wren, blackbird and other town nesters, the song thrush will build its nest wherever it can find a safe, relatively quiet spot. Hedges, shrubs or ivy-clad walls are the usual choice but even metal pipes stacked at the back of a yard may be chosen as a nest site. The mistle thrush, a larger bird, also nests in towns, usually in a tree fork.

while on the wing.

Red admiral, small tortoiseshell, small copper and the white butterflies all occur in town. Honey bees, too, flourish in towns, perhaps flying from a back garden hive or one kept on a sheltered roof terrace. The flowers of the lime tree – widely planted in streets and squares – produce particularly good honey, and attract many kinds of bee.

The common lime also attracts moths. The caterpillars of the splendid lime hawk-moth, the buff tip and the brindled beauty all feed on the leaves. Other moths are attracted by the sugary honeydew produced by the colonies of aphids (such as greenfly) which infest the sappy leaves. In turn, blue tits and great tits feed avidly on aphids.

Town trees can be very colourful. In April and May the pink or white blossoms of flowering Japanese cherries enliven streets and parks. In autumn, the orange, yellow and red leaves of park maples and the red berries of street whitebeams and rowans add a splash of colour.

The tree most associated with towns, however, is probably the London plane. A foreign hybrid, it attracts few insects (the vapourer moth is one) but is planted because it can cope with smoke, traffic fumes and sulphur dioxide gas. Sulphur dioxide – the cause of 'acid rain' – is poisonous to many trees (pines are rather sensitive) and also kills lichens. In the city centre, therefore, a maximum of five types of lichen will be found, while in the suburbs, 30 or more may grow.

The cleaner air has also brought insect-eating pipistrelle bats back to the centre, and hedgehogs may scuffle through the park shrubberies or commute between town gardens. Cities with large rivers may enjoy the occasional seal or dolphin upstream: these may be just poor navigators or they may be pursuing a rich source of food. In the Thames, for instance, over 70 kinds of fish have recently been recorded, including salmon and sea horses.

WINDOWSILL KESTRELS
Kestrels are versatile nesters, rearing broods on tall chimneys, spires, power stations, cranes and the windowledges or balconies of tower blocks, 20 storeys high.

COUNTRY COUSIN
(below) Traditionally a farmland bird, the woodpigeon is quite at home in towns, often building its twiggy nest platform on a branch above the street. In the park it struts importantly, its deep purple chest puffed out, among the tatty town pigeons.

Among the fish in the park lake may be a few large old eels. More visible are the waterfowl, with exotic mandarins swimming alongside native pochard, tufted duck, mallard, coot and moorhen which may all nest near the lake.

Two factors, in particular, bring wildlife into towns. Firstly, the network of green corridors. Viewed from a high building, the lines of railway embankments, road verges, river banks and canals can be seen coming in from the country to link up with the green parks, gardens and churchyards. Foxes use these corridors and there is rough grass for bank voles. Bankside brambles, elder and hawthorn are full of fruit in the autumn and nesting birds in the spring. Urban canals can be surprisingly unpolluted, offering good breeding habitat for dragonflies.

The second factor is the climate – in winter city centre temperatures may be 5°C higher than the surrounding countryside. The kingfisher on an urban canal will still be fishing when the streams and ponds elsewhere are frozen over. And, as night falls on the office workers rushing to catch their trains out of town, the wheeling, chattering cloud of starlings overhead are commuting in reverse, returning to sit out the cold night on the windowsills of centrally heated office blocks.

FRIENDLY SQUIRREL
This popular animal is the mammal most commonly seen in towns. Here, it is little persecuted unlike its country cousin. It eats hazel nuts and sweet chestnuts, if they are available, and bark, leaves and shoots. It will, though, readily visit bird tables or scavenge in litter bins.

TOWN LIMES
The common lime has bushy shoots at its foot and knobbly bosses on the trunk. The small-leaved lime has smaller leaves with noticeable tufts of red hairs where the veins fork on the underside. The leaves of the broad-leaved lime (a species less often found in town) are hairy on both sides.

PEPPERED MOTHS
(below) Since the Industrial Revolution, the dark form of this moth has become more common than the paler form, being better camouflaged against smoke blackened walls.

COMMON LIME

BROAD-LEAVED LIME

SMALL-LEAVED LIME

Tree of Heaven

Flowers

Flowers

Fruit

Lime Hybrid

COMMON LIME *(Tilia x europaea)* Towering up to 130′ (39m), this hybrid of the small- and large-leaved limes is one of Britain's tallest trees. Very hardy and bearing sweet-scented flowers in early July, the common lime is often planted along the roadside, despite its need for frequent heavy pruning. The lime is, however, a rather messy town tree. Aphids infest the foliage and produce a honeydew which coats the leaves and the ground beneath the tree in a sticky film which blackens with mould and dust.

TREE OF HEAVEN *(Ailanthus altissima)* Native to North China, this tree may reach 90′ (30m) and has a graceful, spreading crown. Its tolerance of air pollution and its decorative qualities make it ideal for city parks and gardens in south and east England. The 12-35″ (30-90cm) compound leaves are red when young, turning green as they open. Male and female flowers appear on separate trees in July, and the big bunches of winged seeds turn red as they ripen in late summer. It grows freely from self-sown seed in open spaces and waste ground.

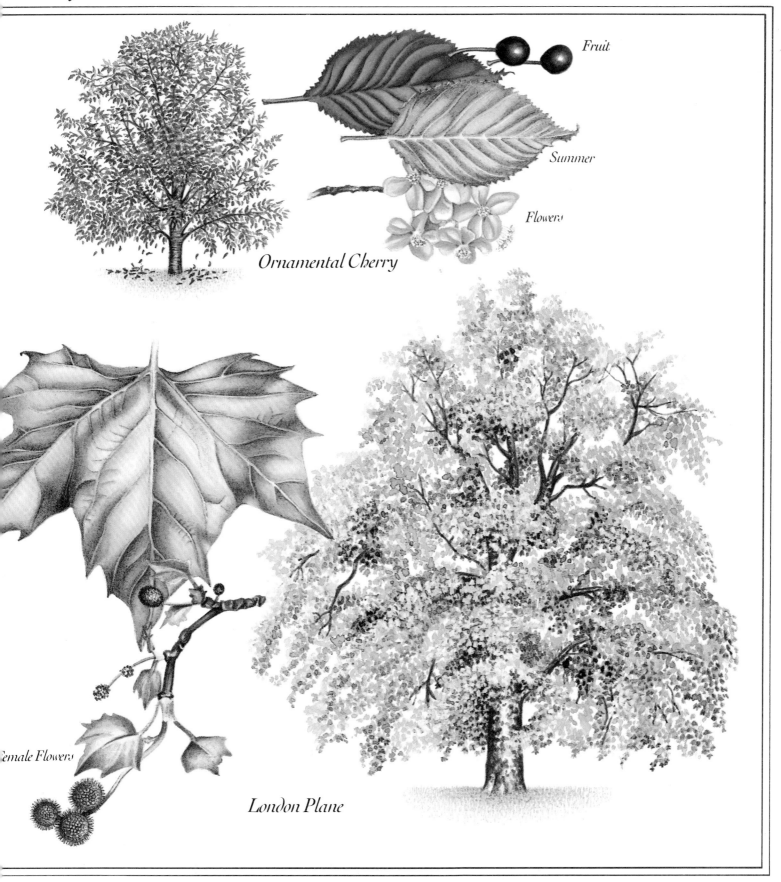

Ornamental Cherry

Fruit

Summer

Flowers

London Plane

Female Flowers

ORNAMENTAL CHERRY (*Prunus sargentii*) Well-named, this highly decorative tree is often planted alongside roads and in parks and gardens, where it gives a fine show of pink flowers in April. The leaves, whch are first purple, turn green in summer, and finally, brilliant red in September. This cherry can grow to 80′ (25m) in its native Japan, but here it is smaller and is often grafted onto the wild cherry (*P. avium*) – white flowered shoots from this rootstock sometimes growing up into the crown. The small black fruits rarely develop.

LONDON PLANE (*Platanus* x *acerifolia*) This vigorous hybrid of the Oriental plane and the American plane first became established in England in the 18th century. A tall tree, reaching 100′ (30m) or more, with a large, spreading crown, it grows well in city streets and urban parks. Damage from air pollution is minimal – rain washes dirt from the glossy leaves, and the bark is continually renewed as the older patches flake away, exposing pale, clean areas. Male and female flowers are borne in separate, round clusters in May.

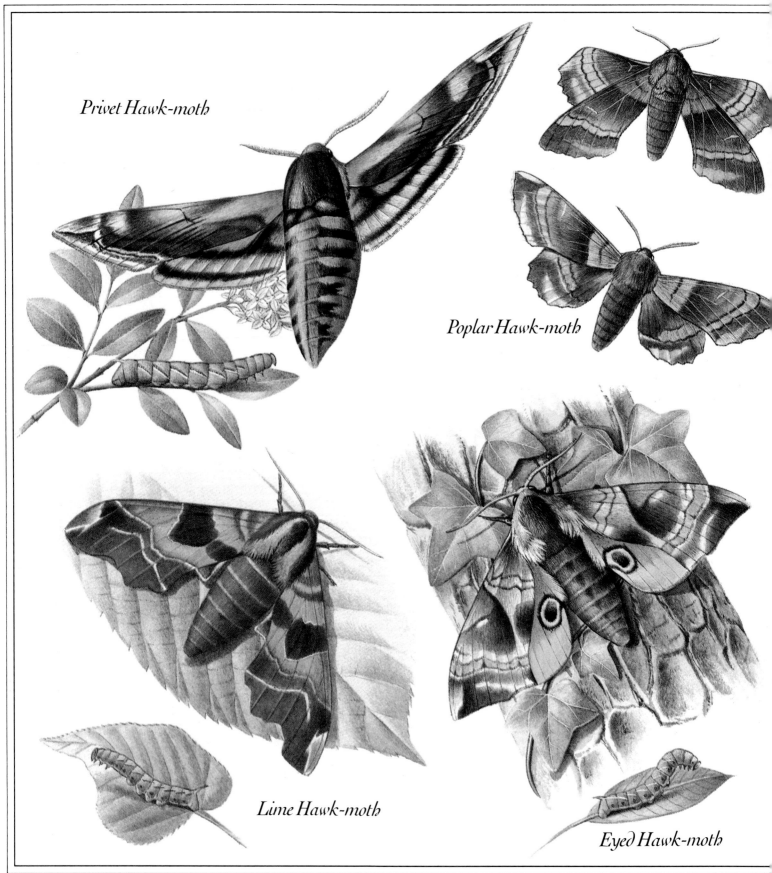

Privet Hawk-moth

Poplar Hawk-moth

Lime Hawk-moth

Eyed Hawk-moth

PRIVET HAWK-MOTH *(Sphinx ligustri)* Although its nulmbers are dwindling, this moth is still to be seen in town and country in south England where privet and lilac grow. It is a fast, strong flier. The caterpillars burrow up to 6″ (15cm) into the ground to pupate.

LIME HAWK-MOTH *(Mimas tiliae)* This is a moth of southern England, especially common around London, where there are plenty of lime trees. The recent loss of so many elms, another important food plant, has reduced its numbers in other parts of the country.

POPLAR HAWK-MOTH *(Laothoe populi)* This moth is common throughout Britain in open, damp habitats where poplars, willows and sallows grow, where it flies at night from May to August. When resting, it brings its hind wings forwards to lie in front of its forewings.

EYED HAWK-MOTH *(Smerinthus ocellata)* The dramatic 'eyes' are concealed while the moth is at rest, but when threatened, it exposes them to distract the attacker. The larvae pupate below ground; the moths emerge in spring and take wing at night until early summer.

Light Emerald Moth

Silver Y Moth

Vapourer Moth

SILVER Y MOTH (*Autographa gamma*) Easily recognized by the 'Y' on its forewings, this moth is a summer migrant from southern Europe. Common throughout most of Britain, they are seen in city parks and gardens by day and flutter around lights at night.

LIGHT EMERALD MOTH (*Campaea margaritata*) In June and July this moth may be found flying at night among trees or resting on foliage by day. It is abundant in both urban and rural areas. The brown 'Looper' caterpillars mimic twigs when at rest.

VAPOURER MOTH (*Orgyia antiqua*) Only the male of this common species can fly; the female vapourer is wingless and scarcely moves, even laying her eggs on her pupal case. The caterpillars, which feed on many trees and shrubs, have hairs which predators find irritating.

Swift

Summer

SWIFT (*Apus apus*) Migrating north from Africa, the swift arrives in Britain in May. This 6½″ (16cm) bird has long, powerful wings and short weak legs, and lives an almost entirely aerial existence, landing only to breed. Parties of fast-flying screaming swifts, swooping to catch insects, are one of summer's most exciting sights. They nest colonially in old buildings or cliffs, making shallow nests from airborne material glued together with saliva. The young stay on the wing until they breed at 3-4 years. In August they all fly south.

FERAL PIGEON (*Columba livia*) This plump, 14″ (35cm), city bird is a descendant of the rock dove. The plumage is extremely variable: some are bluish like the rock dove, while others are chequered brown, white or grey. Feral pigeons can breed all the year round, where there is adequate shelter and sufficient food, and lay two pure white eggs in a rather untidy nest on rooftops and ledges. Consequently in many cities pigeons are present in such huge numbers that they are considered pests and measures are taken to control them.

Starling

Winter

Juvenile

Feral Pigeon

House Sparrow

Female

Male

STARLING (Sturnus vulgaris) With its sharp, long yellow bill and iridescent speckled plumage, shot through with green and purple, the starling is a strikingly attractive bird. Yet its aggressive bullying manner makes this stumpy 8½" (22cm) bird rather unpopular.

Starlings breed from April onwards, laying up to 7 pale blue eggs in a scruffy nest often tucked into a hole in a wall or roof. After breeding, starlings gather in huge flocks which darken the sky at dusk before settling down to roost among the rooftops.

HOUSE SPARROW (Passer domesticus) Possibly the best-known British bird, the perky, 5¾" (15cm), sparrow is highly gregarious, and often lives in close association with man. The sexes are clearly distinguishable, the males being more colourful than the dull brown females, having a black bib and white wing bars. In March both sexes help build a nest, in trees or crevices in buildings, which they line with soft materials such as fur or feathers before laying a clutch of greyish speckled eggs. Usually three broods of 3-5 are produced a year.

AT THE SIDE OF THE ROAD

Largely undisturbed, roadside verges are flourishing nature reserves, often bedecked with meadow flowers, and attracting all our reptiles as well as many insects, birds and mammals.

Roadside wildlife is the most familiar of all. Song birds establish their territories in the hedge, starlings search the grass for insects, while perky sparrows flock to pick grit from the tarmac itself. All are visible from the car windows of passing travellers.

Even motorways have attracted their own wildlife, headed by a most distinctive bird – the kestrel. It is surely the mascot of modern Britain, hovering over the verge or central reservation, heedless of the rushing traffic. With a swoop it falls to a lower, closer observation station. But few drivers catch sight of its final pounce, a quick drop with half closed wings onto an unsuspecting vole running between the grass tussocks.

Alongside quieter country lanes, the banks of cow parsley provide better cover for the voles and therefore poorer hunting for the kestrel which is less often seen. Here, however, voles are only the start of the wildlife tally. Many animals live among the roadside herbage.

From the road can be heard the shrill squeaks of shrews. They have a longer snout and sharper teeth than either voles or mice. They are highly territorial little animals and no shrew will tolerate another on its home patch. Their quarrels can be heard quite a distance away.

Another flurry of action occurs when a rabbit is suddenly disturbed by a questing stoat. Fleeing to its burrow, it hastily scampers along the network of small twisting paths which lies hidden below the taller plants of the verge. The bulkier badgers and foxes out on patrol often make use of the road itself. Dazzled by car headlights at night, this habit sadly means that many are struck by cars.

CRICKETS AND GRASSHOPPERS

In the warmth of the sunshine, the roadside is alive with insects. Not only grasshoppers but bush crickets of different kinds chirrup from the longer grass. Resembling grasshoppers in many ways, bush crickets – sometimes known as long-horned grasshoppers – can be distinguished by their very long antennae. Females sport a formidable looking tail which is not a sting but an egg laying organ.

The colourful wayside flowers attract as many busy hoverflies, bees and butterflies as are found in any meadow. While small but gaudy beetles sun themselves on the flat platforms of the cow parsley; cardinal beetles and soldier beetles are often seen. Nearby, escaping all but the closest inspection, lurks a crab spider, its colour camouflaging it to the exact shade of the white or yellowish flower. It spins no web but jumps at any hoverfly that happens to land nearby.

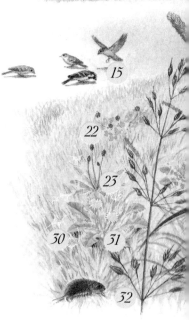

BRIGHT FLOWERING VERGE
Red poppies, white mayweed, yellow ragwort and rape growing beside the M20. Rape, a member of the cabbage family, has invaded from nearby crop fields, while the splash of poppies indicate that the soil has been recently disturbed.

WILDLIFE OF THE ROADSIDE VERGE

On the road, grit aids the digestion of various birds, and road casualties provide easy pickings for crows, magpies and the omnivorous badger. The verge divides into several areas that reflect its management. Nearest the road the grass is regularly mown and the flowers are low growing, while many, like plantains and dandelions, have flat rosettes of leaves. Money spiders sling their webs between the short stems. Further in, a meadow-like swathe is cut twice a year. Taller flowers and grasses flourish here, providing cover for grasshoppers and the runways of voles, as well as perches and egg-laying sites for meadow brown butterflies. Common blues rest head down overnight on grass stems. Where the ground has been dug for pipe-laying, nettles, docks, mayweeds and other strong-growing plants colonize the bare soil. Peacocks lay their eggs on stinging nettles. A ditch provides a habitat for aquatic plants and may attract spawning frogs which, in turn, fall prey to grass snakes. Beneath the hedge the tall vegetation, including cow parsley, may be cut only once a year. Stoats hunt along the hedgerow where chaffinches and magpies may be nesting.

KEY TO THE SPECIES

1	Kestrel	19	Broad-leaved dock
2	Carrion crow	20	Reed canary grass
3	Magpie	21	Stoat
4	Oak	22	Red clover
5	Gorse	23	Ribwort plantain
6	Whitethroat	24	Sheep's sorrel
7	Meadow brown	25	Cowslip
8	Peacock	26	Meadow grasshopper
9	Nesting chaffinch	27	Common blue
10	Badger	28	Hedgehog
11	Timothy	29	Garlic mustard
12	Nettles	30	Money spiders' webs
13	Cow parsley	31	Dandelion
14	Large white	32	Bank vole
15	House sparrow	33	Pyramidal orchid
16	False oat grass	34	Scentless mayweed
17	Meadow cranesbill	35	Grass snake
18	Ox-eye daisy	36	Common frog

TOWNS AND VILLAGES

BROWN BUTTERFLIES
Resting here on fleabane are a female meadow brown (on the left) and the slightly smaller female hedge brown or gatekeeper. Both species are grassland butterflies frequently found on roadsides. Their caterpillars feed on grasses, especially annual meadow grass, and the adult butterflies are on the wing throughout the summer.

FIELD VOLE
(right) A rodent of rough grassy places, field voles are common in Britain but are absent from Ireland. They form runs among the grass stems and are active both day and night, feeding mainly on grasses. Voles form a large part of the diet of kestrels, owls, stoats and weasels.

STOAT AT RABBIT
(below) Hunting by scent along walls, hedgerows and verges, stoats run down rabbits, voles and mice, dispatching them with a bite to the neck. Bounding across the road, stoats are often seen for only a split second.

In the wetter places, which can be easily spotted by the clumps of rushes or even reedmace ('bulrushes'), small frogs abound in spring, and here, too, lurk grass snakes which prey on them. Adders, however, prefer the drier, sunny banks behind the verge, and often hibernate below the hedge.

Surveys have shown our roadsides to be a prime animal habitat, with no fewer than half our mammal species, all our reptiles, a quarter of our birds, half our butterflies and half our different bumble bees having set up home along them.

This variety is matched by an abundance of plant life. Few roadsides would be complete without those umbellifers, the cow parsley and its relatives. They flower in overlapping sequence through the summer. Cow parsley itself flowers from April to June, while the similar looking rough chervil continues into July and hogweed can flower on into the autumn.

But the umbellifers are only the start of the plant story. As with any other habitat, the type of soil along a length of verge is reflected in the flowers seen. And the soil, of course, changes as the road winds across the countryside.

Cowslip and salad burnet, for example, indicate a rather limy soil, while ribwort plantain implies a neutral one. Most verge soils are one or the other, but if heather, bracken, foxglove or sheep's sorrel are seen, the soil is likely to be rather acid.

Moreover, large patches of cowslips, rockrose or meadow cranesbill tell us that the verge has ancient soil, long undisturbed. Another clue

BLACK-HEADED CARDINAL IN FLIGHT
(below) This cardinal beetle – so-called because of its bright red wing-cases – is one of three British species. It can be spotted on flowers at the roadside and in old woodland and parkland. Here it is seen taking off from a head of cow parsley. The yellowish larvae live under the bark on fallen trees and stumps.

CINNABAR CATERPILLARS
(above) Crowds of these tiger striped moth caterpillars festoon ragwort and groundsel plants in July and August, stripping them bare. They can afford to be so conspicuous because they absorb poisons from the plants, making them distasteful to birds.

ADAPTABLE MAGPIE
(below) A familiar roadside bird, the magpie is quick to descend on rabbits, hedgehogs and other animals killed by passing traffic. This easy source of food has replaced the carrion once commonly found on farms and in cities.

to age is the sheer number of flowers – sometimes as many as 20 or 30 different species can be counted in each square yard of the verge.

Older verges, too, will have many more wild grasses, including not only cocksfoot but bromes and Yorkshire fog or even quaking grass with its dainty panicle.

All in all, more than 500 different flowers have been found on verges. This wonderful diversity of often quite small plants very largely relies on regular cutting of the verge, which keeps coarser growth at bay.

The story starts many years ago when each village had a lengthman who maintained local stretches of road. He worked along these throughout the seasons, scything the waysides short and keeping them clear. Wide lanes were counted a bonus as the villagers often grazed their animals on them and even took a cut of hay from the waysides.

In this way, a meadow-like habitat was created along the roads and lanes, filled with the very same flowers and the same grasshoppers and blue and brown butterflies as bedecked the village meadows.

SAVING THE FLOWERY SWARD

This century, when the road itself became tarmacked, motor mowers have replaced the lengthman's scythe on the verges. But if the blades are not set to cut too short, the flowery sward is maintained. If the verge is shaved short, however, only low growing plants such as speedwells, dandelions and plantains can survive.

Very often, verges are mown in swathes. The roadside strip is kept short-trimmed for safety and appearance, and a middle swathe allowed to grow higher, and maybe cut twice a year; this encourages the meadow plants, allowing them to flower and seed. The back swathe, where the cow parsley flowers tall in front of the hedge, will perhaps be cut only once a year.

So rich have some verges become that many counties have roadside 'nature reserves', with a cutting programme to suit the flowers. Nowadays, though, the danger is that cutting is being run down to save ratepayers' money, and the tougher plants will be able to overwhelm the dainty flowers. Chemical sprays which would kill all the plants except for the tougher grasses have, luckily for nature, been found too expensive for regular use.

The rich tapestry of our verges, offering nature at first hand, is a prize habitat in the countryside. And an important one, for verges total no less than half a million acres.

Cow Parsley

Yarrow

Broad-leaved Dock

Sheep's Sorrel

BROAD-LEAVED DOCK *(Rumex obtusifolius)* A tall perennial with stiff, branched stems reaching 39″ (100cm). Lower leaves are large and oval, upper ones more linear. The inflorescence has many whorls of tiny wind-pollinated flowers. It is common on disturbed, open ground.

COW PARSLEY *(Anthriscus sylvestris)* An extremely common plant, flat heads of tiny white flowers are seen by roadsides and hedges almost everywhere from April to June. 24-39″ (60-100cm), the stems are grooved and hollow. Fern-like leaves have toothed leaflets.

SHEEP'S SORREL *(Rumex acetosella)* An upright or sprawling 4-12″ (10-30cm) perennial. Separate male and female plants bear spires of tiny green-yellow flowers, which turn red as they mature, from May-August. Common on acid grasslands and heaths.

YARROW *(Achillea millefolium)* Belonging to the daisy family, this perennial has tough, erect 16″ (40cm) stems and creeping runners. An aromatic plant with long feathery leaves, it bears dense, flat sprays of flowers June to August. It is common in grasslands and waysides.

Treacle Mustard

Rough Chervil

Hogweed

Meadow Cranesbill

ROUGH CHERVIL (*Chaerophyllum temulentum*) Resembling cow parsley, but with rough, hairy, solid 12-39″ (30-100cm) stems that are purple-spotted, and dark green leaves, hairy on both sides. Flowering June-July, widespread but local in Wales and the North.

TREACLE MUSTARD (*Erysimum cheiranthoides*) Locally abundant in cultivated lowland in the South, this 8-24″ (20-60cm) erect annual has stalkless, narrow stem leaves – and a basal rosette that withers before the flowers open June-August. The fruit is a long, thin capsule.

MEADOW CRANESBILL (*Geranium pratense*) An erect hairy 12-31″ (30-80cm) perennial growing from a thick rhizome. Upper stems and buds have sticky hairs. Flowers are borne in pairs June-August, becoming fruit which splits open, shooting out seeds. Widespread.

HOGWEED (*Heracleum sphondylium*) A common 20-80″ (50-200cm), coarse, stiffly hairy biennial with lobed leaves on broad stems. Flowering from June to September, the notched petals are white or pink, those of the outer flowers are larger than the rest.

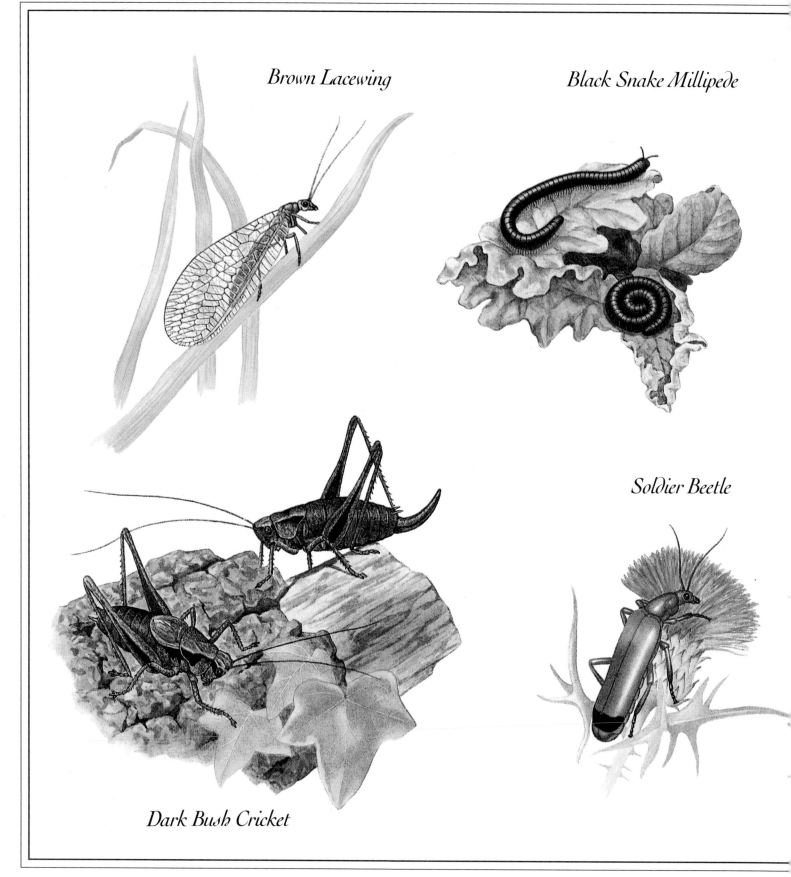

Brown Lacewing

Black Snake Millipede

Soldier Beetle

Dark Bush Cricket

BROWN LACEWING *(Kimminsia subnebulosa)* A small and predatory insect which feeds on aphids, it is common in deciduous trees and tall vegetation. 2-3 generations a year, brown larvae moult 3 times before pupating. Adults have 2 pairs of wings with a 'lacy' network of veins.

DARK BUSH CRICKET *(Pholidoptera griseoaptera)* Males are heard 'chirping' loudly from hedgerows in summer. Common in the South and Midlands, they feed on plants and soft insects. Females place eggs singly into rotting wood with an ovipositor. They cannot fly.

BLACK SNAKE MILLIPEDE *(Tachypodoiulus niger)* Despite its many legs – 96 pairs – this millipede moves quite slowly, curling up and exuding a foul smell when attacked. It feeds on living and dead plants. When hatched, the young resemble the adults and mature in 6 months.

SOLDIER BEETLE *(Rhagonycha fulva)* The adults fly well and are numerous July-August, often seen on umbellifer flowers. They feed on pollen, nectar and aphids. Females lay about 200 eggs – the tiny, predatory larvae overwinter in the ground, resuming growth in spring.

Click Beetle

Pied Shield Bug

Thrips

Speckled Bush Cricket

CLICK BEETLE (*Agriotes lineatus*) A 'clicking' defense mechanism enables this beetle to make huge leaps or to right itself when upside down. Adults feed on pollen and nectar, but the larvae, known as wireworms, attack roots. Common on pastureland and verges.

SPECKLED BUSH CRICKET (*Leptophyes punctatissima*) Living among tall plants, this flightless cricket is most common in the South. Adults are seen in warm weather August-October. Males grip the females with 'pincers' when mating. Eggs are deposited in plant stems.

PIED SHIELD BUG (*Sehirus bicolor*) Attentive parents, females tend their 40-50 eggs, laid on the ground, until they hatch. Adults and larvae feed on dead nettles and related plants. It is common in hedges and waste ground in the South.

THRIPS (THUNDERFLY) (*Thrips* spp.) Inconspicuous but very numerous, these minute insects can usually be found scuttling amongst flower petals. Not all have wings – those that do, fly on hot still days, and are known as thunderflies. Feeding on sap – some are crop pests.

Magpie

Male

Female

Greenfinch

MAGPIE *(Pica pica)* Becoming increasingly numerous, this 18″ (45cm) member of the crow family has an unmistakable appearance and harsh *chak-chak-chak* call. Magpies are omnivorous, usually feeding on open ground but also scavenging on rubbish tips and foraging amongst bushes, stealing eggs and nestlings. The sexes are alike and both build the large nest – domed to prevent predation by crows – of twigs with a cup of mud and finer materials. Nests are made up in trees. 5-8 blue-green, speckled eggs are laid in April.

GREENFINCH *(Carduelis chloris)* A gregarious but argumentative 5¾″ (14cm) finch, widespread and now increasingly numerous as it has spread into recently forested areas. It is a seed eater – with a strong beak. In winter, many flock into towns, enjoying peanuts from bird tables. A bulky nest of grass and moss lined with fine stems and feathers is built deep in a thick bush. Breeding April-August, the somewhat duller female lays 4-6 pale, red-purple spotted eggs in each of 2-3 clutches. Young birds are a pale, streaky brown.

Lesser Whitethroat

Whitethroat

Female

Male

LESSER WHITETHROAT *(Sylvia curruca)* Similar to the whitethroat but paler, greyer and with no chestnut on the wings, this 5¼″ (13cm) summer visitor has a shorter tail. It is a secretive bird usually remaining in dense cover, but often feeding in treetops. A flimsy nest of dead leaves and grass is lined with hair and down. 4-6 off-white eggs with olive and grey spots and marks are laid May-June – sometimes 2 broods. Chiefly insectivorous, berries are eaten prior to migrating. The song is a quiet warble, changing to a rattle. It is locally common.

WHITETHROAT *(Sylvia communis)* A restless 5½″ (14cm) summer visitor often noticed bustling about in the undergrowth, the male with his crest raised. The female can be distinguished by her brown head. Males utter a fast chatter during a dancing song flight. Both sexes build the deep cup-like nest of twigs and dry grass, lined with fine stems and located low down in a bush. Double-brooded, 4-5 pale blue or green, speckled eggs are laid beginning in May. Eating insects most of the year, they take berries and fruit in the autumn.

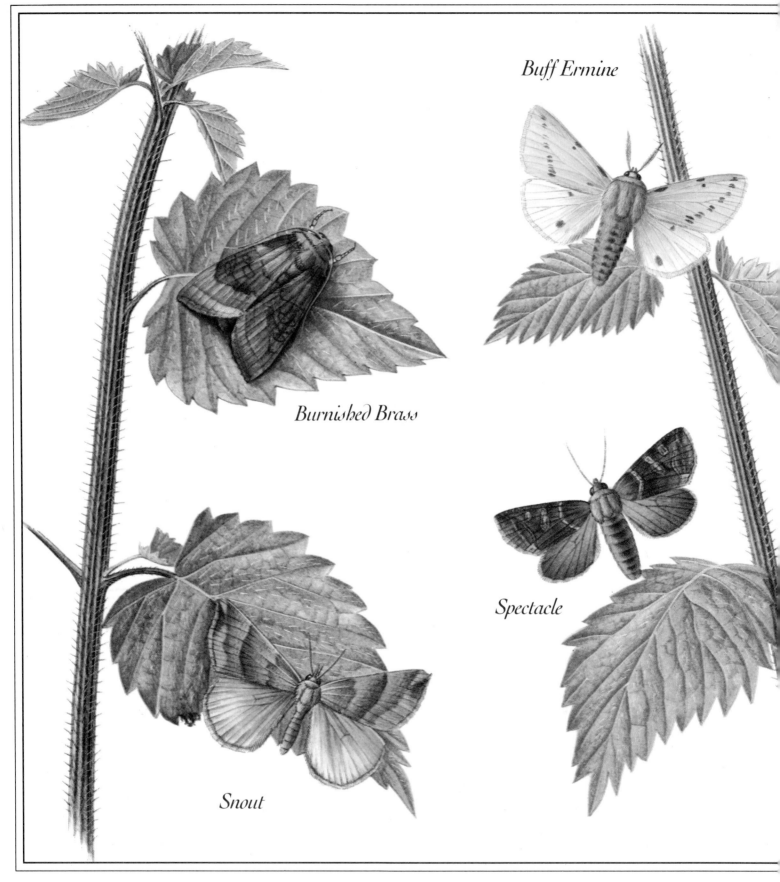

Buff Ermine

Burnished Brass

Spectacle

Snout

BURNISHED BRASS (*Diachrysia chrysitis*) Chiefly active at night in June-September, it also flies by day, easily recognized by brassy bands on the forewings. Common over wasteland and hedges but absent from the far North. Overwintering larvae pupate in May.

SNOUT (*Hypena proboscidalis*) Sensory 'palps' form the snout of this common moth. Flying at night over hedges and wasteland June-July, it always stays near the larval foodplant, stinging nettle. Sparsely hairy, green caterpillars hibernate, pupating the next June.

BUFF ERMINE (*Spilosoma lutea*) Attractive moths, females usually paler than males, that fly at night May-July. Common in areas with lush vegetation – though local in the North and Ireland – the hairy larvae feed on dock and other plants July-September, overwintering as pupae.

SPECTACLE (*Abrostola triplasia*) A nocturnal moth with indistinct 'spectacle' markings on the thorax, the adults are attracted to flowers May-June. Locally abundant, its larvae are also active at night and feed on the foliage of stinging nettles.

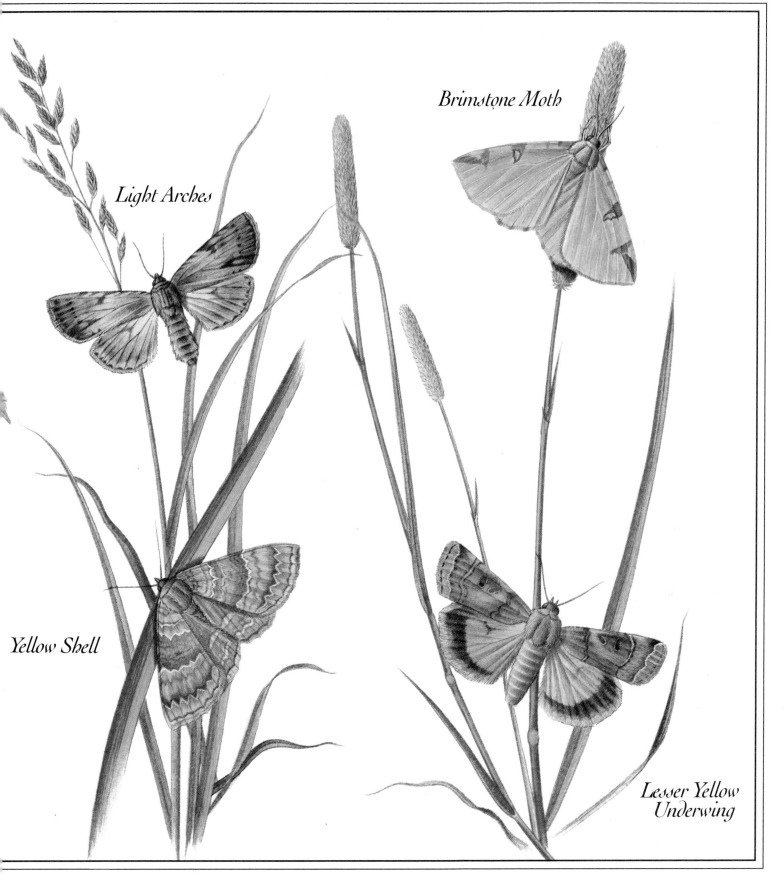

Brimstone Moth

Light Arches

Yellow Shell

Lesser Yellow Underwing

LIGHT ARCHES (*Apamea lithoxylae*) This pale moth flies at night June-July, resting on tree trunks by day. It is generally common but scarce in the North. The female lays white shiny eggs in grass seedheads, the larvae feed low down the stems October-May, pupating underground.

YELLOW SHELL (*Camptogramma bilineata*) This widespread abundant moth has variable markings—a very dark form occurs in Ireland. Adults fly night and day from June-August. The larvae feed on grasses and other plants after dark, hibernating in winter, pupating underground in May.

BRIMSTONE MOTH (*Opisthograptis luteolata*) Flying day and night, it is a moth often Seen in open woodlands. Some of the warty, twig-like larvae hibernate, others overwinter as pupae so adults occur spring-autumn. Foodplants are sloe and hawthorn.

LESSER YELLOW UNDERWING (*Noctua comes*) A widespread moth of hedges and heaths, which flies at night July to September. Young larvae feed on herbaceous plants and grass. After hibernating they eat the leaves of birch and shrubs, pupating underground.

49

ON *THE* COMMON

**Rich in insects and plants, with good numbers of
both birds and mammals, the patchwork mix of the lowland common
is a welcome sanctuary for wildlife and people.**

A stroll with a dog across the grassy common sends rabbits scampering to their burrows among the clumps of dog rose and bramble. From the depths of a thicket, a tentative burst of song betrays the presence of a garden warbler. Orange-brown small skippers fly swiftly over the grass and a bright, 'blue-eyed' peacock butterfly perches, wide-winged, on a thistle. Topping everything the liquid music of a skylark in full song rains down from above.

The common can be an exhilarating place, but it is always more than just a playground for ourselves. Very often it is a wildlife sanctuary, today more precious than ever before. And though it may carry only one name on the map, to the observant eye the common turns out to be a patchwork of different habitats.

The lowland village common can be a wild place, whether it be heathland or grassy. Because it has never felt the bite of the plough and never been drained, the ground retains a prehistoric geography of bumps and ruts, ancient paths and mysterious hollows.

The grazing has always been rather scrappy. There may be cattle or sheep on the common, or the plump bellied ponies of local children, but they hardly ever create the smooth lawn of the regimented grazing regimes in the grassy ley fields alongside (here everything is calculated to put meat onto bone in the shortest possible time). The haphazard munching of the commons' beasts creates a wonderfully diverse grassland.

There is plenty of long grass for the benefit of butterflies, especially the 'browns', which lay their eggs on the grass stems and leaves. One of the most likely to be seen is the meadow brown, one of our commonest species but now much less often seen in large numbers, mainly because of the ploughing of the ancient hay meadows. The small heath is another likely find, as is the marbled white – they are both grassland 'browns' in spite of their names. They may be joined by the moth-like skipper butterflies.

INDUSTRIOUS ANTS

Ant hills are often a feature – meadow ants can nest undisturbed in this casually grazed and unploughed land. These industrious insects rarely make an appearance above ground, but forage in their tunnel systems below the surface, acting as a territory marker.

The ant hills make a rather unusual miniature habitat in their own right. The fine grained soil is desert dry at the top, and here wild thyme and other delicate small flowers may grow; they would elsewhere be smothered by the rank grasses. Into the ant hill bore small mining bees and wasps. And here, too, the strangely shaped

BURNET ROSE
Essentially a flower of coastal areas, this white rose grows on commons with sandy heathland and can form areas of scrub on limestone in the North. Shorter than other roses – about 18in. – it has distinctive black hips in late summer.

ROMAN SNAILS
These large snails –
their shells are 2in.
high – are found on
meadows and
commons in chalk
and limestone areas
of southern England.
The species is not
widespread but can be
locally common in
areas which suit it.

KEY TO THE SPECIES
 1 *Magpies*
 2 *Silver birch*
 3 *Whitethroat*
 4 *Oak*
 5 *Molehills*
 6 *Dog rose*
 7 *Bracken*
 8 *Creeping thistle*
 9 *Hawthorn*
10 *Spindle*
11 *Rooks*
12 *Nettle*
13 *Field mushrooms*
14 *Rabbits*
15 *Garden warbler*
16 *Red admiral*
17 *Sorrel*
18 *Comma*
19 *Sweet briar*
20 *Red admiral caterpillar*
21 *Meadow ants' nest*
22 *Meadow brown*
23 *Bee orchid*
24 *Creeping thistle lacebug*
25 *Hedgehog*
26 *Short-tailed vole*

purse web spider often lurks in its sock-like web.

Some colourful flowers cope well with the long grass. If the soil is somewhat chalky there may be a few wild orchids. The bee orchid is one – its upright spike of flowers is seen in June or July. Its name comes from the resemblance of these flowers to female bumble bees.

Thistles – statuesque but much maligned – are strong growers with intricately tight flower heads that repay a closer look. The creeping thistle is one species found everywhere; it can grow to a sturdy three feet and spreads quickly through its creeping root system.

Goldfinches are well known frequenters of the downy thistle heads in autumn, delicately pulling the individual seeds out one by one.

LIFE ON THE LOWLAND GRASSY COMMON
No longer regularly grazed or mown, many commons are reverting to scrub. Low-growing grasses and flowers, interspersed with taller shrubs and trees, produce a rich mixture of species. At ground level, edible mushrooms appear in late summer; hedgehogs, moles and voles search for invertebrates; butterflies find foodplants for egg-laying; and anthills double as rabbit latrines and fertile sites for downland flowers. Numerous birds frequent the common for its plentiful insect life and safe nesting sites among the scrub.

Apart from these and other seed-eating birds, thistles attract many insects earlier in the year, especially butterflies.

The painted lady is drawn to the sweet, musky odour of thistle flowers. One of our most prized butterflies, it flies here in summer from its birth sites in North Africa. It lays its eggs on thistles growing out in open ground. Home bred butterflies are on the wing later in the year, and while some may begin a homeward migration, many die with the onset of the first cold nights.

Another doughty butterfly traveller is the more familiar red admiral. Those seen flying early in the year come from Europe, those on the wing later are home bred. It is often seen on commons, attracted by the nettles for egg laying, though like all butterflies it needs to top up its energy store, and frequently visits brambles and other flowers, sipping the nectar with its long 'tongue'.

The peacock and the small tortoiseshell butterflies are also highly mobile. Occurring in many habitats, they may well be seen seeking egg-laying sites on the nettles that grow alongside the common's thickets.

These thickets add immensely to the attraction of the common, for such 'wild places' are hard to find in today's manicured countryside. They attract nesting birds, and a good many moths.

Left to itself, most of Britain would become

CUCKOO SPIT ON A CREEPING BUTTERCUP
Appearing in spring, cuckoo spit is the protective froth nest of a young froghopper bug which sucks sap from the host plant.

GIANT PUFFBALLS
(left) Young cattle may or may not be fungophiles but this dramatic fungus, when young and white, is certainly a human delicacy. Giant puffballs frequently grow to a width of over 2ft and can, reportedly, weigh up to 56lb. The brown spore mass in the foreground (revealed when the white outer walls break away) splits from its roots and, blown by the wind, scatters spores (seeds) over a wide area.

MEADOW BROWN BUTTERFLIES PAIRING
(below) Found throughout the British Isles, meadow browns are probably our commonest butterfly and will flutter up from long grass on almost any summer walk through pastures or commons. The larger size of the female can be clearly seen and she is also more brightly coloured than the male, which is unusual among butterflies.

FROSTED HAWS
(left) Hawthorn produces a rich harvest of berries – haws – which form a winter larder for birds and mammals.

FRUITING JUNIPER
(below) The fruits of this native evergreen shrub ripen from green to blue black over a period of 2 to 3 years, and are used to flavour gin.

SCRUBLAND BUNTING
(below left) Yellowhammers are birds of open country, frequently seen in the scrub on commons.

covered with oaks and other mighty trees creating a dense forest. Farming and grazing keep the land open. When land is abandoned the woodland returns, but not at one bound. A rather intricate natural process takes place, seen on many commons.

FROM GRASSLAND TO WOODLAND

As any gardener knows, bare ground is soon covered with a tangle of 'weeds' – small, quick growing plants of many different kinds. In time these are replaced by grasses and are smothered when the grass grows tall. What happens then depends on the seeds that birds or other accidents of nature bring to the site, but quite often clumps of brambles grow. Wild roses, too, are early colonizers, often found on parish commons.

Then it may be that a bird (or a mouse gathering a winter store) brings the seeds of two shrubs, very familiar but of great importance in our countryside. These are hawthorn and blackthorn or 'sloe'. They are both quick growing and prickly, soon forming dense thickets. Blackthorn is particularly able to do this, for it can spread by means of underground suckers.

In time the seeds of trees find their way to the thicket. Some birds (jays, for example) are well known for the way they collect acorns and other seeds and carry them some distance to bury them in a cache. In the thicket, safe from cattle and other grazing animals, and relatively safe from rabbits (the thorns deter them) the tree saplings grow, and in time will overtop the hawthorn and blackthorn pioneers which remain as the underwood in the new woodland.

That is what is happening on many open grassy commons. It takes around 50 years for a low wood to develop. On chalky soils it may be that spindle and dogwood are the pioneers. On chalk hillsides yew or juniper sometimes grow first, to be followed by beech.

On heathy commons in the lowlands, different species are seen. Often gorse is early on the scene as the pioneer tall scrub, but sometimes quick seeding birch creates its own instant woodland. Pine, too, can spread quickly with its light seeds, to be followed by oak at a later stage.

In other words, left to itself, our lowland countryside would change its natural face. The common holds the proof.

Garden Warbler

Chiffchaff

GARDEN WARBLER *(Sylvia borin)*
This 5½″ (14cm) migrant haunts
scrubby undergrowth throughout
England and Wales from April to
September. It feeds on worms,
insects, larvae and berries, and in
May or June lays four whitish eggs
in a cup-shaped, grassy nest.

CHIFFCHAFF *(Phylloscopus
collybita)* Fond of undergrowth and
tall trees, this 4½″ (11cm) bird flits
from twig to twig in search of insects,
larvae and spiders. Most winter in
Africa, though some stay in the warm
South and West. In May, four shiny
eggs are laid in a domed nest.

Willow Warbler

Grasshopper Warbler

WILLOW WARBLER *(Phylloscopus trochilus)* Similar to the chiffchaff in appearance, size and feeding habits, the willow warbler prefers more open ground, and its mournful 'wee-eet' call is distinctive. From April on, six or more eggs are laid in a spherical nest on the ground.

GRASSHOPPER WARBLER *(Locustella naevia)* Heath, conifer woods, marshes and water meadows are the habitats of this widespread 5″ (12.5cm) migrant. In May or June, it lays six eggs in a hair-lined, well hidden nest. It eats insects and larvae, and winters in Africa.

Sweet Briar

Dogwood

Spindle

SWEET BRIAR (*Rosa rubiginosa*)
Also called eglantine, this vigorous,
8′ (2.4m) shrub has arching,
densely prickled branches. Fragrant
flowers appear in July and the
leaves smell of spice. A quick
colonizer of chalky ground, it is
sometimes grown as a garden hedge.

DOGWOOD (*Cornus sanguinea*)
Usually found on chalky soils
especially in the South, this 12′
(3.5m) upright suckering shrub
produces its pungent flowers in
June followed by shiny black
inedible berries. The deciduous
leaves turn wine-red in autumn.

SPINDLE (*Euonymus europaeus*)
This 25′ (8m) shrub, or small tree,
grows in hedges and copses in
chalky soil, especially in the South.
Tiny flowers appear in June or July,
but it is best known for the beautiful
fruit that follow. Much loved by
aphids and caterpillars.

Field Rose

Buckthorn

Burnet Rose

FIELD ROSE *(Rosa arvensis)*
Common on heavy soils in the South
and West, the field, or trailing, rose
makes dense mounds of slender
stems. Its unscented flowers borne
in June and July, even in shade,
are followed by small fruits; the
shiny leaves last well into winter.

BUCKTHORN *(Rhamnus
catharticus)* A native of the Midlands
and the South, this 10′ (3m)
shrub favours hedges and woods on
chalk. The thorn-tipped branches
carry tiny flowers in June followed
by black berries. In autumn the
leaves turn golden-yellow.

BURNET ROSE *(Rosa
pimpinellifolia)* This suckering
shrub, up to 6′ (1.8m) tall, is
usually found on sand or shingle by
the sea, but also forms dense
thickets on limestone. Flowers,
carried in May and June, are
followed by purple-black fruit.

Plate 15.

Buff Arches

Buff Arches Caterpillar

*Copper Underwing
Caterpillar*

*Peach Blossom
Caterpillar*

Beautiful Carpet

Peach Blossom

Copper Underwing

BEAUTIFUL CARPET (*Mesoleuca albicillata*) An increasingly rare woodland moth occasionally found in gardens. By day it rests on the undersides of leaves. The ¾″ (20mm) moth flies from June. Its caterpillars feed at night on bramble, the leaves of wild strawberry and raspberry.

COPPER UNDERWING (*Amphipyra pyramidea*) This 2½″ (55mm) southern moth flies in July and August. Its caterpillars feed on many plants, including bramble, willow, oak and birch. The pointed hump on the caterpillar's rear is its most distinguishing feature.

PEACH BLOSSOM (*Thyatira batis*) Common in woodlands and scrubby places in the South, and locally in Northern Ireland and Scotland, this attractively marked moth has a wingspan of 1⅜″ (35mm), and flies in June and July. Caterpillars feed on bramble and raspberry leaves.

BUFF ARCHES (*Habrosyne pyritoides*) Widespread in the South but absent from Scotland, the caterpillars of this woodland 1½″ (40mm) moth feed largely on bramble, hazel and hawthorn. It flies in June and July, sometimes with a second generation in autumn.

Broad-bordered
Yellow Underwing

The Mouse

Barred Yellow

The Lackey

THE MOUSE (*Amphipyra tragopoginis*) So called because it runs when disturbed, this moth flies at night in July and August. It has a 1½″ (40mm) wingspan and is common in woods, fens, marshes and gardens. Caterpillars feed on willow, thorn and wild strawberry.

LACKEY (*Malacosoma neustria*) Common in the South, lackeys range in colour from yellow to brown. They have a wingspan of 1½″ (40mm) and fly only at night, in July and August. Caterpillars weave silken tents on hawthorn, sloe, oak, birch, willow and some fruit trees.

BROAD-BORDERED YELLOW UNDERWING (*Noctua fimbriata*) Common in woodlands in the South, this 2½″ (65cm) moth appears in July, then rests and reappears in late summer. Caterpillars emerge from their cocoons to feed on hawthorn, willow, birch and dock.

BARRED YELLOW (*Cidaria fulvata*) Common in England and Wales, less so in Ireland and Scotland, this 1″ (25mm) moth flies at night, from June to August. Its haunts are scrub and hedgerows. Caterpillars feed on the leaves of burnet and dog rose, but will eat cultivated types.

AROUND THE GREEN

**Circled by farmland, the village's many habitats
draw in nesting birds, breeding butterflies and feeding moths,
while mice and bats often frequent the buildings.**

The stately trees of the village first catch the eye. So tall that they overtop the church, they bestride the green, dwarfing the cottages below. Often there is one really ancient tree, so old that its bark is riven and split, proving an irresistible lure to nesting birds, bats and other wildlife.

Horse chestnuts are frequently found around the green, often planted in commemoration of some event. They are of foreign origin, occurring in the wild only in the Balkans, and their insect count is lower than that of native trees: only four insect species regularly make use of them compared to the total of 284 for the oak. For all that, their flowers – as intricate as orchids – are a delight in themselves when they bedeck the leafy branches in spring like white tallow candles. And, of course, the conkers – the plump ripe seeds of the horse chestnut which are hidden in spiky green husks – have, for centuries, been the cherished weapons of childhood duels.

The red horse chestnut, a hybrid of North

NESTING JACKDAWS
Chimneys provide ready-made sites for the jackdaw's twiggy nest.

American stock, is often planted alongside its white-flowered cousin. Smaller, with crinkly leaves, a shorter candle of pink flowers, no wicked spines on its husks and no sticky buds in spring, it is something of a poor relation.

More majestic trees are often to be found in the churchyard and the vicarage garden. Here may grow yews, tall pines, the stately Atlas cedar and the spreading cedar of Lebanon. These trees attract collared doves, coal tits and nesting goldcrests. The tall pines may also hold a rookery.

Rooks have long been associated with villages and particularly with stands of elm, but sadly these fine trees are now all but extinct in lowland Britain, killed by disease. Instead, the birds choose any tree tall enough to give a high vantage point for their nests. These are built in February and March, when the broadleaved trees are still bare, and there is much noisy twig stealing and argument.

WILDLIFE OF THE VILLAGE

Daisies, dandelions, speedwells, plantains and clover interleave the grass of the green, attracting bees and butterflies. Starlings, thrushes, sparrows and pigeons probe the turf for invertebrates. The village trees provide feeding, roosting and nest sites for birds, as well as hunting perches for the spotted flycatcher. The woodpigeon, mistle thrush, treecreeper and goldcrest may all nest in the cedar. The rookery is sited in a clump of tall trees. House martins build mud nests under the eaves, jackdaws opt for chimneys or church tower crevices, where the barn owl may also nest, while tits seek holes in trees or thatch. Foxgloves, ox-eye daisies and other garden flowers attract bees, moths and butterflies. The vegetable patch, where white butterflies are drawn to the cabbages, also attracts robins and the insectivorous hedgehog.

KEY TO THE SPECIES

1 *Jackdaw*
2 *Bats*
3 *Rooks*
4 *Barn owl*
5 *Cedar of Lebanon*
6 *Oak tree*
7 *House martin*
8 *Great tit*
9 *Starlings*
10 *Spotted flycatcher*
11 *Horse chestnut*
12 *Silver Y moth*
13 *Peacock butterfly*
14 *Cottage garden flowers*
15 *Hedgehog*
16 *Cabbage white butterfly*

ledge in thick cover – against an ivy clad wall maybe, or up a cracked tree trunk.

Looking at the village as the birds and other wildlife may see it, several different habitats can be distinguished. The churchyard is one, as is the pond and the village stream, too. All in all, nature prefers variety and a bit of disorder, and contenders for the 'best kept village' award are likely to be too spick and span to attract the widest variety of species.

The jumbled, tight-packed cottage garden, on the other hand, can contain a wealth of wildlife. The flowers themselves have often been traditionally grown for centuries. Originally they may have been planted for their medicinal properties. Monkshood, for instance, grows wild in the south-west, but is found in most cottage gardens, and may have been used as rat poison in the old days. Many cottage favourites are, by origin, wild flowers; but the reverse may also be true. Snowdrops have been grown in gardens

SPOTTED FLYCATCHER
(left) Swooping from a prominent perch, the flycatcher captures a wide variety of flying insects. Here it has caught a small tortoiseshell butterfly.

SMALL TORTOISESHELL ON ICE PLANT
(below) Flying from February to October, this butterfly hibernates through the winter, often in a house or garden shed. Adults flock to feed on garden flowers, such as Michaelmas daisy, orpine or buddleia, but lay their eggs on nettles. The colony of young black caterpillars protects itself with a web.

COMMUNAL ROOSTS

Though they nest within the village itself, the rooks feed out on the open fields, congregating on old grassland where there are vast numbers of insects, worms and other invertebrates. Though persecuted for the corn they steal, rooks, on balance, do more good than harm, taking the leatherjackets and the wireworms which damage the roots of grass and cereals. After breeding, rooks tend to spend the nights in large communal roosts, sometimes returning to their treetop rookery in autumn, for a renewed, but abortive, burst of nesting activity.

Jackdaws – close cousins of the rooks – are equally gregarious and just as typical of the village scene. They feed alongside rooks in the fields, and mixed flocks may straggle back to roost together in the evening, with the jackdaws' *chack, chack* calls counterpointing the rooks' deeper *caw* and *kaah* notes.

Nesting in loose colonies, jackdaws seek out holes and crannies in sites as diverse as old trees, castles, churches and cottage chimneys. They are lively, communal birds, and have an interesting and elaborate social language, using not only calls but also postures to communicate. Mentally alert and always inquisitive, jackdaws have a fondness for bright, shiny objects, taking and hiding anything from diamond rings to sweet wrappers.

The village buildings attract innumerable other birds. The thatch of cottage roofs makes a fine nest site for sparrows and starlings. House martins build under the eaves, swifts nest in the roof cavities, while swallows favour the outbuildings. Blackbirds, tits, wrens, robins and other familiar birds all nest and feed in the village gardens.

A rarer village visitor is the spotted flycatcher which is a summer migrant arriving in May. It is attracted by rather open wooded areas, which to its eye the village may resemble. It nests on a

COTTAGE GARDEN
(left) Growing in this richly varied border are angelica, poppies, spurge, ox-eye daisy, geraniums, honesty and foxgloves, many of which can be found growing wild in hedgerows, fields or woods.

CABBAGE WHITES
(right) Feeding on cabbages and Brussels sprouts, these caterpillars are the only British butterfly larvae to damage crops. The adults are best told apart by their antennae: the small white's are ochreous, whereas the large white's are black with white tips. The large white is also noticeably larger than its relative which has a 2" wingspan.

HOUSE MOUSE INSIDE A CAVITY WALL
Although found in fields and hedgerows many mice overwinter in outbuildings or houses.

ROOSTING BATS
These pipistrelles – our smallest and commonest bat – hang, head down, when roosting. They can squeeze into remarkably small cavities and are often to be found in the roof space. They fly out shortly before dusk to feed on flying insects, often congregating over the village stream or pond where gnats, moths and other insects are abundant.

for centuries and, though commonly seen growing wild, they are probably an introduced species rather than a native flower. Gooseberries and currants, too, can be found growing wild, but the bushes may have grown from pips carried by birds raiding the gardens nearby.

Orpine – known also as sedum or livelong – is a native flower typical of cottage gardens. A boon to bees, it also attracts colourful butterflies such as the peacock.

Familiar though it is by name, the house cricket is now rarely heard from within the cottage. Its old haunt, the warm open range, has been replaced by modern stoves, and modern cleanliness has banished it outside. However, its shrill chirps may be heard coming from the cottage compost heap on warm evenings and nights. This insect-rich rubbish heap may also be the refuge of the common toad, or act as an incubator for the eggs of a grass snake.

VILLAGE LIFE

As evening falls the glow from the cottage windows attracts many moths, including the red underwing which flies in from poplar trees in the lane, and the white ermine and angle shades moths which are drawn from hedgerows to the garden flowers. The old lady moth often flutters out too, as the curtains, where it has been resting, are drawn.

It is after dark that the village most seems part of the countryside around. Cottages and fields are joined by the calling of the barn owl, an eerie cry, now sadly not as common as it was. From its nest in the church tower, a hollow tree or nearby farm buildings, it flies out to quarter the fields, in silent pursuit of the nighttime voles, mice and shrews. More common is the quavering hoot of the tawny owl. Adept at flying between trees, this owl hunts predominantly in woodland and prefers to nest in hollow trees.

A hedgehog, snorting through the herbaceous border, stops briefly to sniff the air as a vixen's sharp cry echoes across the surrounding fields, then returns, grunting, to its search for fat white slugs and glistening earthworms.

LARGE WHITE
FEMALE

LARGE WHITE
MALE

SMALL WHITE
FEMALE

CATERPILLAR OF LARGE WHITE

CATERPILLAR OF SMALL WHITE

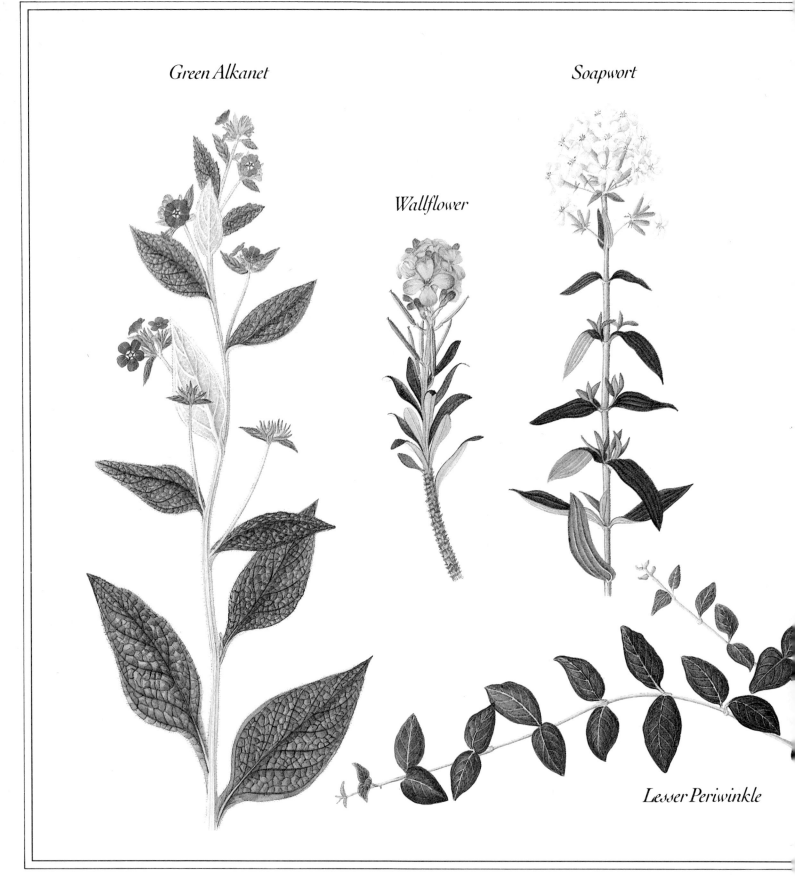

Green Alkanet

Wallflower

Soapwort

Lesser Periwinkle

GREEN ALKANET *(Pentaglottis sempervirens)* The blue flowers of this hairy evergreen plant are like those of the garden forget-me-not. Green alkanet has upright stems 12-40″ (30-100cm) high, and flowers from April to June. Its root is a source of red dye.

WALLFLOWER *(Cheiranthus cheiri)* The fragrant blossoms of the wild wallflower are always bright yellow. They give a splash of colour to dry wall crevices from April to June. This perennial grows to a height of 6-24″ (15-60cm) and spreads by seed from long seed pods.

SOAPWORT *(Saponaria officinalis)* The fragrant flower clusters of the soapwort attract hawkmoths. This perennial grows 12-32″ (30-80cm) high and flowers from August to October throughout England and Wales. The leaves and roots produce a soapy liquid when boiled.

LESSER PERIWINKLE *(Vinca minor)* The trailing stems, 12-24″ (30-60cm) long, of this widespread evergreen plant root wherever they touch the ground. Short upright stems produce flowers from March to May, and in the autumn. The rough blackish seeds rarely mature in Britain.

Borage

Snapdragon

Orpine

Greater Periwinkle

BORAGE (Borago officinalis)
This annual is a garden escape that has colonized waste ground. The bright blue star-like flowers that appear in June and July are edible, as are the young cucumber-flavoured leaves. The plant grows to 20″ (50cm) tall.

GREATER PERIWINKLE (Vinca major) Producing its large violet-blue flowers from April to June, the greater periwinkle is fairly common in the south of England. The plant roots easily from the tips of the stems, and its oval leaves have short stalks.

SNAPDRAGON (Antirrhinum majus) A well-known garden plant, the snapdragon grows well in old walls. The 12-18″ spikes of flowers revert to reddish-purple and yellow in the wild and appear from July to September. The name antirrhinum means snout-like.

ORPINE (Sedum telephium)
This succulent plant – also known as livelong – can survive long periods of drought: the fleshy leaves and upright stems can store water. It grows to a height of 8-24″ (20-60cm) and flowers in late summer through to early autumn.

Wren

Great Tit

House Martin

HOUSE MARTIN *(Delichon urbica)* A summer visitor from Africa, the 5″ (13cm) house martin builds a nest of mud pellets often under the eaves of a house, in which 4 or 5 glossy white eggs are laid. The bird eats insects, catching them on the wing.

WREN *(Troglodytes troglodytes)* A tiny 3¾″ (9.5cm) bird, which eats small insects larvae and seeds. The male builds several spherical nests from grass and leaves in tree trunks, hedges or sheds. The hen chooses one which she lines with feathers and then lays 5-8 eggs.

GREAT TIT *(Parus major)* At 5½″ (14cm) this is the largest and most quarrelsome of the tit family. It feeds on fruit, berries and seeds, as well as insects and scraps. 5-12 eggs are laid from April to May in a cup nest of moss often made in a nest-box, tree or wall.

Mistle Thrush

Barn Owl

Robin

BARN OWL (*Tyto alba*) While hunting at night for rats, mice and voles the 13½" (34cm) barn owl makes its long eerie shriek. It returns each year to the same nest site in a barn or hollow tree to lay its 4-7 white eggs. Heaps of castings reveal the nest site.

ROBIN (*Erithacus rubecula*) The tame 5½" (14cm) robin will often search around the feet of a gardener for insects, larvae and earthworms. The female builds a nest of grass, dead leaves and moss in ivy or undergrowth, or in an old container. She lays 5 or 6 speckled buff eggs.

MISTLE THRUSH (*Turdus viscivorus*) Named for its partiality to mistletoe berries, the 10½" (27cm) mistle thrush eats slugs, snails, insects and earthworms also. A bulky nest of twigs and grass is made high in a tree in February, and 3-5 eggs are laid.

ON THE RESERVOIR

The vast expanses of water held in our reservoirs harbour diving ducks, roosting gulls, introduced fish and, at the water's edge, nesting warblers and attractive flowering plants.

Summer sees reservoirs at their most attractive. On blustery days, gentle breezes ruffle the water, setting myriad reflections of the sun dancing and flashing on the surface; on calm days, the pellucid waters mirror the scene around to serene perfection. Yet even on a grey winter's day, when the water seems dull and lifeless and the concrete trappings seem stark and sterile, there is a rich profusion of wildlife to be seen on many of Britain's reservoirs.

Despite their artificial origin, reservoirs seem to attract a wide range of wild creatures and plants. Numerous species, especially birds, have made their homes in and around these man-made lakes – so avidly, in some places, that several reservoir sites have been established as nature reserves of national importance.

Reservoirs vary enormously – from dammed upland lakes and flooded farmland to urban canal feeders and vast concrete basins storing water near the big cities. Yet they all provide a combination of open water and, usually, shelving shoreline that has proved as attractive to many species as any natural habitat – especially at a time when natural habitats are coming under increasing pressure from man's activities. In the country, reservoirs provide an environment for

wildlife as comfortable as many natural lakes; in the town, they are a unique refuge amid the barren urban landscape.

Reservoirs do, however, present certain difficulties for wildlife. The water level, for example, may fluctuate widely, often in an unpredictable way. Birds such as great crested grebes, which anchor their floating nests to emergent vegetation, and coots, mute swans and other species which nest among reeds, rushes, willows or overhanging bushes, may find that they are flooded out, or left on dry land, dangerously exposed to predators. Indeed, grebes are such poor walkers that, if the nest is left high and dry by a fall in the water level, they are quite unable even to reach it. But breeding birds are not the only interesting species to be found at such sites. Inland waters are visited by thousands of winter visitors, or passage migrants on their way north in spring and south in autumn.

Ideally, the level should be high during the winter, covering the vegetation of the previous summer and autumn, floating off the seeds and making the shallows around the reservoir edge a paradise for dabbling ducks. A warm, dry spring might allow a slow fall in the level, exposing a little fresh, oozing mud to attract

PINTAILS UPENDING
Pintails are rare breeding birds in the British Isles – probably fewer than 50 pairs breed each year. In winter, however, large numbers fly here from northern Europe. The largest flocks occur on estuaries and saltmarshes. But they also visit reservoirs with shallows that allow them to upend in search of underwater plants.

SEASONAL WILDLIFE ON THE RESERVOIR

In winter (left of picture) many birds visit the reservoir. Gulls fly in to roost on the open water. Rafts of tufted duck and pochard dive for food, often dozing during the day. Grebes and cormorants dive for fish. Great grey shrikes are scarce winter visitors associated with scrub areas near reservoirs.
In summer (right of picture) waterside plants bloom. The hatch of insects attracts dragonflies, swallows and the reservoir's many fish. Ringed plovers may nest on the shore, while moorhens, sedge warblers and occasionally pochard and gadwall nest in the vegetation.

KEY TO FEATURES AND SPECIES

1 Cormorant
2 Great grey shrike
3 Swallow
4 Gadwall
5 Willow wood
6 Planted hawthorns
7 Gulls
8 Tufted ducks
9 Mayfly
10 Sedge warbler
11 Great willowherb

12 Shovelers
13 Trout rising
14 Pochard
15 Moorhen
16 Reed canary grass
17 Great crested grebe
18 Grey heron
19 Roach
20 Amphibious bistort
21 Clear shallows

22 Whirligig beetles
23 Pale persicaria
24 Brooklime
25 Brown hawker
26 Scum of red algae
27 Muddy foreshore
28 Little ringed plover
29 Common fleabane
30 Water mint
31 Feeder stream

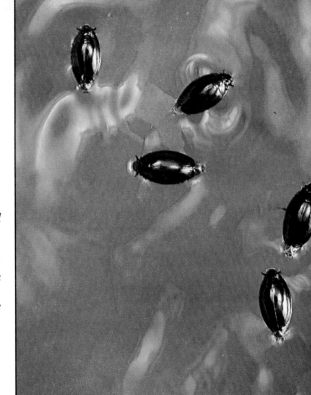

CANADA GEESE
(left) Introduced into Britain in 1678 from North America, these geese are now a common sight on many inland waters. Numbers have increased and the population has spread since the last War. The birds have taken well to reservoirs and gravel pits, nesting on islands and in rough vegetation around the margins. Large flocks fly in V-formation.

WHIRLIGIG BEETLES
(right) At the margins of reservoirs and other bodies of open water – including garden ponds – large numbers of these beetles congregate. Like other beetles they can fly and are often one of the first insects to colonize a new stretch of water. They get their name from the way they whirl in circles on the surface.

SHOVELER PAIR
(below) Shovelers breed mainly on lowland marshes and in water meadows but, where conditions are suitable, they have also taken to nesting around reservoirs. They feed on plant matter in shallow, muddy waters, sieving it through their broad spatulate bills as they swim.

sandpipers on passage, and to encourage snipe and redshanks to settle and breed. During the critical weeks when grebes and coots are brooding their eggs, the level should, ideally, be almost stable, but a fall during the late summer is perfect for the supply of fresh, rich mud on which waders can feed during the weeks of autumn passage. In fact, returning waders may be present as early as July and linger into November – the more mud, the better they like it. Mud also encourages a growth of luxuriant vegetation, slowly covering the more exposed areas as they dry out to give the huge supply of seeds, shoots and roots beloved by the ducks in winter.

MUD LOVERS

On reservoirs created from flooded farmland especially, vast areas of mud can appear where once there was shallow water. These areas soon attract hordes of opportunistic waders. Scores, even hundreds, of snipe and dunlins may be joined by typical passage waders such as greenshank, green sandpiper, ruff and ringed plover. These mud areas may also attract more exotic species in the autumn – little or Temminck's stints, curlew sandpipers, wood sandpipers, even pectoral sandpipers from America. Reservoirs in Cornwall are among the best places in Europe to find rare vagrants from America.

The mud soon becomes covered with rushes, docks, and water mint, which in turn attracts scores of small butterflies, among them tortoiseshells, small coppers and red admirals. Golden dock can spread quickly over drying mud, even after several years of high water; amphibious bistort copes easily with variations in wetness. More established vegetation around the edge – reed canary grass or even beds of reed – have reed and sedge warblers breeding. Wet spots, where streams run in to the lake, may become enlivened by the colourful flowers of brooklime, water forget-me-not and purple loosestrife. Brown hawker dragonflies hunt over the damp vegetation, and damselflies, such as the banded demoiselle, flit across the incoming streams.

Out in the middle, there will often be a

concentration of great crested grebes, already beginning to associate in loose flocks by late summer. They are attracted by the roach and, perhaps, small introduced trout too. Later, herons, cormorants and goosanders may also enjoy the fishing, taking many small pike which abound in such waters. Migrant common and black terns dip to the water surface to take insects, but rarely fish. Black-headed gulls appear as early as July after their breeding season; by winter, their roosting flocks may be numbered in tens of thousands.

Teal, shoveler, gadwall and mallard feed around the reservoir edge, foraging among the water plants or dabbling and upending in the shallows. Tufted ducks dive for snails and other small creatures on the bottom during the day. With them will be sleepy pochards, which dive for bottom-living plants at night. Where there is a sward of close-cropped grass, or meadows nearby, flocks of wigeon begin to appear in the

FLOWERING BROOKLIME
(right) This plant of wet
places may be found growing
in the water or on the damp
margins. It occurs around
shallow-edged reservoirs and
in feeder streams. A
perennial, it flowers from
May to September, producing
four-petalled blue flowers
on spikes that shoot out
from the bases of the upper
leaves. Although bitter in
taste it can be eaten, like
the watercress alongside
which it often grows.

RED ALGAE
(bottom right) Blooms of
algae may be found on the
surface of standing water in
summer, especially in slack
backwaters.

autumn. All winter they will use the reservoir as a safe refuge, but come out to graze on the grass when undisturbed.

In winter the reservoir will have other visiting wildfowl. There may be goldeneyes, diving for shellfish, goosanders, smew and ruddy ducks (North American birds escaped from wildfowl collections and now in flocks hundreds strong on the reservoirs of the Midlands and the West Country). And anything from a group of scoters to a stray long-tailed duck might drop in and stay. Great crested grebes move out to the deeper water in winter, joined by cormorants and harried endlessly by gulls that try to steal their catch.

Each winter evening, long lines and Vs of birds fly to the reservoir – not geese, but gulls, which have spent all day foraging on farmland or on refuse tips and now seek a safe place to spend the night. Thousands of herring, common, black-headed and lesser black-backed

GOOSANDER FISHING
(below) Pursuing a fish
underwater, the goosander is
well equipped to catch its
prey. A strong swimmer and
diver, it can stay submerged
for a minute or more. Its
long, red bill is ideally
designed for holding slippery
fish; as well as being
hooked at the tip, it is
also saw-edged. Goosanders
are commonest in winter and
may be confused with the
red-breasted merganser –
another sawbill duck. The
two can occur together on
reservoirs in winter and may
be joined by a third sawbill,
the smaller smew.

gulls gather in huge rafts, and the dedicated gull-watcher might pick out an occasional glaucous, Iceland or Mediterranean gull with them. Their presence on most reservoirs is innocuous. Where the water is already half-treated, however, water authorities deliberately scare them off with explosives and taped distress calls.

Naturalists, whatever their interest, find that the variety at reservoirs makes them an interesting habitat. The diversity of wildlife lured by the captive waters makes each visit more than worthwhile.

Smew

Male

Female

Ruddy Duck

Male

RUDDY DUCK *(Oxyura jamaicensis)* This blue-billed, 14-17″ (35-43cm) duck was first recorded as breeding wild in the British Isles in 1960, when a pair was found in Somerset. Since then they have spread rapidly. Diving for about 20 seconds at a time, it takes invertebrates and aquatic plant seeds from the mud. It breeds on still waters, anchoring a floating nest of plant material to tall waterside plants, in which 6-10 creamy white eggs are laid. Mainly silent, though the male clucks during courtship. In winter the male resembles the female.

SMEW *(Mergus albellus)* Small numbers of this beautiful 15-18″ (38-45cm) sawbill duck visit the British Isles each winter, diving for fish in fresh waters and estuaries, particularly in south-east England. Its breeding grounds are mainly in Scandinavia and Russia, where it nests in holes in trees, laying 7-9 cream to pale buff eggs. The distinctive male appears almost completely white when on the water but reveals a more pied pattern in flight. The smew is usually a quiet bird, but makes a variety of calls during courtship and when alarmed.

Waterfowl

male

Female

Teal

Male

TEAL *(Anas crecca)* The smallest British duck, only 13-15" (34-38cm) long, the teal is very gregarious. A dabbling duck, it usually finds food at the surface or by upending, and rarely dives. It has a diet mainly of seeds in the winter, but also takes aquatic invertebrates during summer. It breeds in many places in the British Isles, usually nesting on the ground in dense fringes of vegetation; 8-11 yellowish-white eggs are laid in a down-lined hollow. The drake has a whistling call and the duck a high-pitched quack.

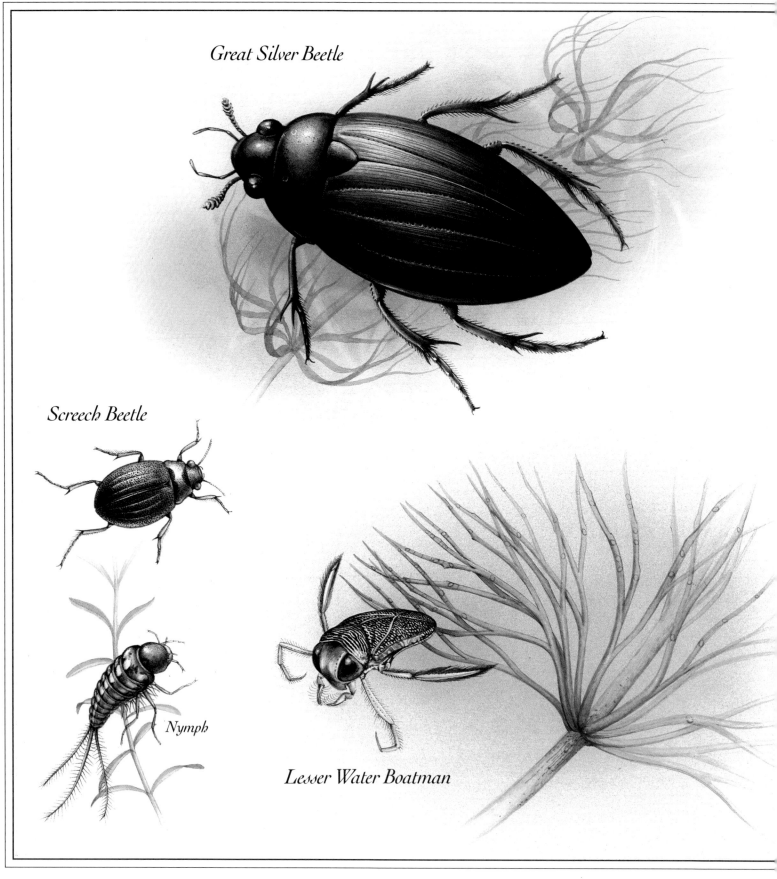

Great Silver Beetle

Screech Beetle

Nymph

Lesser Water Boatman

SCREECH BEETLE (*Hygrobia hermanni*) A common species in still, muddy water, this ¼″ (5mm) beetle announces its presence when captured with a loud squeak, which it makes by rubbing its wing covers against the end of its abdomen. The larva feeds mainly on *tubifex* worms.

GREAT SILVER BEETLE (*Hydrophilus piceus*) Britain's largest water beetle at 1¾″ (45mm), it feeds on water plants in still, weedy water. A layer of air trapped by the hairy body, and breathed underwater, makes the beetle look silver. The larvae feed on water snails.

LESSER WATER BOATMAN (*Corixa punctata*) Unlike the common water boatman, this bug – ⅓″ (8mm) long – swims back uppermost. It spends much of its time on the bottom and swims to the surface to renew its air supply, which is stored in a space between wings and abdomen.

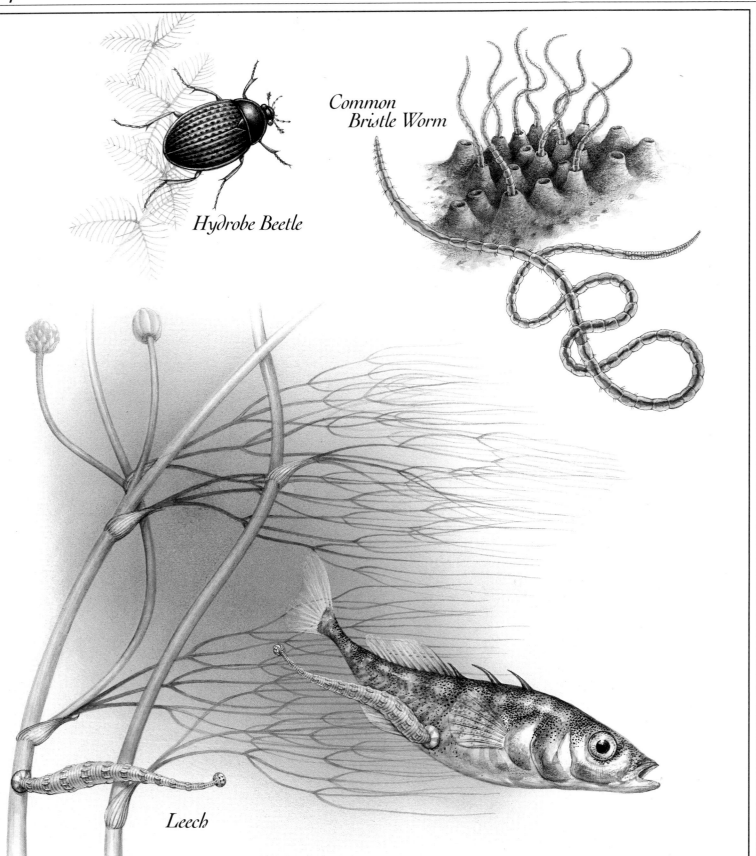

Hydrobe Beetle

Common Bristle Worm

Leech

HYDROBE BEETLE (*Hydrobius fuscipes*) Common in still waters, this ½″ (12mm) water beetle resembles a small great silver beetle. Like many of our water beetles, the hydrobe is a strong flier; this enables it to search widely for suitable new sites for feeding and colonisation.

LEECH (*Piscicola geometra*) This leech is a parasite of fishes, attaching itself to their fins and body. It has two pairs of eyes and its semi-transparent body is about 1″ (25mm) long. It is often found in streams as well as at the margins of still waters.

COMMON BRISTLE WORM (*Tubifex tubifex*) These 1½″ (40mm) worms live in mud; only their tails protrude, and these wave about ceaselessly to extract oxygen from the water. They are often abundant, and provide an important food source for ducks.

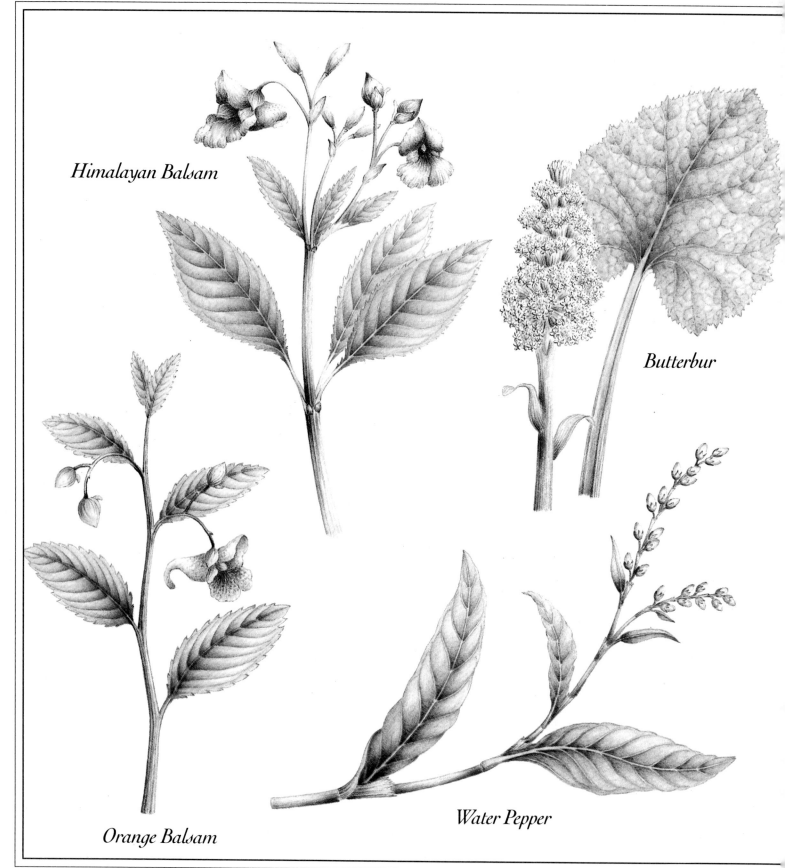

Himalayan Balsam

Butterbur

Orange Balsam

Water Pepper

ORANGE BALSAM (*Impatiens capensis*) A native of eastern North America, this slender, branched 12-20″ (30-50cm) annual bears colourful five-petalled flowers. Naturalized in watery places since early in the last century, it blooms from June until September.

HIMALAYAN BALSAM (*Impatiens glandulifera*) Sometimes known as policeman's helmet, this 5-7′ (1.5-2m) annual is widely naturalized in wet places. Its pale pink to claret flowers appear from June to October and are followed by exploding seed capsules.

BUTTERBUR (*Petasites hybridus*) The stout, 4-16″ (10-40cm), flowering stems of this perennial, a member of the dandelion family, appear in spring, bearing many heads of flowers. The leaves appear later and become huge – up to 30″ (75cm) across – by summer.

WATER PEPPER (*Polygonum hydropiper*) The nodding stems of little greenish flowers of this 1-2′ (30-60cm) hairless annual are familiar during late summer in damp places. The plant is very peppery to the taste and was once used to treat toothache.

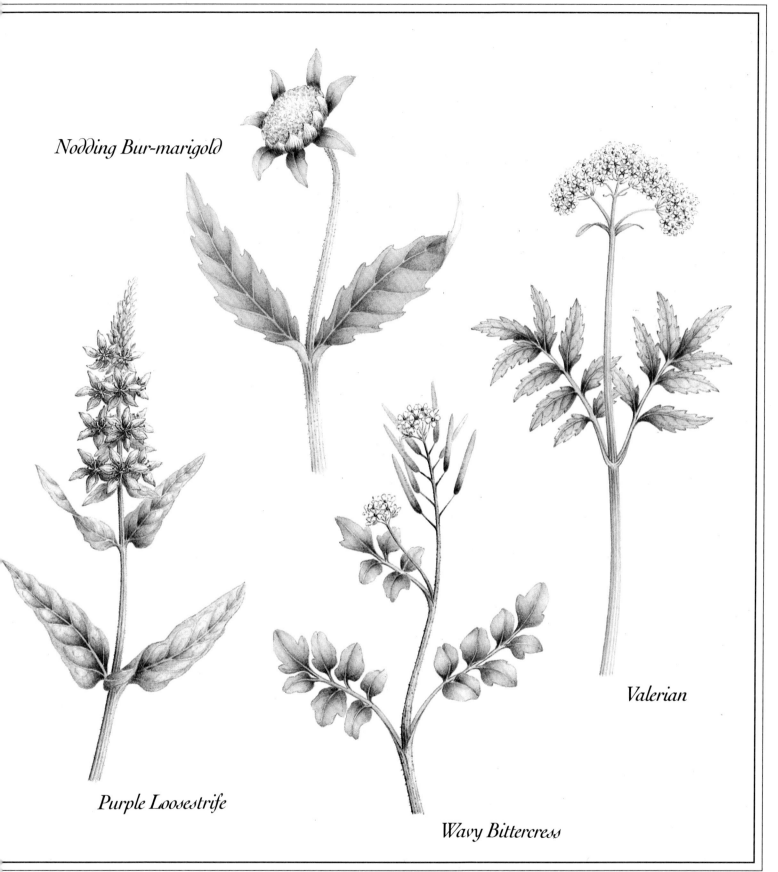

Nodding Bur-marigold

Purple Loosestrife

Wavy Bittercress

Valerian

NODDING BUR-MARIGOLD (*Bidens cernua*) Rather local throughout the British Isles, this 2-24″ (8-60cm) annual prefers places which are wet in winter but dry in summer. The flowers appear in late summer and are followed by seeds which bear small barbed bristles.

PURPLE LOOSESTRIFE (*Lythrum salicaria*) The flowers of this 2-4′ (60-120cm) perennial appear from June to August. Most common in the South, it is a plant of the margins of still and slow-moving waters, where it sometimes forms extensive stands in swampy and marshy places.

WAVY BITTERCRESS (*Cardamine flexuosa*) Abundant in shady places and moist ground, this 8-18″ (20-45cm) biennial produces its little flowers from April till September. Its four-petalled blooms show it to be a member of the mustard family – the crucifers.

VALERIAN (*Valeriana officinalis*) This erect 1-5′ (25-150cm) perennial, whose juice is used as a sedative, is most common in damp places. It blooms throughout summer and the flowers are followed by seeds which bear a feathery 'parachute'.

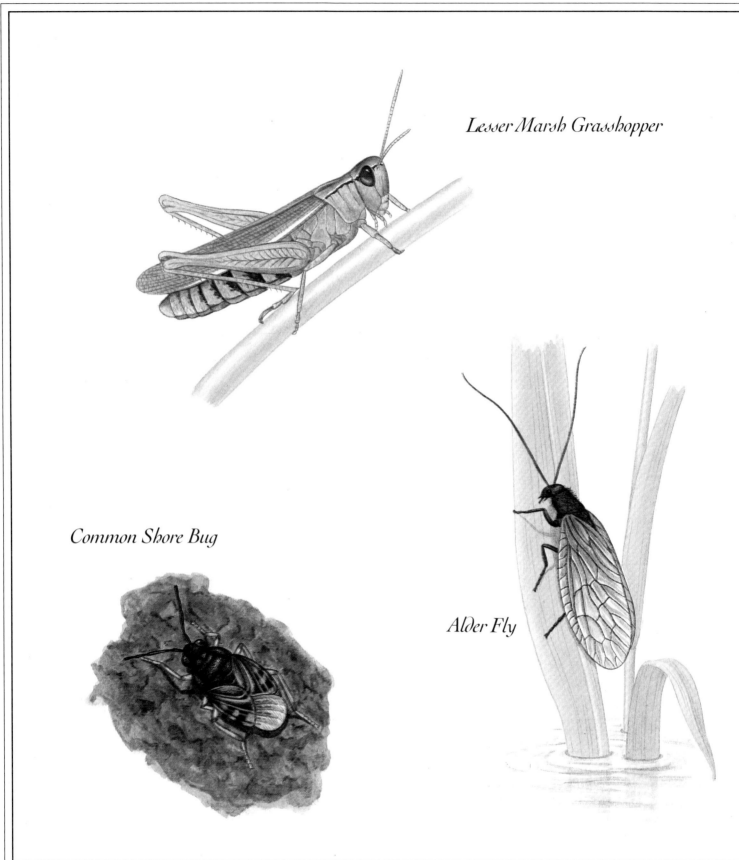

Lesser Marsh Grasshopper

Common Shore Bug

Alder Fly

LESSER MARSH GRASSHOPPER (*Chorthippus albomarginatus*) This ¾″ (15mm) grasshopper is rather variable in the amount of brown and green colouration. Preferring moist, grassy places it is widespread in England, especially near the south and east coasts, but rare elsewhere.

COMMON SHORE BUG (*Saldula saltatoria*) Widespread by the margins of still and slow-moving water, this well-camouflaged ¼″ (5mm) carnivore is one of the commonest British shorebugs, running and jumping restlessly over the mud in search of prey.

ALDER FLY (*Sialis lutaria*) Around the margins of still waters in early summer, this ½″ (12mm) long insect may be seen resting on vegetation or making short, heavy flights from one perch to another. The eggs are laid on waterside plants and the carnivorous larvae are mud-dwelling.

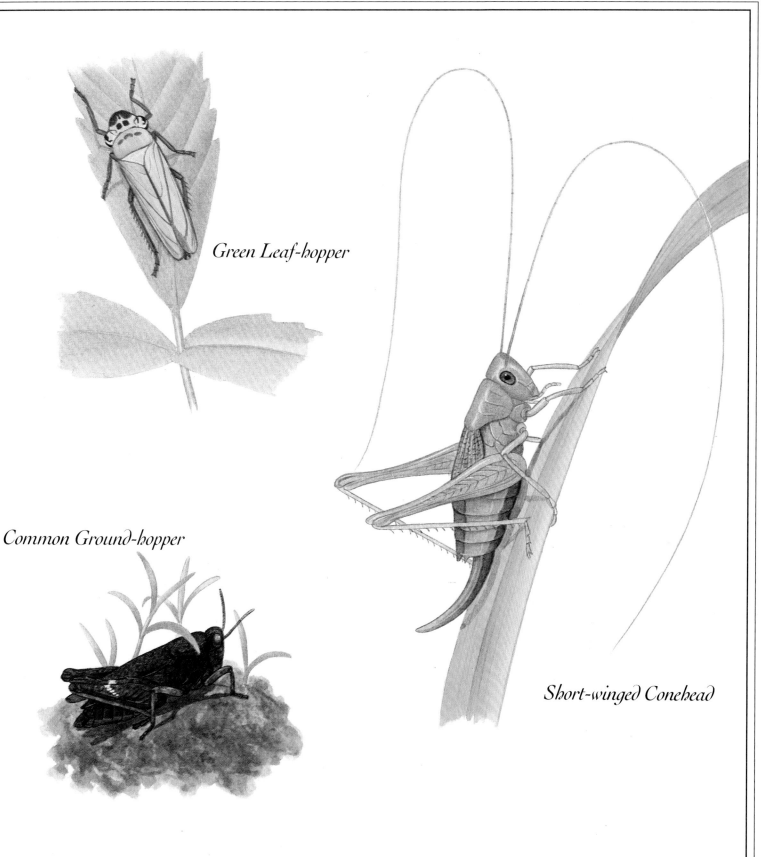

Green Leaf-hopper

Common Ground-hopper

Short-winged Conehead

GREEN LEAF-HOPPER (*Cicadella viridis*) Commonly found in wet, marshy places throughout the British Isles from July to October, this is an extremely active insect, frequently leaping from plant to plant. At rest, the wings are folded, roof-like, over the back.

COMMON GROUND-HOPPER (*Tetrix undulata*) This ½″ (12mm) insect ranges in colour from whitish, through yellows, browns and greys to black, and may be mottled. It occurs in a wide variety of habitats and can jump powerfully and also swim.

SHORT-WINGED CONEHEAD (*Conocephalus dorsalis*) A small ¾″ (15mm) bush-cricket which likes moist habitats, especially near the coast in England. It often inhabits areas of reeds, sedges and rushes and is most frequently seen in late summer.

ALONG THE TOWPATH

Once the bustling byways of cargo laden barges, canals have become peaceful backwater havens for wildlife. Fish and waterbirds have benefitted from fewer boats and fresher water and the banks now abound with plantlife.

Canals may seem like long straight rivers, but their almost still, fresh waters attract a quite unique range of plants and animals. In some ways the canalside habitat more closely resembles a small lake or a deep pool, but because it has a uniform depth and steep banks, there are none of the shallows which are so attractive to certain waterside birds, plants, amphibians and insects.

Canals which are alive with boats can be rather sterile places for wildlife. For the propellers of the boats stir up the bottom mud and though fish and other aquatic animals can survive days of muddy water when a river is in spate, on very busy canals the water is always muddy and this can prevent both plant and animal life. And even if the banks are left untrimmed (they are usually kept cropped along working canals) the heavy wash from modern boat traffic inhibits many of the flowers of the water's edge. So while long stretches of some navigable canals can have great wildlife value, it is the neglected canal or the quiet, disused side cut which are the richest wildlife havens.

Neglected canals are, therefore, home to birds such as the moorhen – common on fields and village ponds – which like to spend much time foraging on land, but close to cover. Young moorhens can be seen from April through the summer for as with many species

NATIVE WATER VIOLET
A flower of early summer.

FLOATING WATER FERN (above) *Introduced from America, this small fern is found increasingly on canals. Its roots hang free in the water and, in winter, the leaves turn reddish.*

DEMOISELLE (above right) *This delightful damselfly, a species of fast running clear streams, may sometimes be seen by canals. Both sexes — the male is shown here – have a fluttering butterfly-like flight.*

two or three broods may be reared each year.

The little grebe or dabchick is also widespread, but prefers some vegetation, maybe a reed bed, close by. It has the habit of suddenly disappearing underwater and sometimes, in order to dive more deeply, it will jump up and break the surface with a splash to bob up again some distance away, after foraging while submerged. Generally, however, it does not like to dive too deeply, and so neglected canals suit it well.

More exciting – and an indication of a canal which has become a really rich wildlife haven – would be the sight of a warbler, a reed warbler maybe, making its beautifully woven cup nest slung between the stems of the reeds. And where this little bird abounds, cuckoos too may

LIFE ON THE DISUSED CUT

From the banks, water violet, yellow flag and great reedmace are encroaching on the open water. Water lilies, amphibious bistort, which grow both on the land and in water, and Canadian pondweed have also begun to choke the channel. The eggs of the roach, laid in early summer, will stick to the underwater stems of the plants. Damselflies and dragonflies lay their eggs directly in the stems: these hunters are attracted by the many water insects. Swallows and house martins are also drawn by this ready supply of insect food. The aquatic moorhen tends to feed on land, grubbing for seeds and insects, as does the mallard, though it often upends to eat underwater plants. The little grebe, though, feeds only in the water, diving for insects and small fish such as sticklebacks. The insect-eating reed warbler nests close to water, artistically slinging its delicate woven cup-like nest between plant stems.

KEY TO THE SPECIES

1 & 7 *House martin*	10 *Water violet*
2 *Swallow*	11 *Moorhen*
3 *Towpath hedge*	12 *Little grebe*
4 *Great reedmace*	13 *White water lily*
5 *Large red damselfly*	14 *Roach*
6 *Reed warbler at nest*	15 *Amphibious bistort, water*
8 *Canadian pondweed*	16 *Common hawker dragonfly*
9 *Mallard*	17 *Amphibious bistort, land*

often startling colours combined with their breathtakingly rapid darting flight makes them exciting to watch as they hunt over the water or lay claim and patrol a territory. It is not unusual to see one of these large insects take a damselfly, its small relative, and consume it in mid-air.

The dragonflies choose undisturbed, clean water with plenty of bankside vegetation for perching and egg laying. In this way, these colourful insects usually signpost a length of canal that has plenty of other wildlife interest too.

Below the surface, such water may be well stocked with fish such as sticklebacks. The three-spined stickleback is commonly found in all types of fresh water in the lowlands, but also occurs in brackish estuaries. The nine-spined stickleback prefers densely weeded fresh water. Rudd are typical of brackish canals and some canals are well known for their giant eels. Eels, like other fish, can reach the canal via its feeder river, although some reaches are also stocked

be common as the reed warbler is one of the cuckoo's favourite host species.

Along stretches of unpolluted canal, bountiful hatches of flies attract screaming hordes of swallows, swifts and house martins. These birds may be nesting in the neighbouring town or village but sometimes a canal bridge – a feature of the habitat – will offer secure cover for swallow and house martin nests. Sand martins, though, need a steep sandy bank as a nest site.

Members of the dragonfly clan – the dragonflies themselves and the damselflies – also indicate water of good quality. Dragonflies rest with their wings outspread and have gigantic eyes which meet across the head. Damselflies are of slighter build, resting with wings held together above their backs, and they have smaller eyes.

Dragonflies are active predators and their

CODLINS AND CREAM
Clumps of great willowherb (above) adorn the bank in stately waist-high masses. The country name likens the flower to rosy apples.

THE ROACH AND THE RUDD
(right) Similar at first sight, the rudd (top) differs from the roach (below) in its jutting jaw and redder fins.

A TASTY MORSEL
The minnow (below) has the misfortune to be a favoured meal for a host of aquatic creatures, from beetles to fish and birds.

RUDD

ROACH

by anglers with carp and other fish.

Frogs and newts like shallowish water for breeding, and their presence may thus indicate that the canal has been neglected for a good many years and has silted up.

The neglected canal can contain an extremely rich variety of plant life. Here one can mark such things as the slight differences between closely related species – the ivy- and celery-leaved crowfoot, for example, which differ from the common water crowfoot not simply by their leaf shape, but by being found in shallow muddy water. As with any undisturbed fresh-water habitat, some submerged plants are likely; the starwort likes these rather muddy conditions. Most submerged plants, such as water violet, push up a flower stalk (often supported by a raft of floating leaves) but hornwort, though a true flowering plant, never appears at the surface. It pollinates underwater. Aquatic plants in general have a poor root system, but hornwort has none!

Identifying water plants by their leaves alone can be difficult, for leaves which float on the surface are generally rounded. This is a good working shape adopted by many different aquatic plants – there is none of the wonderful variety of leaf shape we expect from land plants. The small leaves of the fringed water lily, for instance, resemble those of the larger white water lily, though the species are not related.

Some canals have rather unusual plants, not at all common elsewhere. One such is the water fern, a small fern which resembles duckweed but which becomes red during the summer. It is found, amongst other places, along a stretch of the Basingstoke Canal. Another with a story is Canadian pondweed: introduced from America 150 years ago, it spread rapidly through the canals, and is found everywhere today.

By the banks of neglected canals, beds of reeds grow, along with great reedmace, yellow flag and other plants typical of pond and river edges. Amphibious bistort is one such species which happens to be at home both in the water

VENERABLE BIVALVE
The swan mussel (above left) is a common inhabitant of the mud or gravel beneath slow-moving waters, where it can survive for more than a decade, and at 9" (23cm), it is one of the largest of our many hinged molluscs.

DEFENSIVE DRAGONFLY
(above right) Common in the south of England, the broad-bodied chaser (above right) is a dragonfly whose delicate appearance belies a bellicose nature. Extremely territorial, the male will defend his chosen twig against all-comers. The abdomen is veiled with a bluish bloom.

AN EXOTIC NATIVE
Looking like a tropical visitor, the kingfisher (left) employs a dive-bombing technique of astonishing accuracy in raiding the water for fish.

ACTIVE DIVERS
The lesser water boatman (right) searches for algae and edible debris on the canal bed. It traps an air-bubble between its wings, which it uses as an ad hoc aqualung.

and on land: the water form has rather pointed leaves.

Sometimes the straggling vegetation on the bank of the canal will be found trimmed down as a small, rather untidy lawn. This is the work of the water vole, one of the most charming of canalside creatures. Although rarely seen, it is often heard as it plops into the water when disturbed. Canals are, however, populated by few other mammals, although water shrews are reasonably common, as are brown rats in some areas. Mink, too, may be found along those canals well stocked with fish. Mink catch much of their food in water but they also hunt the waterside. They are usually active at night and the only clue to their presence may be the scattered remains of their prey.

Swallow

Adult

Adult

Moorhen

Juvenile

SWALLOW *(Hirundo rustica)*
A familiar and favourite summer
visitor this 7½″ (19cm) bird with
long tail streamers is often found
near water where it feeds on aerial
insect life and swoops low to sip
water. Returns each year to same
mud and straw nest to lay 4-6 eggs.

MOORHEN *(Gallinula chloropus)*
This common 13″ (33cm) freshwater
bird with red bill-base eats water
plants, seeds, and insects. Its long
non-webbed toes enable it to walk
on floating plants. Nests over water
and lays up to 11 bright buff,
mottled eggs.

Juvenile

Little Grebe

Male

Mallard

Female

LITTLE GREBE *(Tachybaptus ruficollis)* Smallest of the grebe family, this cobby 10½" (27cm) bird, also known as a dabchick, is found on small ponds, slow rivers, canals and sheltered lakes. It bobs and dives for small fish and lays 4-6 eggs in a nest of floating weeds.

MALLARD *(Anas platyrhynchos)* A large, robust duck, 23" (58cm) long. Male is gaudily coloured. Feeds by filtering water with large flat bill for animal and plant matter. Familiar quacking sound is made by female. Lays up to 12 olive eggs in ground or tree nests.

Blue-tailed Damselfly

Female

Male

Male

Common Blue Damselfly

COMMON BLUE DAMSELFLY
(*Enallagma cyathigerum*) Flies, skimming the water, from May to October. Is widely distributed and abundant even in Scotland. Likes large lakes, canals, ponds and streams with plenty of vegetation at the edge. Wingspan of 1½″ (38mm).

BLUE-TAILED DAMSELFLY
(*Ischnura elegans*) The commonest damselfly in England, this insect flies from late May to September, along ditches, canals and over ponds or lakes. Can tolerate even slightly polluted water. Wingspan of 1½″ (35mm).

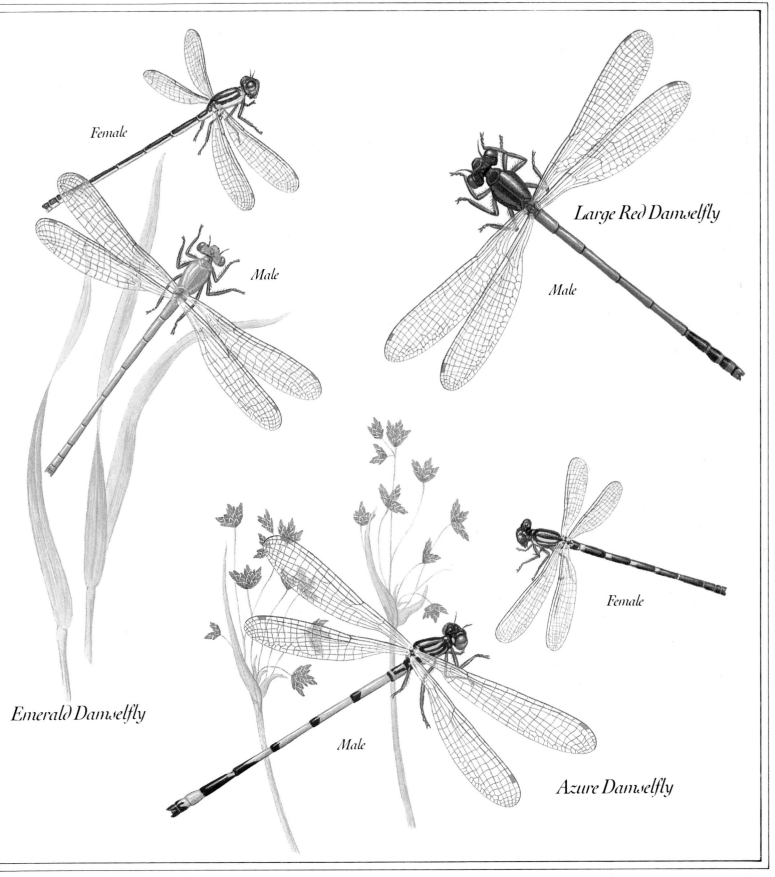

Female

Male

Large Red Damselfly

Male

Female

Emerald Damselfly

Male

Azure Damselfly

EMERALD DAMSELFLY *(Lestes sponsa)* Widespread and common, it flies from mid-June to late September. Likes open ditches, ponds, lakes and canals with rushes or boggy edges. Wingspan of 1¾" (44mm). Rests on grass or heather with half-open wings.

LARGE RED DAMSELFLY *(Pyrrhosoma nymphula)* Distinctive and widespread, it is a large and easily approached species. Common in canals, marshes and peat bogs and even over salty water. Flies from early spring to September. Has a wingspan of almost 2" (50mm).

AZURE DAMSELFLY *(Coenagrion puella)* Adult azure damselflies often fly in pairs, tail-to-head and are common except in the north, flying from May to August. Likes water meadows, canals, ditches and pools with grassy vegetation. It has a wingspan of just over 1½" (35mm).

Brooklime

Gypsy-Wort

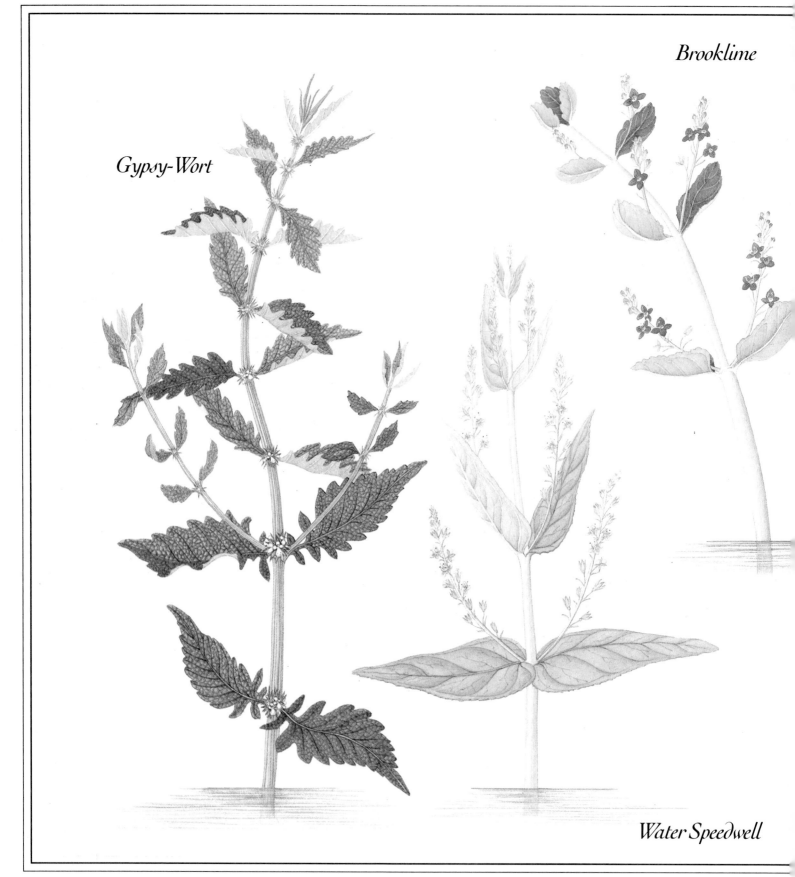

Water Speedwell

GYPSY-WORT *(Lycopus europaeus)*
This 12-40″ (30-100cm) perennial
gives a strong black dye – its name
comes from a mistaken belief that
gypsies used it to darken their skins.
The white or pinkish flowers appear
in summer and the plant is
widespread and common by water.

WATER SPEEDWELL *(Veronica
anagallis-aquatica)* This hairless
speedwell is usually a perennial and
common in muddy places in the
South-east. The branched stems are
8-18″ (20-45cm) tall and their bases
tend to be creeping and rooting.
The leaves are unstalked.

BROOKLIME *(Veronica
beccabunga)* Common and often
abundant in wet places this stout
8-24″ (20-60cm) perennial flowers
in May and June. It has short-
stalked leaves and like water cress,
a plant of similar habitats, it used
to be popular in salads.

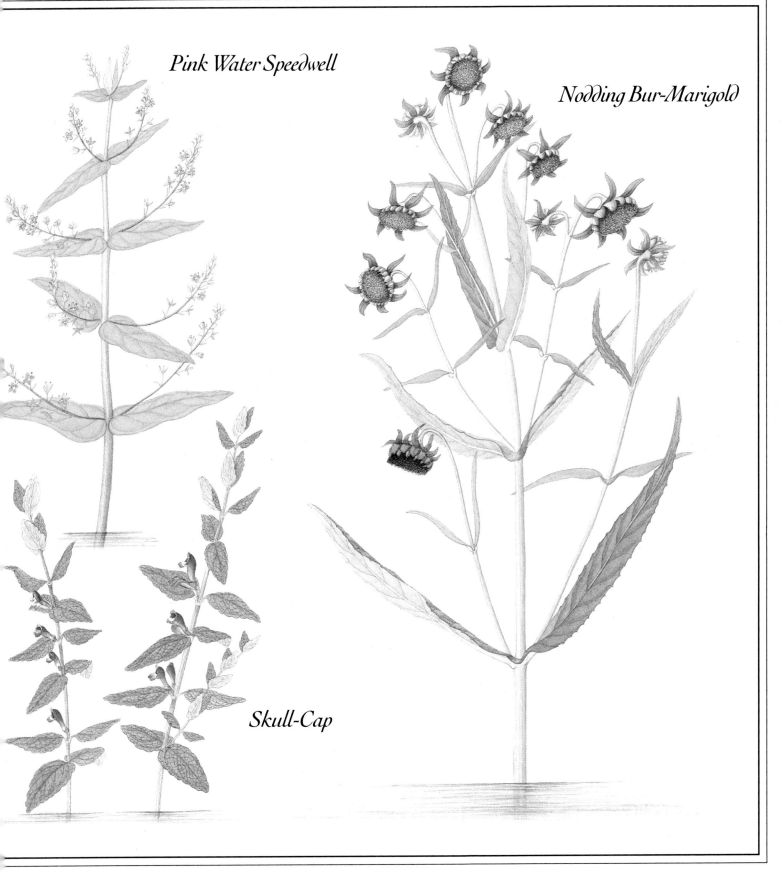

Pink Water Speedwell

Nodding Bur-Marigold

Skull-Cap

PINK WATER SPEEDWELL
(*Veronica catenata*) A stout, hairless
perennial 12-20" (30-50cm) tall,
quite common in shallow water
in the South-east. It has unstalked
leaves and it flowers from mid
June to early August. The stems
are often purple tinged.

SKULL-CAP (*Scutellaria
galericulata*) A perennial with
stout branched stems 9-15"
(22-38cm) tall. Common in wet
places, although absent from the far
North, it flowers from mid June to
early September. In the past it was
used by herbalists to treat fevers.

NODDING BUR-MARIGOLD
(*Bidens cernua*) A member of the
daisy family, this widespread 6-12"
(15-30cm) annual may be found
growing by water, where it is sometimes frequent. Its drooping, solitary
heads of yellow flowers appear from
early June until mid September.

Rudd

Three-spined Stickleback

Ruffe

RUFFE *(Gymnocephalus cernua)*
Usually 6″ (15cm) long, with a
strongly-spined dorsal fin and spiny
gill covers. Ruffe are found widely
in canals and slow rivers. By day
they feed on the muddy bottom.
Ruffe spawn in spring, favouring
warmer shallower water.

RUDD *(Scardinius erythrophthalmus)* A bright and
silvery fish usually up to 12″ (30cm)
long, with large scales and bright
red fins. Found in lakes, canals and
slow-flowing rivers, feeding at
surface or middle depth on tiny
invertebrates and vegetation.

THREE-SPINED STICKLEBACK
(Gasterosteus aculeatus) A common
and tiny, 3″ (8cm), fish of lakes,
rivers, canals and the edges of the
sea. Between March and June the
males build nests in which the
female lays her eggs; the male then
guards the newly hatched young.

Nine-spined Stickleback

Gudgeon

Silver Bream

SILVER BREAM *(Blicca bjoerkna)*
Up to 14″ (36cm) long, this fish
swims strongly and deep in slow-
flowing water and lakes. Feeds on
worms, molluscs and insect larvae;
spawns in shallow water in May
and June. Young mature after
5 years and may live for 10 years.

GUDGEON *(Gobio gobio)* This
6″ (15cm) fish, with its sensitive
drooping barbels lives on the river
or canal bed, for which it has
evolved a flattened belly, and
feeds on small plants and water
creatures. It is found throughout
England and Ireland.

NINE-SPINED STICKLEBACK
(Pungitius pungitius) Usually called
ten-spined but most often has nine
spines. This 3″ (8cm) long fish is
found in both brackish and fresh
water. Males make nests, attract
females with zig-zag dance, then
guard the eggs and young.

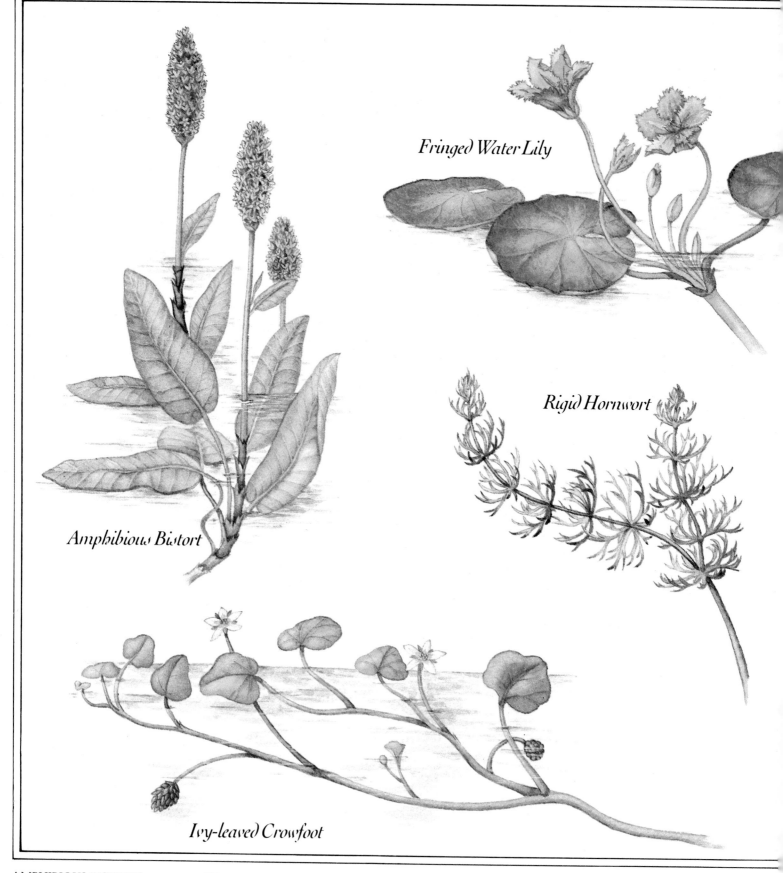

Fringed Water Lily

Rigid Hornwort

Amphibious Bistort

Ivy-leaved Crowfoot

AMPHIBIOUS BISTORT
(*Polygonum amphibium*) This creeping 3′ (1m) plant spreads in large patches. It has tough hairless stems with large floating leaves. Flowering from July to September it is common in still fresh water, where it grows close to the water's edge.

IVY-LEAFED CROWFOOT
(*Ranunculus hederaceus*) Common creeping plant on mud near water and in shallows; this crowfoot has small, star-like ¼″ (12mm) flowers which bloom mostly in May and June above the streamers of floating, ivy-like leaves.

FRINGED WATER LILY
(*Nymphoides peltata*) Not a true water lily, this plant sports 1½″ (4cm) yellow flowers in July and August. Green floating leaves are purple underneath. A relatively scarce plant found in sheltered waters, mainly in the South.

RIGID HORNWORT
(*Ceratophyllum demersum*) A submerged rootless 2″ (5cm) waterweed of still water. It has a bushy and stiff appearance and is decorated occasionally by tiny green or white flowers which are followed by spiny, warty fruits.

Plants of the Canal

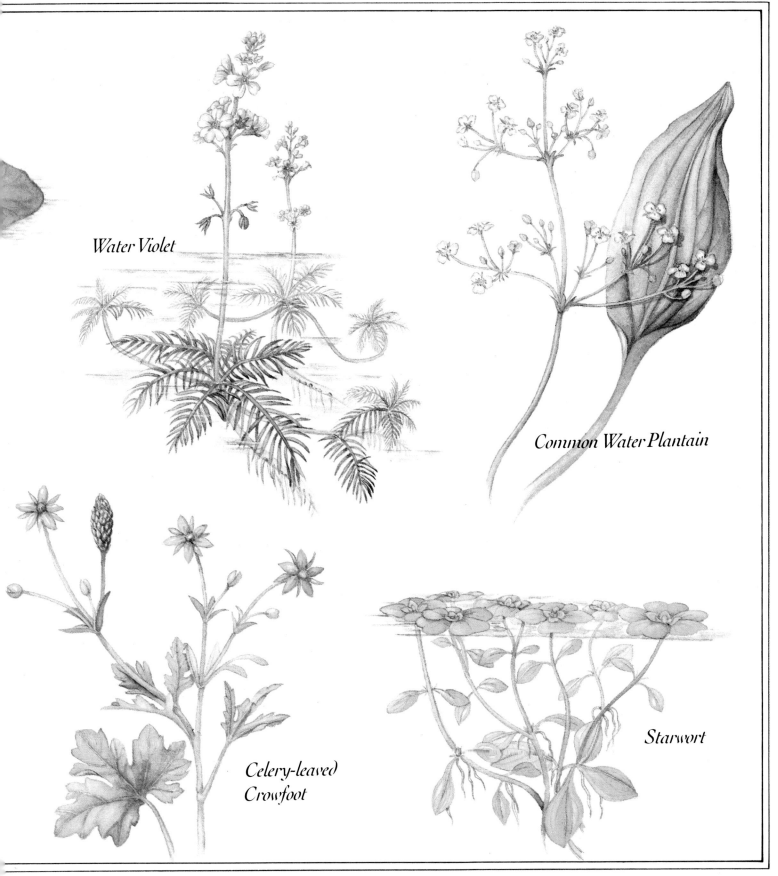

Water Violet

Common Water Plantain

Celery-leaved Crowfoot

Starwort

WATER VIOLET (*Hottonia palustris*) Fairly scarce, this 16″ (40cm) plant is found in ditches, ponds and shallows of canals in the South. Flowering from May to June it is a graceful floating perennial with submerged leaves. Leafless flowering stems emerge above the water.

CELERY-LEAVED CROWFOOT (*Ranunculus sceleratus*) A small buttercup, up to 18″ (45cm) high. Has bright, pale green, branched stems and shiny leaves in tiny bushes with insignificant yellow flowers. Common in wet and muddy places, it flowers all summer.

COMMON WATER PLANTAIN (*Alisma plantago-aquatica*) This stout plant up to 2′ (60cm) high has broad leaves on long stalks. Carries many-branched flower spikes on leafless stems, flowering in July and August. Common in South, it is found in shallow fresh waters.

STARWORT (*Callitriche spp*) A group of very closely related species, each variable and overlapping. This one is a slender, pale water weed found in still water and on dry ground or mud, with 20″ (50cm) stems supported by water, with minute, petalless flowers.

LOWLAND BRITAIN

Lowland Britain is a gentle landscape of rolling downland and broad plains, and amid the patchwork of copses and heaths and fields – often stitched together by mile upon mile of hedgerow – a rich diversity of wildlife flourishes. Few parts of lowland Britain are not farmed or utilized in some way nowadays, yet though many natural habitats have disappeared – and with them many species – there are still myriad wild creatures and plants to see and enjoy on a walk in the countryside.

Much of lowland Britain – essentially southern and eastern England – is built upon sedimentary rocks, rocks created long ago as sand and sediment settled upon the bed of an ancient sea, which then lifted and became crinkled by massive earth movements to form plateaux and hills. Exposure over many thousands of years to the erosive power of wind, rain and running water has moulded these rocks into softly rounded hills and valleys. In many places, rivers, and the ice sheets that covered much of Britain in the past, have deposited rocks and silt eroded from the hills to form broad plains and undulating heathlands.

People have occupied lowland Britain right from the earliest times, and the land has proved remarkably fertile. Over the centuries the vast wildwood that used to blanket much of the landscape has been cleared for farming and an increasing acreage has been brought under the plough, changing the scenery to form the familiar patchwork pattern we see today. Even land cultivated for centuries continues to change as farming methods develop. This century the rows of stately trees and small farms that used to surround the fields have in many places been swept away to create vast open spaces where mechanical harvesters and modern agricultural techniques can maximize crop production.

In late summer lowland Britain can still be tranquil and beautiful, especially as the green corn gradually ripens to gold in the sun. Yet the cornfield is no longer as colourful as it once was, for improved seeding techniques have eliminated many of the wild flowers that used to grow among the crops. Despite this all kinds of plants, birds and mammals continue to live around the cornfield at harvest time, and even in winter, when fields are cold and bare.

Symptomatic of the changes in farming methods this century is the destruction of hedgerows which has proceeded at an alarming rate since the second world war. The vast wild forests of oak and beech that covered lowland Britain have now gone forever too. None of the original wildwood is left in its natural state – except perhaps on a few steep slopes – for it has all been cut down to provide timber for fuel and for construction and to make way for farmland. Yet there are still large pockets of ancient oak and beech wood, such as the New Forest and Charnwood Forest, which are varied enough as habitats to provide a home for many plants and creatures. In summer, the old oakwood teems with life, and, though many species depart in autumn hardier inhabitants and new arrivals ensure there is life even in winter.

Surprisingly, perhaps, the rolling downs and wolds of southern Britain are no more natural a habitat than these managed woods. They are the creation of prehistoric farmers who hewed and burned the beech woods that once grew there to provide pasture for the sheep – which have prevented the trees growing back ever since. Much of even this ancient pasture is now going under the plough and as it shrinks, so gradually we lose another kind of habitat now colonized by wild flowers and butterflies.

Sandy heathlands, too, are under threat. Like the downs, they were cleared of their original timber covering by farmers long ago and were colonized by many species of wildlife. Their value as farmland is limited but heaths too are rapidly disappearing, covered by housing estates and factory complexes as the towns expand, and as industrial 'islands' are built.

The rivers of lowland Britain still meander through the gently undulating landscape. Despite canalization and redirection, and pollution by farm chemicals, sewage and industrial effluents in many rivers, there are still water courses which contain a rich variety of wild creatures and plants. Lowland Britain, one of the most heavily farmed areas in the world, suffers many demands, but this landscape still contains havens for wildlife far from the city.

THE FIELD AT HARVEST TIME

A man-made habitat that changes through the year, the harvest field provides food and shelter for the many plants, birds and mammals that have learned to take advantage of its seasonal face.

Although, at first glance, the cornfield might seem to be a featureless, over-regimented place, compared with other habitats in the countryside, it is by no means lacking in wildlife. Indeed, it provides some fine examples of how wild plants and animals are always poised, ready to take advantage of even the slightest opportunity such as a neglected corner or freshly dug ditch.

In the past, the cornfield was a very colourful place indeed. Not only did the fields blaze red with poppies, but in among the ripening corn were patches of golden yellow corn marigolds, blue cornflowers and stands of corncockle.

These weeds have a story. It is thought that when, some thousands of years ago, our first farmers arrived from the Continent bringing with them stocks of seed wheat and barley – of Mediterranean origin – they also brought the seeds of corncockle and other cornfield weeds which grew alongside the corn in their homelands. Each year, in Britain, these weeds grew with the corn, their seeds poughed into the soil in autumn or even taken in with the seed corn, to be inadvertently planted with the crop the next spring. Eventually, they became a colourful feature of every cornfield, celebrated in the literature, poetry and paintings of the time. They disappeared only with the introduction of weed-killers and with improved cleaning of the seed.

Although many of these cheerful additions to the cornfield were not of significance to the farmer, for the amount of nutrient they stole from the soil was slight, corncockle was a distinct nuisance. Its seeds tainted the ground flour and made it unpalatable and even mildly poisonous. So it was the custom in many places to walk the wheat, pulling up any corncockle that could be seen.

If corncockle, corn marigold and these other handsome plants are to be seen today, it is likely to be only along the edge of the field, where by accident and good fortune they have escaped the sprays applied to the standing crop. Poppies, however, may still be seen, scattered or sometimes in wide sheets, in today's cornfields.

WILDLIFE IN THE CORNFIELD

Throughout the year the cornfield presents a wide variety of habitats for wildlife. In spring the young green wheat provides food for birds, mammals and insects, nest sites for birds and open soil for plants. Grazing animals, like the rabbit, hare and deer nibble at the shoots alongside birds like the partridge and pheasant. Lapwings probe the soft soil for insects while skylarks take insects and seed, and both birds nest among the wheat. By midsummer flowers are in full bloom, while the harvest mouse rears its young in a ball-shaped nest. After the harvest the woodpigeon feasts on spilt grain before the stubble is burnt in readiness for the new sowing.

KEY TO SPECIES AND HABITAT

1 *Lapwing displaying*	12 *Hare*
2 *Skylark*	13 *Cornflower*
3 *Wood*	14 *Ripe wheat*
4 *Roe deer*	15 *Grey partridge*
5 *Pheasant*	16 *Corn marigold*
6 *Combine harvester*	17 *Poppy*
7 *Stubble*	18 *Harvest mouse in nest*
8 *Stubble burning*	19 *Field pansy*
9 *Woodpigeons*	20 *Long-tailed field*
10 *Hedge*	*mouse*
11 *Spring wheat*	21 *Rabbit*

CORNFLOWERS IN A BARLEY FIELD
Known locally as bluebottles or blue bonnets, the rich blue cornflower is now rare due to cleaner seed-grain. It flowers from June to August.

PHEASANTS IN DISPUTE
(right) The colourful cock pheasant gathers a harem of hens and may battle against other males, delivering vicious hacks with the spurs on the back of its legs. Cock birds utter a loud, crowing call as they strut conspicuously about the fields.

SONGPOST
Its speckled crest raised, the skylark sings its liquid, warbling song from a post bordering the cornfield. The song is a characteristic sound of spring and early summer, and usually delivered on the wing as the skylark rises high in the sky. Just visible as a speck in the sky, it then plummets, still singing, towards the ground.

CORNFIELD FLOWERS
White scentless mayweed, red field poppies and yellow wild mignonette in a wheatfield.

Poppies are a wonderful example of the tenacious weed. A weed is, after all, only a plant growing in the wrong place – a place where, as it happens, man is trying by farming or gardening to grow a crop. Many familiar weeds are plants with a quick-growing strategy, able to take advantage of newly exposed or freshly dug soil. In the past they would have been found on landslips and other recently cleared ground, for they are soon shaded out by taller plants in a natural habitat. However, ploughed fields suit them to perfection and during their brief but rapid development they produce vast numbers of small seeds which can remain dormant for long periods. The sheets of poppies in the cornfield today often follow deep ploughing as the long-lived seeds are brought to the warm topsoil where they sprout. It is also noticeable that after land drains have been laid, to improve the drainage of the field, the lines of the filled-in ditches are often marked by lines of red poppies the following year.

THE FARMER'S CROP

Wheat, barley, oats and rye are, of course, different species of grass, and the young cornfield closely resembles a grassy meadow. Sometimes the farmer uses it for grazing: sheep can safely be let on to winter wheat or barley in early spring, and their nibbling encourages the plants to send out side shoots which create a denser growth. Other animals also graze the young leaves. Deer can be seen, especially at dawn, for they are shy and only leave the shelter of the wood when no one is around. Hares and rabbits graze out on the open field, while in some places wintering flocks of geese leave nearby salt marshes to graze the young corn – much to the annoyance of the farmers.

In spring, the grassy looking field attracts the skylark and the lapwing. Lapwings (often known as peewits, due to their distinctive, plaintive *peewit* calls) are one of our most handsome birds, and the exuberant aerobatics of their nuptial flights are an exhilarating spring spectacle. Although by nature a wader of wetlands, lapwings now nest in a variety of other habitats, including ploughed and newly sown fields.

These birds are no threat to the farmer. Indeed, by taking insects and other invertebrates from the soil, they do more good than harm, consuming potential pests. The pheasant's diet also includes insects, although it will take grain and other seeds. Often seen, the conspicuous pheasant keeps close to the shelter of its covert, and rarely ventures far out into the field.

The grey partridge, however, is now seen less often. Once a common bird of cornfields, its numbers have declined over much of Britain. By nature it is a bird of the open field, as its excellent camouflage suggests: when feeding it keeps itself hunched and dumpy, and resembles a large stone or clod of earth. Although some partridges may nest in the open, many rely on the cover of the hedge; the grubbing up of hedges in the corn belt,

CORNFIELD NESTS AND EGGS
The skylark's 3-5 eggs are dull white, covered with smudges of brown, and laid in a neat grass cup beside a tussock. Lapwing eggs are pear-shaped and the nest may be hidden among grass, crops or furrows.

SKYLARK

LAPWING

PARTRIDGE

Partridges make grass-lined scrapes in crops or at the foot of a hedge. The 10-16 eggs of the red-legged partridge are speckled with red-brown; the 9-20 eggs of the grey partridge are unmarked olive. The quail lays 7-12 eggs, whitish with blotches of very dark brown, in a sparsely lined scrape among crops or grass.

QUAIL

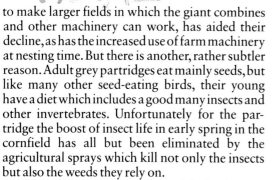

RED LEGGED PARTRIDGE

trees to nest, it feeds on open ground, taking mainly vegetable food in the form of grain, seeds and young shoots. Pigeons are unusual among birds in that they feed their young with a special protein rich 'milk,' called crop milk. As a result, their breeding is not limited only to the spring and early summer, when there is plenty of insect food available for their young. Indeed, woodpigeons can breed strongly in autumn – and here the farming calendar was a prime reason for their past success, for the soil of the autumn fields was scattered with the loose grain dropped from the sheaves of the old harvest.

Other animals may also take advantage of the ripening cornfield. The rabbit, often seen in spring out on the young corn but rarely further than a quick dash from the shelter of the hedge, will continue to snatch any greenery it can find under the shelter of the towering stalks. Under cover of the growing corn, rabbits may venture far out into the field – a fact that was recognized in the past, for the field was first cut around the edge, then slowly worked towards the centre. The rabbits left the uncut patch only at the very last moment, to be caught or shot as they fled across the open field.

Another inhabitant of the old cornfield was the harvest mouse, still to be found sometimes, with its carefully constructed nest woven between the tall stalks. Intriguingly, the wood mouse is just as common in cornfields nowadays. This mouse – also known as the long-tailed field mouse – lives in many different countryside habitats, wandering large distances in search of seeds, berries and other food, which it takes back to a store.

So behind the featureless uniformity of the cornfield lies hidden a surprisingly complex and rich variety of plants and animals, each opportunistically exploiting a habitat dominated by man's tireless quest for ever larger harvests.

ROE DEER BUCK
Deer are shy creatures and usually keep to the shelter of woodlands. Early on spring mornings though, they may venture out to nibble the sprouting shoots of corn.

to make larger fields in which the giant combines and other machinery can work, has aided their decline, as has the increased use of farm machinery at nesting time. But there is another, rather subtler reason. Adult grey partridges eat mainly seeds, but like many other seed-eating birds, their young have a diet which includes a good many insects and other invertebrates. Unfortunately for the partridge the boost of insect life in early spring in the cornfield has all but been eliminated by the agricultural sprays which kill not only the insects but also the weeds they rely on.

This link between man, diet and the bird is even more interesting in relation to that most familiar of all birds, the woodpigeon. Although needing

Corncockle

Corn Buttercup

Rough Poppy

Charlock

CORN BUTTERCUP *(Ranunculus arvensis)* Small pale yellow buttercups on a slim, pale green plant develop into the spiky, burr-like fruits which help to identify this species. It is now a very scarce poisonous weed of waste places and cornfields growing to a height of 20″ (50 cm).

ROUGH POPPY *(Papaver hybridum)* The bristly seed pods identify this 12″ (30 cm) poppy with deep crimson petals. It prefers fields on chalky or limestone soils in the south, but is now uncommon and widely scattered, rarely making a dazzling show like the common poppy.

CORNCOCKLE *(Agrostemma githago)* This annual cornfield weed reaches 3 ft (1 m) tall and has solitary flowers of a delicate purple-pink. It flowers in July and August, above the ripening corn, but is now a rare sight except in a few undisturbed grassy waysides.

CHARLOCK *(Sinapis arvensis)* A very common and invasive weed of cultivated ground, charlock is also known as wild mustard. It grows to about 18″ (45 cm) and produces coarse mop-heads of yellow flowers from May onwards, making a fine show in sunny summers.

Long-headed Poppy

Corn Marigold

Cornflower

Field Pansy

CORNFLOWER (*Centaurea cyanus*) The vivid blue flowers on 2′ (60 cm) stems appear in July or August. The days when this was a common arable weed, covering fields with a blue haze, are sadly gone; it is more likely to be seen as an escape from a garden.

FIELD PANSY (*Viola arvensis*) A 12″ (30 cm) spreading plant, whose flowers are held above a tuft of oval and deeply cut leaves, the field pansy looks like the garden variety in miniature. The yellow, white or purple flowers come in succession from April to September.

CORN MARIGOLD (*Chrysanthemum segetum*) The scientific name gives a clue to the form of the 2″ (5 cm) flowers, like broadly-rayed daisies on a stem up to 18″ (45 cm) tall. Where still common it makes a glorious yellow carpet over cereal fields in summer.

LONG-HEADED POPPY (*Papaver dubium*) This is a pale salmon pink poppy, which grows 18″ (50 cm) tall. It is commoner in the north of the country and is most frequently found on roadsides and waste places. The long, slender seed pods give it its name.

Corn Bunting

Red-legged Partridge

Partridge

Quail

CORN BUNTING *(Emberiza calandra)* This 7″ (18 cm) bird utters a distinctive dry stuttering trill, generally from a prominent perch. It lives in open country, eating insects and seeds. It lays 4-6 lightly speckled pale blue or buff eggs in a grass nest on the ground.

GREY PARTRIDGE *(Perdix perdix)* A stocky 12″ (30 cm) bird, it flies low over the rough or cultivated fields which are its favoured habitat. When startled these birds burst into flight uttering a harsh 'krikrikrik'. Adults feed on leaves and seeds, the young on insects.

RED-LEGGED PARTRIDGE *(Alectoris rufa)* Distinctively marked and easy to recognize, this large, 13½″ (34 cm), bird lives on dry sandy ground, rough or cultivated. It feeds on seeds, shoots and insects taken from the ground. If disturbed, it will run rather than fly.

QUAIL *(Coturnix coturnix)* More often heard than seen, this dumpy 7″ (18 cm) bird lurks concealed among tall vegetation in and around cereal fields. The call is a bright loud three-note whistle, 'whit whit it'. Its diet consists of cereal and grass seeds, and some insects.

Birds of the Field

Skylark

Wood Pigeon

Lapwing

SKYLARK (*Alauda arvensis*) The 7″ (18 cm) skylark is slightly larger than a sparrow, with a small crest. It soars to a great height, warbling constantly, and often leads the dawn chorus. It feeds on seeds, leaves and insects, and is the most widespread of British birds.

LAPWING (*Vanellus vanellus*) This broad-winged 12″ (30 cm) bird of damp fields and ploughed land flickers black and white in flight. On the ground it runs and stops to tilt forward, then run on again, searching for insects and larvae. its call is a mournful 'peewit'.

WOODPIGEON (*Columba palumbus*) This big, 16″ (41 cm), pigeon has a characteristic white wing patch. It is a greedy eater and causes enormous damage to cereal, bean and pea crops, which are its favourite food. Its song is a soothing 'coo'. It lays two white eggs.

THE FIELD IN WINTER

Quiet, but not asleep, the winter field sustains a remarkable
range of wildlife, including birds, mammals – even flowers –
through the cold, bleak months.

Winter is a time of rest for much wildlife. Frogs and toads hibernate, as do snakes and lizards. Many insects are also inactive: some butterflies spend the cold months as dormant caterpillars or chrysalises, ready to emerge fully adult in spring. But in spite of this, the winter field is often a surprisingly busy place.

WINTER WILDLIFE

Rather like white flags portending the snow to come, large flocks of gulls flap and flutter above the fields. Most likely to be seen is the black-headed gull which, of all its relatives, least deserves the name sea-gull, for it now often nests inland. Despite its name, it does not have a black head, but a brownish one and in winter this is lost except for cheek spots. The common gull, which is also sometimes seen in the fields, has a yellow bill and looks rather like a small herring gull. Indeed the herring gull itself, an aggressive bird, is now a frequent visitor to the ploughed fields.

These gulls are scavengers and take almost anything that is edible, and it is the large number of worms, insects and other small animals in the soil that attracts them – they often

HARDY LIFE OF THE WINTER FIELD
The fields at their various stages – ploughed, recently sown or with a kale crop – offer different cover and feeding opportunities. Predators, such as the fox and weasel, all use available cover to stalk their prey; tits and finches search the hedge and verge for insects and seeds; geese graze on grass and crops; and flocks of birds scour the fields or follow the plough for buried insects and worms.

KEY TO THE SPECIES

1 *Rookery*	11 *Pheasant*
2 *White-fronted geese*	12 *Catkins*
3 *Lapwings*	13 *Chaffinch*
4 *Gulls*	14 *Greenfinch*
5 *Kale*	15 *Planted field*
6 *Flooded area*	16 *Hare*
7 *Sheep*	17 *Weasel*
8 *Fox*	18 *Mole tunnel*
9 *Starlings*	19 *Groundsel*
10 *Rooks*	20 *Hare tracks*

follow the tractor to feast on those newly exposed by the plough or harrow.

Rooks have much the same habits – they trek in from their tree top roosts in noisy untidy lines. At this time of year the old saying that it is a crow if seen alone, a rook in company, breaks down – for crows often roost and feed together. Many birds become less solitary after nesting is over and fly together in large numbers and even sometimes in mixed flocks.

Among the rooks are often seen smaller, perky jackdaws, arch communicators, with a language of clucking calls that is quite unlike the harsh cawing of the rook. Feeding groups of starlings may also join them. And along the

HOAR FROST ON COW PARSLEY
One of the carrot family, woody stemmed cow parsley stands statuesquely throughout the winter, attracting seed-eating finches, such as the goldfinch, to its umbrella-like seed-heads.

hedges and the edges of the fields, mixed flocks of finches, tits and other birds busily search for the remaining seeds and small invertebrates which make up their own diet.

In the shelter of the kale being grazed by the sheep, pheasants stalk – they prefer not to stray far from cover and very often kale is planted alongside a sporting covert for the dual purpose of both feeding the sheep and giving the pheasants extended feeding ground.

All these birds do the farmer a service by ridding the soil of wireworms, leatherjackets and other pests which would damage the future crop (even the crow is of benefit here, though treated as a pest in its own right). The flocks of waders which sometimes visit winter fields are equally beneficial. Lapwings, for example – sometimes known as green plovers, or peewits – may be seen in flocks – and such a gathering is likely to be on its way to the milder countryside of the south west; in really cold winters, however, most of our lapwings migrate to southern Europe but are replaced by others from the far north. Indeed, many birds may be involved in regular, large scale winter travel. Many of the starlings, for example, will be continental birds which arrive here in their millions in winter, to take advantage of our milder climate. Even the flocks of tits and finches along the hedgerow travel great distances each day, roosting afresh each night.

This restless movement on the part of many birds is not the same as migration, although linked with it. Many interesting birds migrate here in winter, of course, from breeding grounds far to the north. Geese are among them, and some are occasionally seen in the arable fields.

North of the Wash, pink-footed geese are the most likely to be seen in the winter fields – they come to Scotland and Northern England from Iceland and Greenland. More come to Britain than ever before, though they seem to prefer Scotland – maybe because the stubble which attracts them remains longer. They are also seen on potato fields. These birds tend to spend the night on the coast, but at dawn fly inland to feed, and return

FOX IN THE FROST
(above) Undaunted by all but the hardest weather, foxes hunt throughout the winter and can be versatile scavengers and raiders.

PUSSY WILLOW CATKINS
(above right) A sign that spring is on its way: the silky grey male catkins come out before the leaves on sallow bushes in hedges and field corners. Catkins begin to expand in late winter.

PINK-FOOTED GOOSE
(below) Wintering in Britain from October to April, the elegant pink-foots are the smallest and most numerous of the 'grey' geese.

at dusk – their passage overhead marked by a thrilling honking chorus. They are the most musical of geese. These daily movements, known as 'flightings' are interrupted on moonlit nights when the birds often remain in the fields to feed. This is rather unusual, for ground-feeding birds are not often active at night: even in winter they must gain their food during the short daylight hours.

HUNTERS AND HUNTED

With the mammals, however, activity is usual during the hours of darkness, though both

stoats and weasels course the hedgerows both by day and night, hunting mice and voles, and small birds. A snow patch may reveal the tracks of foxes which mate between Christmas and February and the silent night may be pierced by the weird, unearthly scream of a vixen advertising her presence to potential mates. It is at this time of year (when they are hunted) that foxes are seen at their best with thick, full coats – they are raggedly moulted in summer.

Often to be seen on the winter field are new lines of molehills running from the hedge where the moles took shelter when the field was ploughed. On undisturbed ground, their network of tunnels may be years old, and untraceable from above; here they have to dig anew after the tractor has passed, but the disturbance of the field in spring when the fields are frequently sprayed probably discourages their breeding in this habitat. Moles feed on the worms and other small animals which fall into their tunnels.

The varied climate of our winter, with its occasional warm spells, means that flowers may also be seen, at least around the field's edge. Many quick-seeding 'weeds' typical of open or newly dug ground can be seen in flower at any time of year: groundsel and shepherd's purse among them. Some are annuals which flower, set seed, and sprout again more than once a year and a mild winter encourages these. Ragwort is a biennial with an extended flowering period, and red and white deadnettles (often seen on the waste edge of a field) can flower right up to Christmas. The sight of coltsfoot, however, means that winter is past its worst, and spring is not far away.

WOOD MOUSE
Wood mice are vulnerable in the winter: apart from the perils of the cold, their food supply – berries, seeds and insects – may be frozen away. They also become easy targets for predators.

COCK PHEASANT
(below) This prime lowland gamebird may fall to the guns in winter.

FIELDFARE

REDWING

WINTER THRUSHES
Large flocks of fieldfares and redwings from Scandinavia arrive in the British Isles from October, overwintering until April. They often feed together on hedgerow berries or on insects in the fields. Both species are closely related to our native mistle thrush and song thrush and look similar. On the fieldfare – the larger of the two – look for the chestnut back, grey head and rump and, in flight, the white under-wing. The smaller and neater redwing (easily confused with a song thrush) has a red under-wing and flanks, with white stripes over its eye and under its cheek.

107

Red Dead-nettle

Groundsel

White Dead-nettle

GROUNDSEL *(Senecio vulgaris)* This is an upright, rather weak plant, 3-18″ (8-45cm) tall, found in flower all through the year. With cottony seeds dispersed by wind, it is a weed of both cultivated ground and wasteland. It is controlled by herbicides on arable fields.

RED DEAD-NETTLE *(Lamium purpureum)* A softly hairy annual branched at the base to form a loose, spreading clump 4-18″ (10-45cm) tall, with the upper leaves often tinged purple. It flowers from early spring until autumn and is pollinated by bees.

WHITE DEAD-NETTLE *(Lamium album)* A widespread hairy perennial with erect stems 8-24″ (20-60cm) tall. Pollination is by long-tongued bumble bees which brush past the stigmas and pollen sacs as they suck the nectar from the base of the flower tube.

Common Chickweed

Shepherd's Purse

Common Field Speedwell

SHEPHERD'S PURSE (*Capsella bursa-pastoris*) Very successful on arable and waste land this 1-16″ (3-40cm) tall weed has two or three generations in one year. Both basal and stem leaves vary in shape, but it is known for its seed purses.

COMMON CHICKWEED (*Stellaria media*) A widespread and tenacious weed with bright green leaves and branching semi-prostrate stems 2-16″ (5-40cm) it flowers all year. Growth can be very luxuriant in damp places. It can be eaten as a salad vegetable.

COMMON FIELD SPEEDWELL (*Veronica persica*) An annual, spreading plant with hairy-stemmed branches 4-16″ (10-40cm) long. Introduced from south east Europe in the early 19th century, it is now a persistent weed of arable fields. Flowers can be seen in all months.

Rook

Jackdaw

Black-headed gull

winter

summer

ROOK *(Corvus frugilegus)* A noisy, gregarious 18″ (46cm) bird, nesting in colonies in the tops of small groups of trees. They prefer arable areas where they feed on grain, insects and other invertebrates. Identified by bald face patches and shaggy leg feathers.

JACKDAW *(Corvus monedula)* A handsome 13″ (33cm) bird, social and adaptable, nesting in colonies in suitable holes or crevices in rural and urban localities. It has a varied diet including insects and seeds – and often scavenges. Contact call is a high 'tchak'.

BLACK-HEADED GULL *(Larus ridibundus)* Our smallest resident gull, 15″ (38cm), nesting in colonies near water, from coastal sites to sewage farms. Often seen following the plough to feed on insects in lowland fields, though many scavenge in cities during winter.

Fieldfare

Female

Pheasant

Male

FIELDFARE *(Turdus pilaris)*
A gregarious 10″ (25cm) bird
arriving here in the autumn,
sometimes in huge numbers, to feed
in fields and hedges on berries and
fruits, often in mixed flocks with
Redwings. In spring they return to
Scandinavia to breed.

PHEASANT *(Phasianus colchicus)*
Brought to Britain by the Romans,
it is now a common bird nurtured
for sport. Colourful males, 33″
(84cm), preside over small harems
of dowdier females, 23″ (58cm).
Flight is fast and noisy but
sustained only for short distances.

IN THE SHADE OF THE HEDGEROW

Providing nest sites for birds and highways for animals, hedgerows attract a diversity of wildlife that few other man-made habitats can match.

A walk beside a hedgerow almost anywhere in Britain will reveal a rich and flourishing gallery of wildlife. Even recent hedge-rows, dating back little more than a century have been swiftly colonized by nature, and have now become havens for an enormous variety of woodland plants and animals dispossessed of natural habitats elsewhere.

The best time to see hedgerows, perhaps, is May, when the white flowers of hawthorn, or may, give the hedges a beautiful snowy mantle and fill the air with the bitter-sweet scent of their blossom. In summer, the dog rose, traveller's joy and other climbers come into bloom. And towards autumn, there is often the reward of hips and wild berries, blackberries and sloes which both decorate the hedgerow and provide a vital source of food for the birds and mammals which inhabit it.

HEDGEROW PLANTS

The variety of plant life depends to a considerable extent on the age of the hedgerow. Older hedges will usually have been colonized by many different species, while a fairly recent hedge may only include the original hawthorn plus elder or ash. In an ancient Anglo-Saxon parish boundary hedge you may see as many as 10 different shrub or tree species, including hawthorn, buckthorn, elder, ash, and, if the soil is chalky, spindle-tree and dogwood.

For the soft green plants, the many different 'micro-climates' that the hedge itself creates, as it snakes alongside a road or neatly crosses the ploughlands, can be as important as the hedge-row's age. Some parts of the hedge may be in permanent shadow, while other lengths are ex-posed to hot sun for much of the year. For plant (and some animal) life a hedge has two very different sides, and important differences also occur when the hedge crosses unseen geological changes in the bedrock, which give rise to different types of soil. The degree of moisture present in the soil also has a significant effect on the hedgerow flora and fauna, and the soil of a valley bottom is likely to be much damper than that of the slopes.

Such factors are reflected in the exact mixture of species of wild plants that you see at the foot of the hedgerow. In one place there may be wild strawberry, ripening on a sunny bank, while further along there are the trumpet flowers of great bindweed or a patch of nettles – both of which can flourish in the shade. Any assembly of plants, at the hedgefoot as elsewhere, is the result of intense competition between the species, and local conditions will always favour some plants over others.

PRIMROSES
(far left) A bright harbinger of spring, the primrose blooms in March, flourishing on open, sunny hedge banks.

HARVEST MOUSE
(left) Frequenting hedgerows bordering cornfields, the harvest mouse is Britain's smallest rodent.

RED ADMIRAL BUTTERFLY
(right) Arriving in April from Europe, this beautiful butterfly makes a colourful addition to hedgerow wildlife.

HEDGEROW WILDLIFE

The hedgerow provides food and shelter for
farmland birds and animals, and acts as a leafy
wildlife highway between the fields. Rooks may
perch in the hedgerow trees; the greenfinch and
chaffinch nest in tree forks; the trees also affect the
micro-climate of the hedgerow, encouraging shade-
loving plants like arum, and moisture-loving frogs.
Beneath the trees, the climbing bryony and bindweed
use the hedge bushes for support.

The plants and animal species have an intimate
relationship. Bees, bumblebees and butterflies
pollinate the flowers and ivy provides a winter roost
for the brimstone. The elm, once the pride of the
hedgerow, has been killed by a disease and becomes
host to numerous insects on which birds feed.
Nettles are a food plant of caterpillars; aphids, are
eaten by ladybirds, spiders, frogs and wrens; and
frogs, in turn, are food for adders.

KEY TO THE SPECIES

1 Rooks	8 Brimstone	15 Caterpillars	22 Wild strawberries
2 Pollarded ash	9 Holly	16 Cow parsley	23 Dunnock
3 Blackbird	10 Blackbird's nest	17 Hoverfly	24 Adder
4 Greenfinch	11 Bindweed	18 Wren	25 Bees' nest
5 Cuckoo	12 Bryony	19 Garden spider	26 Arum
6 Dead elm	13 Aphids	20 Ladybird	27 Bumblebees
7 Ivy	14 Dunnock's nest	21 Frog	28 Bank vole

THE TINY WREN
(above) Skulking among the undergrowth, the wren can often be pinpointed by its loud, rattling song. This perky insect-eater is probably the commonest breeding bird in Britain, at about 10 million pairs.

The way that the hedge was created can also play a part. Bluebells could mean that the hedge was originally a relic of woodland left behind when fields were carved out of the forest. Or it may be that a long time ago, the hedge was planted near to a wood, and in time bluebells and primroses and other woodland flowers migrated down it. Bluebells are rarely seen in a young enclosure hedge.

Few flowers, however, have become typical of hedgerows in the way that hawthorn, blackthorn and some other shrubs have. Of the great number of species to be seen growing in hedges, only wild arum and black bryony and some other climbers are more likely to be seen there than in woods or other habitats. Ivy, although it is most clearly visible in hedges, is just as common in many kinds of woods.

To some extent, the flowers and the climbers you will see reflect how the hedge is being looked after. Where a hedge is layered, for example, the shrubby growth is thinned out and climbers are usually cleared away; when the ditches are cleaned out, many of the soft plants are also removed. On the other hand, if the hedge is simply machine-trimmed by tractor, the climbers and shrubs will quickly grow again from their undamaged roots, while the profusion of flowers which grow at the hedgefoot will be completely unaffected by this type of management.

The blossom and leaves of the hawthorn and other hedgerow shrubs are often busy with insect life, ranging from bees visiting to collect pollen and nectar to ladybirds searching for greenfly and other aphids, which they consume in large numbers. The caterpillars of many moths are often visible on the leaves and twigs of the shrubs, while butterflies may be seen in summer – the beautiful peacock butterfly can be seen fluttering along the hedge in search of suitable nettles on which to lay its eggs. Spiders of many different kinds are also plentiful – a reflection of the busy insect life which they trap and catch, sometimes with webs, but sometimes by simple ambush, jumping out at their hapless prey.

BIRDS OF THE HEDGE

For birds, the structure of the hedge is particularly important. Some, such as crows, use only the hedgerow trees to roost or nest in, and feed in the surrounding countryside. Owls may be able to nest in a large, old tree with holes in the trunk; they too will hunt for food far from the nest, often following the line of the hedge in search of the mice and voles which scuttle in its cover.

The smaller birds, such as greenfinches, may nest in the lower branches of hedgerow trees, but they can equally easily nest in the hedge itself. Other species, however, will only nest in the hedge, never in trees. Some, like the blackbird, will feed out on open ground some distance from the hedgerow, while its cousin the song thrush patrols close to the hedge, looking for snails which are most likely to be found in its shelter. The dunnock

GARDEN CROSS SPIDER
(above) The garden cross spider and its web both grow larger through the summer, reaching maximum size in October. The spider eats the old web every few days and spins a new one overnight.

YOUNG RABBITS
(left) Rabbits, whose numbers peak in midsummer, dig burrows among the hedgerow plants and tree roots, and feed in the adjacent fields.

HEDGEROW NESTS

SONG THRUSH

YELLOWHAMMER

YELLOWHAMMER, CHAFFINCH AND DUNNOCK
The yellowhammer's hair-lined grassy cup is usually on the ground and contains 3-6 whitish eggs with ruddy scribbles. Mosses and lichens camouflage the chaffinch's nest and its 4-5 bluish or browny-white eggs. Hair, wool or feathers line the dunnock's twig, moss and grass nest with its 3-6 bright blue eggs.

CHAFFINCH

DUNNOCK

THRUSH AND BLACKBIRD
The smooth mud lining and spotted light blue eggs distinguish the song thrush's nest. The similar-sized blackbird's nest is made of moss, twigs and grass, and the 4 or 5 eggs are pale blue thickly speckled with brown.

BLACKBIRD

(or 'hedge sparrow') keeps close to the hedgerow while it forages on the ground, but its nest also attracts the far-ranging cuckoo, for the dunnock is one of its favourite hosts. And the diminutive wren rarely leaves the dense, protective shade of the undergrowth at the base of the hedge – its rattling song often the only sign of its presence.

Birds do not come to the hedge only to nest. In autumn and winter you can often see flocks of finches of all kinds seeking hedgerow berries, seeds and other food. Though they range long distances, they usually roost in certain spots, and one part of a hedge may become a kind of hotel in the winter months, housing different flocks of feathered guests each night. You can watch them arrive at dusk, flying into the hedge in small, chattering flocks; for the hedgerows provide invaluable shelter during the coldest months of deepest winter.

Other creatures take similar advantage of the food and shelter the hedgerow can provide. Adders are often seen basking on a sunny bank, or using the hedge as a sheltered highway across the open fields. A small pool in the hedgerow ditch can be a refuge for frogs, now that the cattle ponds once found in the fields have been filled in and ploughed over. Mice and voles flourish in hedgerows as does the hedgehog, while predators such as foxes, stoats and weasels are attracted to the hedgerow and use it both as a thoroughfare and as a hunting ground. And what hedge would be complete without rabbits, feeding close to their burrows dug in its shelter?

BUFF-TAILED BUMBLEBEE
(right) Most bumblebees pollinate flowers as they feed but the buff-tailed bumblebee performs no such service as it bores through the side of the flower to reach the nectar.

THE COMMON FROG
(below) The damp, grassy hedge bottom or ditch provides food and shelter for the common frog.

Red Admiral

Brimstone

Male

Female

Comma

Hedge Brown

RED ADMIRAL *(Vanessa atalanta)* Flocks arrive each spring from the Mediterranean coast and spread throughout the British Isles; they favour nettle leaves as egg-laying sites and seek nectar from autumn-flowering garden plants. The sexes are similar.

COMMA *(Polygonia c-album)* The male butterfly is easily recognized by the jagged outline of the wings: the female has a more rounded silhouette. It lays eggs wherever nettles abound in the South, Midlands and Wales and hibernates in hedges.

BRIMSTONE *(Gonepteryx rhamni)* Once known as the 'butter-coloured fly,' the brimstone is found in the hedgerows and woods of England, Wales and Ireland. It lays its eggs on buckthorn and alder buckthorn leaves, and hibernates through the winter in evergreen plants.

HEDGE BROWN *(Pyronia tithonus)* Also known as the gatekeeper, this butterfly is seen from July to September in the hedges, woods and grasslands of southern England, Wales and southern Ireland. The male of the species is smaller and brighter than the female.

Hedgerow Butterflies

Orange Tip

Male

Female

Peacock

Male

Green-veined White

Female

ORANGE TIP (*Anthocharis cardamines*) Seen throughout the British Isles during May and June, this butterfly seeks out lady's smock and garlic mustard in hedgerows and meadows. With the massive loss of hedgerows it is inevitably becoming increasingly rare.

PEACOCK (*Inachis io*) The spectacular peacock commonly feeds on nectar from buddleia and hemp agrimony flowers, and lays its eggs on nettles. Found throughout the British Isles, it hibernates from September to March in out-houses, sheds and hollow trees.

GREEN-VEINED WHITE (*Pieris napi*) Seen throughout the British Isles, in hedges, woods and meadows where hedge- and garlic mustard grow, this butterfly sometimes visits gardens and allotments. The darker sub-species *britannica* is found more commonly in Ireland.

Common Hawthorn

Traveller's Joy

Blackthorn (Sloe)

Black Bryony

TRAVELLER'S JOY *(Clematis vitalba)* Also known as old man's beard because of its profuse woolly seedheads in autumn. The twining stems which clamber over the hedgerow, can be up to 100′ (30 m) long. In July and August clusters of greenish flowers smell of vanilla.

COMMON HAWTHORN *(Crataegus monogyna)* This small, tough tree, also known as may, brightens the hedgerow in spring with a foam of white, scented blossom followed by red berries. It has a ridged trunk and coarsely toothed leaves 2″ (5 cm) long; unpruned it can reach 50′ (15 m).

BLACK BRYONY *(Tamus communis)* This clockwise-twining climber of hedgerows and woods has loose short spikes of tiny greenish flowers in May to July, which produce clusters of poisonous red berries. Black refers to the colour of its poisonous tuber.

BLACKTHORN *(Prunus spinosa)* This easily suckering small tree can grow up to 20′ (7 m) tall – but is usually much lower. Its bare black thorny twigs are covered in white blossoms from March to May, and produce a crop of slate-coloured sloes in autumn.

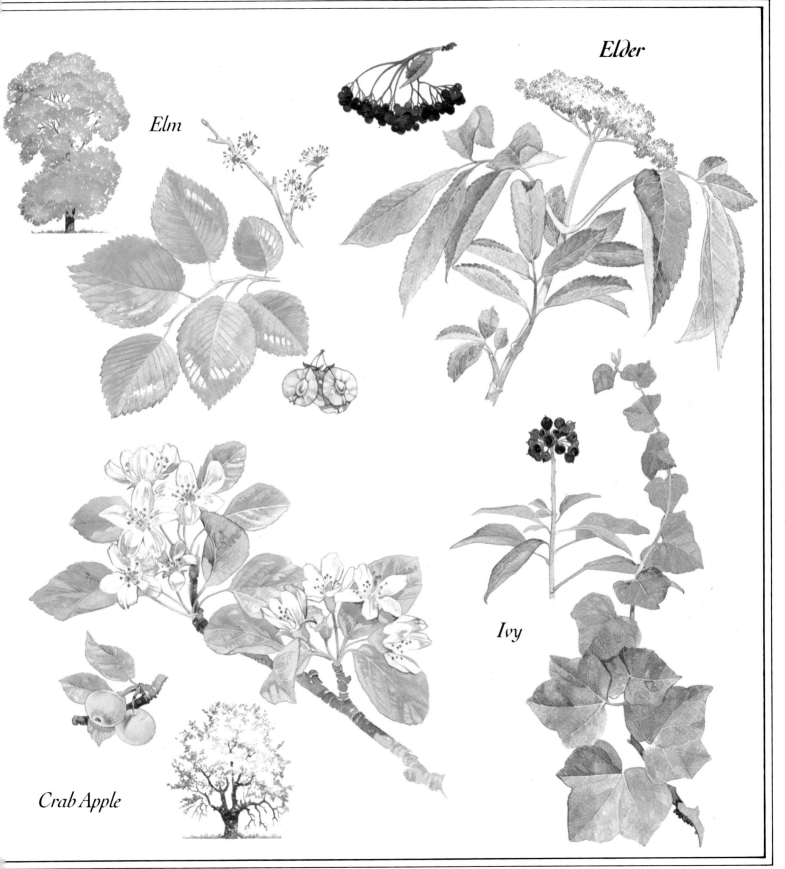

Elm

Elder

Crab Apple

Ivy

ELM (*Ulmus procera*) Standing 130′ (40 m) tall, the elm once punctuated our fields and hedges with its distinctive silhouette. Dutch elm disease has taken its heavy toll, but a few trees remain, and some stools of felled elms, left in the hedgerows, are sprouting suckers.

CRAB APPLE *(Malus sylvestris)* An attractive feature of woods and hedges in May, when it produces loose clusters of white or pink-tinged flowers, and again in autumn with its 1¼″ (3 cm) round yellow fruit. It makes a bushy gnarled tree up to 25′ (8 m) high.

ELDER *(Sambucus nigra)* More familiar as a shrub, in hedges this small tree is often cut back so that it seldom attains its potential 30′ (10 m). The flat sprays of tiny white flowers can be used in wine making, as can the inky black berries which follow.

IVY *(Hedera helix)* This familiar evergreen climber can travel 100′ (30 m) clinging to plants and walls by means of its adhesive aerial roots. From September to November it produces large heads of greenish-yellow flowers, followed by clusters of black berries.

Redwing

Female

Male

Chaffinch

Male

Yellowhammer

REDWING *(Turdus iliacus)* The 8¼"
(21 cm) redwing is distinguished
from the song thrush by its white eye
stripe and red under-wing. Feeding in
flocks, mainly on berries, the redwing
is a winter visitor, but some nest in
Scotland, where they lay 5-6 greyish-
blue eggs.

YELLOWHAMMER *(Emberiza
citrinella)* Famous for its call of 'a
little bit of bread and no cheese,' this
yellow-headed, 6½" (16.5 cm) bird is
usually seen feeding on the ground,
where it searches out seed and
insects. The female lays 3-6 whitish
coloured eggs.

CHAFFINCH *(Fringilla coelebs)* An
extremely common 6" (15 cm) seed-
eating finch, the chaffinch is easily
identified by its white shoulder
patches and its white tail feathers
visible in flight. 4 or 5 blue or brown-
white eggs are laid in a well-
camouflaged nest.

Song Thrush

Male

Female

Linnet

Dunnock

SONG THRUSH *(Turdus philomelos)*
The 9″ (23 cm) song thrush can often be located by the sound of it hammering a snail against a favourite stone, or by its flutey musical song which it sings from a high perch. It lays 4-6 light blue speckled eggs.

DUNNOCK *(Prunella modularis)*
Commonly known as the hedge sparrow, the thin bill and shuffling gait distinguish this bird from the house sparrow. A ground feeder, the dunnock searches out insects at the base of the hedge. It lays 3-6 bright blue eggs.

LINNET *(Carduelis cannabina)* The twittering song and red forehead and breast of the chestnut-backed male are distinctive in summer. These 5¼″ (13.5 cm) finches feed on a wide variety of seeds and breed in noisy crowded colonies, laying 4-6 pale blue eggs.

Red Campion

Dog Rose

Ground Ivy

Sweet Violet

SWEET VIOLET *(Viola odorata)* The flower of Aphrodite – Greek goddess of love – can be recognized in hedge banks and wood edges by the familiar fragrance of its bluish-violet or white flowers which bloom from January to April. It grows 6″ (15 cm) tall.

DOG ROSE *(Rosa canina)* This common, decorative shrub of hedge and scrubland produces a wealth of large sweetly-scented pink or white blooms in June and July, followed by red hips in autumn. The arching stems, up to 10′ (3 m) long, have hooked thorns.

RED CAMPION *(Silene dioica)* This untidy plant is commonly found in hedges, woods and shady places, which it brightens with a mass of carmine flowers in May and June. It can grow to a height of 3′ (1 m), and can be recognized by its hairy stems and leaves.

GROUND IVY *(Glechoma hederacea)* A creeping perennial which grows from 4-12″ (10-30 cm) high. With hairy stems and soft, kidney-shaped leaves, it frequents woods and hedgebanks, favouring damp soils, and produces whorls of mauve flowers from March to June.

Hedgerow Flowers

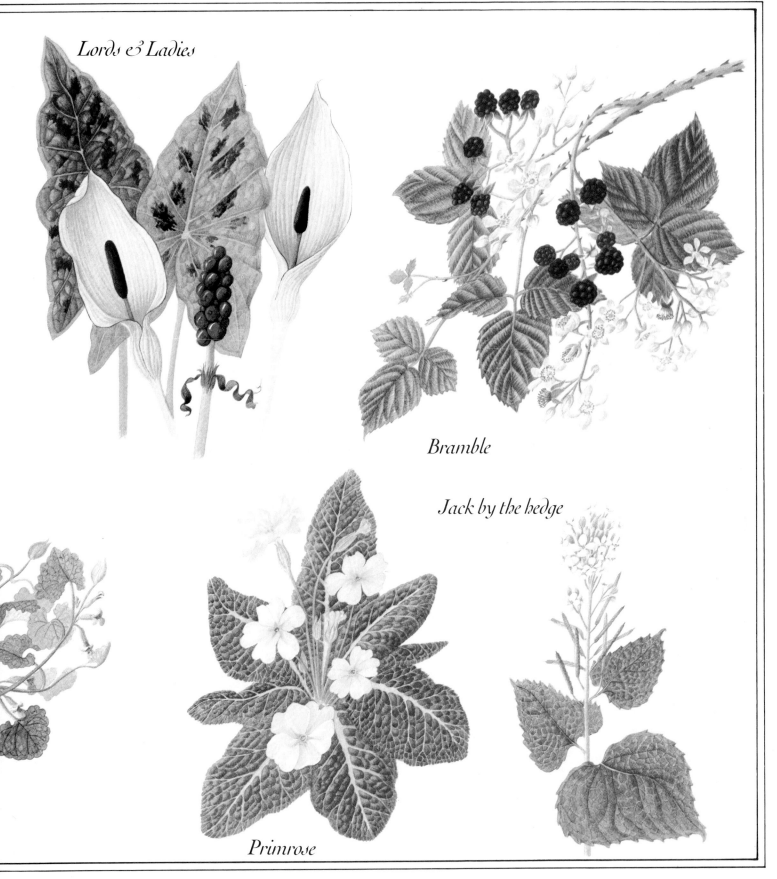

Lords & Ladies

Bramble

Jack by the hedge

Primrose

LORDS AND LADIES (*Arum maculatum*) A tall, 18″ (45 cm), and stately feature of shady hedgebanks, it is first distinguished by the emergence of arrow-shaped leaves in early spring. The purple or greenish flower spike becomes a cluster of poisonous red berries in autumn.

PRIMROSE (*Primula vulgaris*) The pale yellow flowers, each carried on a single hairy stalk, emerge from a rosette of leaves between February and May. Increasingly rare on the hedgebank, primroses grow to 6″ (15 cm), and require both a male and female flower to set seed.

BRAMBLE (*Rubus fruticosus*) The common blackberry is an untidy shrub whose thorny stems sprawl over hedgerows, rooting as they go. The long flowering season, from May to September, results in an abundance of fruit. Its prickly leaves have 3-5 leaflets.

JACK BY THE HEDGE (*Alliaria petiolata*) Also known as garlic mustard – which describes the aroma of the crushed leaves – this biennial plant grows to 3′ (1 m) tall in large groups below hedges and walls. After flowering from April to June, long seed pods are produced.

BENEATH THE LOWLAND OAKS

Carpets of bluebells, the busy hammering of woodpeckers, butterflies flitting through sunny glades, and the sweet song of the nightingale are typical delights of the lowland oakwood.

Although much used (and sometimes abused) by man, the lowland oakwood remains one of the most familiar features of the countryside. Its main characteristics are similar throughout Britain, but no wood is quite like another. Each has its own personality, shaped by local soil conditions, how damp or well-drained it may be, and the way the wood has been used in the past.

A close look at the vegetation of the wood can help us decipher its history. In the oldest woods, for example, you may see small-leaved lime, Midland hawthorn (with blunter leaves than its hedgerow cousin) and the wild service tree. Where these species flourish, they probably mark a direct link with the original wildwood.

Hazel, by contrast, is likely to have been deliberately planted, and coppiced for its useful poles. Parts of the wood may have been cleared for this type of management – honeysuckle, a typical climber of oak woodland, would certainly have been cut out of a worked coppice.

OAKWOOD FLOWERS

Other plants, like the bluebell and other spring flowers which make such a fine sight in the oakwood, benefited from coppicing. After the hazel had been cut, sunlight flooded the woodland floor, replenishing the bulbs so they survived the gathering gloom until the next cut. Today's bountiful display is often the result of centuries of man's use of the wood, and the disappearance of flowers from some woods is due to ending coppicing.

However, soil preferences and other factors may dictate whether you see these flowers or not. On heavy soil, sheets of bluebells, together with wood anemone and the exotic heads of early purple orchid, indicate an ancient fragment of oakwood. But bluebells can spread far more quickly on light soil, so they may simply be picking out a sandy patch. If they are growing on the unmistakable bumps of ancient ridge-and-furrow ploughland, then the wood is certainly one occupying once open land.

When we look for animals in the wood, we may at first be disappointed. Indeed, the oakwood may seem to be an empty, silent place, with none of the busy insect and bird life that we expect of grassy fields and hedges. But this impression is misleading, for the oakwood is truly bursting with life. The oak tree itself gives home to no less than 284 different insect species, the highest total for any native tree or shrub (the figure for hawthorn is 149, for example).

Many of the animals are restricted to one

ROE DEER FAWN
Camouflaged by its dappled brown and white coat, a roe deer fawn lies hidden in the undergrowth. These deer are widespread in Britain today, for the population has increased steadily during the century. The fawns are born in early summer and twins are common.

THE MANY LAYERED OAKWOOD

An environment with a rich variety of plant life, the oakwood is home to many animals. The oak tree itself harbours numerous galls, which contain the young of gall wasps. The purple emperor and purple hairstreak sip honeydew in the canopy, while fritillary caterpillars feed on dog violets. Treecreepers and nightingales hunt insects; jays and squirrels eat acorns; and the wood mouse, feeding on insects and berries, forms part of the tawny owl's diet.

KEY TO THE SPECIES

1 Tree canopy
2 Purple emperor
3 Grey squirrel
4 Purple hairstreak
5 Gall wasp
6 Galls
7 Acorns
8 Oak tree
9 Foxglove

10 Honeysuckle
11 Shrub layer
12 Bracken
13 Bluebells
14 Oak roller moth caterpillar
15 Coppiced hazel
16 Treecreeper
17 Tawny owl
18 Nightingale

19 Yellow pimpernel
20 Pearl-bordered fritillary
21 Dog violet
22 Jay
23 Wood mouse
24 Ivy
25 Lesser celandine
26 Leaf litter
27 Wood anemone

125

SPOTTED FLYCATCHER
(above) Arriving in late April or May, this lively flycatcher may be seen in woodland glades. It nests on walls, in a creeper such as ivy, and usually rears two broods in the South.

EARLY PURPLE ORCHID
(top right) Found all over Britain, this orchid flowers earlier than other woodland varieties. It has traditionally been used in love potions, and even to determine the sex of unborn children.

PURPLE HAIRSTREAK
(right) Large numbers of this butterfly may be seen in the tree canopy. They feed on honeydew on oak leaves, and lay eggs singly on the twigs.

special part of the wood – the undergrowth, for example, or the tree canopy. This is particularly true of butterflies: one or two varieties prefer the canopy, and often remain unobserved unless glimpsed by chance, while bird-watching with binoculars. Others, though they seek woodland plants on which to lay their eggs, are more often seen when they visit sunny clearings to gain refreshment by sipping nectar – bramble blossoms are a magnet for butterflies.

Many moth caterpillars are also denizens of the canopy far overhead. But the caterpillar of the green oak roller moth is frequently encountered in spring, hanging by a thread from the upper branches after being dislodged by a gust of wind or other accident. In warm weather, these caterpillars can all but strip the tree of its leaves; the oak can put out a second flush, but it is severely weakened. Drought and disease may then kill branches in the summer, causing the familiar 'stag head' appearance of many oaks – at the top, dead branches protrude like antlers from a new, lower crown.

The structured wood, with its layers of vegetation and occasional openings and clearings, provides many living grounds. Dead wood, for example, is an important mini-habitat for many insects. Beetle grubs spend their formative months in rotting trunks and timbers, playing a vital role in the cycle of decomposition by which dead matter in the wood eventually disappears, to provide nutrients for new growth. Fungi, too, have an important function in the decomposition cycle. Their dramatically coloured caps and brackets are the spore bodies; their feeding threads run below them, hidden in soil or bark, or in the wood of dead or dying trees.

The oakwood provides a home for many birds. Some species nest and feed in its own preferred layer of the wood, while others prefer the clearings or the woodland edge. Coppicing, by strengthen-

ing the shrub layer of the wood, favoured the nightingale. This shy bird is attracted to young coppice, but tends to leave the shrubs when they become tall, after about eight years. One reason for the songster's steady decline in Britain may be the loss of the coppice it had been accustomed to for centuries.

NUTHATCH AT THE NEST
(above) The nuthatch usually nests in a tree-hole, but will choose a wall or nestbox.

GREAT SPOTTED WOODPECKER
(left) A male leaving the nest – note a young bird's bill poking form the hole. Both parents feed the young.

SHY ROE DEER
(above) Roe deer may sometimes be seen during the day in open woodland glades.

TAWNY OWL AT THE NEST HOLE
This is the commonest British owl, but is not found in Ireland. In woodland it feeds mainly on voles and mice, roosting during the day.

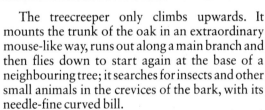

BARKS

SILVER BIRCH

OAK

ASH

HAZEL

Blue tits spend much time searching the topmost canopy for aphids and caterpillars, while their close cousins, the great tits, seek similar food lower down. Much the same division can be observed with the lesser and great spotted woodpeckers. The former (a rare prize for the birdwatcher) tends to make its living along smaller branches, the latter on the massive boughs. Each species has a 'niche' in the wood—not just the place where it is likely to be found, but also its way of life. In this way, competition between the species is reduced or avoided.

LIFE IN THE TREES

Many woodland birds are familiar from hedges and gardens, for woodland species have adopted 'new' habitats created by man. Others are only likely to be seen in the wood, because they require thick tree trunks for nest holes, or because they seek the seclusion the wood provides. The nuthatch is one – it can be recognized from afar by its ability to walk equally easily both up and down the trunk. Its presence may also be revealed by a loud tapping as it hammers the nuts it has jammed into cracks in the bark – (the traditional combination of oak standards and hazel coppice, yielding plentiful acorns and quite a few cob nuts, favours the nuthatch well). This bird has the unusual habit of adopting the nest holes of other species, but narrowing the entrance with mud to exclude other larger birds.

The treecreeper only climbs upwards. It mounts the trunk of the oak in an extraordinary mouse-like way, runs out along a main branch and then flies down to start again at the base of a neighbouring tree; it searches for insects and other small animals in the crevices of the bark, with its needle-fine curved bill.

Jays like the privacy of the wood but will venture out into clearings and, indeed, out of the wood altogether, to cache acorns they have collected. By doing this, the birds may well help the spread of the oak trees, for it is noticeable that acorns rarely seem to sprout and yield strong seedlings under their own parent tree.

Squirrels, too, seek the acorns and hide them away in pockets dug in the soil. And a number of other mammals, among them the dormouse, fox, badger and stoat, both make their homes and hunt in the rich community of the oakwood. Some, like the rabbit and the mole, are more familiar from open habitats in the countryside: in the wood their excavations are hidden.

Voles and mice are ever active, and after dark the latter may even climb up into the coppice or shrub layer in search of berries and birds' eggs, exposing themselves to the watchful owl. Deer, though largely unseen, are surprisingly common, and their two-toed slots or footprints can be found along the tracks that they follow through the wood. Deer can be found in the majority of lowland woodlands today.

Bluebell

Early Purple Orchid

Wood Sanicle

Wood Anemone

BLUEBELL (*Hyacinthoides non-scriptus*) From April to June, bluebells carpet many woods in misty lilac-blue, although there are also white and pink blooms. The fragrant flowers are borne on 12″ (32 cm) stems, and produce ½″ (1 cm) brown seed capsules.

EARLY PURPLE ORCHID (*Orchis mascula*) This stately woodland plant with long speckled leaves produces a 6-24″ (15-60 cm) spike of rosy-purple spurred flowers from April to June. It can be found in shady places throughout Britain, but is more common in the south.

SANICLE (*Sanicula europaea*) Fluffy heads of white or pinkish flowers on 8-24″ (20-60 cm) stalks appear in the woods – especially under beeches – from May to July. Shiny, deeply-lobed leaves form a hammock above which the flowers and bristly seedheads are carried.

WOOD ANEMONE (*Anemone nemorosa*) Clumps of these white or pink flowers are a common sight in deciduous woodland from March to May. They are borne above a collar of deeply-cut leaves and are 2-12″ (5-30 cm) tall. The flowers produce a globular seedhead.

Flowers of the Oakwood

Enchanter's Nightshade

Dog's Mercury

Sweet Woodruff

Yellow Archangel

ENCHANTER'S NIGHTSHADE (*Circaea lutetiana*) Happy in woods and shady places, this plant grows plumes of delicate white flowers from June to August. It varies in height from 8-28″ (20-70 cm), and the bristled fruits hang from the stems, catching on feather and fur.

DOG'S MERCURY (*Mercurialis perennis*) Early in spring the floors of woods throughout Britain (less so in Ireland) become clothed in fresh green as the oval leaves of this poisonous plant emerge. 16″ (40 cm) spikes of insignificant green flowers appear from February to April.

SWEET WOODRUFF (*Galium odoratum*) This small 6-12″ (15-30 cm) erect plant grows mainly in woods on lime-rich soils. The small fragrant white flowers are borne above a ruff of leaves with minutely hooked margins in May and June. The fruits are burr-like.

YELLOW ARCHANGEL (*Lamiastrum galeobdolon*) In May and June the bright yellow flowers streaked with red are a common sight in woods and clearings of South England and the Midlands. It grows up to 24″ (60 cm) high, and the leaves are paired and hairy.

Great Spotted Woodpecker

Spotted Flycatcher

Jay

Lesser Spotted Woodpecker

SPOTTED FLYCATCHER (*Muscicapa striata*) This small, 5½″ (14 cm) summer visitor is commonly seen on the edge of a wood, in a park or a large garden, sitting upright and alert before flying out to catch a passing insect, then returning to its perch. It lays 4-5 eggs.

GREAT SPOTTED WOODPECKER (*Dendrocopos major*) The commonest woodpecker of deciduous and conifer woods is 9″ (23 cm) long, and boldly marked in black, white and red. It feeds on grubs under tree bark, and bores a nest hole in which to lay 4-7 round, white eggs.

JAY (*Garrulus glandarius*) The 13½″ (34 cm) jay is shy and elusive except in town parks, where its raucous 'skraak' call often gives it away; in flight the white rump and laboured wing beats are distinctive. Preferring deep woods, it eats scores of acorns and lays 5-7 pale eggs.

LESSER SPOTTED WOODPECKER (*Dendrocopos minor*) Lacking the red undertail of its larger relative, this sparrow-sized, 5¾″ (14.5 cm) bird is best seen when drumming in March in the bare tops of trees. It has a shrill 'pee-pee-pee-pee' call and lays 4-6 eggs.

Treecreeper

Nuthatch

Tawny Owl

TREECREEPER (*Certhia familiaris*) This tiny, 5″ (12.5 cm) bird creeps quietly up the bark of old trees searching for insects with its down-curved bill, then flies away to the next tree with a shrill 'tseee' call. It nests behind loose bark, laying 5-6 tiny eggs.

NUTHATCH (*Sitta europaea*) The brightly-coloured nuthatch moves around freely on trees, not using its tail for support like the mouse-like treecreeper. At 5½″ (14 cm) long, it has several very loud calls, eats nuts and insects it finds in the bark, and lays 6-9 white eggs.

TAWNY OWL (*Strix aluco*) Some 15″ (38 cm) long, this big, heavy owl is the bird which hoots after sunset, or calls 'kewick' in a town park, wood or churchyard – the large round head and black eyes are distinctive. It lays 2-4 white eggs in a tree hole or old crow's nest.

Hazel

Wild Service

Common Oak

Wych Elm

HAZEL (*Corylus avellana*) The hazel produces its familiar bunches of yellow catkins very early in spring, from Janaury to March. By August these develop into cobnuts – a delicacy both for squirrels and humans. Unpruned, it will reach 30 ft (9 m).

COMMON OAK (*Quercus robur*) This is the great old tree of parks and forests. Its massive gnarled branches support a wide dome; the giant bole may be hollow in ancient trees; the acorns are in pairs on a 2″ (6 cm) stalk. The tree is host to a multitude of flora and fauna.

WILD SERVICE TREE (*Sorbus torminalis*) This rare native of southern England grows on clay or limestone to a height of 80 ft (25 m). The white flowers are borne in May, and followed by elongated brown fruit. The tree has scaly grey bark and deeply-cut leaves.

WYCH ELM (*Ulmus glabra*) Larger leaves and seeds distinguish the common native of the north from the English elm. It has a massive, irregular dome and may reach over 120 ft (38 m). The dark leaves have a very rough, veined surface and the smooth bark is pale grey.

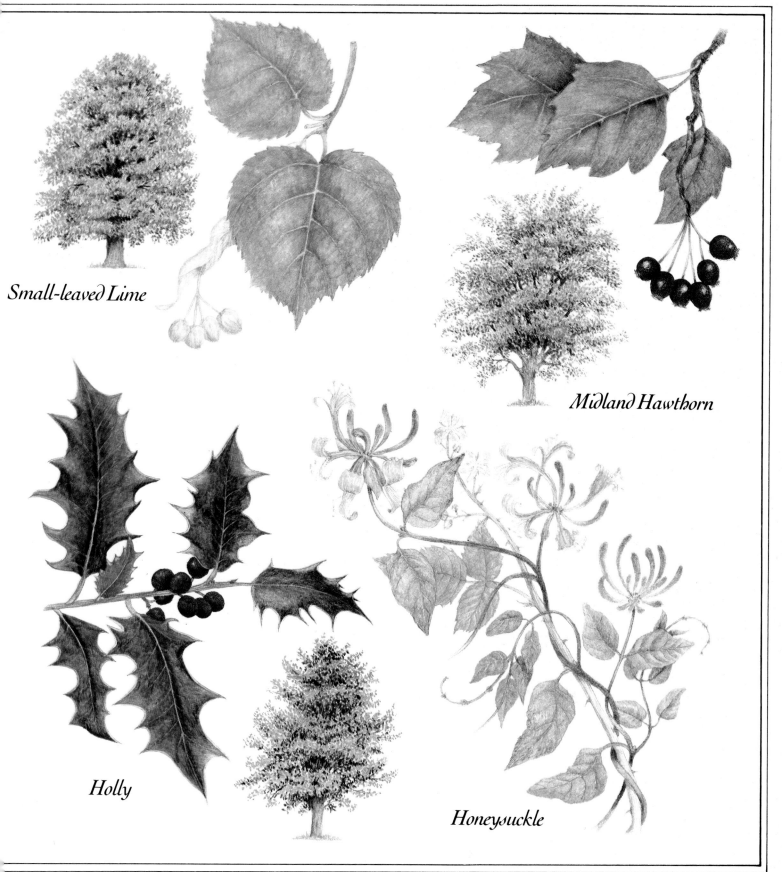

Small-leaved Lime

Midland Hawthorn

Holly

Honeysuckle

SMALL-LEAVED LIME (*Tilia cordata*) A beautiful, 100 ft (30 m) tree with delicate shiny leaves, the lime is found all over the British Isles. The fragrant yellow flowers appear in July, emerging in bunches at all angles, unlike the hanging flowers of the common lime.

HOLLY (*Ilex aquifolium*) An adaptable inhabitant of almost any soil or situation, the holly tree grows up to 40 ft (12 m), with its branches punctuated by small bunches of yellowish flowers from May to August. The familiar red berries form in September.

MIDLAND HAWTHORN (*Crataegus oxyacanthoides*) This differs from the common hawthorn in having two pips in the bright red fruit, and more rounded leaves. It is also much rarer, growing in heavy soils in the south and east of the British Isles to a height of 25 ft (8 m).

HONEYSUCKLE (*Lonicera periclymenum*)This vigorous twining plant, whose stems may be 30 ft (9 m) long, is a fragrant favourite from June until late autumn. The cream flowers deepen to orange and finally explode into clusters of bright red berries.

Plate 38.

ROE DEER (*Capreolus capreolus*)
This small, graceful deer, reaching
24-28″ (61-71 cm) at the shoulder, is
the most attractive deer in Britain,
delicately built and with an
intelligent soft expression; males
have short, forked antlers. The coat
is foxy red from May to September
but turns dark grey-brown with a
white rump patch in winter. Roe
deer are common in parts of
England and widespread in
Scotland, liking plantations and
thickets which are sheltered and dry.
1-3 fawns (but usually twins) are
born in May.

FALLOW DEER (*Dama dama*)
Wild fallow deer of the woodlands are shy, secretive animals. The coat is usually reddish fawn with white spots, but other common colours are light fawn to white or a faintly spotted black. Bucks have broadpalmed antlers and all fallow deer have a white rump patch with a black central line along the tail. Big bucks reach 37″ (95 cm) at the shoulder and weigh 200 lb (90 kg); does are much lighter. Herds are widespread in England and Wales and parts of Scotland and Ireland. One fawn is born in June.

Stinking Hellebore

Spring Snowflake

Winter Aconite

STINKING HELLEBORE
(Helleborus foetidus) A poisonous, unpleasant-smelling plant 8-31″ (20-80cm) tall, seen in open woods of south and west England and Wales. The lower leaves are evergreen. Sprays of drooping flowers open Feb-March. The oily seeds attract ants.

SPRING SNOWFLAKE *(Leucojum vernum)* A very rare bulb, occurring only in a few localities in Dorset and Somerset, in damp scrub and by streams. Single, nodding white flowers, tipped with green are seen February to March on 6-8″ (15-20cm) leafless stems.

WINTER ACONITE *(Eranthis hyemalis)* Early to bloom from January-March, aconites have single flowers on stems 2-6″ (5-15cm), each with a collar of deeply divided leaves. Stalked leaves grow after the flower stem has withered. Naturalised, but found only locally in woodlands.

Barren Strawberry

Spring Crocus

Mezereon

Lesser Celandine

BARREN STRAWBERRY (Potentilla sterilis) Growing in 2-10″ (5-25cm) clumps, this soft hair covered plant with trifoliate toothed leaves flowers February to May. Non-fleshy fruits follow – it also spreads by short runners. Common in open woods and glades.

LESSER CELANDINE (Ranunculus ficaria) Widespread in woods and by streams where its glossy flowers, borne singly on 2-10″ (5-25cm) stems are a common sight March-May. A tuberous perennial, heart shaped, stalked leaves grow from the base and from creeping, rooting stems.

SPRING CROCUS (Crocus vernus) A garden escape, now naturalized in scattered localities in the South. 2-4 linear leaves grow at the same time as the purple or white flowers, March to April. 4-7″ (10-18cm) high, the flower stalk elongates as the fruit, a capsule, matures.

MEZEREON (Daphne mezereum) A rare shrub of chalk and limestone woodlands, growing to 39″ (100cm). Fragrant flowers open before the leaves from February-March followed by extremely poisonous red berries. The light green lanceolate leaves fall in autumn.

Coal Tit

Irish Race

Long-tailed Tit

Juvenile

Juvenile

COAL TIT *(Parus ater)* The smallest of the tits at 4½″ (12cm), the coal tit is fairly common in both coniferous and deciduous woods. The white cheeks and distinctive nape patch are yellower in the Irish race and juveniles and the white wing bars are obvious in flight. The sexes are alike and the female builds a nest in a hole low down in a tree and lays 7-10 white, red-speckled eggs in April-May. Feeding on seeds and insects it often stores both to enable it to survive harsh winters. The call is a thin, reedy 'tsee'.

LONG-TAILED TIT *(Aegithalos caudatus)* Most often seen in small parties flying from tree to tree with undulating flight, this tiny bird – 2½″ (6cm) long with a 3″ (8cm) tail – frequents heaths, hedges and woodlands. In March and April, both sexes take up to 3 weeks to make a large domed nest – moss and spider's webs are bound outside with lichens, inside is a thick layer of feathers. 8-12 finely speckled white eggs are laid. Juveniles are duller than the adults, with shorter tails. Feeding more on insects than other tits, they often suffer badly in harsh winters.

Marsh Tit

Willow Tit

Summer

Winter

MARSH TIT (*Parus palustris*)
Difficult to distinguish visually from the willow tit, this 4½″ (12cm) bird has a glossy black cap and no pale patch on the folded wings. The call is a loud 'pitchoo', the song a repeated 'schip-schip-schip'. Single-brooded, in April-May the female builds a mossy feather-lined nest in a hole in a tree. 7-9 white eggs with brown markings are laid. The sexes are alike and juveniles closely resemble young willow tits. Resident in open woods with shrubs in much of England and Wales, they eat seeds and insects.

WILLOW TIT (*Parus montanus*)
This 4½″ (12cm) bird has a dull, sooty crown and a larger black bib than the marsh tit – the paler patch on the wing is most obvious in winter. Favouring damp woods and thickets, it occurs as far north as southern Scotland. Quiet and seldom seen on the ground, it forages for insects and seeds in the undergrowth. The female excavates a new nest site in rotting tree stumps every year, using some of the wood chips and fibres to make the nest. 7-8 white, speckled eggs are laid in April-May. The call is nasal and buzzing.

Sulphur Tuft

Giant Polypore

Scarlet Elf Cap

Beefsteak

SULPHUR TUFT *(Hypholoma fasciculare)* A common, conspicuous fungus seen in dense clumps on dead tree trunks. Curved stems up to 4″ (10cm) support a domed cap ¾-3″ (2-7cm) across. The closely packed gills are yellow when young, aging to dark brown, and shed brown spores.

SCARLET ELF CAP *(Sarcoscypha coccinea)* Found on rotting wood, most often in the West, this fungus has cup-shaped fruiting bodies up to 2″ (5cm) across, covered in matted white hairs. Spores are produced in these cups as they mature. They grow all through the winter.

GIANT POLYPORE *(Meripilus giganteus)* As much as 31″ (80cm) across, the fruiting body of this bracket fungus can be seen in autumn on the lower trunks of beech or oak trees. Beneath its fan-shaped lobes are spongy, white pores, from which minute spores fall when ripe.

BEEFSTEAK *(Fistulina hepatica)* Causing brown rot of oak and enriching the colour of the timber, this bracket fungus produces a thick fruit body up to 10″ (25cm) across in autumn. When damaged, the pale, veined, edible flesh oozes a realistic blood-red sap – hence its name.

Oakwood Fungi

Coral Spot Fungus

Gregarious Elf Cap

Velvet Shank

Orange Phlebia

CORAL SPOT FUNGUS (*Nectria cinnabarina*) Common on damaged branches and rotting wood, this fungus appears as tiny spots over the bark. Rain spreads asexual spores from pale spots, and sexual spores from deep red spots seen in autumn are wind-dispersed.

VELVET SHANK (*Flammulina velutipes*) Fruiting all through the winter, even surviving frost, these fungi have 1-4″ (2-12cm), slimy caps on tough stems with dark velvety bases. Pale yellow gills shed white spores. It is widespread and common on dead or damaged wood.

GREGARIOUS ELF CAP (*Mycena inclinata*) Clusters of these delicate fungi are frequently seen on oak and hazel stumps in autumn. The bell-shaped, slightly pleated 1″ (2.5cm) cap with whitish gills sits on a thin 2-4″ (5-10cm) stalk. It has white spores.

ORANGE PHLEBIA (*Phlebia radiata*) Common all year on the bark of dead, broadleaved trees, the fruiting bodies are flattish irregular patches up to 4″ (10cm) across, varying in colour from dull to vivid orange. Spores arise on the wrinkled upper surface.

IN THE BEECHWOOD

Beneath the smoothly arching limbs and dense glossy foliage of the beech trees, curiously shaped fungi and delicate wild orchids litter the leaf-strewn floor while flocks of finches and tits search out food among the beech mast.

Late spring shows the beechwood at its very best, when the branches are freshly laden with light green leaves and clusters of yellowy flowers. At this time of year the sunlight still dances on the woodland floor where last year's dead leaves and dried beech mast (the fruit of the beech) lie in crisp copper carpets and crackly drifts.

By high summer the trees' foliage has stolen three-quarters of the sunlight, so holly, yew and spurge laurel are the only woody shrubs to be found. All evergreens, they can live in the shadow of the beech by making up their lost summer growth in winter. No wood is everywhere the same, however, and in the hanger woods on chalk hillsides both wild cherry and whitebeam may grow tall among the beeches. Less densely shaded patches, especially at the top of the slope, are often carpeted with dog's mercury, while wild strawberry, wood anemone and woodruff grow where the sunbeams percolate through.

On the flat tops of the Chilterns and on downs where the soil is deeper the beech trees thrust upwards to their maximum height – around 130 feet – and cherry and whitebeam and oaks and ash grow among them with holly and yew below. The famous Burnham Beeches grow on sandy soil, which is covered with mosses, and here the trees are not tall and stately but rather stunted and gnarled. Once pollarded (see page 154), their boughs have grown massive in their old age. Occasionally, a heavy branch breaks off to create an interesting mini-habitat for the many insects which live in dead wood. Many of the old beeches in Epping Forest have also been pollarded. Here they are accompanied by hornbeams which are better suited to the heavy, often wet, Essex clay.

BEECHWOOD PLANTS

At first glance the typical beechwood seems rather empty below the canopy. The light is too dim for most green plants which need sunshine to grow. Consequently, the beechwood is home to those plants which do not rely directly or entirely on sunlight or which use curious subterfuges to feed and grow. A close look at the

woodland floor can therefore reveal some very interesting plants indeed.

Beechwoods are noted for their wild orchids. These are not luxuriant species but tiny, delicate specimens, inhabitants of the leaf litter. Orchids produce vast numbers of minute seeds, containing nothing in the way of a food store for the seedling plant. To survive, the seedling's root must establish a *mycorrhiza*, an association with a soil fungus. The fungus is a saprophyte, that is, a plant which feeds on decaying organic matter, such as rotting leaves. The orchid seedling gets its essential nutrients from the fungus. It is quite some time before the orchid actually produces green leaves, and even longer before it flowers: 12 years or more in the case of the twayblade.

Orchids tend to have rather bizarre flowers but there is usually a good reason for this. The

AN EARLY ORCHID
The lovely white helleborine growing in a Chiltern beechwood. This orchid flowers in late May to early June, before the tree canopy closes completely over, but it can, in fact, withstand fairly deep shade. A flower of chalk soils, it has a preference for beech and can be found growing under isolated trees well away from woodlands.

142

twayblade, for instance, attracts short-tongued flies and beetles by releasing its nectar into a shallow groove in the lip of the flower. An insect feeding on the nectar follows the groove into the flower where it comes into contact with the pollen sacs. At this point it touches a kind of 'trigger', which shoots a drop of sticky liquid at the insect, gluing a mass of pollen to its back. The startled insect flies off, and when it visits another flower, the pollen it is carrying fertilizes it.

The bird's nest orchid is wholly a saprophyte – it is leafless and relies totally on the breakdown of dead matter for its nutrients. These orchids

LIFE IN THE SHADE OF THE BEECH

A scene typical of Burnham Beeches or Epping Forest where ancient pollarded beeches (centre) are a feature. The wood warbler sings above its ground nest; the green woodpecker has excavated a nest hole in a trunk; and the blackbird may be nesting in the holly. Beech mast provides a feast for squirrels, mice, chaffinches and crows. Chanterelle and oyster mushroom are tasty delicacies. In the shade grow arum, dog's mercury, yellow bird's nest and the tree parasite, beech tuft.

KEY TO THE SPECIES

1 Blackbird	11 Beech tuft
2 Wood warbler	fungus
3 Green	12 Arum
woodpecker	13 Wood
4 Chaffinch	warbler's nest
5 Holly	14 Chanterelle
6 Carrion crow	15 Yellow bird's
7 Wild cherry	nest
8 Oyster	16 Twayblade
mushroom	17 Wood mouse
9 Grey squirrel	18 Beech mast
10 Dog's	19 Wild strawberry
mercury	20 Plaited door snail

are often present in beechwoods but are difficult to find as their muted colours blend in with the brown leaf litter of the beechwood floor.

Equally interesting are the beechwood fungi. They play a vital part in the breakdown of dead timber which becomes soft and crumbly after they have been at work. These timber decomposers are saprophytes but there is a vast variety of other fungi which are parasites, growing on living trees.

Beechwoods are also renowned for their range of truly delicious edible fungi. The most celebrated of all fungal delicacies is the rare truffle – not much sought now in Britain, although truffle hunting is still kept up in France where pigs are used to smell out the underground 'tuber'. The oyster mushroom, which grows on fallen beech timber, is another tasty species.

There is no simple rule for distinguishing between an edible fungus and one that is poisonous – and beechwoods may contain some of the latter. One such is the death cap, which contains some of the deadliest toxins known.

A RICH HOME

The beech itself is home to a great number of invertebrates – many more than the ash, for example – though not quite as rich a home as the oak. Typical of the beech is Britain's most extraordinary looking caterpillar, that of the lobster moth. When threatened it rears up, resembling a tiny lobster, and squirts formic acid at its attacker. The attractive large emerald moth is also found in beechwoods which grow on sandy soil. Among the leaf litter the plaited door snail lurks in disguise – it looks like a fallen beech bud, which helps it avoid attention from predatory birds.

In summer, birds are not all that common, for there is scant undergrowth to provide cover. Sparse ground vegetation and dense canopy

suits the wood warbler, though, and this perky little bird is quite common in beechwoods. It builds a domed nest in a scrap of ground cover and proclaims its territory from a prominent song post in the lower branches of a tree above its nest. The colourful chaffinch is the most common beechwood bird, and where a tangled thicket sprouts, the blackbird may take up residence. Stock doves are attracted by holes in

NIGHT VISITORS
Shy, cautious creatures, badgers are rarely seen out of their intricate underground homes by day. Instead they emerge from their setts at night to begin foraging expeditions which often last until dawn.

BRIGHT REDSTART
This handsome summer visitor arrives from West Africa in April. Flashing courtship chases between the trees, during which the rust-red tail is shown to advantage, are soon followed by nesting. The birds choose a hole in a tree or wall and also readily use nest-boxes. They feed mainly on insects, and the male (shown here) is particularly adept at catching insects on the wing.

old trees, as is the delightful redstart, which can often be seen in New Forest beechwoods.

In winter the picture changes and the beech-wood attracts many birds – flocks of finches, tits and others come from afar to feed amid the beech mast. The hawfinch is also sometimes seen among the beeches of Epping. Bramblings – relatives of the chaffinch – are winter visitors from Scandinavia and northern Russia, and are usually seen in muted winter plumage. Their numbers are unpredictable from year to year and depend on the abundance of beech mast elsewhere in Europe.

The Chiltern woods are home to one of the few mammals found under the arching branches of the beech – the edible, or fat, dormouse. This bushy-tailed, squirrel-like little rodent was only introduced to Britain around the turn of the century; mainly nocturnal, they are rarely seen. A more likely sighting is the wood mouse or ubiquitous grey squirrel.

EDIBLE DORMOUSE
(above) Once regarded as a delicacy by the Romans, this plump rodent is at its fattest in autumn as it prepares for hibernation. It may sleep for up to seven months, emerging again in April or May.

PLAITED DOOR SNAILS
(below) These snails get their name from the plait-like shape of their shell and the plate or door with which they can close the entrance. Found in both beech and ash woods, they rest during the day on the ground, climbing tree trunks at night to feed on lichens.

LOBSTER MOTH CATERPILLAR
(above) This dramatic caterpillar, though not common, is found chiefly in beechwoods where it feeds on the leaves. In defence it can shoot formic acid at an attacker and rears up to look menacing.

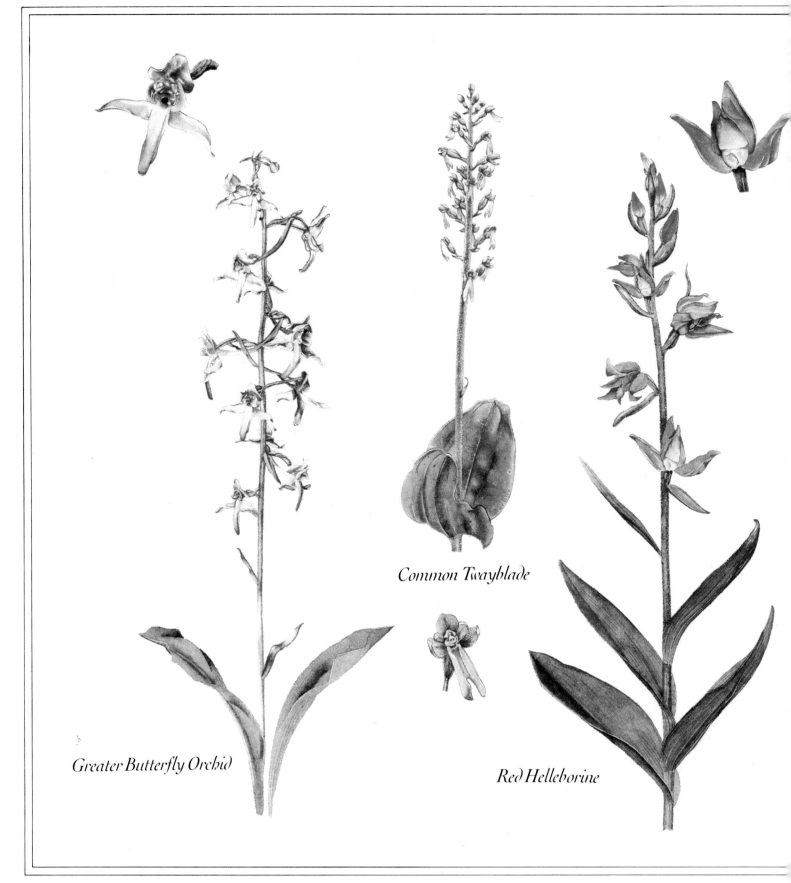

Common Twayblade

Greater Butterfly Orchid

Red Helleborine

GREATER BUTTERFLY ORCHID (*Platanthera chlorantha*) A stout, 12" (30cm), but graceful orchid with a pair of large leaves at the base, and small stem leaves below a broad spike of sweet-scented, creamy-white flowers with long spurs; found in woods and pastures on limy soils.

COMMON TWAYBLADE (*Listera ovata*) Usually found in woods, limy scrub and on dunes, this orchid reaches 24" (60cm). It has two large oval, dark green leaves, which lie horizontal, and opposite each other at the base of a long spike of greenish flowers.

RED HELLEBORINE (*Cephalanthera rubra*) An increasingly rare native perennial, now found only in Cotswold and Chiltern beechwoods, this plant produces its vivid pink 8-20" (20-50cm) flower spikes between May and July above narrow grass-like leaves.

Beechwood Orchids

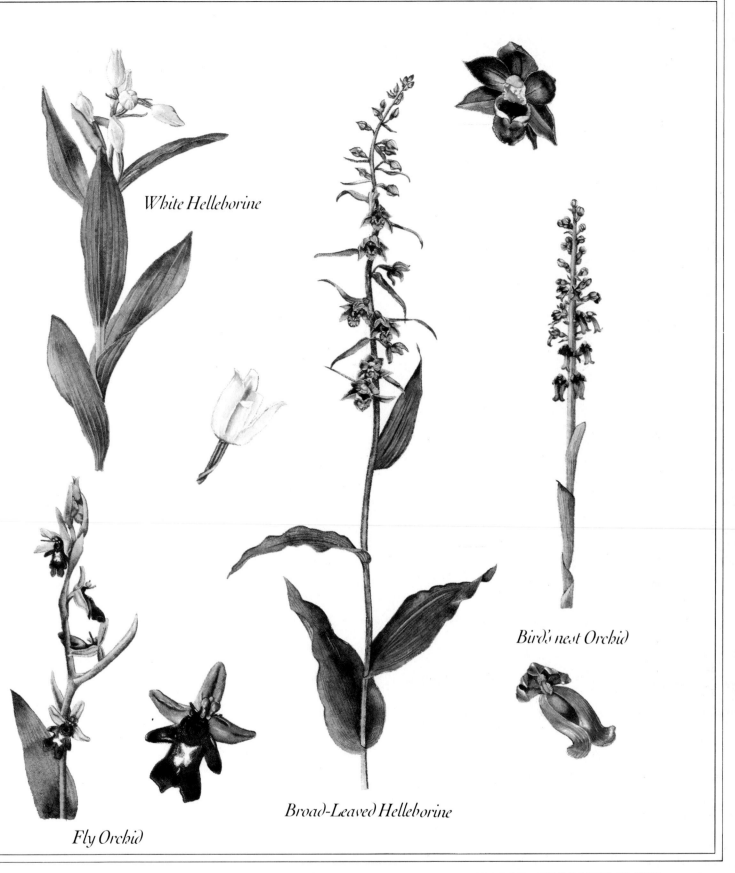

White Helleborine

Bird's nest Orchid

Broad-Leaved Helleborine

Fly Orchid

**WHITE HELLEBORINE
(Cephalanthera damasonium)** Found
in beechwoods in the South, this 18″
(45cm) plant has broad, erect leaves
and creamy-white flowers which
rarely open to reveal a patch of
yelow inside. Each flower is over-
topped by a pointed, green bract.

FLY ORCHID (Ophrys insectifera)
A slender, 12″ (30cm) plant that
prefers the semi-shade at the edge of
woods on limy soils. The flowers
are small, hard to spot, and the
lower lip is brown and blue and
three-lobed. It is rare except in a
few areas in the South.

**BROAD-LEAVED HELLEBORINE
(Epipactis helleborine)** Found in
shady places in woods, this 2′
(60cm) orchid has broad, oval, dull
green leaves which spiral up the
stem. The thick flowers are greenish
or tinged yellow or purple and rather
insignificant.

**BIRD'S NEST ORCHID
(Neottia nidus-avis)** This rarely seen
orchid is found in the deep shade of
beechwoods. It is honey-brown all
over, and lives on dead vegetation
with a fungus partner. The 12″
(30cm) flower spike is sickly
smelling; each flower is two-lipped.

Cep

Hedgehog Fungus

Horn of Plenty

CEP *(Boletus edulis)* This fungus, the 'penny bun' has a thick stem and a smooth, greasy, firm cap up to 7″ (18cm) across. The upper side of the cap is warm brown, and the underside has spongy pores, not gills like a mushroom. An edible variety, delicious to taste.

HORN OF PLENTY *(Craterellus cornucopioides)* In the autumn the floors of beechwoods may be dotted with the brown, grey-stemmed funnels of this fungus. The wavy-edged caps reach 3″ (8cm) across and can be dried and ground for seasoning. Common in some years.

HEDGEHOG FUNGUS *(Hydnum repandum)* Known as the 'wood hedgehog', this species is found in deciduous woods in the autumn. The wavy, orange-yellow cap is thick, fleshy and smooth, and up to 4″ (10cm) across. The white flesh has a spicy, bitter taste.

Beechwood Fungi

Oyster Mushroom

Truffle

Chanterelle

CHANTERELLE *(Cantharellus cibarius)* Fairly common in deciduous woods in the autumn, this 4″ (10cm) all-yellow fungus widens from a narrow base to a broad, flattish cap. It smells of apricot and is delicious, but the similar False Chanterelle is inedible.

OYSTER MUSHROOM *(Pleurotus ostreatus)* The 2-6″ (5-15cm)buff-coloured cap flattens into oyster-shell shaped brackets which attach themselves to deciduous trees, especially beech, in summer and autumn. This abundant species is edible and tasty.

TRUFFLE *(Tuber aestivum)* A rare fungus found underground in beechwoods. Like its more famous and even finer tasting continental relative, it prefers limy soil. The warty, fruiting body is 1-3″ (3-8cm) across, dark grey in colour and pale inside.

Redstart

Male

Stock Dove

Blackbird

Male

STOCK DOVE (*Columba oenas*)
This medium-sized pigeon, 13″
(32cm) long, looks dark and blue
in flight. It nests in a hole in a tree
or cavity, laying two white eggs at
any time in the summer; feeds in
woods and fields on leaves, berries,
grain and buds.

BLACKBIRD (*Turdus merula*)
A 10″ (25cm) thrush, which feeds
on worms and insects, berries and
fruit; common in gardens, parks,
woods and farmland. A superb
songster; females are brown and
indistinctly spotted. Nests in hedges
or bushes, lays 3-5 eggs.

REDSTART (*Phoenicurus
phoenicurus*) A 5½″ (14cm)
songster of old oak and mixed
woods and woodland edges where
it feeds on insects. It nests in a
natural hole or a nestbox, and lays
5-7 pale blue eggs. The flickering
orange tail is distinct at all ages.

Birds of the Beechwood

Wood Warbler

Brambling

Male in winter

Female

Male in summer

Hawfinch

Male

WOOD WARBLER (*Phylloscopus sibilatrix*) This 5″ (12.5cm) bird is rarely seen away from dense beech or oak woods; it feeds on insects in the canopy but nests on the forest floor, laying 5-7 speckled eggs in a domed nest amongst leaf litter. Song is a shivering trill.

BRAMBLING (*Fringilla montifringilla*) Of similar size, 6″ (15cm), and shape to the chaffinch, with which it is often found, this species is a winter visitor in Britain, breeding in Scandinavian birch-woods. Feeds under beeches or in arable fields; population variable.

HAWFINCH (*Coccothraustes coccothraustes*) At 6½″ (16cm), this large, stoutly built finch has a very large head and a strong bill that can crack a cherry stone. It eats beechmast and hornbeam seeds. Shy and not often seen, it lays 4-6 blotched eggs in a nest of twigs.

Hornbeam

Winged Fruit

Flowers

Ripe Berries

Whitebeam

HORNBEAM *(Carpinus betulus)*
A neat, medium-sized tree, 80′ (25m), found in woods of oak and beech, mostly in the South-east; it is beech-shaped with grey bark but its leaves are toothed like hazel and fruits hidden by long, three-lobed bracts in the autumn.

WHITEBEAM *(Sorbus aria)*
A native of the South on chalk or limestone or light, sandy soils, but now frequently planted in towns. The shallow-toothed leaves vary in size and shape but are always white with hairs beneath, briefly bright yellow in autumn. 65′ (20m) max.

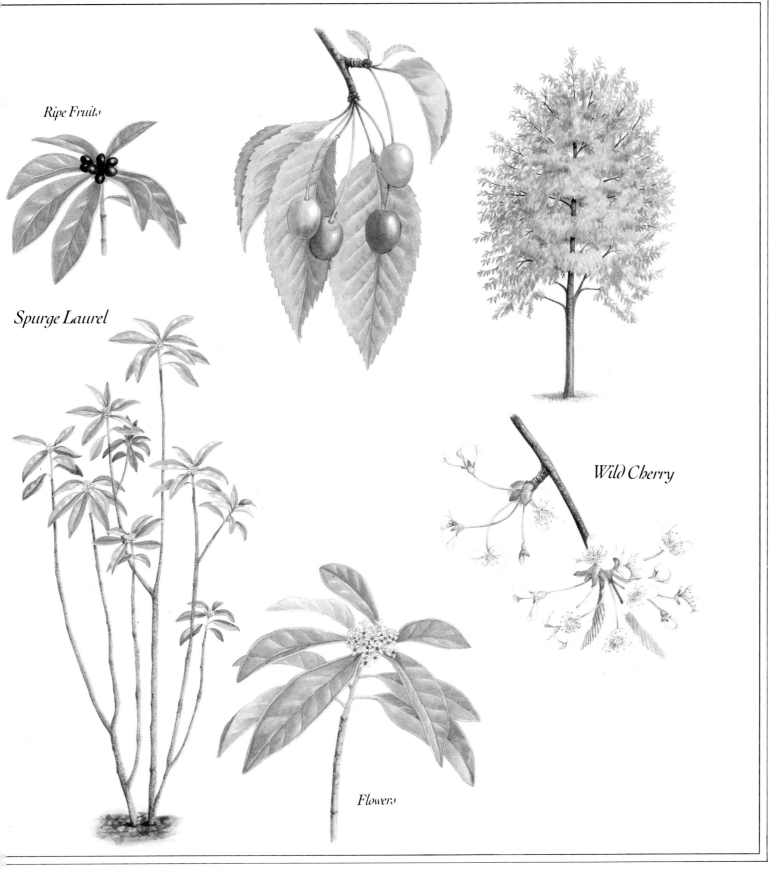

Ripe Fruits

Spurge Laurel

Wild Cherry

Flowers

SPURGE LAUREL *(Daphne laureola)* Widespread in woods on chalk and limestone, this small, 2′ (60cm) shrub has leathery, shiny evergreen leaves rather like those of laurel. Bunches of small, green flowers develop into round black berries which are poisonous.

WILD CHERRY *(Prunus avium)* Widespread in hedges and beechwoods, this small tree flowers as the leaves appear in April and produces small red cherries in autumn. The bark has horizontal peeling bands; the leaves are pointed oval and sharply toothed.

ALONG THE RIVERSIDE

The winding lowland river is a favourite haunt for naturalists and ramblers alike, for its banks and waters support an exceptional range of wildlife.

The gentle lowland reaches of Britain's rivers support a wealth of wildlife that is almost unmatched elsewhere in the countryside. The waters themselves, enriched with minerals washed down from the hills and turbid with microscopic plants, provide a home for fish and numerous tiny animals, while birds and mammals, flowers and trees flourish on the bankside. Each river, winding through the fields, forms a jigsaw of many different habitats, some reflecting the impact of industry or agriculture, some completely natural. From time to time, these local habitats may suddenly change as floods or droughts – even pollution – have an effect on the wildlife of the river.

A LINE OF TREES

The course of a river is often marked by a line of trees, waving in the breezes crossing the open water – a reminder of the wetland wilderness long since cleared for farmland. Some will be ancient alders, easily recognizable in winter when myriad cone-like fruits hang starkly against the tracery of twigs. Later the unopened buds give the trees a purplish tinge, and masses of yellow catkins droop from the branches; in summer the cones are green and the trees can be identified by their bluntly rounded leaves.

Another classic feature of the riverbank is the crack willow, so-called because its fragile twigs snap sharply when bent back. These trees can often be recognized by their mop-shaped heads, caused by pollarding – a form of pruning which dates back to the days when willow poles were used for sheep-hurdles; nowadays willow rods are often used for baskets. Pollarding involved cutting back the branches to the trunk, encouraging the growth of a thick head of straight new shoots, which could be harvested every few years.

The same result could also be produced by cutting the trees back almost to ground level – a process known as coppicing – but pollarding was preferred where meadows ran down to the river, for it put the tender shoots out of the range of browsing cattle. Pollarding is still carried out today, but for different reasons: water authorities may cut back the branches to prevent them from obstructing the river.

RIVERSIDE FLOWERS

Beneath the trees, a profusion of flowering plants have each adapted to their own favoured habitat. In high summer, the pinkish-purple flowers of the great willowherb are a common sight on the bank itself. Below them, with their roots just underwater, you may see the bur-reed, which provides

COMMON ALDER *(left) A quick-growing waterside tree, it is easily recognised by the dark, woody cone-like fruits which can be seen all year. In winter, the leafless tree has purple male catkins which turn yellow in spring. Both siskins and redpolls are fond of its seeds.*

THE SISKIN *(right) This small black and yellow finch has flourished with the spread of conifers on which it feeds. In winter, when numbers are swollen by birds from Scandinavia, the siskin readily takes to the birch and alder trees along the banks of lowland rivers.*

LIFE IN THE LOWLAND RIVER

The lowland river and its banks provide a fertile habitat for a wide variety of plant and animal species, each adapted to its own particular niche. Thus yellow flag and reedmace grow in the stiller waters on the inside of bends and provide cover for the water vole and nesting birds, while the otter digs its burrow among the roots of the willow and alder trees which line the banks.

Many creatures are dependent on the species living in the river itself: swallows are attracted by hatching mayfly; kingfishers swoop for small fish and crustaceans; the swan dabbles for plants and insects; and the wary heron spears voles and frogs as well as fish.

Beneath the surface, freshwater snails feed on the aquatic plant life, such as arrowhead and yellow water lily. Small insects are drawn in by swan molluscs, so called because they too make up part of the swan's diet. The caddis larva makes itself a protective case from plant stems. Bream eat these, while pike prey on fish, water shrews, water voles and even small water birds.

KEY TO THE SPECIES

1 Water vole
2 Crack willow
3 Yellow flag
4 Reedmace
5 Kingfisher
6 Swallow
7 Grey heron
8 Arrowhead
9 Yellow
   water lily
10 Mute swan
11 Alder
12 Otter
13 Mayfly
14 Water
   crowfoot
15 Swan mussel
16 Bream
17 Water snail
18 Caddis larva
19 Water shrew
20 Pike

THE AMERICAN MINK, AN INVADER
The mink, originally an escapee from fur farms, is now widespread along rivers.

nesting and roosting places for wildfowl; in autumn the ripe fruits of the bur-reed provide food for smaller birds. Further out, on a clay river, the plate-like leaves of the yellow water lily may be seen floating where the current is sluggish: the seed cases, smelling like stale alcohol, are sometimes called 'brandy bottles' because of their distinctive scent and shape.

Water lilies and willowherbs are rarely found on the muddy slips where cattle go to drink, for they cannot survive trampling. Instead water mint – easily distinguished by the smell of its leaves – and water forget-me-not, looking a little paler than the garden variety, may flourish. Where the shingle nudges to the surface and the flow is fast and rippling you may see masses of the little white flowers known as water crowfoot.

SWALLOW, SWIFT OR MARTIN?
These birds are often hard to distinguish, but the colour and tail shape give crucial clues. Swallows and martins are both pale underneath, but the swallow has a long, thin tail-fork; the swift's tail is shorter and the bird is larger and darker.

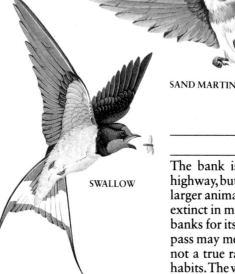

SWIFT

SAND MARTIN

SWALLOW

RIVER CARNIVORES
(below) Among the biggest and most voracious river predators are the perch (back), which eats smaller fish, and the pike (front), which preys on fish, frogs, voles and waterbirds – and other pike.

ANIMAL HIGHWAYS

The bank is an important animal habitat and highway, but few mammals are ever visible. Of the larger animals, the shy otter, now sadly rare if not extinct in many lowland districts, prefers tangled banks for its nightly forays. A sudden plop as you pass may mean you have disturbed a 'water rat' – not a true rat, but a vole, with vegetarian eating habits. The water vole creates close-cropped lawns on the bank; its burrow is dug deep with an entrance hole low down, sometimes below water level. Nest holes higher up a steep bank may belong to kingfishers and sand martins: here they are out of reach of the voracious brown rat, a 'true' rat that will take eggs and young.

Rivers and riversides are a bird watcher's paradise. Many different species are attracted to the water, such as the swifts, swallows and martins, visiting migrants that feed on the newly hatched mayflies in June. Wagtails, grebes, the coot and moorhen feed in the water or close by.

Ducks especially are easy to observe searching for food out on the open surface. Two main kinds of duck can usually be seen – the dabblers which up-end and reach down from the surface for scraps of plants and small animals, and the divers which forage deep under water before reappearing some distance away. Many of these birds nest on quiet and well vegetated stretches of bank, but the mute swan, also typical of lowland rivers, builds its large nest boldly in full view.

The fact that ducks are equally at home on land, paddling across the river and diving underwater is a reminder that the surface is not quite the impenetrable barrier it first appears. Many small aquatic animals, water beetles for example, fly regular sorties out of the water. Numerous insects spend their formative larval months feeding underwater, to emerge into the air, fly, mate and then quickly die once the new generation of eggs has been laid. Mayflies (the 'drakes' and 'olives' of the fisherman) we see for only a short part of their total lives. In the early summer, the warm weather brings vast numbers of them to the surface, where they shuck their larval skins and fly free. This, called 'the hatch,' is one of the spectacular sights of the lowland river, and acts like a magnet for trout and anglers alike.

'GAME' AND 'COARSE' FISH

The trout is the classic 'game' fish, living in clear water and catching its food by sight. Each inhabits its own territory in the river, often in a pool or behind a large stone, and lies head to current, snapping insects from the water. Flowing clumps of weed, or hollows beneath tree roots, provide shady resting places for the fish. Trout require cool water with plenty of oxygen – upland reaches and the clear chalk rivers of southern England are their stronghold today, although they also live in many other rivers. Different fish prefer warmer, murkier water.

In the gentle lowland reaches, large shoals of bream spend much time head down, searching for worms, snails and insects on the muddy bottom, clouding the water as they do so. It takes bream some time to accumulate a meal, and while feeding they are at high risk from predators like the pike. There is an advantage in numbers: if one hapless member of the shoal falls victim, the others can dart away to safety.

The pike, like the bream, tench, roach, perch and other fish which share the lowland reaches, is known as a 'coarse' fish. It can tolerate turbid water even when it is low in oxygen, and it takes full advantage of the gloom to seize its prey from ambush. It waits alone among the weeds – hunting in numbers would soon betray its presence – then shoots out to take other fish up to a fifth of its own size, or a water shrew preoccupied with snapping up caddis from the river bottom. Pike may even snatch young coots and ducklings.

THE CASE OF THE CADDIS

A close look at the water may reveal caddis fly larvae in their extraordinary cases. The larvae living by riffles and other fast flowing sections make themselves a protective shell of heavy sand grains which they fasten to a stone. On the inside of a bend, however, where the current is slow and even a small obstruction can create a pond-like condition, caddis larvae can be seen with their cases constructed of pieces of plant leaf or stem. They can safely crawl in this placid water and often do so, carrying the case with them. The larval stage lasts about a year and large numbers of adult flies emerge in summer.

But the most dramatic river insects are the dragonflies and damselflies, with their brilliant iridescent wings. Throughout the summer, these can be seen flitting past the vegetation on the river bank. Unfortunately, they tend to be quite sensitive to pollution and are usually found only by fairly clean rivers. Indeed, their presence is itself an indicator of the condition of the water.

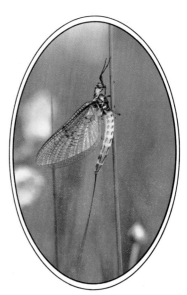

THE MAYFLY
(above) Mayfly nymphs may take a year or more to reach adulthood. The life of the adult is very brief – lasting just a few days – but it provides one of the most spectacular river sights. From May to September, the shining insects form brilliant shimmering swarms over the water, rising and falling in a dancing nuptial flight. They form a rich harvest for swifts, martins, swallows and a number of fish, particularly trout.

SAND MARTIN COLONY
A favourite site for sand martins (above) is bare sand cliffs (right), often on the outside of river bends. The birds excavate burrows up to three feet (1m) long, lining the end chamber with straw and feathers. From May, well-feathered chicks can be seen at the entrance, clamouring for food as the parents dart over the water to catch flying insects.

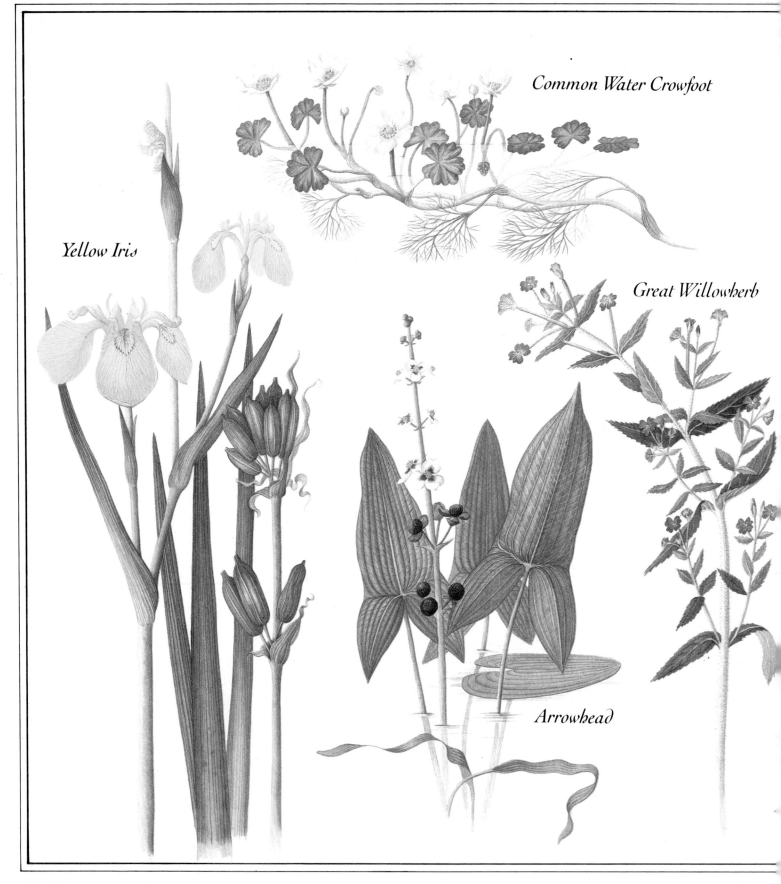

Common Water Crowfoot

Yellow Iris

Great Willowherb

Arrowhead

YELLOW IRIS (*Iris pseudacorus*)
Better known as yellow flag, this iris
grows along the banks of slow-
moving rivers. Usually 3ft (1m) tall,
though it can grow to twice that
height, between June and August it
produces 2 or 3 flowers per stem,
from which seed capsules develop.

COMMON WATER CROWFOOT
(*Ranunculus aquatilis*) Like many
aquatic plants, this crowfoot has two
distinct types of leaf –thread-like
beneath the water and lobed above.
It forms large masses in still or slow-
running water up to 3ft (1m) deep,
and flowers from April to September.

ARROWHEAD (*Sagittaria
sagittifolia*) Easily recognized by the
shape of its leaves, the arrowhead
colonizes the banks of slow-moving
rivers and ponds. Its stems root as
they go, producing 3ft (1m) spikes of
three-petalled white flowers from
July to August.

GREAT WILLOWHERB
(*Epilobium hirsutum*) A common
inhabitant of river banks and damp
places, which it graces from June to
August with 7ft (2m) spikes of
purplish-pink flowers. The Latin
name *hirsutum* refers to the soft hairs
which cover stem and leaf.

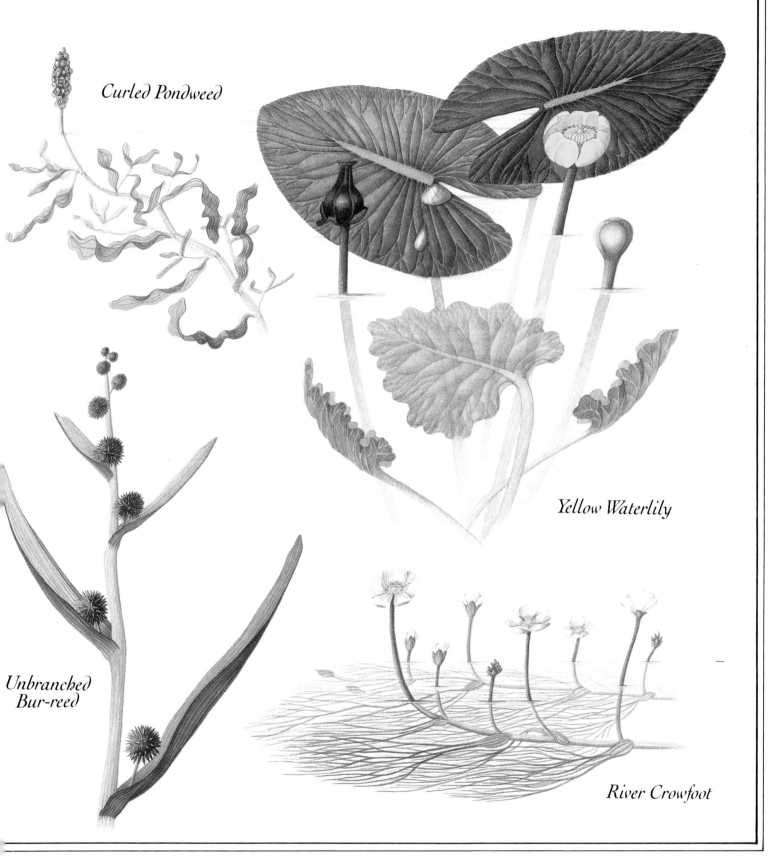

Curled Pondweed

Yellow Waterlily

Unbranched Bur-reed

River Crowfoot

CURLED PONDWEED
(Potamogeton crispus) The wavy translucent leaves of this unobtrusive plant are all submerged beneath the water. The stems may reach 4ft (120cm), and from May to September produce small spikes of flowers, which break the surface.

UNBRANCHED BUR-REED
(Sparganium simplex) A discreet plant found in shallow rivers and ponds, this bur-reed blooms between June and August, producing small green tuft-like flowers on stems up to 2ft (60cm) tall. Above the water the leaves are folded like ships' keels.

YELLOW WATER LILY (*Nuphar lutea*) Flowering from June to September, this is a common embellishment to stagnant and slow-running water, with golden blooms, leathery floating leaves, and stalks up to 10ft (3m) long, which bear cabbage-like submerged leaves.

RIVER CROWFOOT (*Ranunculus fluitans*) In fast-moving water, the river crowfoot grows stout submerged stems up to 20ft (6m) long, which are festooned with dark green tassel-like leaves. From June to August it produces white flowers with 5-10 overlapping petals.

Perch

Roach

Carp

Common Bream

PERCH (*Perca fluvialitis*)
Distinguished by its spiny dorsal fin, the perch is common in slow-flowing rivers, ponds and lowland lakes. It feeds on insect larvae, small fish and shellfish, reaching a maximum size of about 20″ (50cm) and 4½lb (2kg). Young perch live in shoals.

COMMON CARP (*Cyprinus carpio)* A large fish with four barbels around the mouth, the carp lives in slow-moving rivers and lakes; it feeds on crustaceans, worms and algae. Adult fish – some over 40 years old – can reach a size of 22″ (55cm) and 40lb (18kg).

ROACH (*Rutilus rutilus*) A common shoal fish with orange fins and reddish eyes, the roach is widespread in chalk streams, lowland rivers, reservoirs and ponds. It feeds on plants, algae, insects and molluscs, and rarely exceeds 14″ (36cm) and 3½lb (1.5kg).

COMMON BREAM (*Abramis brama)* The lumpy, deep, flattened body and small head distinguish the bream, a bottom feeder, which browses on worms, snails and insect larvae. At home in slow-flowing rivers and canals it grows to 30″ (80cm) and a weight of 11lb (5kg).

Bleak

Pike

Tench

Eel

EEL (*Anguilla anguilla*) Spawning in the Sargasso Sea, off Bermuda, eels migrate to Europe and inhabit inland waterways from ditches upwards. Mainly nocturnal, they eat snails, frogs and live or dead fish. They live for up to 30 years and reach 50″ (130cm) and 20lb (9kg).

TENCH (*Tinca tinca*) A stillwater fish also found in sluggish rivers. It has two barbels on the upper lip, a red eye and a thickset, dark olive body. Reaching 28″ (70cm) and 8lb (3.5kg), it feeds on the bottom, taking insect larvae, crustaceans, snails and mussels.

PIKE (*Esox lucius*) A streamlined, large-jawed predator which lives in ponds, lakes, canals and slower-moving rivers. Built for speed, it ambushes smaller fish, frogs, rodents and waterbirds. Growing to 55″ (1.4m) and 50lb (23kg), it can live for 20 years.

BLEAK (*Alburnus alburnus*) This slim, silver-sided fish – whose scales were once used to make artificial pearls – lives in English rivers and canals. It swims in the top yard of water, feeding in shoals on flying insects and their larvae, and reaches 7″ (18cm) and 3oz (85g).

Water Shrew

Otter

OTTER (*Lutra lutra*) Playful, shy, mainly nocturnal and usually solitary, the otter is a graceful swimmer. Otters have extensive territories along rivers, lakes or the coast and their spraints (droppings) are the clearest sign of their presence. They feed on fish, frogs, crayfish, crabs and birds, and the female raises 1-5 young in a bankside burrow, known as a holt. The larger male grows to 4′ (120cm) and weighs 23lb (10.3kg). Otters are now mainly restricted to the South-west, East Anglia, Scotland and parts of Wales.

WATER SHREW (*Neomys fodiens*) A true river dweller, the water shrew has bristles on its back feet which serve as webs, and a ridged, keel-like tail; when it dives, a trail of air bubbles are released from its fur. Unlike the water vole, the water shrew is a carnivore, eating insects and their larvae, shellfish and fish fry, and reaching a body size of about 6″ (150mm) including tail, and a weight of ½oz (20g). Its lifespan is less than 2 years, during which a female will produce up to 6 litters of 3-8 young in a nesting chamber tunnelled into the river bank.

Riverside Mammals

American Mink

Water Vole

AMERICAN MINK (*Mustela vison*) At 22-34″ (55-85cm) long, the mink is smaller than the otter and is a newcomer to the British Isles, having established wild populations after escaping from fur farms. Dark brown except for white on the chin, it is less aquatic than the otter but is an agile climber and often stalks fish from the bank or an overhanging branch. The mink is especially fond of eels, but also eats other fish, voles, crayfish and birds and even rabbits. The female raises one litter a year of 5-6 young which are born in April or May in a bankside den.

WATER VOLE (*Arvicola terrestris*) Commonly but inaccurately known as the water rat, the water vole lives all over Britain from the lowlands to the mountains. More than twice the size of water shrews, at up to 14″ (36cm) including tail, and weighing up to 7oz (200gm), it feeds on green shoots above and below the water, swimming and diving with remarkable skill considering that its body shows no special adaptation to aquatic conditions. During a life of up to 4 years, females produce between 3 and 5 litters of 4-5 infants each year in their bankside burrows.

Kingfisher

Mute Swan

Great Crested Grebe

Coot

KINGFISHER (*Alcedo atthis*)
Widespread on lowland rivers, lakes and canals, the kingfisher may move to the coast in hard winters. It dives, usually from a perch, for small fish, tadpoles and insects. 5-7 white eggs are laid in a bankside burrow. Adults reach 6½″ (16.5cm).

MUTE SWAN (*Cygnus olor*)
A larger black knob on the bill distinguishes the male; young birds are brownish. They feed on aquatic plants and vigorously defend the large nest, up to 10ft across, containing 4-7 eggs. The wings of this 60″ (150cm) bird hum in flight.

GREAT CRESTED GREBE
(*Podiceps cristatus*) Dives for fish, tadpoles, insects and weed. The ruff and 'ear' tufts, raised for courtship, are absent in winter. 3-8 eggs are laid on a floating platform of weeds, and the young are carried on the parents' backs. Size 19″ (48cm).

Grey Heron

Sand Martin

COOT (*Fulica atra*) The white bill and forehead – origin of the phrase 'as bald as a coot' – are distinctive. Coots are quarrelsome but form large flocks in winter; they dive for weed and insects. Size: 15″ (38cm). 5-10 eggs are laid in a conspicuous reed nest.

SAND MARTIN (*Riparia riparia*) Distinguished from the dark blue and white house martin by its all-brown back, this 5″ (12cm) bird is an insect-eating summer visitor, much scarcer due to the African drought. It nests in colonies, laying 4-5 eggs in a tunnel in the river bank.

GREY HERON (*Ardea cinerea*) The stately heron – size 30″ (76cm) – is a patient hunter, stabbing fish, frogs and water mammals with its sword-like bill. In flight the neck is hunched and wings flap slowly. Herons build large stick nests in tree colonies, laying 3-5 eggs.

ON THE OPEN HEATH

Enlivened by purple heather and bright yellow gorse, the sandy heath is home to rare birds, interesting insects, and reptiles such as the adder.

The heathland habitat is a very varied patchwork. Slight paths wend through the sprawling purple heather and behind the banks of yellow flowering gorse. Though the sun turns the sand pits into a desert, close by lurk permanent pools of deep shade beneath the woody heather tussocks.

In places where the heather cover is scattered, flowers such as wood sage, yellow tormentil and delicate blue sheep's bit scabious can grow. The pale pink spikes of heath spotted orchid may also pulse skywards.

Elsewhere greens catch the eye – of fresh fine-leaved grass or the vivid green of the bog mosses which mark out patches of wet soil that can be found even in the midst of the dry heath. But sometimes the green is composed of curling fronds of bracken and this can be an ominous sign. Although bracken is to be expected, dense stands of it usually mark ground which has been carelessly or accidentally fired, and the heather killed. Bilberry, which is often found on heaths, is quite sensitive to fire and rarely recovers.

Heather itself is able to put on surprising amounts of woody, tussocky growth in such dry, poor surroundings because its roots are home to a fungus. Jointly they can tap the sparse nourishment of the soil.

One plant has adopted a very different strategy. This is dodder, seen as thread-like reddish stems which scramble among the heather stalks. Dodder is a true parasite; it cannot make its own food but relies on the heather sap which it steals. It has quite small, delicate pink flowers.

INSECTS AMONG THE HEATHER

The sun-struck scent of the heather attracts many bees. Some of them are honey bees flying in from hives placed at the edge of the heath (for heather honey is much prized). But many are bumble bees, from smaller colonies in burrows dug out in the dry soil nearby. One of these, the heath bumble bee, relies on heather and bilberry and is only found where they grow.

An unusual wasp crawling on the heather may be the heath potter wasp which uses small

DARTFORD WARBLER
The most colourful of Britain's warblers, the Dartford warbler is confined to the Channel Islands and southern English counties from Devon east to Sussex. The small population of about 500 pairs is found almost exclusively on lowland heaths where it is at the northern edge of its European range. Unlike all our other warblers, except the recently arrived Cetti's warbler, it does not migrate south and the population can be badly hit by severe winters. It fell to about 12 pairs after the 1962–3 freeze-up.

soil pellets to build its brood a flask-shaped nest attached to a stalk of heather.

Small solitary mining wasps abound on heathland, so much so that firm sandy banks or well trodden paths can be pin-pricked with their excavations.

Wasps, unlike bees (which collect nectar and pollen) provide their grubs with a larder of insects, often collecting the caterpillars of moths which are extremely common among the heather. Heathland moths are, however, generally dull in colour. One exception is the emperor moth, bearing large eye spots on its wings. Its bright green caterpillar is equally striking but is unexpectedly well camouflaged when it rests among the heather leaflets.

The busy insect life is matched by many canny spiders which spin their webs between the heather stems. Their webs can resemble the one spun by the garden spider, but the heathland

WILDLIFE OF THE SANDY HEATH

With its low cover of lichens, mosses and tussocky grass, along with areas of shrubby heathers and gorses and taller birches and pines, the heath's warm, dry soil is alive with insects and spiders. Turf ant colonies war with each other and fall prey to the green tiger beetle, but both are eaten by lizards and adders. Moths and butterflies visit flowers and lay their eggs on heather and gorse. The bats and many heathland birds are insectivorous, often catching their prey in flight. The birds nest in shrubs or on the ground and wheatears may breed in vacant rabbit burrows.

KEY TO THE SPECIES

1 *Silver birch*	10 *Gorse*	18 *Lichen* Parmelia *species*
2 *Wheatear*	11 *Bracken*	19 *Adder*
3 *Bats*	12 *Heath spotted*	20 *Moss*
4 *Nightjar*	*orchid*	21 *Green tiger beetle*
5 *Dartford warbler*	13 *Silver studded blue*	22 *Lichen* Cladonia
6 *Scots pine*	14 *Emperor moth*	*species*
7 *Heather*	15 *Tormentil*	23 *Turf ants*
8 *Rabbit*	16 *Common lizard*	24 *Wolf spider* Arctosa
9 *Green hairstreak*	17 *Bell heather*	perita

spider creates something very different. It makes a curtain of threads which hang to the ground to trap unwary ants. Heathland is also a home for the purse web spider, which spins an unusual sock-like web in the soil, within which it waits. Any insect that touches the camouflaged web is drawn into the clutches of the hidden spider.

Other spiders, however, do not spin webs. Notable is a pink crab spider which sits motionless in ambush, matching the bells of the heather flowers. The wolf spiders, often seen on heaths, run down their prey across the dry ground beneath the heather tussocks.

Many insects find that the sparse, warm soil of the heath suits them, for they are more active in hot surroundings. The strange miniature forest of mosses and *Cladonia* lichens, which covers much of the ground, can be as busy as a grassy field. Here scuttles the green tiger beetle, an active hunter armed with large jaws. Its grub, too, is a fierce predator. Lurking in a vertical burrow in the dry soil, it darts its jaws out to seize passing prey.

On the wing over the heather will be seen hawker dragonflies – they like the warmth of the midday heath for they are, by origin, insects of tropical climates. They breed in the boggy pools but tend to roost some distance away and can often be seen crossing the heath in sunshine.

Also active is the beautiful green hairstreak butterfly, the only resident butterfly whose underwings match the greens of the countryside. It flies in early summer and is attracted by the gorse and broom of the heath. On them it lays its eggs.

COCOON ON HEATHER
(above) The silken cocoon of the emperor moth is built with an opening at the top that allows the emerging moth to exit easily but prevents predators entering.

GREEN HAIRSTREAKS
(right) This mating pair reveal their green underwings which camouflage them well. The upperwings are a dull brown. Adults visit many flowers in early summer.

STONE CURLEWS
(left) These extraordinary, beady-eyed birds have declined in numbers since the 1950s due to loss of habitat. They are summer visitors which breed on heaths, downland and, increasingly, on dry ploughed fields. Not easily seen, they are best located at dusk or dawn when they are most active and emit penetrating coor-ee calls.

FLOWERING GORSE
(right) Gorse, growing here alongside heather, is a species typical of heaths. Commonly called furze or whin, it can be seen flowering all year but is at its brightest in spring. The flowers smell of coconut.

The green hairstreak is found in other habitats but the silver studded blue butterfly is more closely linked with heathland. It is on the wing in July and August and several are often seen together, flying with a light fluttering flight. The males are blue but, as with many 'Blue' butterflies, the females are dull brown. They seek gorse, broom and heather on which to lay their eggs.

The warm heathlands benefit cold blooded reptiles, such as the adder, whose sloughed skin can often be found, preserved in the dry condiions. The common lizard and the rare sand lizard also occur on heaths, as does the slow worm, which is a lizard, in spite of its name.

HEATHLAND BIRDS

Skylarks and meadow pipits are numerous, as they are in many rough places, and here, too, can be seen the wheatear – one of the earliest of the migrant birds to arrive in spring. Wheatears are restless birds, often seen on the ground bobbing nervously and flicking their wings, but they also have a hovering, fluttery song flight. They seek disused burrows or holes in the ground for their nest.

The closely related stonechat and whinchat are also typical of heaths – the former, named after its sharp clicking call, is resident all year, but the whinchat is a summer visitor.

Both of these delightful birds are less widespread than previously. A major cause has been the disappearance of the lowland heaths and other rough land on which they breed. But both birds – the whinchat in particular – have taken to new habitats, and now also nest in young conifer plantations.

For two birds, however, the loss of heathland has been particularly damaging. One is the shy Dartford warbler, attracted by the combination of heather and gorse. Warblers are insect eaters, and usually migrate to Africa in winter when flying insects are scarce here, but the Dartford warbler remains with us. Apart from the loss of its heath habitat, it also suffers severly in cold winters.

Its song is a mixture of liquid and chattering notes, less musical than that of many of the other warblers; it scolds intruders with a harsh rattle before flitting back into cover.

For the nightjar, also, the heaths are an important habitat. This bird has an odd jarring song, like the revving of a small engine for minutes at a time, which is heard at night, when the nightjar is active. It feeds by catching moths on the wing in its wide open bill. In daytime it squats motionless on the ground, its curious posture and mottled brown plumage making it well nigh invisible.

Rabbits are also fond of heathland; for though it does not offer much herbage to suit them it has plenty of cover. Seeking them and the voles and mice come occasional foxes, but badgers are unusual as the earthworms on which they prefer to feed are relatively scarce in the thin heath soil. But roe deer often seek sanctuary in the quiet and cover of the heath to add still further to its peaceful charm.

GREEN TIGER BEETLE
Found throughout Britain, the green tiger beetle frequents heaths and coastal dunes. It is a fast runner when in pursuit of its insect prey which is securely held in formidable, overlapping jaws (just visible here). The adult beetle can be seen in spring and summer after emerging from its larval burrow where it has spent up to 18 months.

FEMALE CRAB SPIDER
Blending well with the flowers of cross-leaved heath, this spider waits on the plant for its prey. Unsuspecting insects, coming to the flowers for nectar, are swiftly seized. These spiders can change from pink to yellow or white to match their background.

Sheep's Bit

Tormentil

Heath Bedstraw

TORMENTIL *(Potentilla erecta)*
A perennial with 4-12″ (10-30cm) high, upright but weak stems, this plant is very common on both dry and moist acid soils. The deeply lobed leaves are toothed and those on the stem are stalkless. Long thin stems bear 4-petalled flowers from May to September and attract pollinating insects. In wet conditions, however, the flowers close and self-pollination occurs after which tightly packed aggregate fruits are formed. The roots of Tormentil were once used as a herbal remedy to cure diarrhoea.

SHEEP'S BIT *(Jasione montana)*
An erect plant growing 18″ (45cm) high. The hairy stems each carry a head of narrow-petalled blue flowers from May to August. Common, except in the North, on light, sandy lime-free soils, it has wavy-edged leaves arranged spirally up the stem.

HEATH BEDSTRAW *(Galium saxatile)*
A lime-hating plant found on acid soils mainly in the North and West. It has four square 4-8″ (10-20cm) stems bearing flowers on semi-erect shoots from June to August. Whorled leaves bear tiny, forward-pointing prickles along the margins.

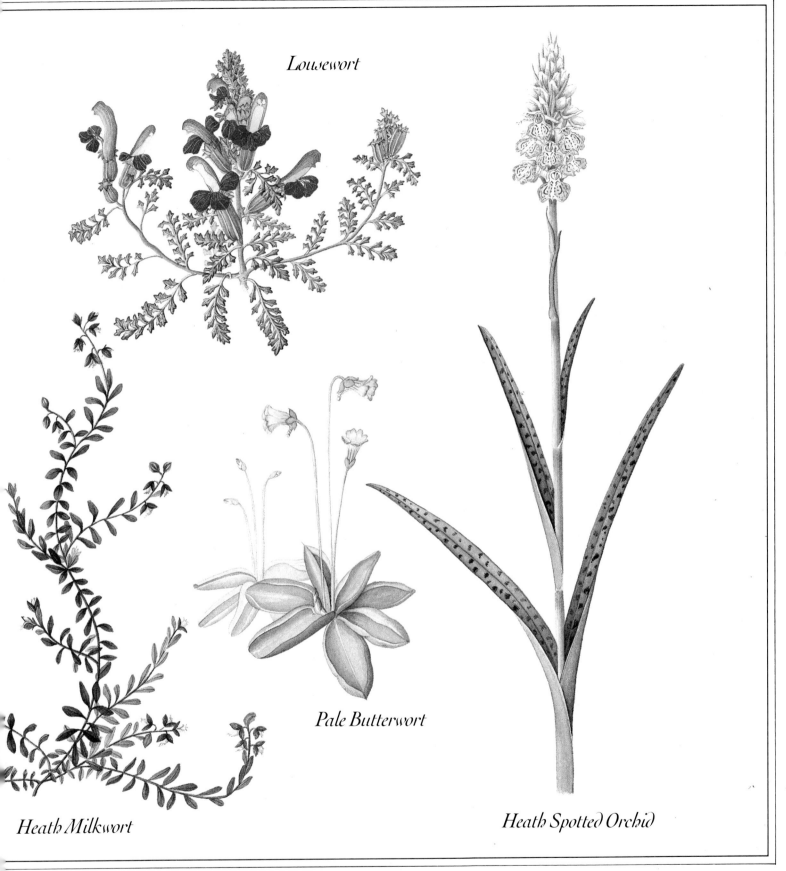

Lousewort

Pale Butterwort

Heath Milkwort

Heath Spotted Orchid

HEATH MILKWORT (*Polygala serpyllifolia*) Small, oppositely arranged leaves distinguish this 3-8″ (8-20cm) plant from other milkworts. It is widespread and common on open acid grasslands and moors where its 3-8 flower clusters may be seen from May to August.

LOUSEWORT (*Pedicularis sylvatica*) Widespread and common on damp heaths and marshes this is a perennial with semi-erect 3-8″ (8-20cm) branches arising from a tap-root. Hooded flowers arranged in spikes around the stems appear from April to July.

PALE BUTTERWORT (*Pinguicula lusitanica*) An insectivorous plant which traps its victims with sticky glands on the rosette of inrolled leaves. Frail 1-2″ (3-5cm) stems bear single small pale flowers from June to October. A rare plant found on wet heaths and bogs in the West.

HEATH SPOTTED ORCHID (*Dactylorhiza maculata*) A common orchid of damp acid soils, the 6-20″ (15-50cm) slender stem is crowned from June to August with a densely packed flowerspike. Purple-spotted leaves are open at the plant base and fold around the stem.

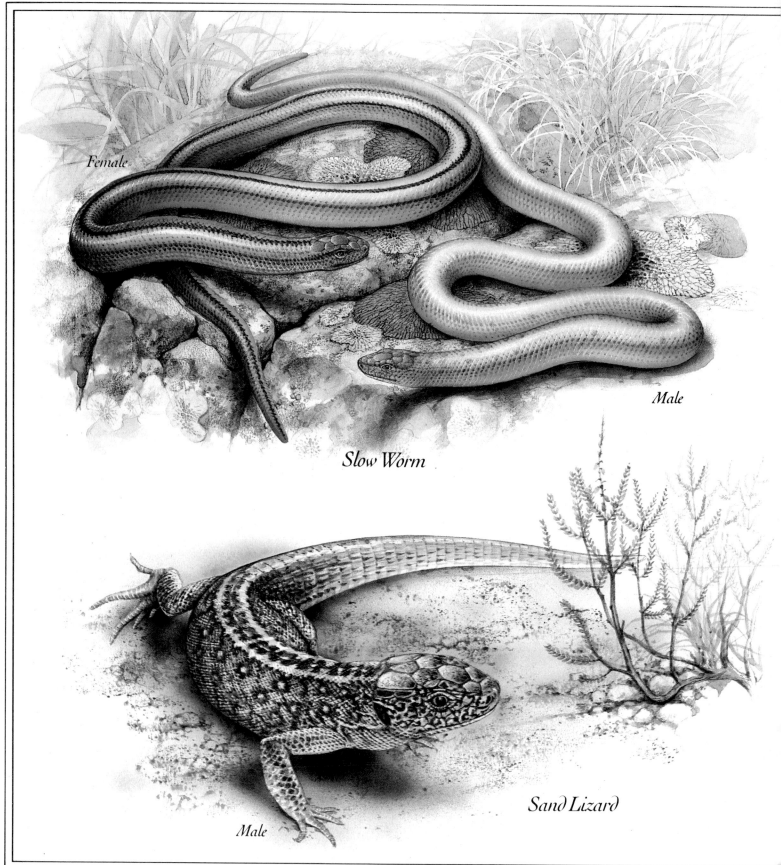

Female

Male

Slow Worm

Sand Lizard

Male

SLOW WORM *(Anguis fragilis)*
A legless lizard which, despite its name, can move quickly to escape from predators. It reaches 18″ (46cm) when full grown but is commonly less as the tail may be shed as a defence. Adults mate in early summer, the females giving birth to 5-26 young in August or September. Silvery-gold with black markings, they take 3 years to mature and can live up to 30 years in captivity. Slow worms eat small slugs, spiders and insects, feeding mainly at dusk and basking in the sun during the day. They hibernate underground over winter.

SAND LIZARD *(Lacerta agilis)*
Eaten avidly by the smooth snake, this 8″ (21cm) lizard only occurs in Lancashire, Cheshire and a few localities in the South, preferring sunny, dry, sandy places. Males have bright green sides, particularly in the breeding season, and fight to defend their territory. The duller purplish-brown females lay 5-15 white eggs in a hollow, which they then cover with sand – these take about 5 weeks to hatch. They feed on insects and grubs. Like other lizards, they can shed their long tail when threatened.

Smooth Snake

SMOOTH SNAKE (*Coronella austriaca*) An uncommon 22-25" (56-65cm) non-venomous snake of southern England, which may bite if handled, it lives at the edges of woods and on heaths – often near water – feeding on other reptiles, nestlings and young mammals.

Smooth, unridged scales give it a glossy and distinctive appearance, but some more heavily patterned individuals may be mistaken for adders. After hibernating, they mate in April – up to 15 young are born in late summer, the egg 'shell' rupturing just prior to birth.

Male

Male

Dartford Warbler

Nightjar

Female

Female

NIGHTJAR *(Caprimulgus europaeus)* A 10½″ (27cm) summer visitor from Africa, which catches flying insects on the wing after dark. Has an unmistakable insect-like churring call. The female lays 2 clutches of 2 pale eggs in a simple scrape nest on the ground.

DARTFORD WARBLER *(Sylvia undata)* A rare resident British warbler found in southern heathlands, this dark, 5″ (13cm) bird has a cocked tail. It has a darting flight and a cheery song. Two clutches of 3-4 speckled eggs are laid in a mossy nest from May.

Birds of the Heath

Woodlark

Tree Pipit

Male

Female

Stonechat

WOODLARK (*Lullula arborea*)
An increasingly rare 6″ (15cm) bird of wooded heaths in the south, this lark with its clear white eyestripe, and a short tail has a liquid and trilling song. The females makes a grassy nest on the ground for 3-4 spotted, buff eggs.

STONECHAT (*Saxicola torquata*)
A conspicuous 5″ (13cm) bird, most common on bushy heaths and moors in the West, it feeds on insects on the ground. It lays 5-6 mottled, bluish eggs in a nest at the base of a bush. The call sounds like two stones clinked together.

TREE PIPIT (*Anthus trivialis*)
A summer visitor to heaths and clearings, where it breeds, this 6″ (15cm) pink-legged bird gives voice to a lovely trilling song in a steep then floating song flight. It lays 4-6 grey-brown flecked eggs in a grassy ground nest in May.

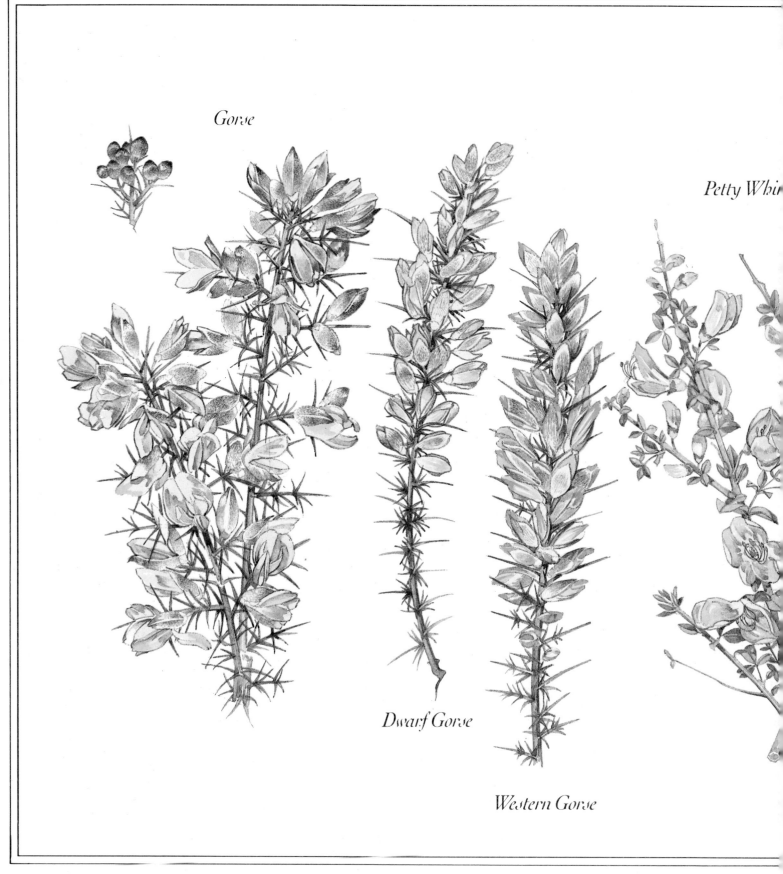

Gorse

Petty Whin

Dwarf Gorse

Western Gorse

GORSE *(Ulex europeaus)* A common, spiny shrub which grows up to 6' (2m), to form dense thickets. The mature plant has no flat leaves but bears sharp, branched, furrowed spines. Coconut-scented flowers bloom in spring, followed by black, hairy seedpods.

DWARF GORSE *(Ulex minor)* A smaller, weaker shrub than common gorse, it grows to 3' (1m) with branches trailing along the ground, on acid heaths, chiefly in the South-east and East. Small flowers are produced from July to October, close to soft, slightly furrowed stem spines.

WESTERN GORSE *(Ulex gallii)* A sharply spiny gorse, with more or less upright, dark green branches reaching heights of up to 6' (2m). Golden flowers appear July to September followed by pods which burst in spring. It grows on open acid soils mainly in the West.

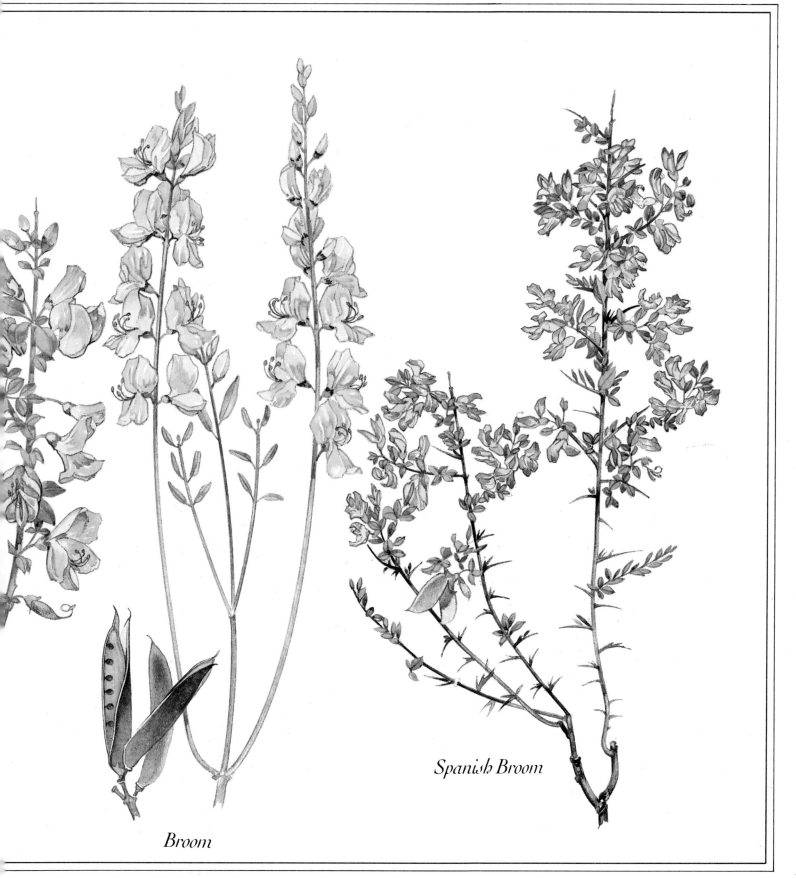

Broom

Spanish Broom

PETTY WHIN *(Genista anglica)*
This sprawling 12-24″ (30-60cm)
shrub has unbranched, curved
spines and waxy, oval leaves. Short
spikes of small flowers open in May
and June, followed by pointed seed
pods. It has a scattered distribution
on heaths and moors.

BROOM *(Cytisus scoparius)*
Widespread on dry, acid soils, this
6′ (2m) erect, spineless shrub has
short-lived simple and trifoliate
leaves. The long straight 5-angled
stems remain green. Flowers, some
with red markings, are borne on
short stalks in May and June.

SPANISH BROOM *(Spartium
junceum)* A Mediterranean shrub,
now established on sunny banks in
the South, which may reach 10′
(3m). Its simple, lanceolate leaves
soon fall, leaving tall smooth stems
and terminal sprays of fragrant
flowers from July to September.

ON ROLLING DOWNS

Carpeted with flowers and alive with clouds of brilliant butterflies the hum of insects and the rhythmic rasping of countless grasshoppers, the sunny slopes of the downs are crowded with delights.

COWSLIPS
*Cowslips are common
on grasslands.*

Old, unimproved chalk downlands are renowned for their astonishing abundance of flowers, with some 60 species found exclusively in this habitat. It is often possible to discover as many as 30 different species growing within one square yard. Not all the plants flower at the same time, of course, so the patterns and colours of the downland turf change as the year progresses. By early summer the downs are aglow with bright yellow flowers, quickly followed by pinks, whites and blues. Then as summer draws slowly to a close, the faded

grassland is brought to life once more by blooms of purple and mauve.

One factor to explain this great variety is that chalk is of benefit to much plant life: the lime neutralizes many of the toxic substances produced when dead plant and animal matter decay in the soil. Chalk also provides plenty of calcium and magnesium, which some plants need. But perversely, it is the very poverty of the soil that helps further to explain the profusion of chalkland flowers. Chalk-based soil is thin, very dry, lacking in nutrients like nitrates and phos-

178

phates and bakingly hot in summer. These harsh conditions prevent plants growing too strongly and so the quick-growing grasses and other natural bullies of the plant world do not have the chance to overwhelm the more delicate plants and flowers. The variety of plant life which results is further encouraged by the selective grazing of sheep and rabbits.

Many of the downland flowers have strategies to cope with grazing. Some, like the dwarf thistle and plantain, hold their leaves in flat rosettes very close to the ground; others grow in small, tight cushions while others, such as lady's bedstraw, are trailing plants which can be nosed aside by sheep seeking tastier leaves.

The lack of surface water on the permeable chalk means that downland plants are often especially adapted to dry conditions. The roots of the common yellow rock-rose, horseshoe vetch and the edible salad burnet reach quite considerable depths, taking advantage of the many fissures in the chalk, and some grasses cope with periods of drought by folding or rolling up their leaves to reduce the surface

PYRAMIDAL ORCHID
Orchids grow freely in chalky soils.

WILDLIFE ON THE DOWNS
The warm, dry slopes of chalky downland, close-grazed by sheep and rabbits, are host to an abundance of flowers, grasses and insect life. Bright blue butterflies and brown, moth-like skippers are lured by golden vetches, wild thyme and the wonderful diversity of grasses. High in the sky the lark soars, while the swallow swoops to catch a tasty insect and the hobby soars, alert for insects or small birds on the wing.

KEY TO THE SPECIES
1 Skylark
2 Beech knoll
3 Sewn grass
4 Hobby
5 Swallow
6 Lynchets
7 Sheep
8 Adonis blue (female)
9 Horseshoe vetch
10 Chalkhill blue (male)
11 Banded snail
12 Clustered bellflower
13 Squinancy wort
14 Rabbit
15 Bee orchid
16 Hoary plantain
17 Wild thyme
18 Lady's bedstraw
19 Ant hill
20 Yellow-wort
21 Marbled white (male)
22 Large skipper
23 Knapweed

DOWNLAND VISITOR
(left) Rooks are sociable birds which prefer to nest in colonies in tall trees. But they will visit the downs in search of insect food, especially the wireworms and leather-jackets which are common in downland soil.

available for water loss through transpiration.

Orchids, with their food-storing tuberous roots, are more plentiful on downland than anywhere else in Britain. The common spotted, early purple and twayblade are all relatively common and even the bee orchid may be found occasionally.

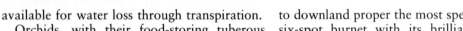

BUTTERFLIES

The butterflies of chalk grassland are as vivid and colourful as the flowers. Blue butterflies, in particular, are associated with this type of terrain, most of them feeding on plants of the pea family such as horseshoe and kidney vetch. The common blue and small blue are also found in many other places but the adonis blue and chalkhill blue, as the latter's name suggests, are restricted to ancient chalk grasslands. But there is a considerable difference in their distribution even in this limited area. The chalkhill blue is quite common whereas the adonis is extremely localized. The reason is that although both butterflies lay their eggs on horseshoe vetch, the adonis blue will only lay on plants barely an inch tall growing in hot pockets of short turf in south-facing sunspots; the chalkhill blue on the other hand is less choosy, laying on taller plants even on north-facing slopes.

The chalkhill blue and some other blue butter-flies – notably the virtually extinct large blue – enjoy a fascinating, sometimes mutually bene-ficial association with ants, which will park a caterpillar on a convenient clump of its favourite food plant and 'milk' it for a sweet liquid secreted from a gland in its back.

In patches of downland where the grass has escaped grazing and grows taller, other butter-flies can be seen. The marbled white and large skipper caterpillars feed on grasses, especially cocksfoot, while food plants of the silver-spotted skipper, which is exclusive to the downs, are sheep's fescue and tufted hair grass. Skipper butterflies are rather moth-like in appearance and behaviour, with their whirring darting flight and their habit of folding their wings back down along their body. Among the true moths common

to downland proper the most spectacular is the six-spot burnet with its brilliant black and crimson colouring.

Butterflies are, however, not the only insects to exploit the rich variety of downland plantlife. Cunningly camouflaged grasshoppers and crickets proclaim their presence in the taller grasses by the noisy stridulations of the male of the species striving to attract a female. Snails are also common, particularly the striped snail,

FEARSOME PREDATOR
(above) The common shrew is a noisy and belligerent creature which tolerates the company of others only when mating. It has an inexhaustible appetite, especially for earthworms which are prolific in grassland soil.

FEASTING KESTREL
(left) Attracted to the downs by a plentiful supply of voles and shrews, this sharp-eyed hunter can often be seen hovering in the sky as it searches the ground for likely prey.

SONG BIRDS
(below) Linnets were once kept in cages for their musical warbling. Though not typical downland birds, they will colonize patches of open scrub.

as the chalk supplies the minerals they need to help build up their shells. Earthworms also need calcium and are abundant in chalky grassland soils. Spiders are also common on chalky grasslands, in particular the merciless purse web spider – often found on the sunny side of anthills – which catches its insect victims in a silken tube-like trap. The dry sun-baked slopes of the downs are also attractive to reptiles like the slow worm and common lizard.

Until the flea-borne plague of myxomatosis, rabbits were by far the commonest downland mammal, helping to keep the turf cropped short and, along with the aggressive grass-eating field voles, providing food for carnivores like stoats, weasels and kestrels. The dry grasslands of the downs, with their abundant insect and earthworm life may also be home to moles and the voracious and hyperactive shrews which daily consume the equivalent of their own body weight. Brown hares, whose speed and alertness help them survive in open country, may also be seen.

DISAPPEARING WILDLIFE

As a result of changes in the traditional downland habitat a number of birds, once widespread there, are now uncommon. The stone curlew with its eerie unmistakable long shrill call is now rarely seen, while the wheatear, once so prolific that it became symbolic of the downlands, is now more often seen on moors. Hunters like the hobby and Montagu harrier also became less common though the numbers of the former bird, at least, are now increasing once again. It is an

SOUND OF SUMMER
The rasping song of the grasshopper begins as the days become hotter towards the end of June and July. As the temperature rises on warm summer afternoons, the chirruping actually seems to speed up. The sound is made by the grasshopper rubbing its hind leg against tough veins on its forewing.

attractive sight, sliding past the ground or tumbling far overhead.

The only nesting bird to be seen today on the downs in summer may well be the ubiquitous skylark, though in some places meadow pipits are as numerous. In winter the scene is much more bleak with rooks and starlings scavenging a meagre living from the desolate landscape.

LOVE SONG
Skylarks sing their exuberant songs not only to mark out territory but also to attract females for breeding. When a pair has formed the skylark hen lays 3-4 eggs in a grass nest on the ground.

Stone Curlew

Hobby

Meadow Pipit

HOBBY *(Falco subbuteo)* A small dashing falcon, 14″ (35cm) long, which is a scarce summer visitor to farmland and heaths in the south, feeding on large insects and small birds – a diet which demands expert flying. It commandeers deserted crows' nests to lay its 2 or 3 eggs.

STONE CURLEW *(Burhinus oedicnemus)* A rare and furtive bird, whose plumage blends well with the bare and stony downland of its chosen habitat, where it searches at dusk for insects and worms upon which to feed. It is about 16″ (47cm) long. Two eggs are laid in May.

MEADOW PIPIT *(Anthus pratensis)* A small, 5¾″ (14cm), insect and worm-eating bird which inhabits downs in summer, and lowland fields and coasts in winter. In spring males perform a parachuting display flight with a long trilling song. It lays 3-6 eggs on the ground.

Wheatear

Male

Female

Montagu's Harrier

WHEATEAR *(Oenanthe oenanthe)*
A summer visitor from Africa,
the wheatear is a small 5¾″
(14cm), bird which feeds entirely on
insects. It inhabits open country
and bleak moor and coast, laying 6
eggs, usually in a disused animal
burrow.

MONTAGU'S HARRIER *(Circus
pygargus)* During courtship, this
harrier performs an impressive
aerobatic display. It reaches 18″
(46cm) and feeds on small mammals
and birds. It inhabits open grass and
heathland, and lays its 3-6 white
eggs in a grass nest on the ground.

Lady's Bedstraw

Dropwort

Cowslip

LADY'S BEDSTRAW (*Galium verum*) This widespread native of hedge and grassland produces clusters of honey-scented flowers from June to August on stems which may reach 28″ (75cm), and which are collared with tufts of filament-like leaves at regular intervals.

COWSLIP (*Primula veris*) This pretty and delicately fragrant perennial of meadow and bank, bears 12″ (30cm) tall nodding heads of yellow flowers in April and May. These are held above a rosette of crinkled bright green leaves. They are common everywhere except Scotland.

DROPWORT (*Filipendula vulgaris*) This inhabitant of chalk grassland in the south and east of England produces slightly scented heads of cream flowers from May to August. These are borne on bare stalks which vary from 12-28″ (30-70cm) in height, above fronds of dark leaves.

CLUSTERED BELLFLOWER (*Campanula glomerata*) Stately heads of violet bell flowers from May onwards distinguish this inhabitant of grassland, common in parts of England, Wales and southern Scotland. It grows to 8″ (20cm) in spreading clumps.

Clustered Bellflower

Thyme

Carline Thistle

Dwarf Thistle

Small Scabious

THYME (*Thymus drucei*)
This straggling 3″ (7·5cm) aromatic herb is covered in terminal heads of pinkish-mauve flowers from May to August. It is found throughout the British Isles, particularly favouring well-drained grasslands and dunes.

DWARF THISTLE (*Cirsium acaule*) Otherwise known as stemless thistle, this plant produces solitary purple-pink flowers from June to September contained in a rosette of grey-green prickly leaves. It is found on grazing land or short grassland in the south of England.

CARLINE THISTLE (*Carlina vulgaris*) This stiff 2′ (60cm) plant bears brownish-yellow flowers with narrow radiating bracts from July to October. The prickly leaves and seed heads of this plant remain throughout the winter on the chalky grassland where it thrives.

SMALL SCABIOUS (*Scabiosa columbaria*) This common plant of dry chalky grassland in England bears pincushions of pale lilac flowers on bare stems from June to August. It grows to a height of 22″ (65cm) and is said to have cosmetic properties.

185

Silver-spotted Skipper

Common Blue

Male

Female

Male

Male

Female

Adonis Blue

COMMON BLUE *(Polyommatus icarus)* This small butterfly (wingspan 1⅜", 35mm) is found throughout the British Isles in wild grassy places from April onwards. The colour is very variable, but usually the males are bright lilac-blue, and the females brown with a blue cast.

ADONIS BLUE *(Lysandra bellargus)* A rare butterfly of chalk downlands in the south of England, the Adonis feeds exclusively on horse-shoe vetch, and can be distinguished from the Common Blue by its brighter colour, and bi-coloured wing fringes. It flies from May.

SILVER-SPOTTED SKIPPER *(Hesperia comma)* This is a rapidly declining species, now found only in the chalk hills of the south of England, where the larva feeds on grass. It flies swiftly and close to the ground, almost exclusively in mid-August.

Male

Large Blue

Male

Chalkhill Blue

Male

Brown Argus

Female

Female

LARGE BLUE (Maculinea arion) Unfortunately this butterfly has been brought to the edge of extinction by its complex need for wild thyme on which to feed, and a certain kind of ant to provide food and shelter. It has a 1½″ (40mm) wingspan, and flies from June.

BROWN ARGUS (Aricia agestis) Found in the chalk and limestone downlands of the south of England and Wales, this 1⅛″ (30mm) butterfly flies between April and August. It is active in sunny weather. The larva feeds on rock rose and stork's bill.

CHALKHILL BLUE (Lysandra coridon) Like the Adonis blue, this butterfly is limited to areas where horse-shoe vetch – its larval food plant – grows. It is an active 1⅜″ (35mm) butterfly, which likes to bask, wings outspread in the sun, and flies in July and August.

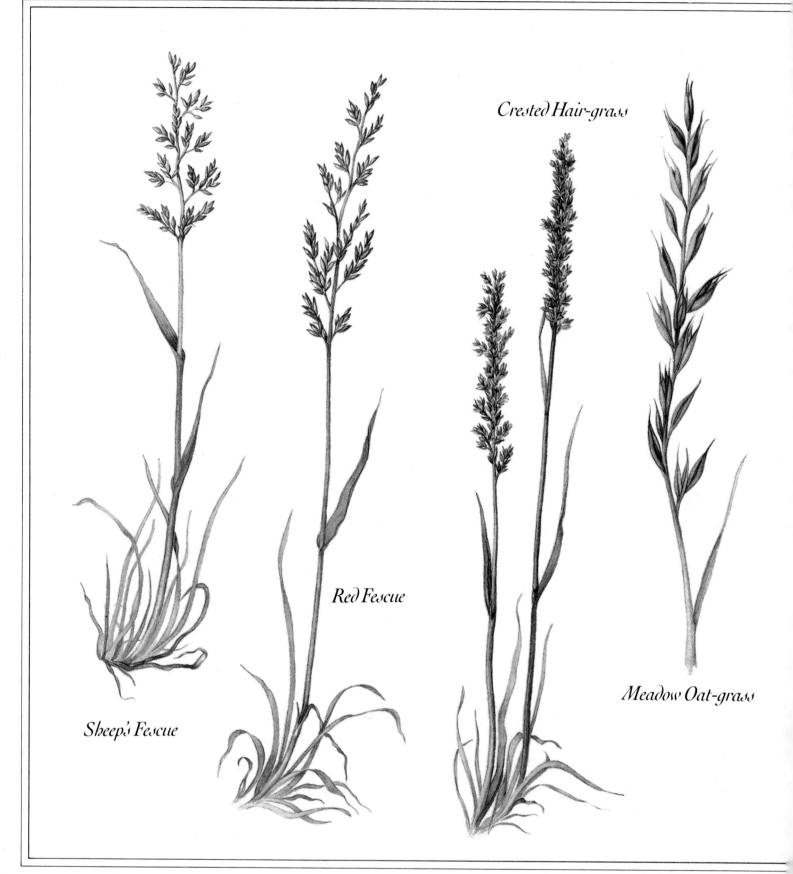

Crested Hair-grass

Red Fescue

Sheep's Fescue

Meadow Oat-grass

SHEEP'S FESCUE *(Festuca ovina)*
Abundant in dry grassland over chalk
or limestone, sheep's fescue grows to
24″ (60cm) tall, with short leaves and
branched flowerheads, making
dense tufts of good grazing grass.
The flowers are green or purplish,
from May to July.

RED FESCUE *(Festuca rubra)*
A common and ubiquitous grass
throughout the British Isles, which
provides excellent grazing. Its
spreading stems can be up to 36″
(90cm) long, and produce branched
flower heads from May to July,
which may have a reddish tinge.

CRESTED HAIR-GRASS *(Koeleria cristata)* Common throughout the
British Isles on chalk and limestone
and on dunes, this grass grows to a
height of 2′ (60cm) and has bright
green leaves with hairy sheaths.
The flowerheads are narrow and
silvery green.

MEADOW OAT-GRASS *(Avenula pratensis)* A common grass of chalk
and limestone, growing up to 32″
(80cm) tall. It is slender and elegant
with stiff blue-green leaves and
spikes of whiskered flowers held
tight against the stem throughout
June and July.

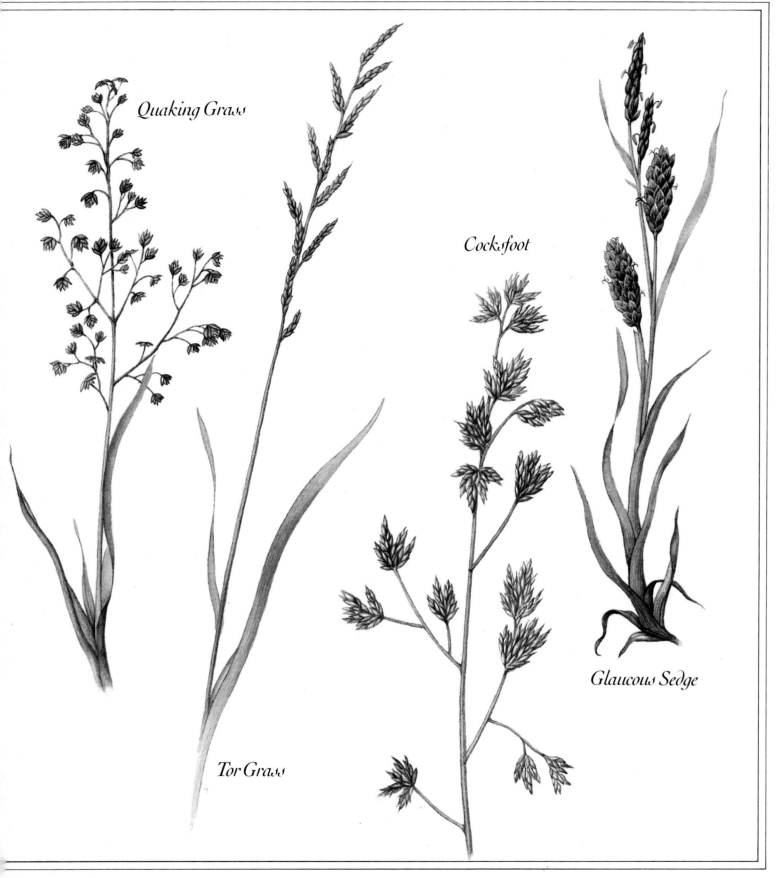

Quaking Grass

Cocksfoot

Glaucous Sedge

Tor Grass

COMMON QUAKING GRASS (Briza media) Common in dry chalky pastureland, this graceful grass grows to a maximum of 30″ (75cm) tall, and produces fronds of quivering flowers on threadlike stems from June to August. It is also called rattle and doddering dickies.

TOR GRASS (Brachypodium pinnatum) A tall – up to 48″ (120cm) – grass with stiff creeping stems, which spreads over large areas of chalk and limestone grassland in the south of England. The flowers are borne in angular spikes from June to August.

COCKSFOOT (Dactylis glomerata) A useful grass for grazing and fodder, this can reach 56″ (140cm), and from June to September produces bunches of tuft-like flowers at the end of stiff greyish stems. It is a widespread feature of pasture and roadside.

GLAUCOUS SEDGE (Carex flacca) Dark cylindrical flowers appear on this 24″ (60cm) sedge in May and June. It can be found throughout the British Isles and adapts to damp or dry conditions, open country or woodland. Plants bear male and female flowers.

189

UPLAND BRITAIN

The uplands are Britain's wild places, far away and high above the towns, villages and farms of the lowlands, exposed to the wind and weather. In many places, just a few stunted trees and gaunt rock outcrops break up the bleak, open landscape of rough grass and heather, and only the hardiest creatures seem to brave the winter, when howling gales sweep across the moors and snow piles deep in every gully. But they are not the natural wildernesses they seem.

Shaped by glaciers and ice in the time of the Ice Age, Britain's rugged uplands were once covered in a thick forest that left only the highest hills and the wettest and rockiest places exposed. The Highlands of Scotland, for instance, were once clothed by great forests of Scots pine, juniper and other hardy trees. At its greatest extent, the Caledonian forest probably covered more than three million acres of the Highlands. Further south, vast woods of ash and birch, oak and elm covered the hills.

Well into the Dark Ages, wolves and wild boars, along with brown bears, lynx and elk, roamed the shadowy vastnesses of the great Caledonian forest and many of the other forests of northern Britain and Wales, and few people ever ventured far into their trackless deeps. But as the population of Britain grew, so the pressure on land increased, and soon acre upon acre of these ancient wildwoods were falling to axe and torch as settlers created grazing land for their cattle and goats. On Dartmoor, for instance, the traces of ancient farms from the earliest days of forest clearance can still be seen outlined in the turf. Later, trees were felled for timber and charcoal.

By the Middle Ages, most of the forest in upland England was completely cleared, though much of the Caledonian forest remained intact well into the 18th century. But no sooner had the forest been cleared than many of the settlers began to leave, for the effects of removing the trees proved disastrous in this marginal environment. Exposed to wind and rain, the soil was quickly drained of nutrients and became acid, and all but useless for anything but rough pasture. Grazing sheep and goats prevented trees from recolonizing in many

places, once the land was abandoned for cultivation. Yet because the soil was thin and poor and wet, trees could rarely grow even on ungrazed moors.

The result is that much of Britain's uplands remain bleak open moorland, wandered by sheep and clothed only in tough grass and heather. The weather here is seldom mild, and in winter it can be extremely harsh. Yet though the landscape is largely a human creation its very remoteness makes these wildernesses safe refuges for many wild birds and plants. The moorlands of upland Britain are the last refuge of many of our rarest and most spectacular birds, such as the hen harrier and the golden eagle. The clear, tumbling upland streams provide a focus for plants and wild birds and the drier hills a home for lizards.

Over many upland moors, vast plantations of conifers have been created in the last 50 years to grow timber for sale. Great conifer forests have been planted in the lowlands, too, but it is in the uplands where the dense, dark ranks of trees have made the most impact, marching over the landscape like an invading army. Yet though the gloom beneath the tall trees seems deadly there are many plants and creatures to be seen in both upland and lowland conifer plantations.

In a few places on limestone outcrops, such as in Lathkill Dale, Cressbrook Dale and Dovedale in Derbyshire and around the South Wales coalfields, natural ashwoods grow. Very few of these are ancient, and many were planted comparatively recently on grassy slopes. But the ash is a quick growing tree, its delicate leaves block out little light, and the combination of shelter and light encourages a rich and diverse undergrowth that harbours many fragile plants – which in turn contribute nutrients to the soil.

The Highlands of Scotland and the Welsh Mountains have much in common with the uplands of the rest of Scotland and England, and share the same bleak scenery of rugged hills, tumbling streams and windswept grass, dark conifer plantations and pockets of ashwood. But they also provide unique habitats for plants and wild creatures, found in few other places in Britain, and remain our last great wildernesses.

ON THE WILD MOOR

The harsh 'go-back, go-back' call of the red grouse, the evocative cry of the curlew and the busy humming of bees are characteristic sounds of the moorland – a windswept upland habitat carpeted with heather.

Moorland is typically high, wet and wind-swept. Heather is the dominant plant and a rolling landscape of its massed purple-pink flowers creates one of the headiest botanical spectacles in the whole of Europe. Heather is well adapted to a moorland existence and can tolerate damp soil around its roots but seems to need rather drier conditions when it is flowering. It is an evergreen shrub and this can be an advantage on the often gloomy moorland, for it can snatch at what sunlight there is all year round. Its leaves are narrow and leathery, which cuts down water loss. On the face of it, it might seem a surprising feature for a plant growing in damp surroundings; but during the long moorland winters, water is locked up in the frozen soil, and the sweeping winds would soon dry out plants not so well adapted.

The drainage of the soil determines the types of plant to be seen on different parts of the moor. Bilberry likes a quick draining soil, and although it grows among the heather it can flourish on dry ground. Like heathers, it has leathery leaves, though it is not an evergreen. In the damper areas, cross-leaved heath may accompany the heather, growing alongside rushes and purple moor grass. Mat grass is another distinctive grass, with its unusual one-sided panicle or flower head. Although common on most of Britain's bleak moorlands it grows best where the soil is richer, its wiry bristly leaves forming dense tussocks.

Where the ground is waterlogged large bogs can become established and many interesting plants are to be found on their springy surfaces. One is the sundew, which gains nutrients that are absent from the bog by trapping insects on sticky hairs and then digesting them. Butterwort (bog violet) with its striking flowers is another plant which catches insects on sticky leaves that curl around their prey. Rather than growing on the bog itself it will probably be found where a flush brings a supply of minerals to the surface soil.

Cowberry and cranberry may both be found creeping out across the surface of the bog. Like

HEN HARRIER AND CHICKS
This large moorland bird of prey nests on the ground in well-grown heather or rushes. It glides low over the ground as it hunts. Once it bred only in Ireland and remote Scottish islands, but in the past 40 years or so it has moved into Scotland, northern England and Wales. Males may mate with several females.

MOORLAND WILDLIFE

Few trees grow on upland moors, except planted conifers, as grazing sheep or deer prevent them growing. Rowan, though, is a hardy species which may survive, rooted in a rock crevice. Thus, ground-hugging shrubs – heather, cowberry, bilberry, cranberry and crowberry – provide food and nesting cover for grouse, harriers and meadow pipits. Grasses and rushes are ideal nest sites for curlew, dunlin, other waders and the skylark.

Bogs, with their mosses, rushes and bog asphodel, attract dragonflies, waders and the carnivorous sundew. Heather provides nectar for bees, food for the emperor moth's caterpillar, and cover for voles on which harriers and short-eared owls prey. (Plants not to scale in illustration).

KEY TO THE SPECIES

1 Conifer plantation	11 Cross-leaved heath
2 Curlews	12 Dry stone wall
3 Rowan	13 Grasses
4 Burnt heather	14 Bog moss
5 Red grouse	15 Sundew
6 Sheep	16 Bog asphodel
7 Hen harrier	17 Bilberries
8 Dragonfly	18 Emperor moth
9 Heather	19 Emperor moth
10 Stream	caterpillar

UPLAND BRITAIN

DUNLIN AT NEST
The dumpy little dunlin is an active bird and our most abundant coastal wader in winter, when numbers are swollen by birds from Russia. They nest in damp areas, often on upland moors in Britain. In the Cairngorms, they breed in areas up to 3000 ft. Dunlin are at the edge of their breeding range in the British Isles and those nesting on Dartmoor are the southernmost population in the world.

FLOWERING COWBERRY
(below) Also known as red whortleberry, this is a low evergreen shrub common on northern peat moors, especially in the Scottish Highlands. The pink or white flowers appear from May to August. The edible red berries occur in early autumn and can be made into a very tasty jelly.

bilberry they carry edible berries, though rather bitter ones.

Another flower which can hardly escape being noticed is the beautiful bog asphodel, whose orange-yellow flowers make a vivid contrast with the green of the bog moss. It was once regarded with great suspicion, for it was thought to be the cause of foot rot which afflicts sheep grazing on boggy land. It has since been found that the lack of minerals in the bog is a more likely cause of the problem. The somewhat rarer bog rosemary is another pretty plant.

MOORLAND BIRDS

Much of Britain's moorland is, in fact, maintained solely for the benefit of the red grouse. This bird is totally adapted for life on the open moor and is rarely found elsewhere. While other birds have to leave the moor at the onset of winter, the grouse is well adapted both physically and behaviourally to

HUNGRY GOAT
These hardy animals are sometimes let loose to graze wild on grassy moorlands.

survive. Its behaviour in a snowstorm illustrates this. It crouches with its head to the wind, and avoids being buried by constantly treading the falling snow so that it becomes surrounded by a melted patch. At the end of the storm it can then reach food by burrowing into the drifts.

For many people the true call of the wild is the haunting cry of the curlew. In summer the curlew along with several other waders – notably the dunlin, greenshank and golden plover – come to the moors to nest. The soil around the bogs is soft enough to be probed with their delicate bills, and there are plenty of insects to be caught for their broods. The summer days are longer in the North than in the South so, living on the northern moors give the birds more time to feed.

Other birds are also common: skylarks and meadow pipits nest on the ground between the heather tussocks, and the cuckoo is often heard, for it lays its eggs in meadow pipits' nests. The small birds may be hunted by merlins and hen harriers – this bird, although still comparatively rare, is known to have increased in numbers in recent years: it often hunts the moors. As well as birds, the hen harrier will prey on voles, which can reach plague numbers in some years on dry moors. During such plagues short-eared owls often appear on the moors where they are easily spotted as they hunt in daylight.

HUMMING WITH LIFE

Where the ground is dry, bumble bees and other insects which dig nest holes may be found. The honeybees, however, which make the heather hum, are more likely to come from hives taken to the edge of the moor in spring by beekeepers who want their bees to produce heather honey, but 'wild' colonies of these bees are not uncommon. Many spiders frequent the plants, and woodlice like the humid conditions beneath the foliage. Grasshoppers, too, can be heard – usually the

green grasshopper which lives higher and further north than its relatives. Dragonflies may also add a dash of colour to the moorland scene as they patrol the boggy pools, catching the midges that hatch in vast numbers.

Some of the grass-loving butterflies of the lowlands appear on the moors – the gatekeeper, small heath and meadow brown, for example. The prize insect sighting is, however, the emperor moth. Related to the silk moths, it has a complicated cocoon which can be found fastened to heather stalks.

Frogs can be surprisingly common around the pools, though the cool climate may mean that the tadpoles take two years to grow up. The palmate newt and common lizard can also be found on some moorlands.

The more southerly moors may also offer good hunting grounds for the adder – not in the wetter parts, however, for waterlogged soil restricts the burrowing of the mice and voles on which it preys.

In midsummer, the moorland, filled with the scent of heather, the busy humming of bees and the bubbling call of the curlew, is an exhilaratingly rich and varied habitat, full of surprises.

THE CURLEW, OUR LARGEST WADER
The long, curved bill allows the curlew (above) to probe for food that is out of reach of others. It is one of our commonest breeding waders.

EMPEROR MOTH
(right) A moth of moors and heaths, seen from March to July, its green warty caterpillar feeds on heather but the adult moths do not feed at all as they lack sufficiently developed mouth parts.

FOUR-SPOTTED LIBELLULA ON HEATHER
(below) The damp moorland areas – streams, pools and bogs – are a naturally attractive habitat for the insect eating dragonflies.

MOORLAND ROCKS

The hard rock underlying Britain's moorland can often be seen in scattered outcrops. Look out for:

Schist

Slate

Basalt

Millstone Grit

Dartmoor Granite

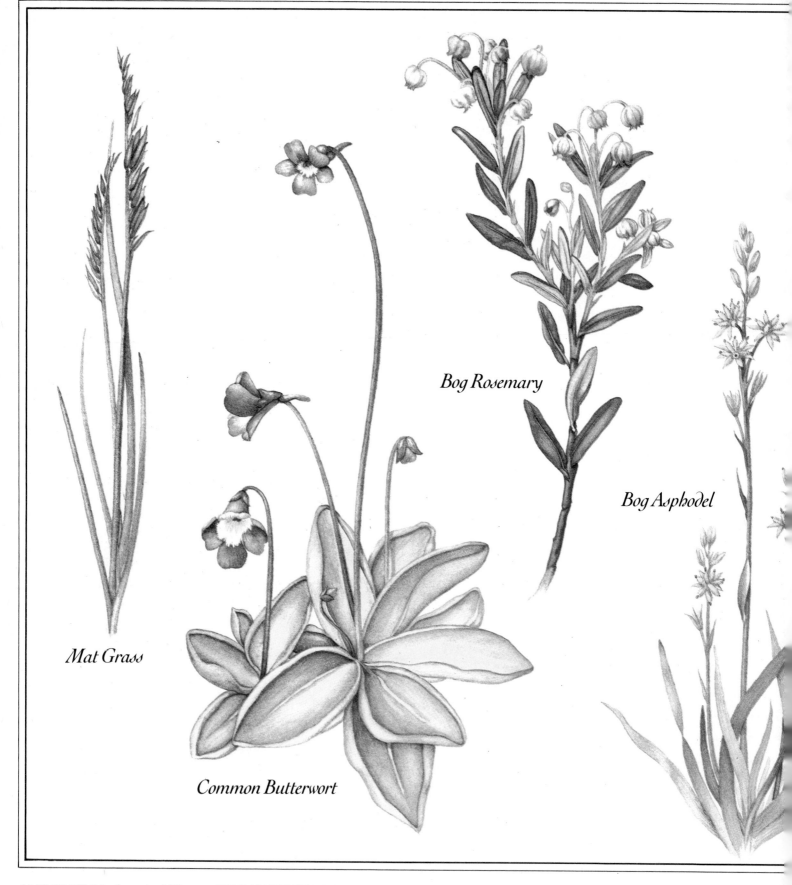

Mat Grass

Common Butterwort

Bog Rosemary

Bog Asphodel

MAT GRASS (*Nardus stricta*) Often abundant on poor soils of moors and peaty ground, this grass reaches 9″ (22 cm). It grows in dense tussocks with wiry, bristly leaves which are too tough for grazing. It produces one-sided livid purple flower spikes from June to August.

COMMON BUTTERWORT (*Pinguicula vulgaris*) Like the sundew, this plant of bog and moorland traps insects with its sticky leaves, which grow in a flat lime-green rosette. The pale violet flowers are borne singly on 4″ (10 cm) leafless stalks from May to July.

BOG ROSEMARY (*Andromeda polifolia*) This small, 12″ (30 cm), evergreen shrub is a rare feature of bogs in the North and in central Ireland. The dark shiny leaves have pale undersides, and help set off the globular pink flowers which appear between May and September.

BOG ASPHODEL (*Narthecium ossifragum*) Between July and September, this plant produces stiff spikes of fragrant yellow flowers, which mature to brick red, and can be up to 16″ (40 cm) tall, held above clumps of grass-like leaves. It grows in wet moorland and bogs.

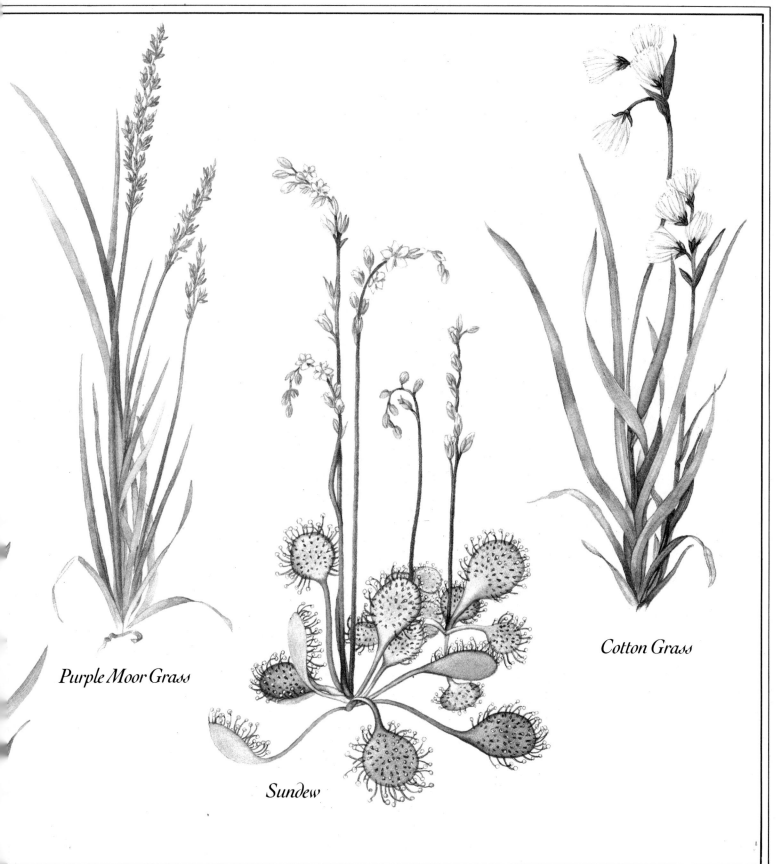

Purple Moor Grass

Sundew

Cotton Grass

PURPLE MOOR GRASS *(Molinia caerulea)* This grows freely in poor marshland and moor, and can reach 3′ (1 m) tall. It grows from dense tussocks, with shiny wiry stems. The leaves are flat, slightly hairy, and greyish. It produces small purple flowers in spreading spikes.

SUNDEW *(Drosera rotundifolia)* This strange inhabitant of wet moors and bogs has round red-tinged leaves, which are covered with red hairs tipped with blobs of sticky 'dew' to which passing insects adhere. The 6″ (15 cm) plant then digests them through its leaves.

COTTON GRASS *(Eriophorum angustifolium)* This grass is common in wet places with acid soil. It produces fluffy tufts of white cotton after flowering, at the tips of 12″ (30 cm) round or grooved stems. The leaves are spiky and triangular in cross-section.

Common Lizard

COMMON LIZARD *(Lacerta vivipara)* A small, delicate lizard of warm, grassy or heathery places, this species reaches 6″ (15 cm) or so in length. Its skin is coloured various shades of brown with broken, longitudinal lines of dark spots. The males are orange or red beneath the black dots, while the slightly larger females are paler and unmarked. Diet consists of spiders and small insects. Pregnancy lasts about three months and three to fifteen young are born still in their egg membranes, but they quickly struggle out to fend for themselves.

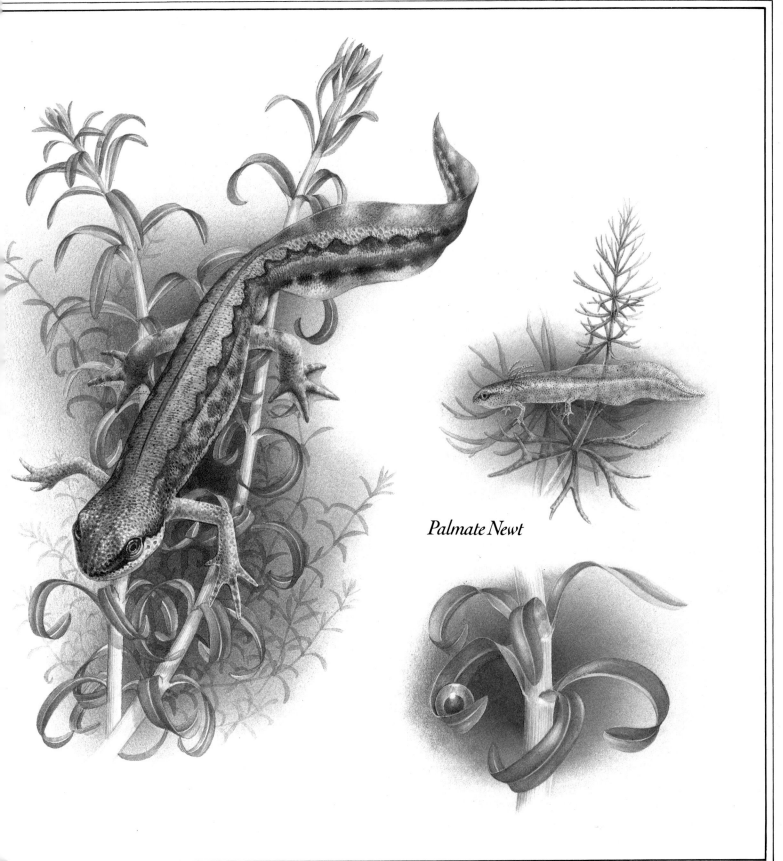

Palmate Newt

PALMATE NEWT (*Triturus helveticus*) A 3″ (7.5 cm), smooth-skinned newt, resembling a small aquatic lizard. In spring the breeding male has a smooth-edged, low crest along his back and tail, and webbed hind feet. The female has a pinkish throat. Adults spend most of their life on land, migrating at night to a breeding pool in February or March. The female lays up to 300 eggs, wrapping each one in an underwater leaf. The tadpoles (efts) breathe through branch-like gills behind the head. Newts feed on slugs, snails, worms, insects and tadpoles.

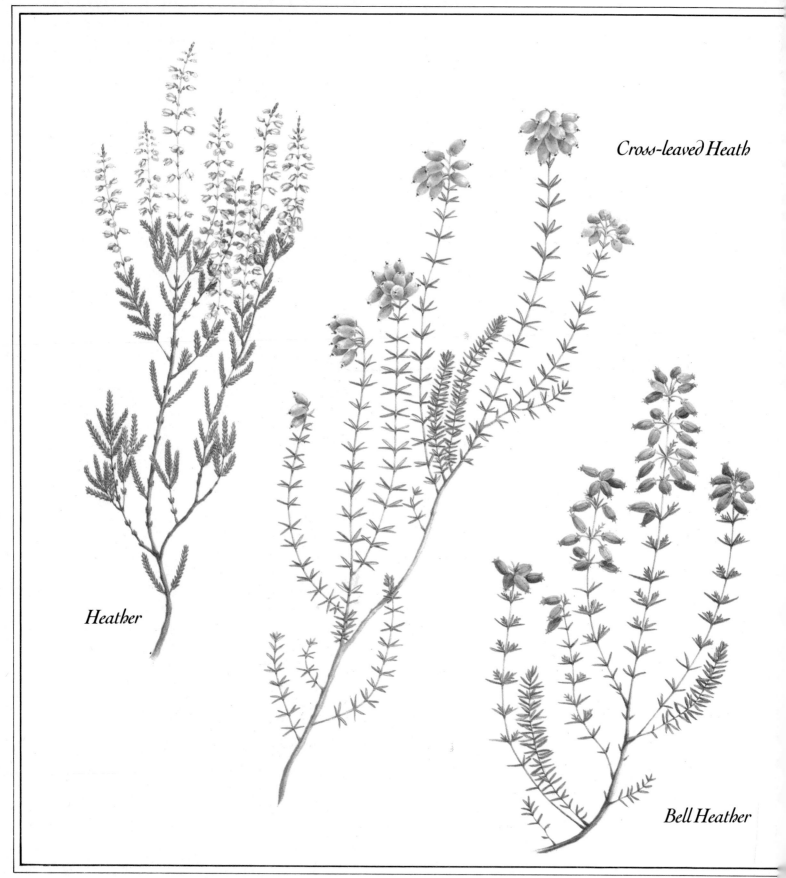

Cross-leaved Heath

Heather

Bell Heather

HEATHER *(Calluna vulgaris)* Also known as ling, this 24" (60 cm) evergreen bush carpets great areas of moorland with its spikes of purple or sometimes white flowers between July and September. Individually, the plants are straggly and many-branched.

CROSS-LEAVED HEATH *(Erica tetralix)* Similar to heather, but with larger flowers and evenly spaced whorls of four leaves, this plant thrives on wet moorland and bog. It grows up to 24" (60 cm) tall, and produces its clusters of pink-purple flowers from July to September.

BELL HEATHER *(Erica cinerea)* This plant enjoys poor dry soil, which it embellishes with its spikes of bright purple miniature bell-shaped flowers from July to September. The evergreen leaves grow in evenly spaced tufts from the fine brown stems. It reaches 24" (60 cm).

Cowberry

Bilberry

Cranberry

COWBERRY *(Vaccinium vitis-idaea)* An evergreen 12″ (30 cm) plant found mainly in Scotland which produces white or pink flowers at the end of its leafy stems between May and August. The glossy dark green leaves make a good foil to the small bright red edible berries.

BILBERRY *(Vaccinium myrtillus)* This is a common inhabitant of highland moors. It grows to 24″ (60 cm), and produces globular pink flowers along its deciduous branches, which develop into edible slate-coloured berries. It flowers between April and June.

CRANBERRY *(Vaccinium oxycoccus)* This bog plant produces its exotic looking flowers at the end of sparsely leaved evergreen stems between June and August. These become edible russet berries which dangle from the ends of the 12″ (30 cm) stems. Common in the North.

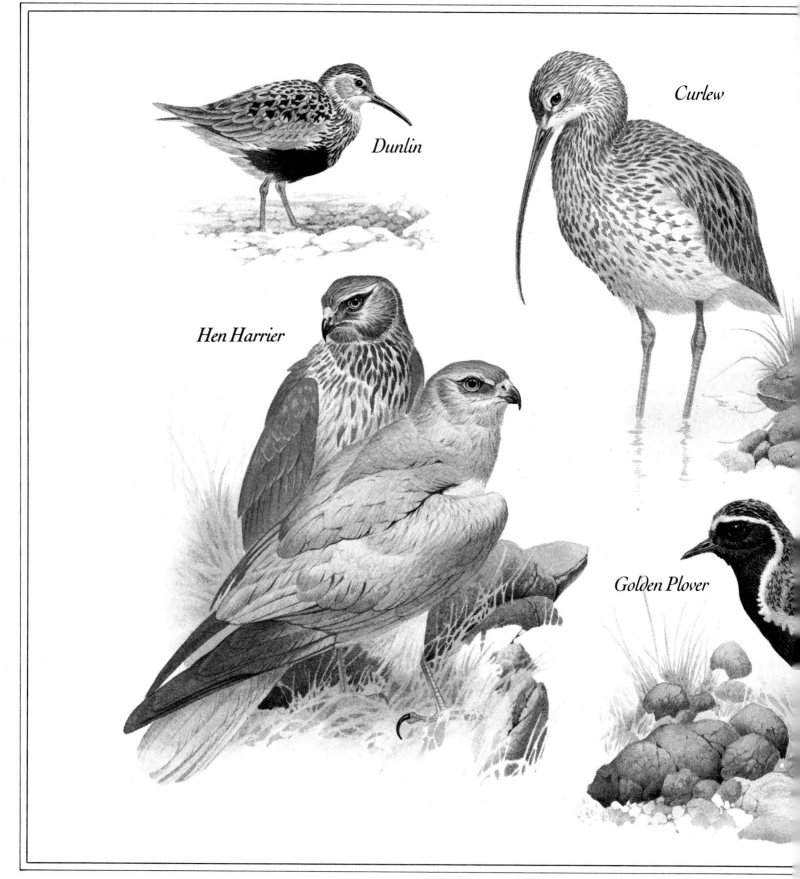

Dunlin

Curlew

Hen Harrier

Golden Plover

DUNLIN *(Calidris alpina)* A small, 7″ (18 cm), round-shouldered, thin-billed wader which breeds on moors and coastal grasslands. In summer, the chestnut back and black belly distinguish it. It feeds on flies, molluscs and worms, and lays 4 mottled eggs.

HEN HARRIER *(Circus cyaneus)* A large, 18″ (45 cm) bird of prey which hunts over moors in summer, floating on uptilted wings looking for small birds and mammals. Males are pale grey with black wingtips, females are streaky brown. 4-6 white eggs are laid.

CURLEW *(Numenius arquata)* The very long, downcurved bill makes this large, 22″ (56 cm), bird unmistakable. In summer it feeds on insects, worms, small frogs and snails, and its bubbling song is clearly heard on the moors. It lays 4 mottled olive eggs on the ground.

Moorland Birds

Short-eared Owl

Buzzard

GOLDEN PLOVER (*Pluvialis apricaria*) This short-billed, 11" (28 cm) wader breeds on high moors where its 'Klew-ee' call is a familiar sound. Its plumage is a rich pattern of yellow, black and white. Males are blacker below. It lays 4 well-camouflaged eggs.

SHORT-EARED OWL (*Asio flammeus*) A fierce expression and big, yellow eyes characterize this large, 15" (38 cm), British owl which hunts in daylight or at dusk for short-tailed voles, which form its main prey. It lays 4-7 white eggs in a concealed ground nest.

BUZZARD (*Buteo buteo*) A majestic, 20" (50 cm), bird of prey, whose mewing 'kiew' is a familiar sound in the north and west of Britain. The buzzard is rich brown with a strong pattern under the wing. It feeds on rabbits and voles and lays 2-4 eggs.

IN CORRIDORS
OF CONIFERS

The mature conifer plantation is dark and forbidding within, but is home to some unusual species. The best chance to see the wildlife is from the cleared corridors, or rides, which criss-cross the forest.

A mature conifer plantation, with its serried lines of bare trunks, is cool, dark and quiet. Wildlife is largely conspicuous by its absence. There are no flowers and little undergrowth, no buzzing insects or calling songbirds, indeed almost no sign of the busy wildlife to be found in a mature broadleaved wood is apparent.

Then, from the green, dense canopy overhead, comes the rapid twittering of an approaching party of goldcrests. These, the tiniest of all European birds, flit restlessly among the needles in search of spiders and other small invertebrate prey.

Much of the plantation's wildlife is to be found in the canopy. Crawling here are the green and white-striped caterpillars of the pine beauty moth and other invertebrates that may become forestry pests if present in large numbers.

Coal tits, like goldcrests, will be drawn to this invertebrate feast. They may be joined by a family party of early-breeding crossbills in search of the seeds held in pine or spruce cones. These birds are not readily visible but their presence may be revealed when a cone sprung open by their curious crossed bills falls with a plop to the ground.

Carpeted with dead needles and dry twigs, little grows on the floor of the wood, though various fungi, including the delicious saffron milk-cap, burst through as summer rolls into autumn.

A CHANGING HABITAT

Quick-growing conifers have a pace of change that other trees cannot match and, as they grow, so the range of wildlife they attract changes. In the early days, some 40 years ago, the ground may have been rough upland, grazed by sheep, before it was fenced and planted with seedlings.

With the sheep excluded, densely set tussocks of grass soon grow tall, threatening to smother the young pines. A skylark trilling overhead seems stationary in the air. It welcomes this new low cover for its scrape of a nest on the ground. The rough grass also attracts meadow pipits. The meadow pipit's display flight is quite

NESTING OWL
A female short-eared owl settles herself on the nest. She lays 4-8 eggs but, in years when voles are numerous, may lay a dozen or more. She incubates the eggs alone but is fed by the male, who hunts by day. The reafforestation of moorland has contributed to an increase in owl numbers. New plantations, with large vole populations among the long grass, provide plenty of food and nesting sites for several years until the tree canopy closes over.

WILDLIFE IN THE CONIFER PLANTATION

Fencing around the newly planted compartment keeps rabbits out and the grass grows tall. Yellow underwing moths rest among the tussocks, skylarks nest here and short-tailed voles breed. The thicket stage attracts nesting whinchats, yellowhammers, chaffinches and warblers. The small birds provide good hunting for sparrowhawks and for long-eared owls which prey also on voles. Both these birds and the scarce hobby often nest in mature conifers. Rutting roe deer bucks face up to each other on the undisturbed ride. Among the mature trees crossbills and squirrels feed on the cones. The female giant wood-wasp lays her eggs deep in the wood of dead conifers: the larvae take up to three years to emerge. Bluebells, wood anemone and dog violet – on which the fritillary lays its eggs – are relics of the old oak forest. The flowers of harebell, tormentil and heather indicate that the area was once heathland.

KEY TO FEATURES AND SPECIES

1 Long-eared owl
2 Goldcrest
3 Male crossbill
4 Female crossbill
5 Clearing
6 Skylark
7 Mature trees
8 Hobby
9 Oak
10 Thinned and brashed compartment
11 Ride
12 Blue tit
13 Female sparrowhawk
14 Sitka spruce
15 Male chaffinch
16 Red squirrel
17 Yellowhammer
18 Compartment at thicket stage
19 Brambles
20 Male roe deer
21 Un-brashed compartment
22 Male bullfinch
23 Turtle dove
24 Saffron milk-cap
25 Male whinchat
26 Newly planted compartment
27 Bluebells
28 Giant wood-wasp
29 Large yellow underwing
30 Tormentil
31 Heather
32 Small pearl-bordered fritillary
33 Harebell
34 Short-tailed vole
35 Small copper
36 Dog violet
37 Corner of old oak forest
38 Wood anemone

and lapwing all leave. Whinchats may return, but find new neighbours in the shape of garden warblers and yellowhammers which sing their songs as they do from many a hedge and copse. Robins and dunnocks are also attracted to the plantation at this low stage.

When ten years old, the conifers offer taller song perches, and bullfinches, chaffinches, blackbirds and turtle doves are lured in. The redpoll, too, is seen. The coniferization of our hills and heaths has helped it, and it can be found nesting in loose colonies among the thick young trees.

As the trees grow taller, these scrub birds will be joined by the goldcrests that first greeted us, and by the tree pipit, a summer visitor. Its 'parachuting' song flight is very like that of its resident cousin, the meadow pipit, but starts and ends on a tree top. So, while one pipit

different from the lark's. The pipit climbs steeply, cheeping all the while, and then it 'parachutes' down with wings and tail outspread, singing a liquid song. Both birds will also nest in shortish grass, but the young plantation is a prime site, and is quickly occupied. It is also attractive to the curlew and lapwing.

A bird matching the meadow pipit in size sallies from its perch on the fence and, after a swerving chase for a fly, returns to wait another chance. It is a whinchat, a summer visitor, and young plantations attract quite a few, now that tangled wildnerness is harder to find in today's countryside ('whin' is another name for gorse).

Among the tussocks, short-tailed voles flourish, to the benefit of their predators. The short-eared owl is one of these, and a female swoops to scare off the whinchat and take its place on the post. Though it hunts by daylight, this bird relies on sound as much as sight to locate the voles.

The thick cover with its larder of young voles attracts stare-eyed adders. Sometimes a sloughed skin is found as the only clue to their presence, for they are retiring creatures. Lizards and slow worms also frequent the long grass. The latter, snakelike though they seem, are actually harmless legless lizards, and if handled will blink in surprise (lizards, unlike snakes, have eyelids).

Other creatures, particularly moths, like the young coniferous habitat. Footsteps kick up a yellow underwing from the tall grass. It flies off erratically, flashing its bright colour before plunging into another tussock, there to haul its wings close and seemingly disappear. This visual trick confuses birds which would take it if they could.

These and many other animals bask in the security of the young plantation for only a few years. The trees grow fast, and soon their branches meet, creating a new habitat.

In many ways the plantation now resembles a thicket; and the skylark, meadow pipit, curlew

MALE REDPOLL
(above) Perched here on a larch twig by a drinking pool, the redpoll has taken readily to conifer plantations. Numbers have increased rapidly in recent years.

SAFFRON MILK-CAP
(right) This attractive fungus grows under pines and spruces in summer and autumn. An edible species, it occurs in England but is commonest in Scotland.

BRIGHT TORMENTIL
(below) Tormentil – a plant of grassland, heaths and mountains – may be found growing in open rides or at the edge of a plantation.

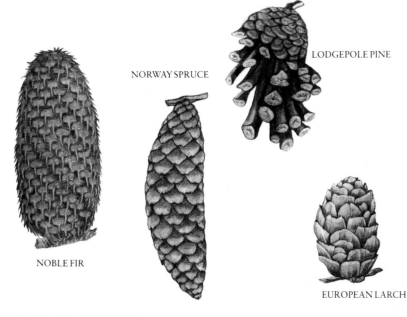

NORWAY SPRUCE

LODGEPOLE PINE

NOBLE FIR

EUROPEAN LARCH

CONES OF PLANTATION CONIFERS
The main conifer groups can be distinguished by their cones. Those of the pines and spruces hang downwards, while those of the silver firs and larches grow upright. Douglas fir – not illustrated here – is not a silver fir and its hanging cones are akin to those of spruce.

– a rare falcon – and heather-loving invertebrates, cannot adapt to the young plantation and, indeed, those species that do so are crowded out in 10-15 years as the canopy closes over.

And although mature plantations have, in some areas, encouraged the spread of rarer species, such as crossbills, pine martens and wild cats, these species may be spreading at the expense of the varied wildlife of the open patchwork that plantations have replaced.

VOLE AND YOUNG
(above right) A short-tailed, or field, vole suckling her young in the breeding nest at the base of a grass tussock. These voles breed rapidly, producing successive litters of 4-6 young from spring until autumn.

PINE BEAUTY MOTH
(right) A night-flying moth, it rests by day among pine branches or on the trunk where it is well camouflaged. It is scarce in Ireland but widespread in Britain. The caterpillars feed on species of pine and can be a pest.

comes to the young plantation, the other only arrives in later years.

Brashing and final thinning of the 15 year-old trees removes the boskiness that attracts many of these songsters. Most are deterred by the dark empty space between the trunks, though coal tits often arrive to nest in holes or mouse burrows among the roots. However, the goldcrest remains to hunt insects in the canopy, and here, too, magpies, jays, crows and woodpigeons may nest. Sparrowhawks and long-eared owls (their short-eared cousins have long gone) also breed in the canopy, taking over deserted nests of crows or pigeons.

Many of today's plantations are vast and little disturbed. Deer like the seclusion and may find enough grazing on the rides. Roe deer are most likely to be seen but red deer occur in some areas, such as Thetford Forest. Their presence may be revealed by well-worn paths which cross the open rides. The pine marten and wildcat – both rare species – have taken to mature plantations and have increased their range in recent years.

But a plantation is more than just trees. The rides and firebreaks form habitats in their own right. The ride is often a kind of open air museum occupied by plants which grew there before the trees were planted. Heather, bilberry, harebell and tormentil all occur in this way.

Though apparently similar, the firebreak is often quite different. Because it is not used as a path, the grasses grow tall and rank, and the heather and bilberry may be overwhelmed by impenetrable brambles. If it is regularly ploughed to keep it clear, the weeds of arable fields may grow. In Thetford Forest it is on this open ground that the rare stone curlew nests.

THE WILDLIFE BALANCE

There is much debate about afforestation, particularly among those who value the open heath, upland grazing or moorland which is often taken for new plantations. Although new plantations are full of wildlife, they attract few species that would not have been present before. Open ground species, such as the merlin

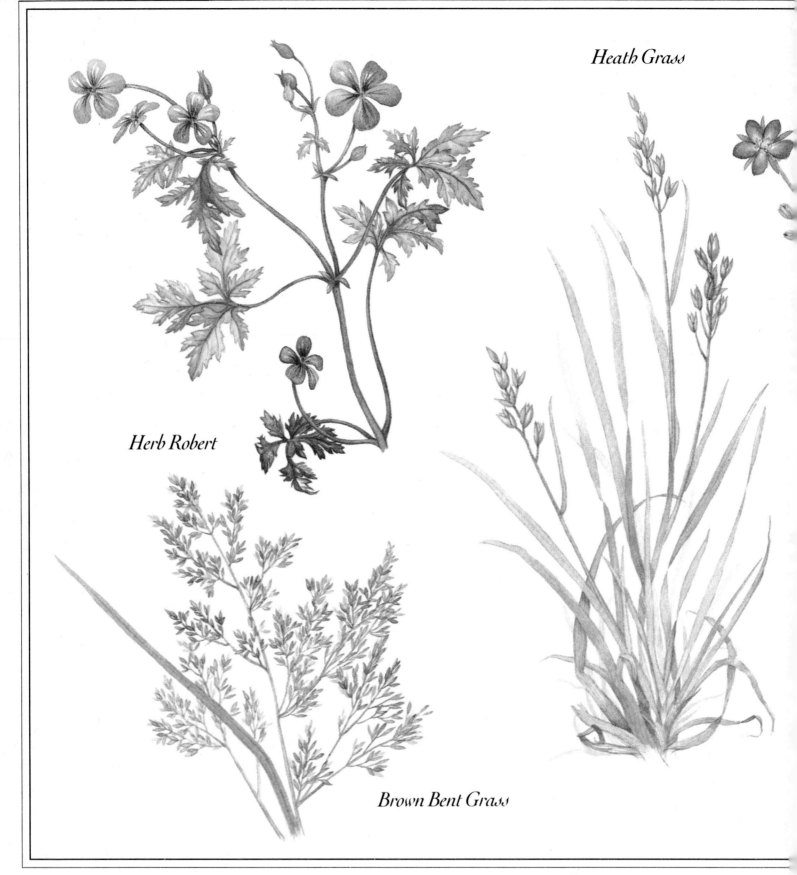

Heath Grass

Herb Robert

Brown Bent Grass

HERB ROBERT *(Geranium robertianum)* Named after a French abbot, this 4-20″ (10-50cm) annual or biennial is common everywhere in woods and hedgebanks. It is usually tinged with red. The flowers appear from May to September and are followed by seed capsules.

BROWN BENT GRASS *(Agrostis vineales)* A tufted perennial, 4-24″ (10-60cm) high, widespread on sandy and peaty soils. It often grows with common bent grass, but is usually less abundant. It flowers in summer and the flat, hairless leaves taper to a fine point.

HEATH GRASS *(Danthonia decumbens)* A pretty, tufted little 4-24″ (10-60cm) perennial: widespread and often common, especially on poor sandy and peaty soils, although sometimes also found on chalk. The leaves are sparsely hairy and the plant flowers June-August.

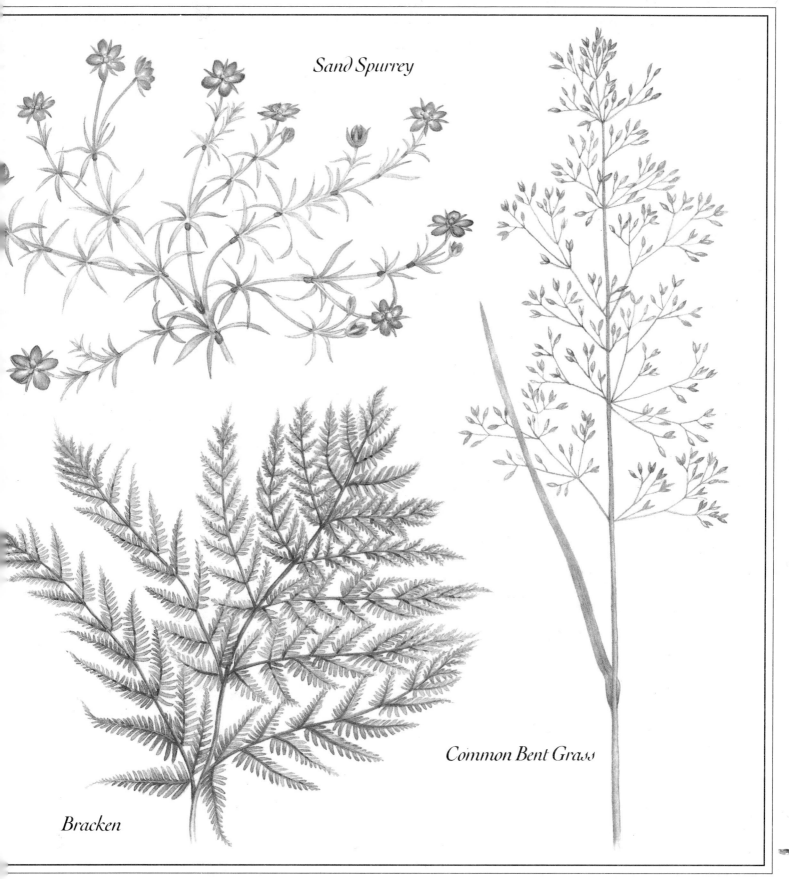

Sand Spurrey

Common Bent Grass

Bracken

SAND SPURREY (*Spergularia rubra*) Widespread and common in open sandy and gravelly places, this little annual or biennial has several straggling 2-10″ (5-25cm) stems. The flowers appear from May until September and are followed by capsules containing brownish seeds.

BRACKEN (*Pteridium aquilinum*) Our most familiar fern, 20-70″ (50-175cm) tall; widespread and frequent on acid soils. The reproductive spores appear in late summer. A perennial refused by sheep and rabbits and resistant to fire, it often invades heath and moor.

COMMON BENT GRASS (*Agrostis capillaris*) An abundant grass, 4-24″ (10-60cm) tall, widely distributed in the British Isles and usually found in acid places. A perennial, it flowers from June until September. The flat, hairless leaves are often inrolled.

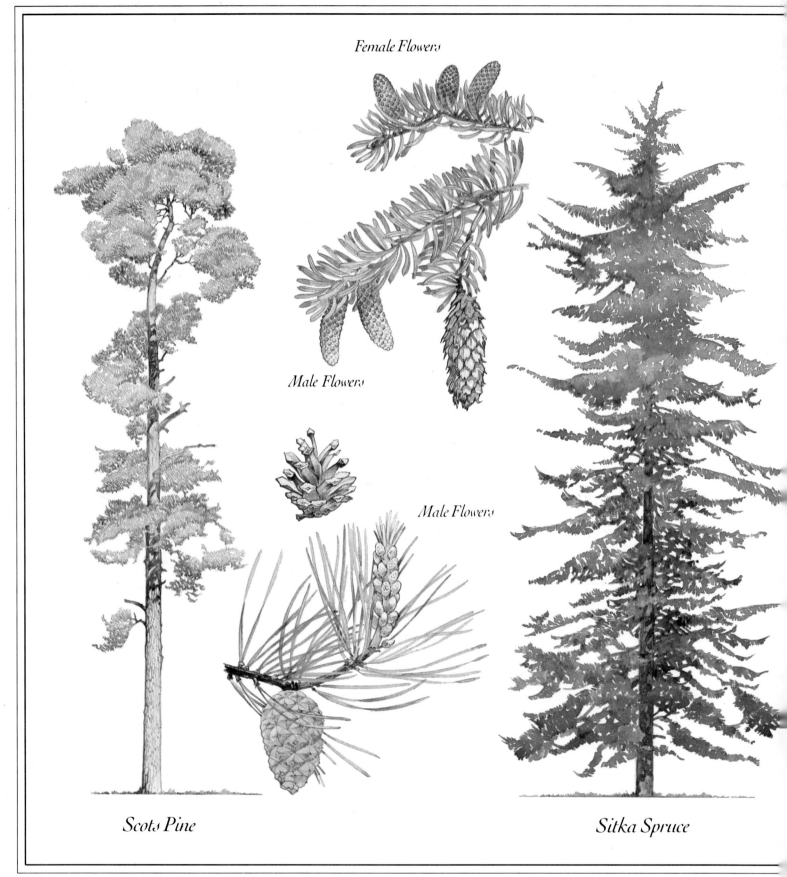

Female Flowers

Male Flowers

Male Flowers

Scots Pine

Sitka Spruce

SCOTS PINE *(Pinus sylvestris)*
Native only in the ancient pine forests of the Highlands, this is a traditional and widespread forestry tree. In time, the lower branches die or fall, leaving a flattened crown on a bare, straight bole of 115' (35m) or more. The bark, often fissured and scaly, is usually pinkish or reddish, with a tinge of grey. The leaves are often twisted. Flowers appear in spring; female flowers become cones which take two years to ripen from green to brown. The timber – yellow deal – is valued for building.

SITKA SPRUCE *(Picea sitchensis)*
A native of the west coast of North America, the Sitka spruce takes its name from a place in Alaska. Moisture-loving, it thrives in the wet valleys of Scotland and has become, this century, the most common forestry tree of western Britain. Fast-growing, it reaches more than 150' (45m) and yields good wood. The needles are very sharply pointed and often bear narrow parallel white bands. The flowers appear early in the year and the cones, which ripen in their first year, have thin, papery scales.

210

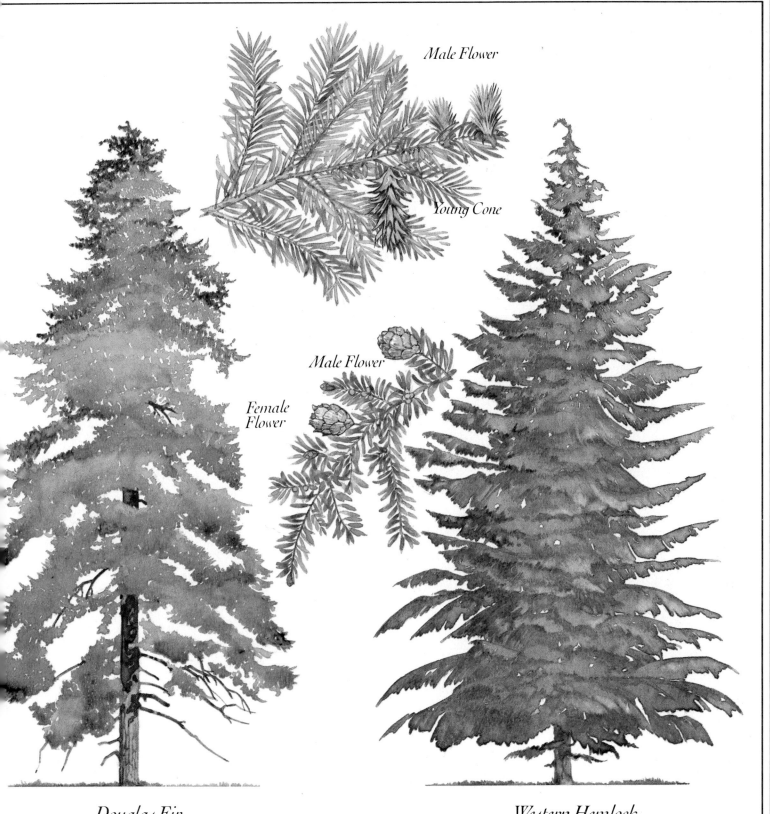

Male Flower

Young Cone

Male Flower

Female Flower

Douglas Fir

Western Hemlock

DOUGLAS FIR (*Pseudotsuga menziesii*) Brought from western North America in the 19th century by Scottish explorer and botanist David Douglas, having been discovered earlier by another Scot, Menzies, this conifer is widespread. Tall and straight, it reaches 170′ (50m) and more here, and makes good masts and flagpoles. Solitary trees are a fine sight, with their huge trunks and masses of plume-like branches. The foliage has a sweet resinous aroma. The flowers appear in spring and the cones ripen to a dull brown.

WESTERN HEMLOCK (*Tsuga heterophylla*) This lofty conifer of 150′ (45m) and more, with its graceful tapering crown, always with the leading shoot drooping, is most often seen in wetter areas; it is not frequent in the East. The leaves, which are variable in size, are parallel sided and round tipped. The flowers appear early in the year and the cones are found at the ends of small branches. The bark is used for tanning; in the tree's native home – the west coast of North America – its inner bark has been eaten as a vegetable by Alaskan Indians.

Female

Male

Scottish Crossbill

Male

Female

Parrot Crossbill

SCOTTISH CROSSBILL *(Loxia curvirostra scotica)* A 6½" (16cm) resident of the Highlands, where its distribution follows that of the ancient pine forests. Its bill – deeper and stouter than that of the common crossbill – is thrust open into pine cones and then closed to lever out a meal of seeds. Despite being brightly coloured, crossbills are often difficult to detect in a wood. The first sign of their presence is often a shower of falling cones discarded by a group of crossbills feeding acrobatically in the upper branches.

PARROT CROSSBILL *(Loxia pytyopsittacus)* Sometimes known as the pine crossbill, this 7" (17.5cm) bird is mainly an occasional winter visitor. Similar in most respects to the common and Scottish crossbills, it is distinguished from them by its strikingly massive curved beak and also by its call, which is deeper and louder. It feeds mainly on pine – the small differences between the several European crossbills, which are all rather similar, may be associated with the slight differences in their feeding preferences.

Male

Common Crossbill

Female

COMMON CROSSBILL *(Loxia curvirostra curvirostra)* A 6½″ (16cm) resident which inhabits conifer woods and plantations in Scotland, East Anglia and the New Forest. In some winters, large numbers of birds arrive from northern Europe, probably as a result of food shortages there. The distinctive call consists of a series of loud, incisive 'chips' uttered both as flight call and contact note. The nest is made of dry grass on a base of twigs. It is lined with fur and feathers and four white or pale blue eggs, speckled with reddish brown, are laid.

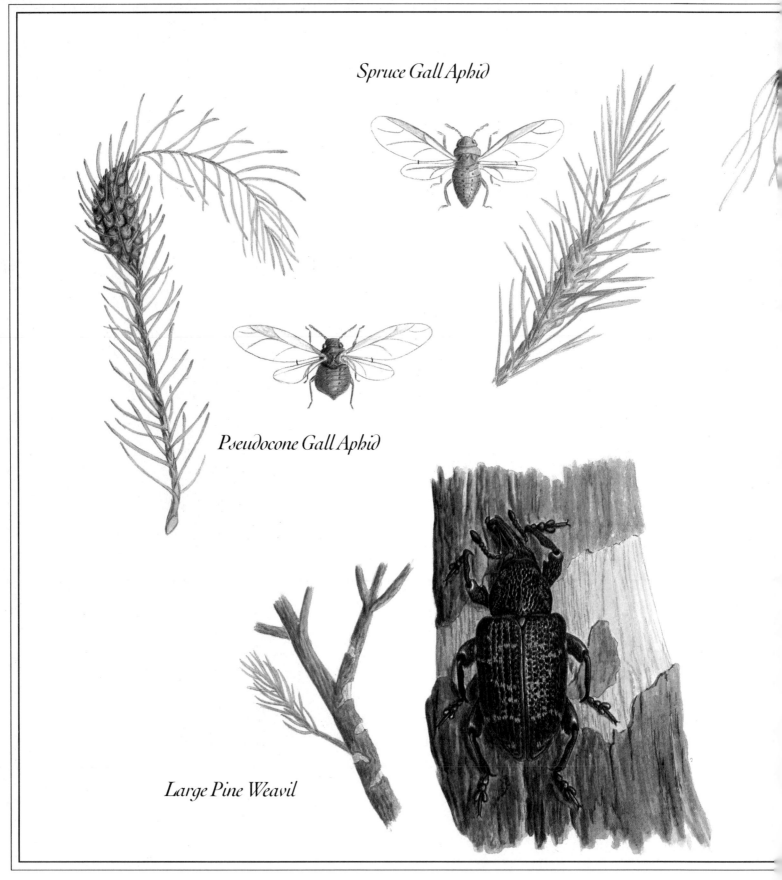

Spruce Gall Aphid

Pseudocone Gall Aphid

Large Pine Weavil

PSEUDOCONE GALL APHID (*Adelges abietes*) This aphid feeds on spruce shoots causing greenish swellings or galls, about 1½" (35mm) long. The galls later turn woody and hard and resemble cones. The aphid also lives on larch without having the same effect.

SPRUCE GALL APHID (*Gilletteela cooleyi*) This aphid causes galls about 2½" (6cm) long by feeding on young shoots of spruce trees, particularly Sitka spruce. The galls are often bent. The aphid also attacks Douglas fir, but without causing galls.

LARGE PINE WEEVIL (*Hylobius abietes*) The adult weevil feeds on the bark of young conifers, damaging or killing them. In large numbers they may cause the complete loss of a crop. The larvae feed in old stumps or logs, forming tunnels between the bark and the timber.

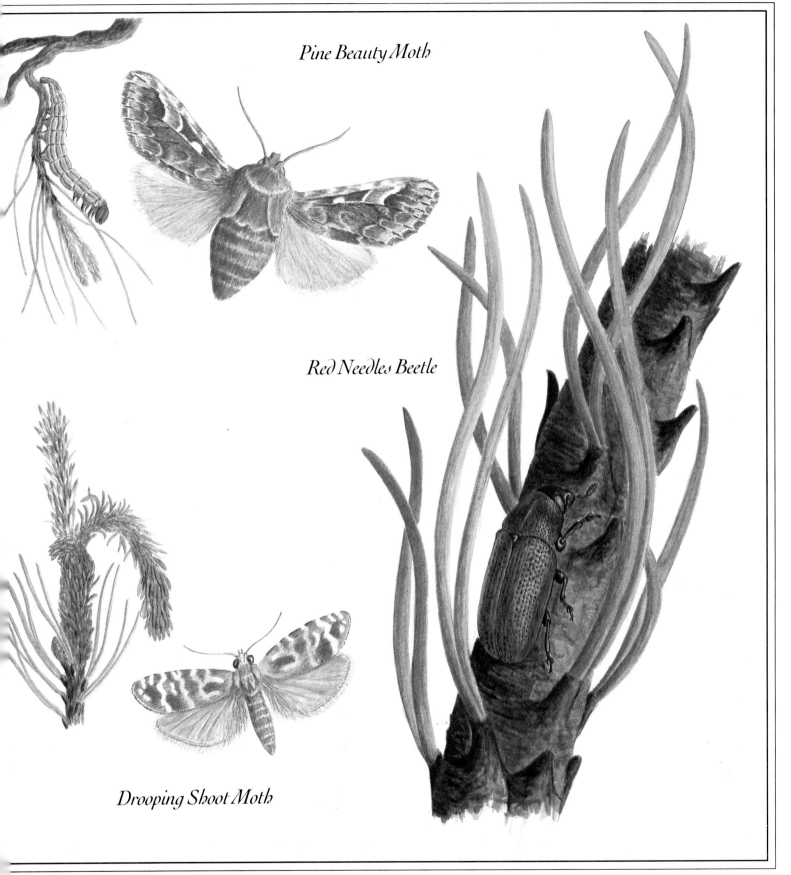

Pine Beauty Moth

Red Needles Beetle

Drooping Shoot Moth

DROOPING SHOOT MOTH (Evertia buoliana) A common moth, on the wing in summer, which can be a serious pest in plantations because the larvae feed on conifer shoots, hollowing them out and killing them; young trees are particularly susceptible to attack.

PINE BEAUTY MOTH (Panolis flammea) A well-known pest in continental Europe, the larvae eat the leaves of conifers. The species is widespread here and has become a threat to plantations in northern Scotland in recent years. The adult is on the wing in spring.

RED NEEDLES BEETLE (Blastophagus piniperda) The adults of this widespread beetle often bore into, and eat the pith of, young pine shoots; the shoots then die, and may fall off, leaving conspicuous red needles. The larvae feed on the wood of pine, leaving long tunnels.

THE UPLAND ASHWOOD

Sunlight filtering through the light-leaved ashwood encourages a lush undergrowth of shrubs and flowers, attracting swarms of insects which are pursued by warblers, tits, voles and shrews.

An ashwood in early summer is a green, airy, sun-dappled place. Light filtering through the open canopy encourages the growth of shrubs and a luxuriant ground flora. The greenery overhead is frosted with the flowers of whitebeam, and, lower down, hawthorn, privet and guelder rose foam with blossom. Underfoot, lilies-of-the-valley peep from their green cowls, and the star-like flowers of wild garlic float above their pungent leaves.

The varied and vigorous shrub layer is particularly colourful in autumn, with the shiny, red stems and crimson leaves of dogwood, lurid pink berries of spindle, pinky-brown nut clusters of hazel, and bright red sprays of guelder rose fruits. At this season, orange-peel fungus brightens the paths and, as the leaves fall, shaggy, rust-brown bracket fungi are more readily visible on the ash trunks. On dead wood grow the rounded, black balls of the King Alfred's cakes fungus.

Glades beside the clear, tumbling rivers of the Derbyshire Dales are busy with activity in early summer. Dapper coal tits and impudent blue tits search the bunches of developing ash keys for caterpillars and other insects. Bursts of musical chatter betray the presence of a whitethroat, and a treecreeper inches its way, mouse-like, along a branch arching over the dancing water. A dipper bobs on a boulder, its white breast bright in the sunlight, then slips into the water to hunt along the bottom for insects. With a scolding squawk, a jay swoops across the glade flashing the blue on its wings.

Suddenly the ashwood seems to hold its breath. A streamlined, barred sparrowhawk darts silently, and very fast, across the glade and twists and turns with remarkable agility through the trees, to be followed by an abusive torrent of scolding and chattering alarm calls from the other birds alerted by the danger.

In a marshy patch by the river's edge, bees hum around the bright yellow 'faces' of monkey flowers. A stone fly, its netted wings folded over its back, rests on a rush stem, seemingly oblivious to the alert and rapacious robber fly on a

MALE WHITETHROAT
This crisply coloured warbler bursts readily into song following its arrival in Britain in late April. The male, particularly, is a conspicuous bird – unlike many warblers – perching in full view on a twig or delivering his ebullient notes in a bouncing song flight. The nest is built among thick undergrowth, usually close to the ground, and two clutches of 4-5 eggs are often reared after incubation by both parents.

WILDLIFE IN THE ASHWOOD

Set in a streamside dip among limestone hills, the ashwood attracts a wide range of species. Both the buzzard and the sparrowhawk may be found building their twiggy nests high in the ashwood canopy, which may be broken here and there by standard trees of other species such as oak and, in newer woods, sycamore. Lower down, the green woodpecker excavates its nest hole in a trunk. Below the trees, shrubs such as hazel and guelder rose provide fruit and nest sites for smaller birds. The lightly shaded floor of the wood is carpeted, in the drier areas, with lily-of-the-valley and, nearer the stream, swathes of garlic-smelling ramsons. Among the flowers, blue butterflies may pause to feed, while voles and shrews busily hunt their insect prey. Cutting through the wood, the foraging paths of badgers fan out from a sett. Nearer the stream, ash trees give way to damp-loving alders from which neat grey wagtails fly sorties out over the water catching insects on the wing.

KEY TO FEATURES AND SPECIES

1 Yew
2 Buzzard
3 Juniper
4 Limestone cliff
5 Ash
6 Whitebeam
7 Oak
8 Female sparrowhawk
9 Wych elm
10 Sycamore
11 Badgers at sett
12 Field maple
13 Green woodpecker
14 Hazel
15 Guelder rose
16 Marbled white

17 Hart's tongue
18 Privet
19 Lilies-of-the-valley
20 Young alder
21 Male common blue
22 Female common blue
23 Common rock-rose
24 Wild thyme
25 Wren
26 Polypody
27 Ramsons
28 Grey wagtail

MARBLED WHITE
(left) This handsomely marked butterfly can be seen visiting flowers along the woodland edge in June and July. The female scatters her eggs, often while flying, among the grass on which the caterpillars will later feed.

ASH FLOWERS AND BUD
(below) Male and female flowers emerge before the leaves shoot out from the distinctive black terminal bud.

HERB ROBERT
(right) These attractive candy-striped flowers are common in woods and hedges.

PYGMY SHREW
(below) Weighing only about 6g, the tiny pygmy shrew can often be found in the same habitats as its larger cousin, the common shrew.

searching by night for insects and fruit, or gnawing the ash bark.

In some lowland ashwoods, the erect green shoots of dog's mercury form continuous ground cover – a sure sign of an area of long-established woodland. Here and there are the dark-centred, green flowers of herb Paris, each among a quartet of leaves, atop an otherwise bare stem. Here, too, can be found the sparse, white umbels of sanicle. A careful search may reveal the slender flower spikes of fly orchids and the delicate spires of red helleborine or of the inconspicuous, green-flowered helleborine. Close by, in a grassy glade, are the more obvious sturdy pink or purple flower masses of spotted orchids, with their dark-blotched leaves.

A monotonous, churring noise in the glade suggests there are grasshoppers about, but it is actually a grasshopper warbler, a little, streaked, brown bird. This summer visitor is so skulking in its habits, it is more often heard than seen. Male long-horned grasshoppers and bush-crickets, living among the ash foliage, produce shorter bursts of sound, by rubbing together strengthened areas of their forewings.

ASHWOOD BUTTERFLIES

On a bramble leaf perches a fearsome-looking male scorpion fly, with beaked head and up-curled abdomen. It feeds mainly on carrion, and the bulbous, scorpion-like tail is harmless. A speckled wood butterfly flutters rapidly up

nearby figwort, poised to launch its long body into the air and pounce. Besides the robber fly, small wasps are busy around the tiny, odd-smelling, red flowers of figwort.

A sprawl of brambles shelters the white-throat's nest in its thorny tangle. The bramble's sunlit leaves swarm with little, black, ant-like flies that twist and turn with outstretched wings as though driven by clockwork. Hoverflies hang, seemingly motionless, above the pinky-white bramble flowers. Alongside familiar yellow and black banded hoverflies, there is a dark one with pairs of greyish spots on its black abdomen, and a robust, furry, narcissus fly. Narcissus flies occur in a variety of colour forms, each mimicking a different species of bumble bee. Their larvae feed within bulbs, destroying the growing point, and in the ashwood they may develop in bluebells, in ramsons (wood garlic), or in the delicate-flowered star of Bethlehem.

Where the grey, limestone boulders tumble down the hillside, feathery fronds of hard shield fern and polypody cluster around a damp trickle among the rocks. Hart's tongue pokes out of a shady crevice, and the delicate sprays of maidenhair spleenwort caress the hard surface.

VOLES ON THE SLOPES

High above, a buzzard soars over the grassy slopes, alert for the movement that betrays a field vole hiding amid the thyme and rock roses. A field vole on the slopes may be a stray youngster that has wandered away from the shelter of the trees in its nocturnal foraging; its litter-mates will be among the lush grass and sedges of the glade by the river in the valley. Here, there are red-brown bank voles, too,

RELATED TREES
(right) These trees –
members of the Sorbus
family – can all be
found growing in ash
woodland. The silver
leaf characterizes the
whitebeam. The many
leaflets distinguish the
rowan, while the wild
service tree can be
identified by its leaf
shape and wrinkled,
brown berries.

WILD SERVICE TREE

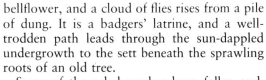

ROWAN

WHITEBEAM

NODDING
BELLFLOWER
(below) The flowers
of nettle-leaved
bellflower nod gently
at the top of the stem,
some 2-3 feet above
the ground. The leaves
superficially resemble
those of the nettle but
lack any sting.

from a patch of sunlight to investigate another speckled wood. On a nearby leaf, a newly-alighted white-letter hairstreak butterfly shuffles around, rubbing together its closed wings so that their conspicuous orange marks and antenna-like white-tipped 'tails' appear to be its head and so distract attackers from its real one.

A striking marbled white butterfly sips nectar from the pink flowers of herb Robert, bees investigate the tall, lilac spires of nettle-leaved bellflower, and a cloud of flies rises from a pile of dung. It is a badgers' latrine, and a well-trodden path leads through the sun-dappled undergrowth to the sett beneath the sprawling roots of an old tree.

Some of the ash branches have fallen and, beneath the bark, small, blunt-headed bark beetles are excavating their breeding galleries. From holes in the wood which they chewed as larvae, shiny, black rhinoceros beetles emerge, the males armoured with a curved horn. The beetles' activities let in fungi, which contribute to the breakdown of the wood, and eventually the fallen bough will distintegrate and its nutrients recycled through the rich community of the ashwood.

NESTING BUZZARD
(below) Incubating its eggs
here in the crotch of an ash
tree, the buzzard is a highly
adaptable bird – although
the rise in buzzard numbers
was temporarily halted in
the 1950s by the crash
in the rabbit population
due to myxomatosis. Since
then, the population has
recovered well and is now
expanding into new areas
of the British Isles.

Fungus Gnat

Sweat Fly

Robber Fly

Owl Midge

FUNGUS GNAT (*Mycetophila ornata*) These small ¼" (6mm) flies are found in damp shady places throughout the year. The males congregate in dancing swarms close to the ground in woodland clearings and under bushes. Larvae and adults feed on fungi and mould.

ROBBER FLY (*Asilus crabroniformis*) At approximately 1¼" (30mm) one of the largest British flies, inhabiting drier localities from mid to late summer. It hunts by darting from a vantage point on to beetles, grasshoppers and other prey. The larvae develop in dung.

SWEAT FLY (*Hydrotaea irritans*) Large numbers of these small ¼" (6mm) flies feed on the sweat and open sores of cattle and other livestock on warm summer days. They do not bite but annoy man and other animals by their persistent attentions. Larvae develop in dung.

OWL MIDGE (*Psychoda alternata*) In spring and autumn these distinctive ⅛" (4mm) hairy flies run around jerkily on leaves and tree trunks, after rain, with wings folded roof-like over the body. The white cylindrical larvae develop in wet decaying matter.

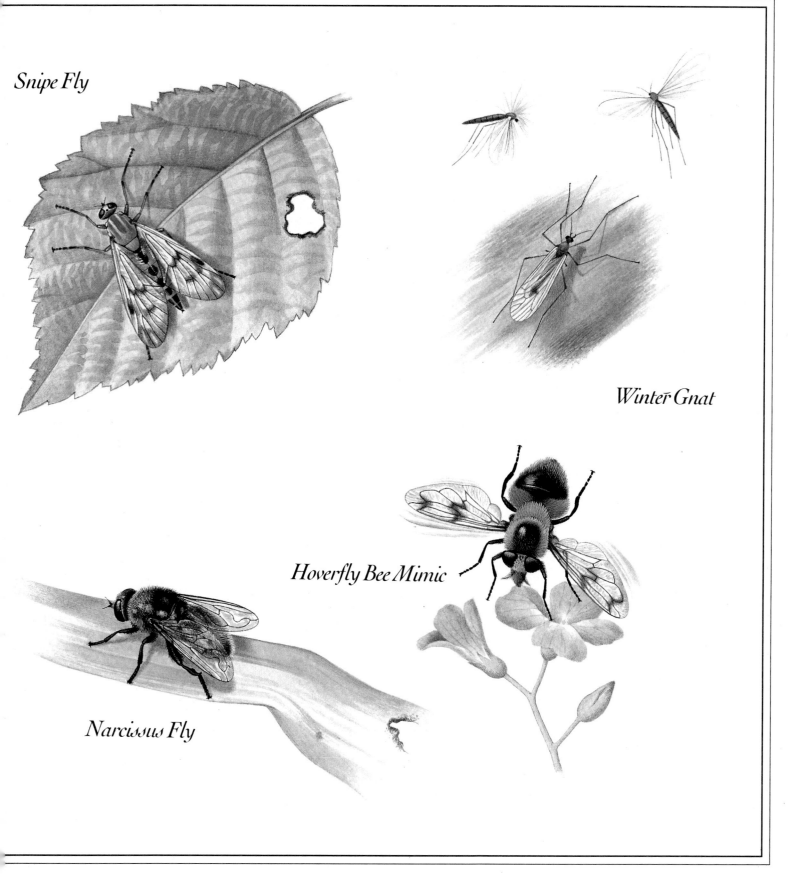

Snipe Fly

Winter Gnat

Hoverfly Bee Mimic

Narcissus Fly

SNIPE FLY *(Rhagio scolopacea)*
This long-legged ½″ (12mm) fly can be seen in summer sitting on trunks and leaves. Whether or not it is a predator is uncertain but the larvae are definitely carnivorous, preying on insects in leaf mould and decaying wood.

NARCISSUS (BULB) FLY *(Merodon equestris)* A variable ½″ (12mm) hoverfly, the adults can be found in the summer on many different flowers. The larvae develop in the bulbs of narcissus and related plants, usually singly, sometimes destroying the plant.

WINTER GNAT *(Trichocers relegationis)* Although these small flies are found throughout the year, they prefer the colder months, the males congregating in dancing swarms on still, damp afternoons in winter. The larvae feed on decaying vegetable matter.

HOVERFLY BEE MIMIC *(Volucella bombylans)* This ½″ (12mm) fly is variable enough to mimic different species of bumble bee. In summer it hovers apparently motionless over flowers and makes short darting flights. The larvae develop in bumble bees' nests.

Field Vole

Pygmy Shrew

FIELD VOLE *(Microtus agrestis)*
Blunt-nosed rodents that are found widely in Britain – except Ireland – in fields, open woods and hedges amongst tall, undisturbed grass. They make a network of tunnels just under ground and feed on stems and roots of plants. Females breed from 6 weeks, rearing many litters of 4-6 in grass-lined nests spring to autumn. Populations are limited by voles' aggressive, territorial behaviour and predation by birds of prey. About 4" (10cm) long, adults are dark with pale underparts and a short tail.

PYGMY SHREW *(Sorex minutus)*
At 2¼" (6cm) with a 1½" (4cm) tail, this busy insectivore is Britain's tiniest mammal. To maintain body temperature, it needs an almost constant food supply, with only short rests between meals. Although not abundant, it occurs throughout Britain in fields, woods and moorland, living in crevices and the burrows of other animals and feeding on small invertebrates. It has a distinctive domed head and short, thin snout. Nests are made underground – many litters of 4-7 are born April-August.

Common Shrew

COMMON SHREW *(Sorex araneus)* More numerous than the pygmy shrew, but not as widespread, this 3″ (7.5cm) insect-eating mammal spends most of its time underground, foraging for food night and day. It is absent from Ireland and exposed moorland, preferring woods, hedges and dunes. Each has its own fiercely defended territory, detecting intruders by smell and sound – it has weak eyes. Females have many litters of 5-7 in well-hidden nests, spring-autumn. They fall prey to larger predators but are distasteful to some. They live only about one year.

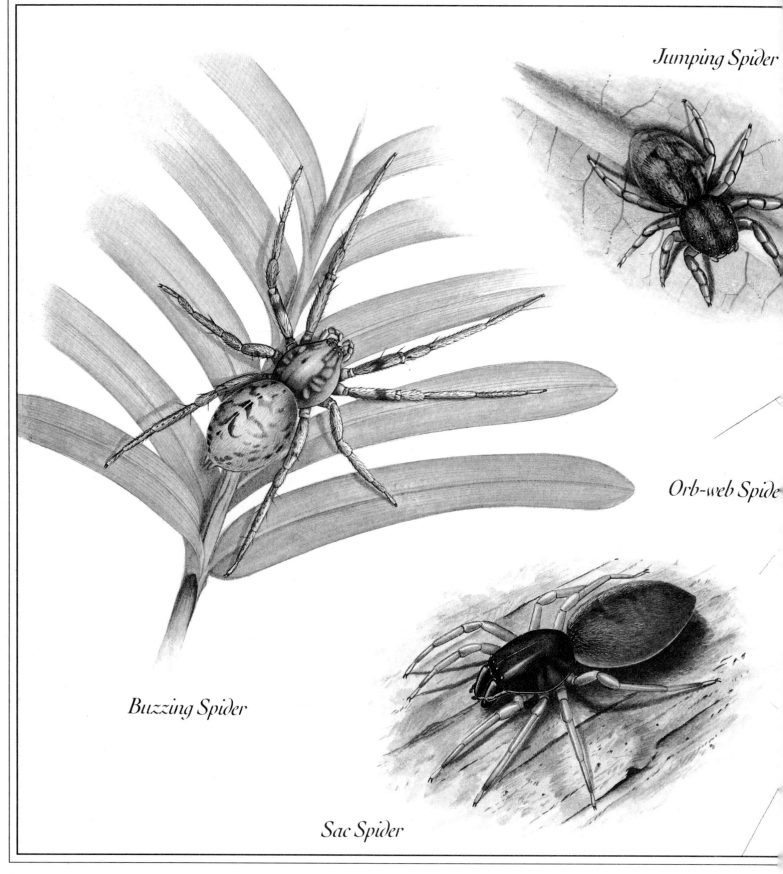

Jumping Spider

Orb-web Spide

Buzzing Spider

Sac Spider

BUZZING SPIDER *(Anyphaena accentuata)* Found throughout Britain, this spider, about ¼" (6-8mm) long, can be seen, particularly in May and June, hunting small flies and leaf hoppers on branches and leaves. The male makes a buzzing noise during courtship.

SAC SPIDER *(Clubiona terrestris)* This is a very common nocturnal hunter, about ¼" (5-7mm) long, which hides during the day in its silken sac-like retreat under the peeling bark of tree trunks. Sexes are alike; eggs are laid in the retreat during summer.

JUMPING SPIDER *(Ballus depressus)* True to its name, this ³⁄₁₆" (4-5mm) daytime spider stalks and leaps on to its insect prey among the tree foliage. Uncommon in England and Wales, seen during early summer. The male is distinguished by its metallic sheen.

Woodland Spiders

Money Spider

Crab Spider

ORB-WEB SPIDER (*Araneus marmoreus pyramidatus*) Seen late summer and autumn, this spider spins a large, attractive orb-web between shrubs in a wood to catch wasps and other flying insects. The male at around ¼″ (5-9mm) is smaller and duller than the female.

MONEY SPIDER (*Drapetisca socialis*) At a bare ⅛″ (3.5-4mm), the tiny common money spider constructs an extremely fine silk web among the fissures on tree trunks to snare insects such as aphids. Sexes are similar and eggs laid in crevices hatch in spring.

CRAB SPIDER (*Xysticus lanio*) This spider, around ¼″ (6-7mm) long and common throughout Britain, lies in wait among tree foliage for passing insects. In early summer the male ties down the larger female with silk threads prior to mating. Young are born late summer.

225

Baneberry

Herb Paris

Purple Gromwell

Stone Bramble

BANEBERRY (Actaea spicata)
Unpleasant-smelling and poisonous, this 12-24″ (30-60cm) perennial is a rare plant of northern limestone ashwoods. The long-stalked leaves are toothed and spikes of many-stamened flowers appear in May, followed by black berries.

STONE BRAMBLE (Rubus saxatilis) Scrambling over rocky slopes, creeping runners send up 3-16″ (8-40cm) flower stems with small blooms June-August. The sharp-tasting red fruit has 2-6 segments. It is local to rare in limestone woods of the North and West.

HERB PARIS (Paris quadrifolia) The single 6-16″ (15-40cm) stems are topped with a whorl of 4 broad leaves, a central flower, with prominent stamens, May-July, and a round black fruit. It is local in damp, chalky woods, over most of England, except the South-West.

PURPLE GROMWELL (Buglossoides purpureocaerulea) This is a rare, downy plant of open limestone woods in west England and Wales. Stems are mostly long and trailing except for upright, 24″ (60cm) flowering shoots open May-June. Leaves are narrow and rough on top.

Voodland Flowers

Upright Spurge

Green Hellebore

Common Figwort

GREEN HELLEBORE (*Helleborus viridis*) This very poisonous 8-16″ (20-40cm) perennial produces green flowers in March-April. Both the basal and the stalkless stem leaves have radiating, toothed leaflets. Local in damp, limestone woods of southern England and Wales.

UPRIGHT SPURGE (*Euphorbia serrulata*) A very rare annual of limestone woods in west Gloucester and Monmouth. The smooth stems 6-20″ (15-50cm) tall, have clasping, finely toothed leaves. Tiny yellowish flowers appear June-September, followed by small warty fruits.

COMMON FIGWORT (*Scrophularia nodosa*) A stiff, 16-31″ (40-80cm) perennial, widespread in wet hedges and woodlands. The four-angled stems bear pairs of opposite, coarsely toothed leaves and branched, open heads of flowers June to September.

ALONG THE MOUNTAIN STREAM

The fast-moving waters of upland streams hold wild trout, occasional salmon, plentiful insects and birds well adapted to plucking food from the tumbling current.

As spring brushes the late April hills, meltwater tumbles and swirls down the troutbeck's rocky gully. The bubbling call of a curlew flows off the moorland, a siskin twitters and wheezes in a twisted pine and a clipped *tchip* call accompanies the bounding flight of a grey wagtail before it lands on a boulder, nervously flicking its tail and displaying brilliant yellow underparts.

The moor is alive with meadow pipits, parachuting groundwards in their song flight. Twigs, branches and an old sheep carcass wedge between the stepping stones below the waterfall's deep plunge pool, on whose edge a smart common sandpiper, newly returned from Africa, prospects a potential nest site, bobbing all the while. The tiny, white flowers of blinks loosely carpet a damp flush, and hurtling past them a tubby dipper, beak crammed with insects, flies upstream and through the waterfall's silver curtain. Here, behind the falling water, a pair of dippers have built a ball-like nest of mosses and grass and will be feeding their first brood.

At the hint of a footfall, wild brown trout dart from the pool's shallows to the deep centre. Creeping over the clear, pebbled bottom, stonefly nymphs search for caddis fly larvae.

A few trees line the course of the troutbeck, growing from cracks in the rocks inaccessible to the mowing machine sheep which have cleared the surrounding hills, nipping off all saplings at an early stage. Catkins dangle from damploving alders, and creamy-white flowers are about to open on the delicate rowan. Silver birch, willow, hazel, oak and pine may also grow along the banks.

BECKSIDE FLOWERS

Woodland flowers sometimes accompany the stream – wood sorrel is one, though it chooses well drained sites. The poor acid soil of much of our mountainous country discourages many flowers, but several can be found where springs or flushes bring minerals to the surface: here willowherbs can grow, and dainty eyebright. The damp ground alongside the stream suits rushes and sedges. Like grass they shoot from below, close to the ground, and so can survive grazing.

Many boulders in the stream carry green caps of moss. Mosses can survive being immersed when the stream is in full spate, while the more delicate fronds of ferns would be torn away. Ferns, however, are usually to be seen above the spate line, either growing on the ground close by or from pockets of soil lodged in rock crevices. Many ferns resemble bracken, but differ in the exact pattern of their fronds (and those of the mountain fern are easily recognised for they smell of lemon when crushed). Other ferns, such as black spleenwort, are rather delicate, attractive plants. Bracken itself does not like waterlogged roots and only grows on quick draining soil.

Few plants grow in the beck itself, though plant slimes can coat the rocks and make the pebbles slippery. Only where the current eases and beds of silty sand are found can the floating leaves of pondweeds be seen – but there is never

PERKY COMMON SANDPIPER
Breeding along upland streams, this summer visitor often perches on a boulder, bobbing its tail and calling loudly.

WILDLIFE OF THE TUMBLING BECK

*The underwater insect larvae provide food for
the fish and birds of the beck. Trout also take
flying insects, minnows, salmon fry and their
own young. The kingfisher dives for minnows
and fry; the dipper wades underwater for larvae
and small fish; the sandpiper picks off larvae
and limpets; and wagtails deftly catch flying
insects. The adult dragonfly catches mayflies
and black flies but may itself fall prey to the ring
ouzel or wagtail.*

KEY TO SPECIES

1 *Rowan*
2 *Buzzard*
3 *Scots pine*
4 *Sheep*
5 *Alder*
6 *Common sandpiper*
7 *Polybody*
8 *Ring ouzel*
9 *Rushes*
10 *Moss*

11 *Kingfisher*
12 *Trout*
13 *Mayfly*
14 *Dipper*
15 *Pied wagtail*
16 *Wood sorrel*
17 *Golden-ringed
   dragonfly*
18 *Minnows*
19 *Salmon parr*

20 *River limpets*
21 *Mayfly larva*
22 *Black fly larvae*
23 *Bullhead*
24 *Web spinning caddis
   larva*

alkaline water where a tributary flows in over basic rock. These changes in acidity can be reflected in a slight change in the proportion of male to female fish.

Smaller fish are found where the level of the stream rises and falls rapidly. Larger fish are found in milder reaches and often where the stream runs past trees. Here the leaves fall into the water, collect in drifts in the pools and decay, so increasing the nutrient content of the water. In the end this means more insects and thus more food for the trout. The dung from grazing cattle can have the same effect.

Salmon or their young can sometimes be seen in the gravel reaches of the troutbeck. The young parr remain in the headwaters, in which they were born, for two or three years before moving down river to the sea.

Very often, however, the trout is the only permanent fish of the turbulent troutbeck, though it may be joined by the bullhead (or 'miller's thumb'). This fish, which prefers deepish water with a gravelly bottom, seeks shelter from the current under a stone or rock, emerging to feed at night.

UNDERWATER INSECTS

Close inspection of the stream will show the insects on which these fish feed. There are often many different types of caddis. Some of the aquatic larvae of these flies spin themselves a net to catch food particles being swept past by the current. Others construct a protective case of grains of sand or even pebbles, and crawl around dragging this home with them. One builds its case onto the underwater surface of rocks and boulders. Some caddis also make cases from leaves but they are found in quieter water and are not so typical of a troutbeck.

The young, or 'nymphs', of mayflies may also be seen in the gentler reaches, either swimming with up-and-down strokes of their three long

GREY WAGTAIL
This elegant bird nests by fast-running water on a rock ledge, in tree roots or under a bridge. The noisy adults are easy to find.

ALDER CATKINS
New catkins and last season's woody, cone-like fruits can both be seen in March on this waterside tree.

the variety of aquatic plants that can be seen in a lowland river. And where the pondweeds grow is, in fact, not quite the troutbeck proper, but what is called a 'minnow reach', slacker water where these fish swarm.

The trout, though, is made of sterner stuff and can survive in the faster reaches. Here, the well-oxygenated water is what the trout needs, but the quality of the water can change in ways which affect the fish. By and large, troutbecks carry acid water, but some may receive rather

STONEFLY NYMPH ON STREAM BED
Nymphs spend three years in the water but winged adults live for less than a month.

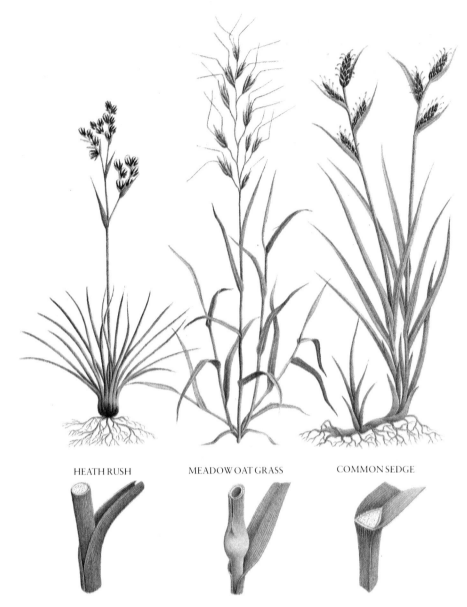

HEATH RUSH   MEADOW OAT GRASS   COMMON SEDGE

the migrant yellow wagtail of the lowland meadows, the grey wagtail is present all year but tends to move to lower ground in winter.

Other birds fish the stream itself – not only dippers, with their quaint habit of walking below the surface in search of caddis, but kingfishers too, can also be seen, though they are scarce in many parts of Scotland. Another bird of this habitat is the common sandpiper. This wader picks insects and their larvae from stones or waterside vegetation, and probes the mud for worms. It also takes tadpoles and young frogs (frogspawn is often seen in the waterlogged, boggy ground in spring).

And from time to time, of course, other birds of the uplands are glimpsed – the ring ouzel, the 'blackbird of the hills', for example, or the stately buzzard wheeling overhead as it scans the ground for prey.

UPLAND MAMMALS

As for mammals, foxes are common enough in hill country, and weasels and stoats are great travellers. Short-tailed voles sometimes reach plague numbers in the uplands. Red deer make use of the troutbeck not only to drink but also to mark a boundary between their territories. Otters, which are now rare in the lowlands but have found sanctuary on the moors and in the uplands, will travel alongside the smallest streams on their far-ranging journeys, pausing awhile to fish.

tails, or crawling. The nymphs of stoneflies also crawl, but painfully slowly – they are known as creepers – which makes them easy to recognise. The larvae of the black fly attach themselves head and tail to a boulder when at rest, and can occupy sites in the teeth of the current. They become the fiercest of the biting flies in the hills.

All these young insects are at risk not only from fish, but also from the golden-ringed dragonfly's predatory nymphs, which frequent fast-flowing water. Also of interest is the pearl mussel, once collected for its pearls, though they are in fact very small and of poor quality. Another mollusc, the small river limpet, may sometimes be seen clinging tight to a stone.

BIRDS OF THE BECK

The mayflies and other insects that breed in the troutbeck are caught by the grey wagtail which dances gracefully into the air after the flies. This long-tailed, striking bird is very much a species of fast water and may be found near weirs or mill-races in the lowlands. Unlike

RUSH, GRASS AND SEDGE *(above) Rushes have cylindrical, pith-filled stems. Grasses have cylindrical, hollow stems with lumpy nodes; the alternate leaves are flat. Sedges have triangular, pith-filled stems with leaves emerging on all sides.*

MALE DRAGONFLY *(top right) Flying during the summer, the golden-ringed dragonfly can be readily identified by the yellow bands on its black abdomen.*

MOUNTAIN ASH *(right) Better known as the rowan, this attractive tree is ablaze with red berries in autumn.*

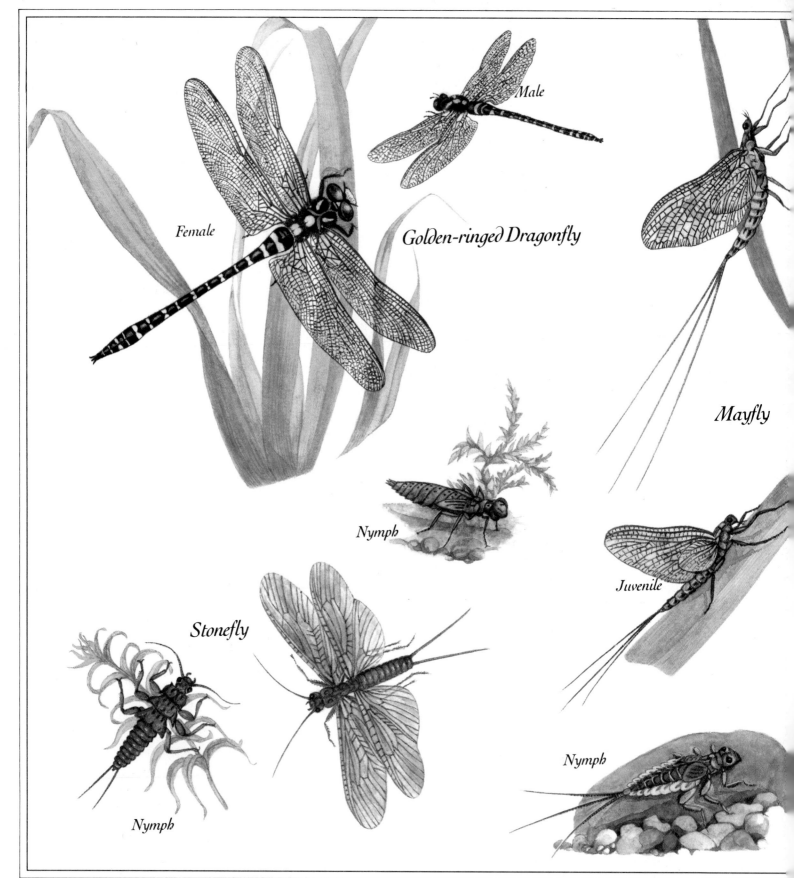

Female

Male

Golden-ringed Dragonfly

Mayfly

Nymph

Juvenile

Stonefly

Nymph

Nymph

GOLDEN-RINGED DRAGONFLY (*Cordulegaster boltonii*) This is the longest-bodied British dragonfly, measuring up to 3⅜″ (86mm) long, with a 4″ (100mm) wingspan. The female's ovipositor – her egg-laying organ – protrudes conspicuously from her abdomen.

STONEFLY (*Perla bipunctata*) This weak flyer, with a 2″ (50mm) wingspan spends most of its adult life hiding among stones at the water's edge. The 1¼″ (30mm) long carnivorous nymph, known as a creeper, crawls among the stones on the beds of fast-flowing rivers.

MAYFLY (*Rhithrogena*) Known to anglers as the March Brown. The winged insect that emerges from the nymph in March is known as the dun, and struggles out of the water to pursue a short life on land. It has one further transformation to an adult spinner which breeds, then dies.

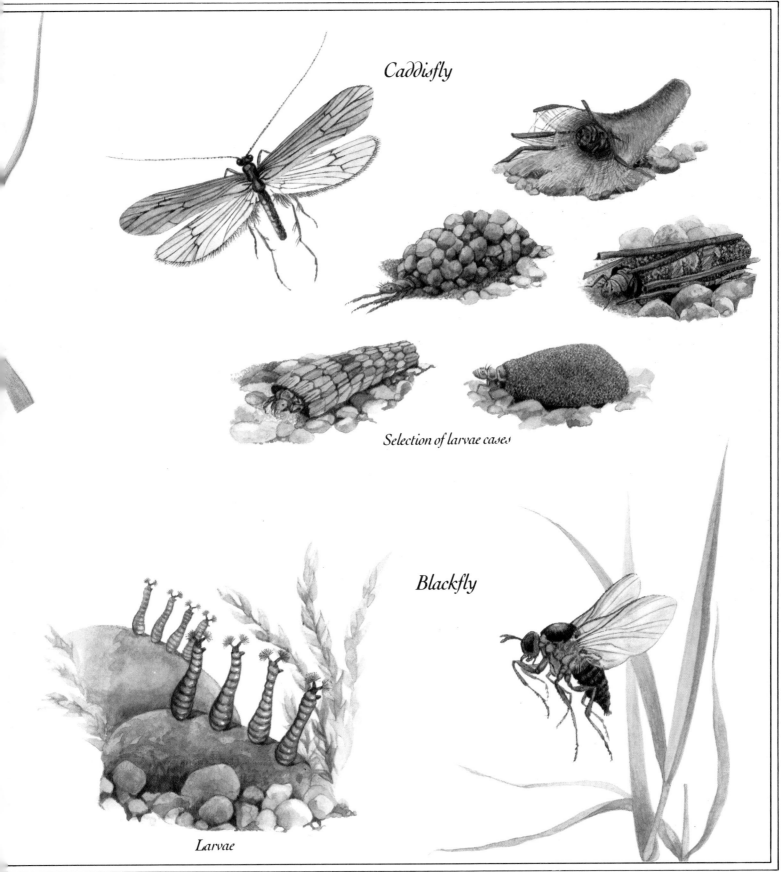

Caddisfly

Selection of larvae cases

Blackfly

Larvae

CADDIS FLY (*Hydropsyche angustipennis*) Most caddis flies are nocturnal, but this species flies in bright sunlight. Each of the 200 species of caddis fly nymph builds a different kind of cylindrical case using sticks, sand, or a web – from which its head emerges to feed.

BLACKFLY (*Simulium*) This is one of the swarming biting flies that pesters waterside visitors especially in early autumn. The ½″ (13mm) larva resists the current by attaching itself to a rock with its tail-hooks. It filters food with filaments on its head.

Dipper

Juvenile

Common Sandpiper

DIPPER *(Cinclus cinclus)* This short-tailed stout 7″ (18cm) bird can walk under water, undaunted by the fastest current, to search for insect larvae and crustaceans. In late March the female lays a batch of white eggs, followed by another in June.

COMMON SANDPIPER *(Actitis hypoleucos)* This summer visitor often nests beside trout streams. The nest is a hollow in the ground lined with grass and dead leaves. The 8″ (20cm) adult feeds on insects, snails and worms. The female lays 4 glossy spotted eggs in May.

Streamside Birds

Grey Wagtail

Male

Female

GREY WAGTAIL (*Motacilla cinera*) Half the length of this colourful 8″ (20cm) bird is taken up by its constantly bobbing tail. The grey wagtail lives close to rushing streams and rivers and is adept at snatching insects from the air as it flies over the water. Breeding begins in April, and two broods may be produced in a year. The female builds a nest of moss and grass in a hole near the water's edge, in which she lays 4-6 russet speckled eggs which she incubates alone for 12 or 13 days. Both parents feed the chicks.

Filmy Fern

Holly Fern

Parsley Fern

Mountain Fern

FILMY FERN *(Hymenophyllum wilsonii)* A delicate plant that grows in a tangled mass on damp boulders. It looks very moss-like and curls up when dry as most mosses do. The frond blades are only one cell thick, apart from the veins, and are quite translucent.

MOUNTAIN FERN *(Thelypteris limbosperma)* In late spring tufts of mountain fern appear on steep banks by streams. The fronds may be 4′ (120cm) long and 10″ (25cm) wide, and wither away in autumn. If crushed or bruised it gives off a pleasant lemon scent.

HOLLY FERN *(Polystichum lonchitis)* The dark green, tough, shiny fronds of this fern are edged with sharp prickles. The fronds grow in spring and summer, and remain green through the winter. They grow in upright tufts to a height of 6-18″ (15-45cm).

PARSLEY FERN *(Cryptogramma crispa)* The dense tufts of this fern closely resemble parsley leaves. The fronds, which grow in spring and wither in autumn, are 3-8″ (7-20cm) long and of two kinds – the outer ones are sterile, and the inner erect ones are fertile.

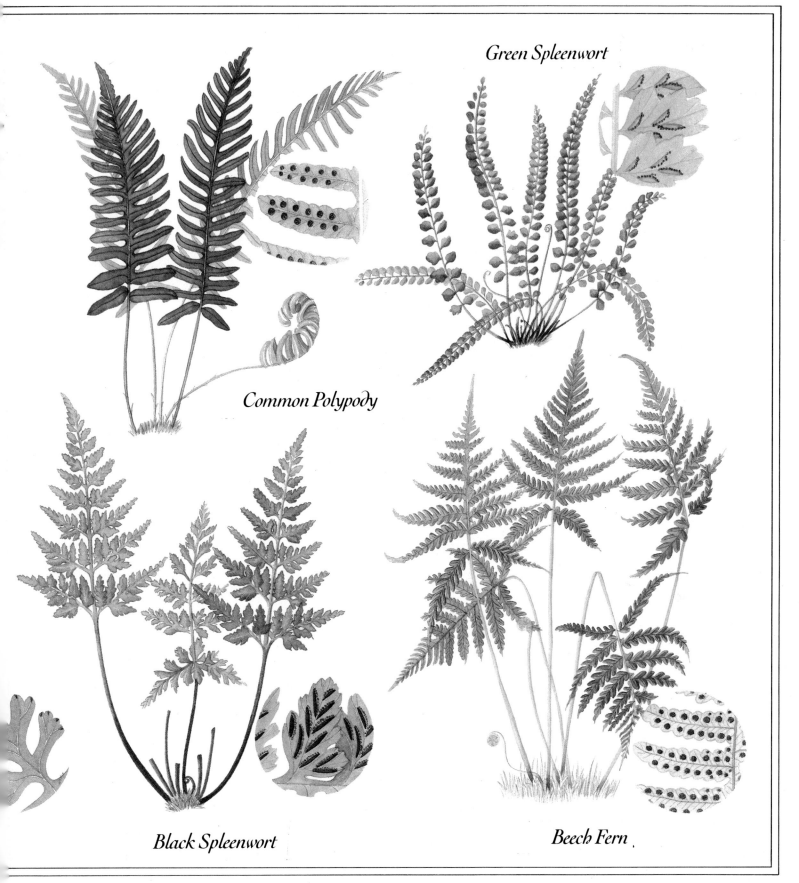

Green Spleenwort

Common Polypody

Black Spleenwort

Beech Fern

COMMON POLYPODY (*Polypodium v lgare*) The 2-30" (5-45cm) fronds of this fern grow on rocks and tree-stumps in summer, and stay green throughout the year. The fronds are flat and oblong or triangular in shape. The long leaf-stalk has no lobes at the base.

BLACK SPLEENWORT (*Asplenium adiantum*) This small tufted fern grows among boulders and in walls. The shiny dark green fronds are 2-12" (5-30cm) long and appear quite late in the year. They are not fully unrolled until mid-summer, and remain green through the winter.

GREEN SPLEENWORT (*Asplenium viride*) Each frond of this wall fern is divided into about 30 pairs of leaflets. These are arranged alternately on the slender green stalks. The fronds grow 1-6" (2-15cm) long, appearing in spring, and withering in early autumn.

BEECH FERN (*Phegopteris connectilis*) A common fern of damp mixed woodlands, that has no special association with beech woods. The 6-18" (15-45cm) fronds grow in late spring, with triangular blades on a very long slender stalk. They die down in autumn.

Salmon

Smolt

Grilse

SALMON *(Salmo salar)* After spending up to 4 years in the Atlantic the salmon makes its way back to its native fresh water birthplace to spawn. For the six or so breeding months it does not feed, and many die. From late November, the female lays her eggs, which hatch in March or April. The young fish, known as parr, stay in fresh water for up to 3 years, and then migrate as smolt to the sea. A grilse is a fish that comes back to spawn after only one year. Others stay longer at sea, and return as very large fish – up to 4′ (120cm) long and 60lb (29kg).

Minnow

Salmon *Parr*

Brown Trout *Parr*

Brown Trout

BROWN TROUT *(Salmo trutta)*
There is great variation in size and colour among trout. Those of upland becks are about 8″ (20cm) long; the pale lake trout grows to 2′ (60cm), while the migratory silver sea trout of inshore waters grows up to 4′ (120cm). All spawn upriver in winter.

MINNOW *(Phoxinus phoxinus)*
Not itself a game fish, the minnow is commonly found in close association with trout and salmon. This slender 4″ (10cm) fish spawns in spring, its small egg-clumps sticking to the gravel and hatching after 5-10 days. Minnows eat shrimps, insects and plants.

IN THE
SCOTTISH HIGHLANDS

Wild and remote, the mountainous country of the Highlands, ranging from the wet grasslands and grouse moors to the craggy peaks, is home to some rare species.

Although grandly picturesque, the Highlands, at first sight, may seem rather empty of wildlife. Closer inspection, however, reveals a fascinating diversity of both plant and animal life. Climate is one key to this diversity, as weather conditions fluctuate widely across the large area which the Highlands occupy.

The basically cold climate, which affects the vegetation so strongly high up in the hills, is markedly milder in coastal areas, even in the far north. Inland the weather is more 'continental', and the hills tend to have less rain but are subject to greater extremes of temperature, and often are very cold. Rainfall can vary dramatically from one side of a mountain mass to the other, and the wetter sides of the mountains are not only more waterlogged but are often sunless and gloomy, as clouds hang over them. The wind is also an important factor in mountainous country. On Ben Nevis, for instance, a wind blowing at 50 miles an hour or more whips across the slopes for more than 200 days in the year. In the lowlands, sea-borne gales lash the coast with even greater ferocity.

Such conditions affect the natural tree line – the height to which trees will grow up the hillside. Because of the gales, trees near the coast may not grow above 200ft (60m) above sea level but, inland, where the wind has lost some of its sting, the same species can be found growing at heights up to 1800ft (550m) on some mountainsides.

In addition to the effects of climate, the varying bedrock (of which there are many kinds) and man's historical and current uses of the land affect the vegetation of both the glens and the slopes above them. These three factors – climate, bedrock and man's usage – have long determined the pattern of natural life in the Highlands.

On the grouse moors, which usually lie above

OUT OF REACH
Large herds of red deer roam the high ground to escape the incessant biting of midges.

SUN WORSHIPPER
The mountain ringlet (above) only flies when the sun shines.

HIGHLAND WILDLIFE
The exciting wilderness of the Highlands is a stronghold for species rarely seen elsewhere in the British Isles, such as the golden eagle, mountain ringlet, alpine lady's mantle and the ptarmigan.

KEY TO FEATURES AND SPECIES
1 *Immature golden eagle*
2 *Snow buntings*
3 *Summit heath*
4 *Late snow*
5 *Grouse moor*
6 *Ptarmigan*
7 *Red deer*
8 *Sheep*
9 *Boggy 'flow'*
10 *Tumbling stream*
11 *Grassland*
12 *Mountain ringlet*
13 *Dipper*
14 *Sandpiper*
15 *Cowberry*
16 *Thrift*
17 *Starry saxifrage*
18 *Alpine lady's mantle*

WHITE-TAILED EAGLE

BUZZARD

GOLDEN EAGLE

LARGE HIGHLAND BIRDS OF PREY

White-tailed sea eagles are characterized by their broad wings – only the adults have white tails. Buzzards have brown and white underparts and short, broad heads. Adult golden eagles are huge, dark and have fingered wing tips. Ospreys have pale heads and black and white underparts.

the sheepwalks, there may be extensive bogs, called 'flows', in addition to the dominant mosaic of old and new heather. Apart from the red grouse, meadow pipits abound here, as do the highly vocal greenshanks which make their virtually untraceable nests both in the young heather and on the flows. Among the moorland heather, berries – such as cowberry and bilberry – are common and provide additional food for the grouse, while wet-loving shrubs such as cranberry lurk in the flows.

ABOVE THE TREES

The deer forests, despite their name, are usually located above the tree line far beyond the sheepwalks and grouse moors, at heights over 2000ft (600m). Here trees are scant, except for a few birch. Heather may be absent, too, and grasses and sedges often cover much of the ground. The red deer would naturally retire to such places to avoid man, but they are also driven this high in summer by the midges which infest much of the Highlands. On well-managed estates, regular culls take place to keep the herd healthy and in balance with the foraging.

Up here you may see a blue hare and sometimes a pine marten, perhaps occupying a lair in open ground. Wild cats, however, tend to remain on the lower wooded slopes. Equally unexpected may be the sight of feral goats, domestic stock which has taken to the wild, though they are more often seen lower down. Small mountain reindeer roam parts of the Cairngorms where their special diet can be found. They were hunted to extinction in the Middle Ages and today's herds were introduced from Lapland some thirty years ago.

Few butterflies take wing in the thin cold

OSPREY

SHORT-TAILED VOLE
(above) This widespread vole is a staple food for many Highland birds and mammals.

CHANGING PLUMAGE
Male ptarmigan in summer (below) and (inset) in winter plumage.

mountain air, but on sunny days the mountain ringlet may be seen fluttering around a patch of boggy grass high above the grouse moors. In Britain, it is found only in the Highlands and the Lake District, and its nearest cousins are in the Alps. Another mountain grass butterfly, the Scotch argus, is less restricted and may be seen on somewhat lower ground.

In areas of extensive soft boggy land, waders come to breed in summer as they do on other moors, while the lively dipper follows the tumbling streams. The ring ouzel, the blackbird of the mountains, is also seen – as it breeds almost exclusively on high ground. The raven and the hooded crow (the northern race of the crow) are both Highland birds, although they also breed on lower ground elsewhere.

The magnificent golden eagle is the bird most associated with the Highlands. Much of the mischief laid at its door by gamekeepers and shepherds is probably the work of foxes, which are not uncommon in highland areas. Nevertheless, continuous persecution, not least by egg collectors, has forced the bird to take sanctuary in the deer forest. Sadly, increasing disturbance by tourists is a threat to its recently improved breeding success. Pairs require an immense area of largely undisturbed ground – up to 30 square miles – for their hunting territory.

LIFE AT THE TOP

High up the mountains, and indeed on the high plateau land too, there is another catalogue of wildlife. Here, far above the last heather, are found alpine plants which grow only or mainly on mountains. If they are also found to the north, in arctic Europe, they are known as arctic-alpines. Mountain azalea and snow gentian are two such species.

In parts of northern Scotland, some typical alpines are also seen down by the sea, but not between coast and mountain. Mountain avens is one such. Conversely, some familiar seashore flowers, such as thrift, are found growing high up in the mountains. Woodland flowers, such as bluebell, campion and violets, are also sometimes seen quite high up, in places where sheep or deer do not graze.

There is a logical explanation for these odd distributions. Capable of surviving a rigorously cold climate, the arctic-alpine and alpine flowers were among the first plants able to colonize the bare open ground at the end of the last Ice Age. Forests of trees later grew on the middle ground, shading them out. When the

YELLOW MOUNTAIN SAXIFRAGE
(above) A bright perennial, this is one of numerous saxifrages found in the Highlands. It grows among rocks or by streams.

NESTING DOTTEREL
(above right) Less than 100 pairs of this charming and remarkably tame plover nest in Britain, mainly in the Highlands. Interestingly, the male incubates the eggs.

PINE MARTEN
(right) This beautiful hunter not only takes mountain hares and black grouse but also has a fondness for fruit. It is at home both on the open hillside and in the forests.

CLOUDBERRIES
(below) Related to the bramble, the attractive autumn fruits of cloudberry are just as edible as blackberries. The white flowered plant grows on peat bogs and moors.

trees were cleared, some of the woodland flowers survived in small pockets.

The tops are also home to some intriguing bird life. One breeding species is the ptarmigan, the grouse of the heights, which retreats to lower ground in winter. The male is unusual in having three coats, the brown of summer and white of winter being separated by a third greyish autumn plumage. The dotterel, a summer visitor, chooses land over 3000ft (900m) to nest, selecting rounded summits or plateaux where strong cross winds will sweep away any snow. The snow bunting, on the other hand, is never far from snow and ice, and tends to choose those craggy tops where snow lies late. Essentially an arctic bird, it is one of Britain's rarest breeding species. Probably fewer than 10 pairs nest each year – all in the Highlands. The fact that birds can flourish at this height shows that life can exist even in the most inhospitable conditions.

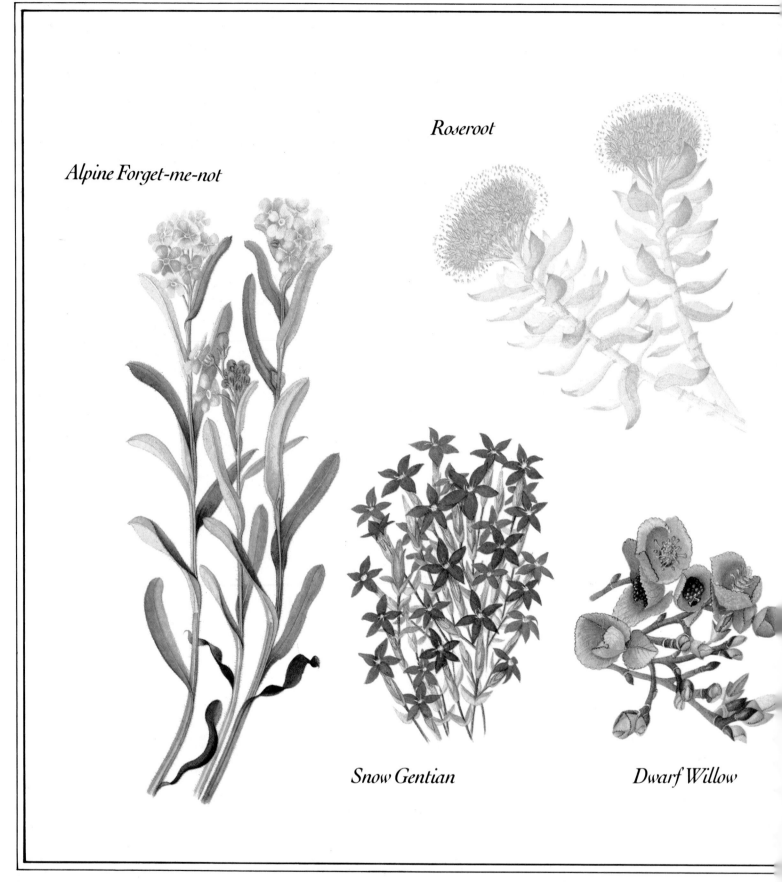

Alpine Forget-me-not

Roseroot

Snow Gentian

Dwarf Willow

ALPINE FORGET-ME-NOT
(Myosotis alpestris) Up to 6″
(15cm) tall, stiff but elegant, this
perennial has scented flowers in July
and August, becoming tiny black
fruit. A true alpine rarity in
Britain – found only on limestone
in Teesdale and Ben Lawers.

SNOW GENTIAN *(Gentiana
nivalis)* An extremely rare annual
alpine, found only on a few rocky
ledges in the eastern Highlands.
It flowers in July and August,
producing single brilliant blue
flowers on 4″ (10cm) unbranched
stems above a tuft of leaves.

ROSEROOT *(Sedum rosea)* Also·
known as Midsummer-men, this
succulent produces fleshy stems with
terminal flower-heads from May to
August, which become dense
clusters of orange fruits. It is quite
common on mountain ledges and
sea cliffs from Wales northwards.

DWARF WILLOW *(Salix herbacea)*
Also known as least willow, this
shrub grows to barely more than 2″
(5cm) tall. It is a prostrate plant
which creeps over the ground in
large patches favouring sheltered
mountain ledges in the north. The
catkins appear in June.

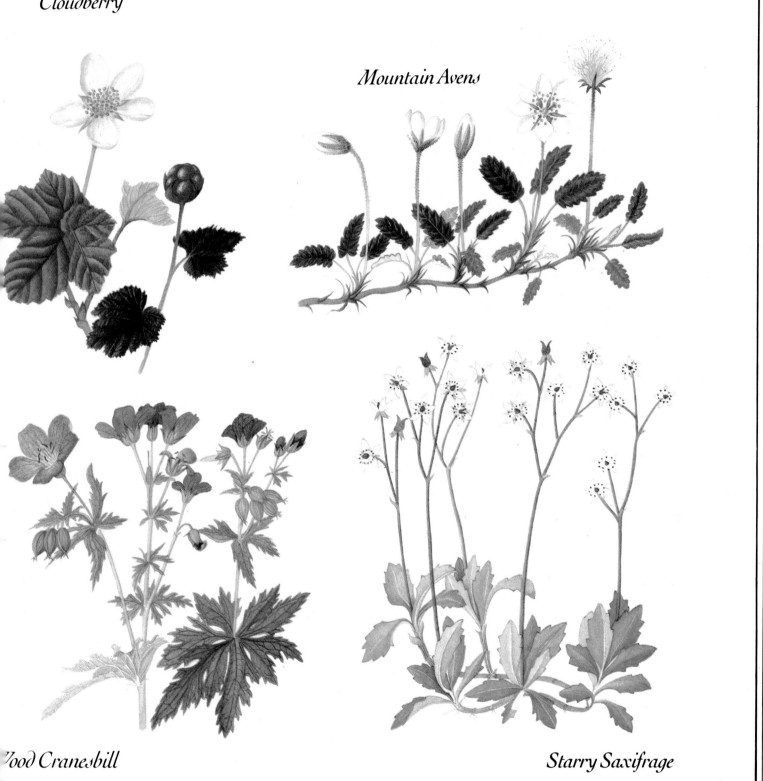

Cloudberry

Mountain Avens

Wood Cranesbill

Starry Saxifrage

CLOUDBERRY *(Rubus chamaemorus)* Up to 7″ (18cm) high, this perennial creeps in loose patches among heather in damp areas on moors and hills. It has solitary white flowers, and orange raspberry-like fruits. Found in the far north of Britain.

WOOD CRANESBILL *(Geranium sylvaticum)* A native of Scotland, where it embellishes meadows, damp woods and mountain ledges with its flowers from May to July, which become the characteristic long pointed fruit (hence cranesbill) on 28″ (70cm) stems.

MOUNTAIN AVENS *(Dryas octopetala)* A 4″ (10cm) creeping plant with 1″ (2.5cm) flowers in May and June, which become feathery clematis-like seedheads. It grows on limestone, high up on rocky ledges from Snowdonia northwards, and in Ireland.

STARRY SAXIFRAGE *(Saxifraga stellaris)* One of the commonest highland saxifrages, this delicately formed 3″ (7cm) plant flowers from June onwards in northern mountains, where it favours wet spots near streams and boggy places.

Golden Eagle

Dotterel

Male in winter

GOLDEN EAGLE *(Aquila chrysaetos)* Between 250 and 300 pairs of this magnificent bird inhabit the Scottish highlands. They are 34″ (85cm) long, with a 7′ (2m) wingspan, and feed on hares, grouse and even sick lambs. They lay 2 eggs in a large nest.

DOTTEREL *(Charadrius morinellus)* A rare breeding bird of Scottish mountains, which lays its 3 mottled eggs on the ground, on broad whaleback ridges and stony barren plateaux. It is a summer visitor, 8½″ (21cm) long, and feeds on insects.

PTARMIGAN *(Lagopus mutus)* An inhabitant of high mountaintops, mostly above the heather grouse moors, this 13″ (33cm) bird lays up to 12 eggs on the ground among short vegetation or stones. It eats shoots, leaves, berries and seeds. It turns white in winter.

Snow Bunting

Greenshank

Ptarmigan

Male in summer

SNOW BUNTING *(Plectrophenax nivalis)* A tame little 6½" (16.5cm) bird which inhabits mountaintops in summer, and beaches in winter, searching for insects and seeds. It lays 4-6 blotched pale blue eggs in a cup-like nest of moss and grass in late May.

GREENSHANK *(Tringa nebularia)* An elegant 12" (30cm) wader, which visits northern moors in summer to lay its 4 beautifully mottled eggs on the ground. In winter it frequents estuaries and marshland, where it feeds on worms, molluscs and fish, as well as insects.

Pine Marten

Blue Hare

Winter Coat

PINE MARTEN (*Martes martes*)
27″ (69cm) from nose to tail, this
elusive and rare creature inhabits
woods and open ground in the far
north. It is an agile, nocturnal
hunter of birds, squirrels and voles,
which it supplements with beetles,
berries and eggs.

BLUE HARE (*Lepus timidus*)
Grey-brown, turning white in
winter, the blue, or mountain hare,
is found on heather moors and high
ground in the north. Smaller and
with shorter ears than the brown
hare, it grows up to 24″ (60cm)
long. It feeds on grasses and shrubs.

Red Deer

RED DEER *(Cervus elaphus)*
Magnificent creatures in their
rutting finery in early autumn,
when the crags resound with their
bellowing courting-cry, red deer
stags stand 48″ (120cm) tall at the
shoulder, and weigh 400lb (180kg).
Their antlers which are grown
annually and shed in early summer,
weigh 20lb (9kg), and are used as a
weapon against rivals to assert
superiority. Generally, stags and
hinds live in separate groups in
open deciduous woods and moors.
A single white-spotted calf is
born in May or June.

IN THE
WELSH HILLS

The late return of spring unlocks the snow-bound Welsh hills to reveal rare flowers and ferns, unexpected butterflies, dashing birds of prey and elusive mammals, such as the polecat.

Amid the Welsh hills winters are long and bleak. Snow and frost take an early grip and last well into the spring. Peaks are white, and upland lakes are locked beneath thick, glassy ice. The scenery is spectacular, but the conditions are harsh for wildlife and few wild creatures spend the winter on the hills. Domestic stock, too, find the going tough and many sheep succumb to the extremes of winter. All too often at lambing time, a late fall of snow or long spell of stormy weather will take its toll of both lambs and ewes.

Few living things benefit from this severity, but the raven appears more successful than most. This great black crow of the hills nests early, no matter how harsh the weather. Pairs show interest in breeding from January and will

have laid by late March. By the time the young hatch there will be an abundance of food in the form of dead sheep and other carrion.

Spring sees the drab brown of the upper slopes grudgingly turn to green. Lower down, the orange-brown of dead bracken takes a long time to change as the new, vivid green fronds slowly uncurl. In some areas, now declining and increasingly precious, the moors remain dark brown with a thick carpet of heather which only blooms in late summer, tinging the slopes with pink.

With the warmer weather, meadow pipits return to the moors, pursued by merlins – rare and dashing falcons which feed on small birds. On the rushing streams in the small side valleys, the first spring migrants are the grey wagtails and dippers, moving up from the larger lowland rivers where they have spent the winter. Common sandpipers are later arrivals. Having flown back from Africa, they are the first of the true summer migrants from overseas.

Down in the little valleys, cowslips, primroses and celandines greet the increased warmth, while brimstone butterflies flicker along the lanes and woodland edges. Later, orange tip butterflies look for lady's smock on damp verges and in the wet meadows where early purple orchids flower.

SCREE LIFE

At the foot of the slope there may be a patch of larch or spruce, or one of the fragments of oakwood still left on the Welsh hills. Such woodland often merges into bracken slopes and areas of very rough ground, where big, loose boulders form block scree, matted with luxuriant green mosses and lichens. In sheltered cracks, where sheep cannot reach, grow ferns, including, in isolated places, the parsley fern and holly fern. On a few screes in Snowdonia, juniper – once abundant – spreads in mats across the blocks. Where the screes are composed of smaller stones there will be flowers, including rarities such as mossy and starry saxifrage, alpine meadow-rue and alpine enchanter's nightshade.

Where the slopes level out there may be tracts

MALE WHINCHAT
(left) Flying in from its winter quarters south of the Sahara, the whinchat arrives in the Welsh hills in late April. It is common on bracken-covered hillsides and in young forestry plantations where it can find its two nesting requirements – tussocky grass and a prominent song post. Once frequent in southern and eastern England, it is now mainly found in the hills below the high moorland.

THE HARDY LIFE OF THE HILLS

Feeding chiefly on carrion in winter, the raven haunts the hills throughout the year, breeding early to take advantage of the mortality at lambing time. The red kite, too, is resident in the hills, nesting in the valley-side oakwoods and feeding on prey ranging from sheep carrion to small mammals, birds and frogs. Both the merlin and its principal prey, the meadow pipit, return from lower ground in spring to breed in the hills, while the insect-eating ring ouzel and wheatear are migrants from Africa, arriving to nest in April. On the lower slopes the polecat hunts mice, voles and frogs. The frogs themselves may lay their spawn in the boggy streamside. Caterpillars of the antler moth feed on grasses and rushes and may devastate large areas of upland grazing. The trees and flowers of the hills often grow in rocky crevices out of reach of grazing sheep and feral goats.

KEY TO THE SPECIES
 1 *Red kite*
 2 *Aspen*
 3 *Raven*
 4 *Rowan*
 5 *Merlin*
 6 *Sheep*
 7 *Juniper*
 8 *Meadow pipit*
 9 *Ring ouzel*
10 *Feral goat*
11 *Wheatear*
12 *Lichen*
13 *Golden saxifrage*
14 *Moss campion*
15 *Parsley fern*
16 *Mesh-web spider*
17 *Polecat*
18 *Antler moth*
19 *Short-tailed vole*
20 *Bilberry*
21 *Common frog*

of purple heather moorland, but where it has been burnt too often and then overgrazed, carpets of bilberry and sorrels will colour large areas brilliant crimson.

BIRDS OF THE SLOPES

Rock is usually not far from the surface and frequently bursts through the thin, poor soil. Such outcrops are popular perches for wheatears – busy, bright little birds which flit from rock to rock flashing the pure white of their rump and tail and calling sharply. On bigger rocks and crags, or in deep, rocky gullies with thick heather below and the odd rowan or hawthorn growing out from the side, there may be ring ouzels too.

Slopes which are covered with heather and bracken and scattered with scrubby hawthorn and tall larches are the favourite haunt of nesting whinchats. Tree pipits are also commonly seen as they parachute down to the bush tops during their early summer song flights. The familiar call of the cuckoo also resounds among the hills.

There may be more exciting finds on these slopes. A black grouse might be flushed from the bracken, making off in low, fast flight across the valley, beautiful in blue-black and white. Old stick nests of carrion crows, which are also common in the hills, are appropriated by pairs of merlins, or even long-eared owls where the scrub is dense.

From the edge of an old, remote wood a foraging polecat may venture out in search of

PEREGRINE AT NEST
Though still at risk from egg collectors and rogue falconers, the peregrine is returning to breed on ancestral crags in the Welsh hills.

PARSLEY FERN
(below) This attractive plant of the mountains grows both on stone walls and on the loose rock screes where drainage is good.

short-tailed voles on the more open slopes. Less likely to be encountered, and very much rarer, is the pine marten whose dwindling population is still holding on in the face of increased disturbance.

Huge areas of the lower slopes, and increasingly the higher ground too, are devoted to growing conifers. The new plantations provide a home for whinchats, grasshopper warblers and meadow pipits, but are rarely occupied by short-eared owls or hen harriers, species which take readily to similar plantations in Scotland. The harriers like the heather moors, which survive

SMALL PEARL-BORDERED FRITILLARY
(left) Seen here on the purple flowers of bugle, this handsome butterfly is mainly a woodland species but can often be seen on moorlands — it has a fondness for heather — and high up on mountain slopes.

WARY POLECAT
(below) The farming country of the Welsh hills and valleys is the polecat's stronghold. Once ruthlessly trapped for its fur, the population is now recovering and spreading slowly into England. Mainly nocturnal, this fearsome hunter is rarely seen but might be glimpsed on the lower hill slopes.

only where they are managed for grouse; merlins too, prefer the tall heather but will hunt in the plantations so long as some open ground remains.

Where the land is flatter and the bobbing white heads of bog cotton mark out the swampy, marshy ground, there may be a special butterfly of the hills — the large heath.

In Snowdonia and one or two places elsewhere, the undulating, extensive plateau of sheepwalk or heather moorland, so characteristic of mid Wales, is replaced by higher, bolder countryside. Among the rocks, rowans and aspens may grow from crannies where they are inaccessible to sheep — the rowan seeds perhaps deposited in the droppings of a ring ouzel. High on these mountains there are feral goats — not true wild animals but domestic goats gone wild, they can be found from Cader Idris in the west to Snowdon in the north but they are becoming an increasingly rare sight as their numbers are declining.

Apart from ravens searching for carrion, buzzards may be seen high above the hills, wheeling for minutes on end, searching the ground below for prey such as voles, small rabbits and even

BRIGHT WELSH POPPIES
Found in damp, rocky places, this plant grows in Wales, Ireland and south west England.

worms. Many hunt by sitting quietly on a stump or post, watching carefully for a careless mole to break the surface or a mouse venturing unwisely into the open.

In mid Wales, the uplands are hunted by the splendid red kite — once nearly wiped out and still, at barely 40 pairs, one of our rarest birds of prey. Yet the merlin, in Wales, is now rarer still. In a much healthier state in the Welsh hills is the peregrine, which may be seen soaring high over the peaks or flashing out of sight across a moor.

On the very high tops, it is bleak, wild and, above all, wet. If the summit is rounded and smooth, there could be golden plovers breeding. In spring, a party of dotterels may stop a day or two on their way north, although occasionally a few have stayed to breed. Meadow pipits and skylarks reach nearly to the top, but nowhere in Wales is quite high enough to have the special birds of the Scottish peaks — ptarmigans, golden eagles or breeding snow buntings. But there are other, more familiar birds — swifts everywhere in summer, sweeping the skies for insect prey; and, right to the very top of Snowdon, gulls will scavenge for the scraps left by tourists.

Much less evident are the rare plants of the high tops — alpine woodsia, mountain avens, Snowdon lily, hoary whitlow-grass, alpine cinquefoil and others — all remarkable little gems well worth the climb and the close searching.

Mossy Saxifrage

Alpine Cinquefoil

Snowdon Lily

Northern Rockcress

MOSSY SAXIFRAGE *(Saxifraga hypnoides)* Forming moss-like clumps, or mats of prostrate stems, this rare perennial grows on ledges and stony slopes of limestone mountains. The erect 2-8″ (5-20cm) flowering stems bear 1-5 white, five-petalled blooms from May to July.

SNOWDON LILY *(Lloydia serotina)* A slender perennial up to 6″ (15cm) tall, this rare lily is a protected species growing on precarious rock ledges throughout Snowdonia. Each plant has 2-4 fine leaves and produces 1 or 2 white, purple-veined flowers in June.

ALPINE CINQUEFOIL *(Potentilla crantzii)* Growing on ledges and in crevices in rocks where it is safe from grazing animals, this is a fairly erect plant 2-10″ (5-25cm) high, flowering June to July. It is found only locally on limestone mountains from N. Wales to Scotland.

NORTHERN ROCKCRESS *(Cardaminopsis petraea)* An early colonist of the bare, rocky slopes of high, limestone mountains, its flowering stems 4-10″ (10-25cm) arise from a basal whorl of leaves – the flowers open from June to August.

Mountain Sorrel

Crowberry

Northern Bedstraw

NORTHERN BEDSTRAW
(Galium boreale) Distinguished
from other bedstraws by three veins
on the rough-edged leaves, this
8-18″ (20-45cm) plant can be quite
common on rocky mountain slopes.
After flowering in July and August,
fruits with hooked bristles appear.

MOUNTAIN SORREL *(Oxyria
digyna)* A characteristic plant of
damp mountain flushes, this rare
2-12″ (5-30cm) perennial has fleshy,
kidney-shaped leaves and bears
red-edged, greenish flowers in
July and August. It requires a
light, open aspect.

CROWBERRY *(Empetrum
nigrum)* This is a low, 6-18″
(15-45cm) spreading, heather-like
shrub which grows on acid, peaty
soil often in very harsh conditions.
It produces small, pink flowers with
six petals in May and June and
round, black berries July-September.

Female

Juvenile

Merlin

Male

Raven

MERLIN *(Falco columbarius)*
These rare, small 10½-13″
(26-33cm) falcons fly low over open
country after small birds, chattering
a shrill 'quik-ik-ik'. 3-5 buff,
heavily red-brown blotched eggs
are laid among the heather
in May.

RAVEN *(Corvus corax)* The largest
member of the crow family, the
25″ (64cm) raven has a very
impressive 4′ (1.2m) wingspan. It
lives in bleak mountains, where its
harsh, deep 'kronk' can be heard
as it soars high in the sky. Its
diet consists of carrion, plant
material and live prey – insects,
young birds and small animals.
Breeding often as early as February,
ravens choose remote sites and
make a deep twiggy nest thickly
lined with wool and moss. 4-6 pale
green or blue eggs with dark
markings are laid from March.

Hillside Birds

Red Kite

Male

Chough

CHOUGH (*Pyrrhocorax pyrrhocorax*) A member of the crow family, the 15″ (38cm) chough is a social bird with a strong, soaring acrobatic flight. Juveniles are not as glossy as the adults and have orange-yellow bills. The chough feeds on flat, short-tufted pastures digging up insects with its long, curved beak. Its call is a range of shrill and tuneless notes. Territorial when breeding, nests are well hidden in caves or old mine shafts in hills and cliffs near the sea. 3-6 white eggs tinted with green and blotched with brown are laid April-May.

RED KITE (*Milvus milvus*) Giving its name to the kite we fly, this rare and protected 24″ (61cm) bird of prey is easily identified in its effortless flight by a deeply-forked tail, narrow wings sharply bent back and white patches on the underwings. The red kite feeds on rabbits, birds, insects and some carrion and calls a shrill, mewing 'weeoo-weeoo-weeoo'. It builds a nest of sticks and earth, often on an abandoned bird's nest, high in the trees in the wooded valleys of central Wales, and lays 2-3 white eggs with red-brown speckles in April or May.

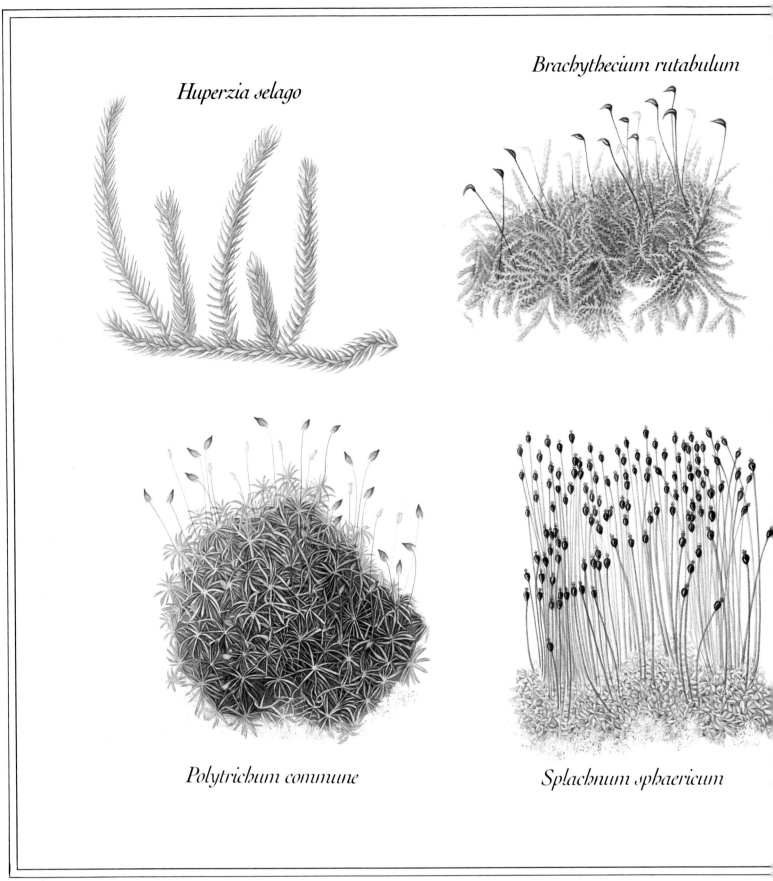

Huperzia selago

Brachythecium rutabulum

Polytrichum commune

Splachnum sphaericum

FIR CLUBMOSS *(Huperzia selago)*
Clubmosses are more highly developed than mosses and more closely related to ferns. This species forms erect 2-10″ (5-25cm) clumps on the open, drier areas of the mountainsides. Small capsules in the leaf axils contain spores.

POLYTRICHUM COMMUNE An easily identified moss which forms large mounds in wet mountain grassland and peaty bogs. The individual plants can reach 16″ (41cm). Female plants have four-sided capsules on long stalks, males are topped by pink, flower-like cups.

BRACHYTHECIUM RUTABULUM A bright glossy green creeping moss ¾″ (2cm) tall, growing in loose carpets on trees, rocks and walls in wet areas. The leaves are sharply pointed and finely toothed. Spore capsules are borne on red stalks just over 1″ (3cm) high in winter.

SPLACHNUM SPHAERICUM
This is an upland moss of wet pastures in mountainous areas where it grows in tufts on sheep's dung. The shoots are short, up to 1½″ (4cm), with numerous capsules each borne on a reddish-yellow stalk of 3″ (8cm) – these appear in summer

Aulacomnium androgynum

Orthotrichum stramineum

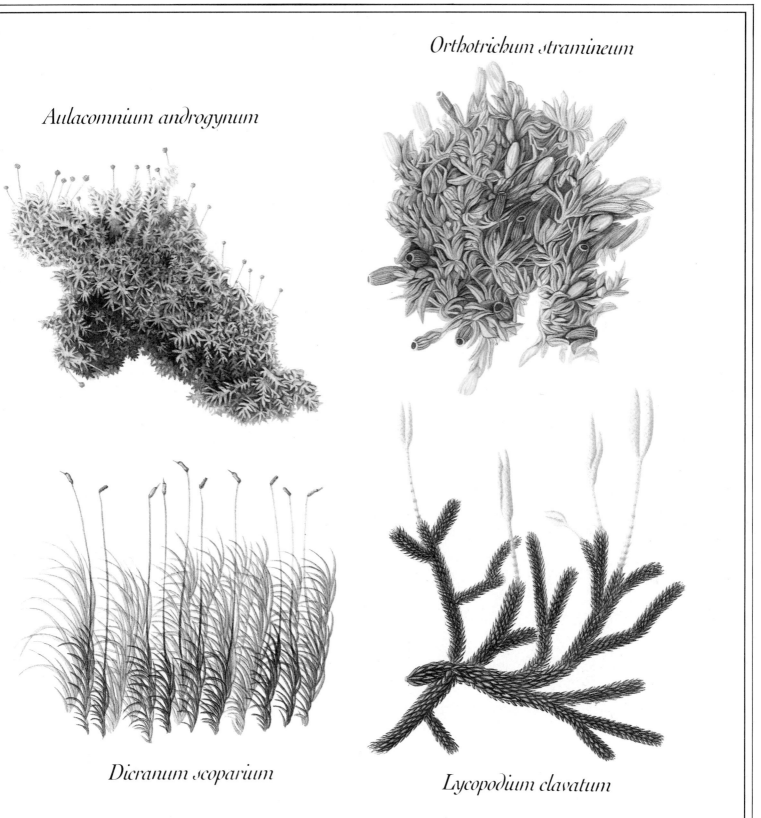

Dicranum scoparium

Lycopodium clavatum

AULACOMNIUM ANDROGYNUM
An unusual bright green moss which has clusters of 'gemmae' – bud-like structures which detach and grow into new plants – borne on the end of stalks. 1-1½" (2.5-4cm) tall, it is commonly found on rotten wood or dry peat.

DICRANUM SCOPARIUM
A sturdy moss growing in long, stringy, dull green matts in rocky crevices, at the base of trees and on heaths. The leaves are usually all curled in one direction and small male plants are found between female plants.

ORTHOTRICHUM STRAMINEUM
A tiny moss growing in low yellow-green clumps less than 1" (2cm) high on the trunks and branches of oak, ash and rowan trees in open woodland. Rigid yellow-brown capsules are set on short stalks close to the leaves.

STAGSHORN CLUBMOSS
(*Lycopodium clavatum*) So-called because of the paired 'cones' which release clouds of bright yellow spores in summer, this is a common plant of upland moors. The spreading, much-branched stems reach 40" (100cm).

THE COAST AND OPEN SEA

Britain's coastline is thousands of miles long, and immensely varied. In some places, towering cliffs and jagged rocks provide a mighty bulwark against the huge winter seas that crash against the coast. At other sites waves lap gently upon sandy beaches in sheltered coves, or great Atlantic waves roll upon a long golden strand. Each of these different habitats harbours its own range and individual species of wildlife uniquely adapted to life by the sea.

Coastal habitats have perhaps been less changed by human activity over the centuries than either upland or lowland habitats, and they owe their character largely to natural forces. The shape of the coast reflects the geological structure and the shape of the land behind, and the way by which rainwater, the sea and coastal winds have altered natural features.

At hundreds of places all around the coast, rugged headlands thrust out into the sea, bearing the full brunt of the stormy seas. For centuries the tough rock, of which these headlands are made, has withstood the relentless battering of the waves. And at their tip great gaunt cliffs often stand, wet with spray, while the weaker rocks either side are gouged out to form coves and bays. Eventually, the headland cliffs will crumble away, but in the meantime they form a fascinating habitat, often supporting a unique community of plants and seabirds, and attracting many other migrant birds making their first landfall after a long journey from as far away as Africa or Scandinavia.

In the turbulent seas around the headland, strong currents swirl, stirring rich nutrients up from the sea bed, providing sustenance for countless billions of plankton which, in turn, provide food for many marine fish. The birds which rest upon the headland cliffs are frequently fish eaters, exploiting the marine life which flourishes in the sea below. From low down at the foot of the cliffs, where lichens take nutrients from the rain and sea spray, to high on the cliff face where pockets of soil support plants able to tolerate salty conditions, there is a surprisingly large wildlife community. Even at the top of a blustery headland the short turf,

cropped by rabbits, often encourages the growth of wild flowers and attracts visiting butterflies.

Much of Britain's rugged North and West coast, whether headland or bay, is rocky and jagged, for the savage power of the Atlantic has torn from the cliff even the toughest of rocks. Here boulders and rocks lie strewn along the shore at the bottom of the cliff and out in the sea. It is a harsh environment, a surface of bare, ragged rocks, battered constantly by waves, sprayed with salt water, alternately submerged and desiccated by the sun's rays. Yet many hardy species of wildlife have become adapted to this exacting habitat, and make the most of the nutrients provided by the sea. All kinds of creatures and seaweeds cling to the rocks and survive the pounding of the waves.

Around much of Britain's South and East coast, however, and in between the rocks, sandy beaches lie like ribbons of gold along the shore, softening the endless crashing of waves. The sand may have been washed down to the sea by rivers when the great glaciers of the Ice Age melted, or the sea may have pounded the rocks, that once formed the cliffs, to sand. But whatever its origins, sand piles up into beaches wherever the coast is sheltered from the power of the sea.

No natural feature or habitat is permanent, but the beach is more unstable than most, and changes almost daily, as the sea scours away sand from one place and deposits it in another. Yet many kinds of small sea creatures thrive in this changeable habitat and provide ample food for birds which forage along the shore, drawn to the rich pickings among the lines of rotting seaweed and other refuse from the sea.

Out in the open sea beyond the coast, seabirds wheel and dive over the waves. Always moving, as gusts and eddies of wind send shivers across the continually rolling surface, and tides raise and lower the water, while currents drift to and fro, the open sea, at the surface, has many moods. Beneath the surface the marine world is equally active, busy with creatures and plants which, like their land based relatives, depend upon each other and form part of a complex environment.

AROUND THE HEADLAND

**Exposed and towering above the sea, headlands
provide excellent natural observatories from which to study the hardy and
adaptable wildlife which thrives on and around them.**

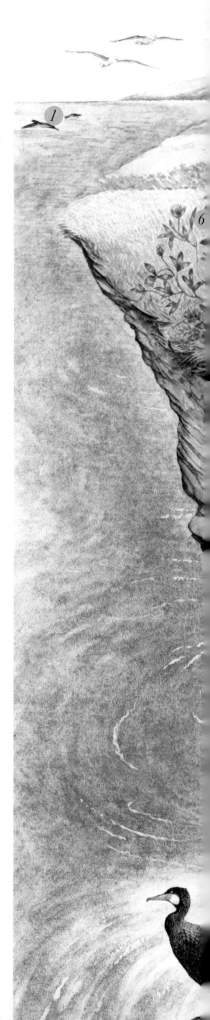

Jutting out into the sea, assaulted by wind and wave, headlands are usually wild, weather-torn places. Yet they are surprisingly rich in plants and wildlife, many species finding a niche between the extremes of sea level and the windblown cliff top.

At the foot of the headland cliff, regularly doused by the lashing spray, there is little if any soil. Rooted plants cannot grow here, but the rock face may be covered with some rather special plants called lichens. Lichens lack roots, and gain nutrients directly from the spray or rain falling on them. Lichens can also be found inland, of course, on walls, roofs, tree trunks and branches, some-times growing profusely, and many different kinds and colours can be seen. Here at the foot of the headland, however, the seashore lichens zone themselves up from the tide mark in three bands, coloured black, orange and (at the top) grey. These bands can be very noticeable if the headland rock

is hard. Chalk, however, is too soft to carry them.

Above the lichen zones, pockets of soil collect in cracks and crevices in the rock. These pockets are within reach of the spray, and rooted plants must be able to cope with salty conditions. One of the plants often seen is rock samphire – it has fleshy stems and leaves, as do many plants found growing in salt marshes. It is interesting that this plump fleshiness is also typical of cacti and other plants living in very dry surroundings. In fact, both cacti and these salt habitat plants face the same problem – they have to control the loss of fresh water from their cells, and their fleshiness is a parallel adaptation.

Further up, and out of reach of all but storm-tossed spray, the cliff may become a blaze of colour at certain times of year. In early summer, the pink cushions of thrift or sea pink may be common, together with white cascades of sea campion. Indeed, the cliff may look rather like a

YOUNG RABBITS
(left) Young rabbits are a common sight in the spring and early summer, gambolling on the fine turf close to their burrows.

THE HEADLAND HABITAT
Although grazing rabbits and strong winds keep the vegetation short, the top of the headland attracts butterflies such as the migrant clouded yellow, large skippers and colonies of small blues whose caterpillars depend on kidney vetch. Kittiwakes nest in small niches in the cliff, guillemots lay their single eggs on wider ledges while cormorants occupy broad ledges with their large nests. Lichens and flowers add bright splashes of colour to the cliff face.

KEY TO THE SPECIES
1 *Common dolphins*	10 *Rabbits*
2 *Gorse*	11 *Kittiwake on nest*
3 *Lovage*	12 *Manured roost*
4 *Swallow*	13 *Tree mallow*
5 *Large skipper*	14 *Guillemot*
6 *Clouded yellow*	15 *Lichens*
7 *Heath ·*	16 *Thrift*
8 *Kidney vetch*	17 *Cormorants*
9 *Small blues*	18 *Sea campion*

well stocked rock garden. The plants growing will, of course, reflect where you are on the coast – the South-west is much milder than the North-east, and every headland has two sides, one much more exposed to the prevailing weather than the other.

A PROFUSION OF FLOWERS

Elsewhere on the cliff, conditions may be very different. The soil below favourite gull roosts may be deep but probably over-rich. The result is not usually an extraordinary profusion of flowers in these places, but sturdy growths of leafier rank plants which often shade out the colourful flowers. Even so, on some Cornish headlands particularly, the colourful tree mallow can be seen growing from these fertile pockets of soil.

The top of the headland is a blustery habitat. As a result, any trees or woody shrubs that do root are severely wind pruned into contorted shapes. Nevertheless, although windy, the climate may be mild as well as wet, especially on western coasts. This brings surprises, for here, in spring, bluebells and perhaps primroses flower right out in the open. Inland, they restrict themselves to the woodland floor, where the trees protect them from biting cold winds, and conditions are often mild and damp. On western headlands, another speciality is spring squill, a delightful flower.

The mild climate can also encourage exotic plants – the hottentot fig grows on some headlands in the South-west. The plant is South African in origin, but can be grown hereabouts in gardens, and has escaped to flourish in the wild.

Sometimes the top of the headland is covered with fine, short-grazed turf, kept down by rabbits, and, in some places, sheep. Even without grazing, the persistent breeze tends to keep the flowers dwarfed. In parts of the South-west and other

OYSTERCATCHERS
(above) The evocative, piping call of the oystercatcher is a common sound on seashores. These waders hunt through the seaweed for mussels and cockles.

CORMORANT AND SHAG
The shag is smaller and darker than the cormorant which it resembles, and in summer it has a distinctive tufted head crest. In winter, the cormorant loses its white thigh patch.

areas, ground hugging heath grows on headlands, with local heathers and gorse pressed into a mat by the wind. Apart from producing dwarfed plants, the unusual conditions of headlands have other effects: the kidney vetch, for example, which often grows here, frequently has crimson-purple flowers; inland they are usually yellow or orange.

Some of these plants attract butterflies. Small blue butterflies lay their eggs on the kidney vetch, while the large skipper is also often seen among the longer grasses of the headland. Some coastal butterflies are very localized – the glanville fritillary relies on sea plantain, but although this plant can be found in many coastal areas on cliffs and headlands, the butterfly is restricted to really warm sunspots on the south coast of the Isle of Wight. It is one of our rarest butterflies.

The resident birds can also be rather specialized, each species choosing particular places on the headland to nest: kittiwakes and guillemots breed on the precipice. The guillemot does not even bother to build a nest, but lays unusually elongated eggs which do not easily roll off the cliff ledge. Rock pipits also choose the cliffs of headlands for their nests, while the rock dove nests in sea cliffs in western Scotland. The rock dove is the ancestor of the familiar town pigeon and has similar plumage, with iridescent neck, two dark wing bars and a white rump. Oystercatchers can often be seen on

fly along the coastline. Birds can see the protruding headland from far out to sea, and home in on it. Many make it their first landfall, resting and feeding on the headland after their long journey across the sea.

But migrants are not the only excitement for the headland birdwatcher, for really rare vagrants are also recorded at these vantage points. These are birds that have been forced far from their usual migration routes by bad weather. One such is the red-flanked bluetail, blown by storms from Siberia to capes on the east coast.

LONG DISTANCE BUTTERFLIES

Migrant butterflies, including red admirals and clouded yellows, often turn up, and the painted lady is another frequent visitor, arriving here after a long journey from North Africa. The splendid Camberwell beauty is a rare visitor, occasionally crossing the North Sea from Scandinavia. In some years the death's head hawk-moth crosses from Europe in large numbers, as do the striped and

the rocks at the foot of the cliff. They take mussels and other shellfish and either hammer open the shells or shear through the muscle of the shellfish with a quick stab of the bill, according to the technique taught them by their parents. In winter, the purple sandpiper is another bird seen feeding busily at low tide among the rocks and pools at the foot of the cliff.

Headlands are particularly noted for their migrant birdlife and are regularly visited by birdwatchers, hoping to catch a glimpse of a storm-driven rarity or see migrating flocks as they

FLOWERING THRIFT
(right) Rounded clumps of thrift – also known as sea pink – hug the ground. This form of growth not only protects them from strong winds but also prevents soil erosion and keeps their roots moist. On cliff tops thrift gives the turf a springy feel.

convolvulus hawk-moths. But the prize sighting must be that of the monarch butterfly; individuals are sometimes seen along western coasts, blown here, almost unbelievably, right across the Atlantic by storms. Their true migration route is between Canada and Mexico.

Headlands also make excellent vantage points for observing whales, dolphins and porpoises, which can be seen offshore. But the basking shark, another denizen of the open ocean, and the world's second largest fish – up to 30 ft (9 m) long – might come close inshore. Where the water is deep enough this harmless giant will sometimes approach the foot of the headland, scratching its belly on the rocks below your feet.

PAINTED LADY
A painted lady feeding on rock sea lavender. These strong-flying butterflies cannot survive British winters but are frequent visitors, migrating here from Africa. They each patrol their own territory, returning time and again to the same spot.

Small Blue

Camberwell Beauty

Clouded Yellow

Monarch

SMALL BLUE *(Cupido minimus)*
This tiny butterfly can be seen on the wing in May and June. It favours grassy places and sand dunes in the south of England and Wales. Its caterpillars feed on kidney vetch which grows in limy soil, and it overwinters as a larva.

CAMBERWELL BEAUTY *(Nymphalis antiopa)* This big, handsome migrant can sometimes be seen in the south and east of England. It likes sunny, open grasslands dotted with trees. The caterpillar eats willow, birch and elm leaves. It hibernates as an adult.

MONARCH *(Danaus plexippus)*
This spectacularly large migrant butterfly is a rare late summer or autumn visitor blown here from North America. There the caterpillar feeds on milkweed, from which it extracts a poisonous deterrent to would-be predators.

CLOUDED YELLOW *(Colias croceus)* In spring this lovely species moves north from Spain and Africa, sometimes crossing into Britain in large numbers, where it frequents chalk grassland until late autumn. It overwinters as a larva; the caterpillar feeds on clover.

Death's Head Hawk-moth

Glanville Fritillary

Painted Lady

Large Skipper

DEATH'S HEAD HAWK-MOTH (Acherontia atropos) The grim name of this very big moth refers to the skull-like mark on its back. It is a regular migrant from Africa, and is on the wing from May to September. The caterpillars feed on potato leaves; the moths raid bee-hives.

PAINTED LADY (Cynthia cardui) A large butterfly, strong and fast on the wing, which inhabits sunny open places and gardens, where it is partial to buddleia. It flies from May to October throughout Britain, after migrating from North Africa. The caterpillars eat thistles.

GLANVILLE FRITILLARY (Melitaea cinxia) Found on the Channel Islands and the Isle of Wight, where the caterpillars weave a silky web over the plantain on which they feed. They overwinter in this web, to emerge as butterflies in May, and fly until the end of June.

LARGE SKIPPER (Ochlodes venata) The name describes the rapid darting flight of this butterfly, which is commonly seen in grassy places throughout England and Wales on sunny days from June to August. It overwinters as a larva, feeding on a variety of grasses.

Rock Dove

Waxwing

Rock Pipit

ROCK DOVE (*Columba livia*)
Ancestor of the domestic pigeon, this 13″ (33 cm) sociable bird is distinguished by its white rump and black-banded wings. It is a rapid flyer, and feeds inland on grain, fruit and seeds. It lays two white eggs in cliff-side crevices.

ROCK PIPIT (*Anthus spinoletta*)
Only 6½″ (16.5 cm) long and rather dark, this bird blends into its usual habitat of seaweed covered rocks. It feeds on insects and tiny crustacea and produces 4-6 greyish brown spotted eggs in its grassy hair-lined nest.

WAXWING (*Bombycilla garrulus*)
A handsome, crested, starling-sized – 7″ (18 cm) – bird, the waxwing breeds in Scandinavia. If the home autumn berry crop fails, large flocks may invade Britain. They are tame and visit gardens for rowan, holly, cotoneaster and other berries.

Purple Sandpiper

Oystercatcher

Red spotted Bluethroat

BLUETHROAT *(Luscinia svecica)*
In spring and autumn, this 5½"
(14 cm) robin-like bird turns up in
small numbers on British headlands.
There are two types – red-spotted
and white-spotted – and both breed
in mainland Europe. They have a rich
song and keep to thick cover.

PURPLE SANDPIPER *(Calidris
maritima)* This stocky little wader, 8"
(21 cm) long, breeds on the Arctic
tundra, but spends much of its life
rooting for periwinkles and insects
around our rocky coasts. It is
remarkably tame, and likes to
congregate in small flocks.

OYSTERCATCHER *(Haematopus
ostralegus)* This large, 17" (42 cm),
gregarious and noisy wader gathers
in great flocks to feed on shellfish, for
which it has a specially adapted bill.
It lays three camouflaged eggs in
summer in a bare scrape on the
ground.

Common Dolphin

Atlantic White-sided Dolphin

White-beaked Dolphin

WHITE-BEAKED DOLPHIN (*Lagenorhynchus albirostris*) This is a powerful, stout 10′ (3 m) animal which migrates from Portugal to sub-polar waters in search of herring, cod and whiting. Its markings are very variable and some, confusingly, do not have the white beak.

COMMON DOLPHIN (*Delphinus delphis*) Up to 8′ and (2.4 m) in length, this is a small, and sociable dolphin, which lives in large schools, often seen accompanying ships. A fast swimmer, it can reach 25 mph. It eats herring, mackerel, cuttlefish and octopus.

WHITE-SIDED DOLPHIN (*Lagenorhynchus acutus*) Roaming the North Atlantic seeking herring, cod and whiting, this is a sturdy dolphin up to 9′ (3 m) long. It sometimes lives in groups of up to 1000, particularly in summer, when it migrates to Norway.

Hunters of the Headland Sea

Bottle-nosed Dolphin

Risso's Dolphin

Calf

Common Porpoise

Female

Male

BOTTLE-NOSED DOLPHIN (*Tursiops truncatus*) A highly intelligent and friendly dolphin which frequents British coastal waters in summer, particularly in the south and west. It feeds on many kinds of fish and cuttlefish, and grows to 12′ (3.7 m) long.

RISSO'S DOLPHIN (*Grampus griseus*) A large, 13′ (4 m), and aggressive dolphin, its body is often marked with conspicuous scars. It is usual for this dolphin to be seen in small family groups when in British coastal waters. It feeds entirely on cuttlefish.

COMMON PORPOISE (*Phocoena phocoena*) Small, 6′ (2 m) and slow, the porpoise frequently falls victim to killer whales and predatory sharks. It can be seen in small groups all round the British Isles, where it feeds on various fish, crustaceans and cuttlefish. It can live up to 15 years.

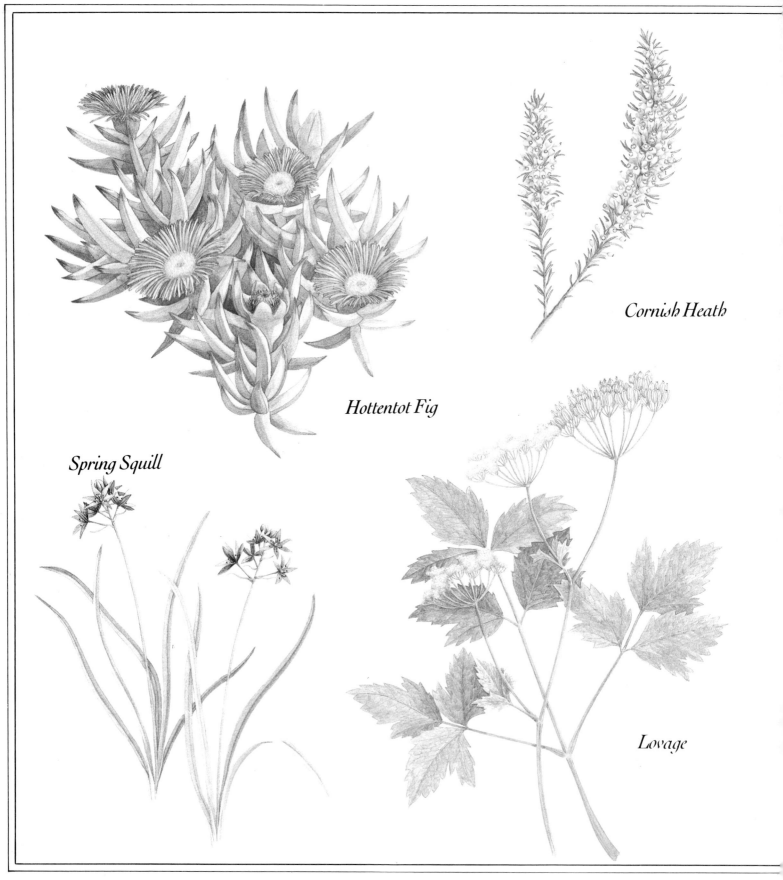

Cornish Heath

Hottentot Fig

Spring Squill

Lovage

HOTTENTOT FIG (*Carpobrotus edulis*) The many-petalled flowers of this 3-4″ (7-10 cm) plant are yellow, purple or pink with yellow centres, and open only in full sun between May and August. They produce acorn-sized fleshy fruit, and flourish in southern England and Ireland.

SPRING SQUILL (*Scilla verna*) A locally rare native of grassy seaside places, producing a bunch of star-like flowers on a bare stem from April to June. The plants spread to form clumps, and can be found in the north and west of Britain. It grows 6-8″ (15-20 cm) tall.

CORNISH HEATH (*Erica vagans*) Found only in one area of Cornwall, and one part of Ireland, this stout heather forms a bush up to 40″ (1 m) tall. The tiny, globular, pink or lilac flowers are carried on a broad spike and cover the bush from August. It has fine grey-green leaves.

LOVAGE (*Ligusticum scoticum*) Hollow ruddy stems and glossy segmented leaves with a strong smell of celery distinguish this Scottish and Northern Irish cliff-dweller. It reaches 18″ (45 cm) and grows in large clumps from rock ledges. It flowers in July and August.

Headland Flowers

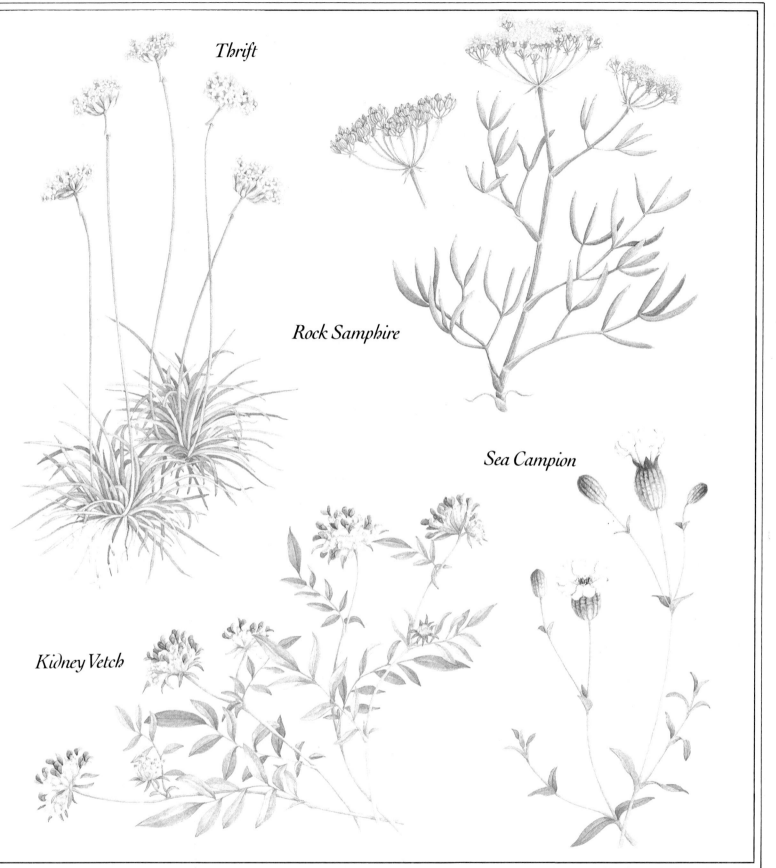

Thrift

Rock Samphire

Sea Campion

Kidney Vetch

THRIFT *(Armeria maritima)* From March to October this plant is covered with fragrant pink flowers held well above cushions of narrow blue-grey leaves. The flowers are 6″ (15 cm) tall, and are cupped in a papery sheath. Thrift can thrive in salt-laden winds.

ROCK SAMPHIRE *(Crithmum maritimum)* Fleshy finger-like leaves with thick skins are this plant's defence against salty sea winds. It forms 6-12″ (15-30 cm) mats, which flower from June to August, making brown corky seed-heads. It grows on south and west coasts.

KIDNEY VETCH *(Anthyllis vulneraria)* Between June and September, the silky leaves of this plant are smothered in bright yellow, orange, red or purple flower heads growing up to 24″ (60 cm) tall. It grows in dry, grassy places throughout the British Isles.

SEA CAMPION *(Silene maritima)* Grassy cliff tops and shingle ridges by the sea are the home of this plant. It reaches only 6″ (15 cm), but spreads in bushy clumps with masses of large, broad petalled white flowers, from May to July, producing brown seed capsules.

ON THE BEACH

**Apart from holidaymakers a flat sandy beach may seem almost lifeless.
In fact it teems with wildlife, though in this exposed habitat it is
well hidden to avoid both predators and the crashing waves.**

Sea breezes and the sound of crashing breakers. Raucous gull cries filling the air and, right down by the tideline, the clockwork scurry of sanderlings keeping their toes just dry as they hunt sandhoppers ahead of the incoming ripple. Early in the morning or out of season, the sandy beach evokes a heart-stirring atmosphere which evaporates with the onrush of trippers, deckchairs and damp children.

The beach is a tough environment and its natural inhabitants live by the patterns of time and tide. The human intrusion is almost the least of their worries. The shifting sand, the ebb and flow of the tide and foul weather are nature's obstacle course, and the wildlife of the beach has learnt to live with these conditions since time immemorial.

As you walk towards the sea, perhaps the first noticeable feature on the beach is the storm ridge, a line of pebbles thrown up parallel to the sea by storm tides. Only occasionally does the sea reach this far up the beach. Without a regular sousing of sea water and its suspended food, little beach life chooses to live here. It is, though, a good spot to look for shells and perhaps semi-precious stones, such as agate

or onyx or to hunt for dried cuttlefish shells.

The real hub of visible life on the beach lies nearer the sea. The strand line – that unlovely mix of rotting seaweed, plastic bottles and other flotsam and jetsam – is a damp haven refreshed by each high tide.

The seaweeds here are not growing: they have been washed loose from rocks and dumped ashore by the sea. Here you may find several broad-leaved kelps such as oarweed, furbelows and the aptly named sugar kelp which has a dusting of sugar when dry (not to be confused with dry salt – you can safely taste the difference). Small red seaweeds – dulse is the best known – will also be found in the strand-line – they often grow like a sock on the stems of the kelp.

As these seaweeds rot on the strand line, they make a mini habitat of their own. Many flies breed here. The strand line makes a good foraging ground for birds, and if turnstones are on the beach, they'll be seen to spend their entire time investigating it. Gulls, starlings, sparrows and carrion crows also find rich pickings here – insects and perhaps a dead fish or seabird.

URCHIN
(left) The heart urchin buries itself to about a hand's depth in the sand as the tide goes out and lines its hole with slime to stop the sand grains collapsing. Its spines fall away when it dies and the attractive brittle case that remains – known as a sea potato – is often seen blowing along the beach.

ON A QUIET SANDY BEACH

The sand dunes in the background are covered by coarse marram grass and perhaps a few hardy flowers. Along the storm ridge are strewn sea-polished pebbles, perhaps the odd semi-precious stone and some empty shells. Visible beach life crowds around the strand line: gulls pick it over, crabs lurk under the damp seaweed, and sandhoppers jump busily about. The herring gull finds the groyne a convenient perch, and from here lets out its evocative 'fishing boat' cry. Beneath the groynes seaweeds grow, providing hiding places for crabs. On the open beach the masked crab scuttles from cover, and the retreating sea exposes the sand mason tubes, while the oystercatcher is on the lookout for cockles. Starfish and, perhaps, shrimps inhabit the pool. Fish are close inshore and under the damp sand the burrowing starfish, lugworm and razor await the next tide.

KEY TO SPECIES

1 Great black-
   backed gull
2 Herring gull
3 Sea wall
4 Lesser black-
   backed gull
5 Strand line
6 Groyne
7 Oarweed
8 Cockles
9 Masked crab
10 Razor shell
11 Sand mason worms
12 Starfish
13 Oystercatcher
14 Lugworm cast
15 Dab
16 Shrimp
17 Lesser weever
18 Burrowing starfish
19 Heart urchin
20 Sandhoppers
21 Lugworm
22 Pod razor

hollow, marking the other end of the U-shaped tube in which the animal lives. Like the earthworm, it eats its silty surroundings, and is more likely to thrive in muddy sand which contains innumerable specks of decaying matter.

On the damp sand near low tide mark, forests of small worm tubes can often be seen: the sand mason worm constructs a tube of coarse sand grains, the peacock worm a smoother tube of silt. Both are collapsed when the tide is out, but become erect when covered, and from the end of the tube the worm extends a fan of tentacles to strain food from the sea.

Shrimps live in the shallows. By day they prefer to remain buried in the sand, emerging at night to feed in the shallow water. Varying from grey to dark brown, they are well camouflaged to match the sand (they only turn red when boiled). Like many active beach animals, shrimps are scavengers rather than predators, though they take small fish fry.

A good catch of shrimps can be a warning signal for they attract the lesser weever, or sting fish. This is our only truly venomous fish, its back fin being supported by very poisonous spines. These fish lie buried in the sand with only the tips of the spines projecting.

Many other fish flock to the shallows and follow the tide in. Dabs and flounder can feed by nipping off the ends of the mason and peacock worms (these quickly grow new sets of tentacles, however). Apart from these flatfish,

A SNORKELER
(above) When buried the male masked crab breathes through a tube formed by interlocking antennae. It feeds when the tide comes in.

STARFISH
(above right) The common starfish finds food in pools.

SMALL CRUSTACEANS
(below) If disturbed, hordes of sandhoppers leap from the cover of rotting seaweed.

Unusual sand dwellers include the burrowing starfish. It resembles other starfish, but the tube feet which cover the underside of its arms are pointed to aid digging – as a result it cannot use them to climb rocks or grasp the shells of mussels and other bivalves to pull them open (the normal way that starfish feed). It has to rely on finding worms or small shellfish to eat whole. It usually lies buried in the sand until covered by the tide.

Towards the low tide mark, where the sand remains wet, some interesting worms are found. Lugworms live under the sand and are well known to anglers who use them for bait. These eight-inch reddish worms leave tell-tale sand casts on the surface. Near each cast is a slight

SEA ROCKET
(right) One of the few plants able to grow on exposed stretches of sand – particularly on beaches undisturbed by holidaymakers – is the aptly named sea rocket.

A FAMILIAR FACE
(left) Joining the many other birds that take advantage of the rich supplies of food on a sandy beach, the distinctive black-headed gull alights on the water to fish.

which are well camouflaged on the sandy bottom, lesser sand eels can occur in large shoals. Not true eels, they are a favourite food of many sea birds. On estuaries, or beaches where a freshwater stream flows into the sea, elvers (young eels) may be found, preparing to migrate upstream from the sea.

Several types of shellfish live buried in the sand between the mid water level and the low tide mark. The bivalves (molluscs which have two shells – like the cockle, for instance) have successfully colonized sandy beaches, and may be there in enormous numbers – some cockle beds have 10,000 to the square yard. The cockles (and the razors, whose familiar empty shells are often found thrown up in the strand line) are both suspension feeders. Buried in the sand, they extend a couple of siphons and suck in water and suspended food through one, and

expel the filtered water from the other. Another method of feeding is adopted by tellins and others: an inlet siphon ranges the surface of the sand like a miniature vacuum cleaner, sucking in any fragments of food it can find.

The man-made groyne, running down the beach into the sea, is a solid habitat (unlike the shifting sand) which can attract species more usually found on rocks. Winkles and barnacles may encrust the timber, and seaweeds hang from the woodwork. Gulls, notably the herring gull and lesser black-backed gull, find it a convenient perch to scan the beach for food.

Though much of the wildlife of the beach is hidden from immediate view it is certainly worth searching out, whether you hold your nose and rummage through the strand line, scan the damp sand, or indeed, simply pause to watch the life on the groyne.

SAFE IN THE SAND
(right) With the tide out only the frilly tops of sand mason tubes are visible.

WADERS
(below) Sanderlings rest after feeding in the sand.

JET

CORNELIAN

ONYX

AMBER

AGATE

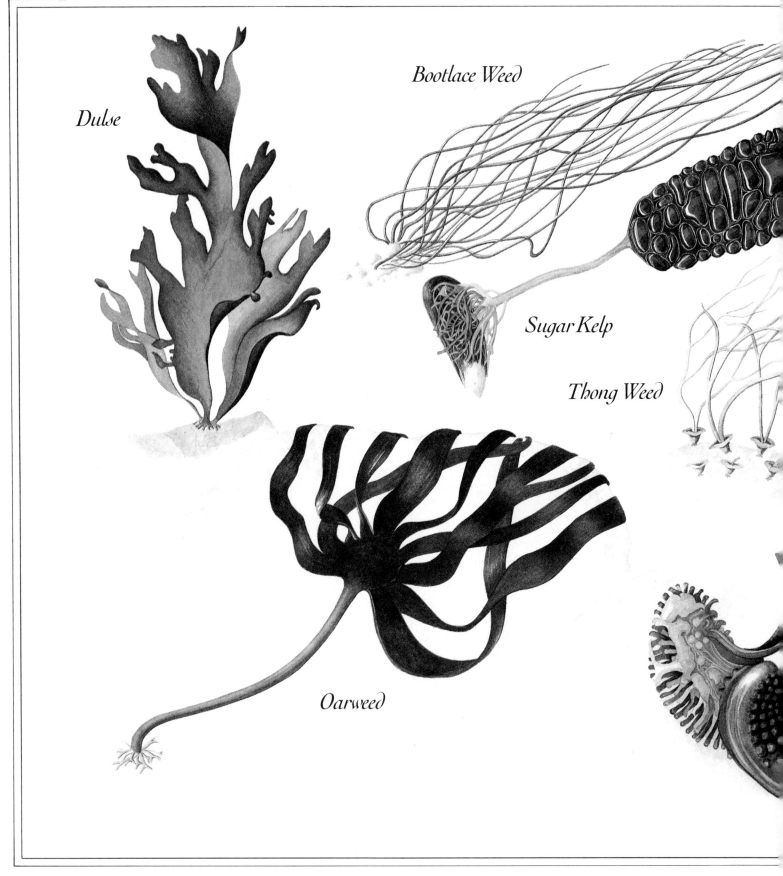

Dulse

Bootlace Weed

Sugar Kelp

Thong Weed

Oarweed

DULSE *(Palmaria palmata)* Tough, thick leathery fronds, indented like fingers characterize this common dark-red seaweed abundant on middle and lower shores. The 12″ (30cm) long fronds grow stemless from the disc-like holdfast, attached to rocks.

OARWEED *(Laminaria digitata)* One of the largest seaweeds of cold waters, often called tangle, this seaweed reaches over 10′ (3m) in length, with 24″ (60cm) wide fronds. It forms dense beds on the lower shore or deeper, clinging to rocks with a rootlike holdfast.

BOOTLACE WEED **(Chorda *filum)* A round slippery undivided frond reaching 20′ (6m) in summer, like a huge bootlace, this plant is attached by a small disc to stones on the lower shore. It is often plentiful, and is found growing freely on all coasts.

SUGAR KELP *(Laminaria saccharina)* Producing long undivided fronds up to 13′ (4m) with wavy or crinkled edges, sugar kelp is a very common ubiquitous seaweed, usually attached to small stones. The 'sugar' is a white dust on the dry fronds.

Seashore Seaweed

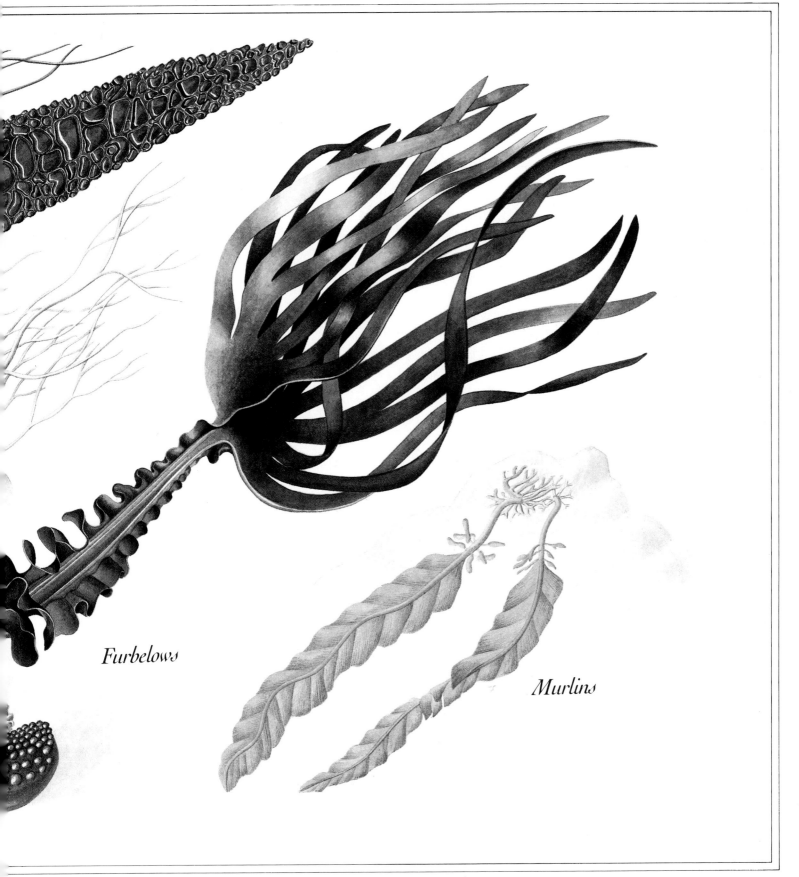

Furbelows

Murlins

THONG WEED (*Himanthalia elongata*) This is a long olive-brown strap-like divided frond growing from a button like a toadstool. It is widely distributed and abundant in places on the lower shores of exposed rocky coasts, where species of laminaria cannot get a hold.

FURBELOWS (*Saccorhiza polyschides*) Like oarweed, but with a rounded knobbly, stiff and hollow holdfast, and a flattened stalk with frilled edges. The fronds grow up to 6' (2m) and are torn off by winter gales, to be replaced annually. It is common on lower ground.

MURLINS (*Alaria esculenta*) Like sugar kelp, but the thin fragile frond has a midrib and less wavy margins. The rib is yellow, the frond browner, and the plant is common only where the shore is too exposed for oarweed to thrive on the wave-washed lower beach.

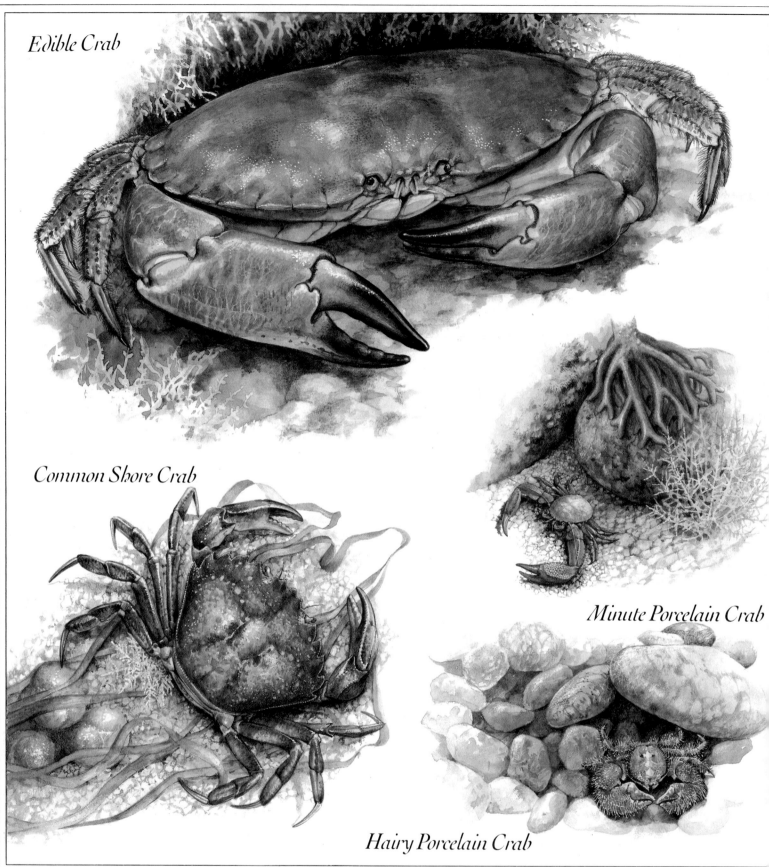

Edible Crab

Common Shore Crab

Minute Porcelain Crab

Hairy Porcelain Crab

EDIBLE CRAB (*Cancer pagurus*)
Up to 8″ (20cm) broad; this is a
bright rough-textured crab; the
front rim of the shell has a
'pie-crust' indentation. It can live
up to eight years, starting life
among the seaweed in the shallows,
and progressing to deeper water.

COMMON SHORE CRAB
(*Carcinus maenas*) Up to 3½″ (9cm)
across, and usually dark olive green
or red, this crab is widely distributed
and very common on sandy, muddy
and rocky beaches and estuaries,
where it is an omnivorous scavenger
from its weedy hiding place.

HAIRY PORCELAIN CRAB
(*Porcellana platycheles*) Lurking
under stones, particularly in muddy
water, this ½″ (1cm) crab clings to
its home with a ferocious grip.
Similar to the minute porcelain crab
except for its brush-like texture, it
has long antennae.

MINUTE PORCELAIN CRAB
(*Porcellana longicornis*) Only ⅜″
(8mm) across, with nippers twice as
long, this shiny brown crab is also
called long-clawed porcelain crab.
A filter feeder, it scoops organic
material from under rocks, which it
then sifts with its mouthparts.

Crabs of the Beach

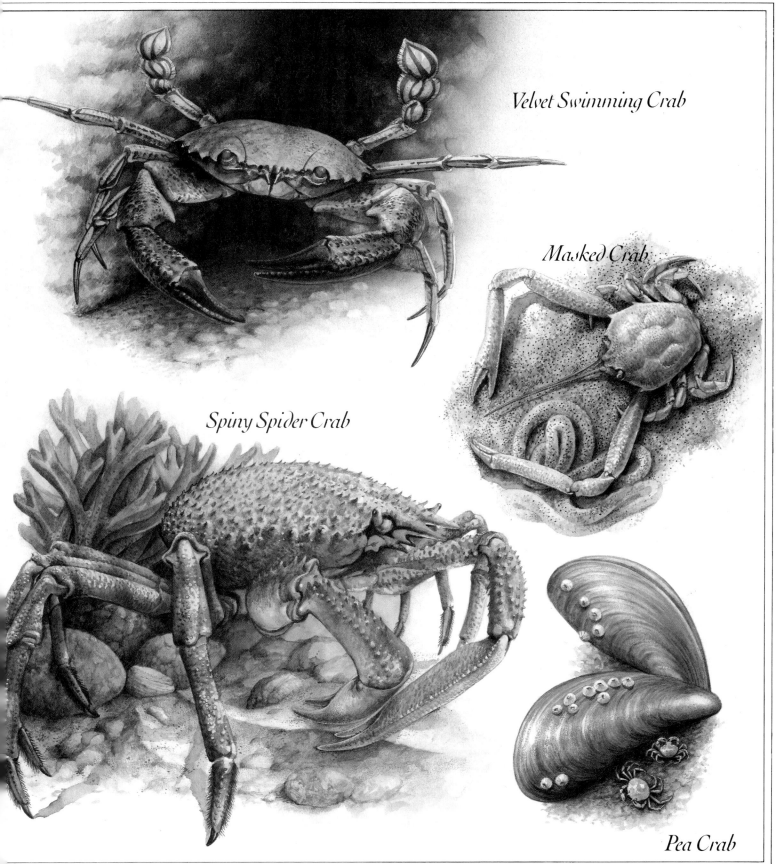

Velvet Swimming Crab

Masked Crab

Spiny Spider Crab

Pea Crab

SPINY SPIDER CRAB *(Maja squinado)* Congregating in great clumps inshore to mate, these 8" (20cm) crabs live in the south and south-west feeding on seaweeds and small creatures. They camouflage themselves with stray fronds of seaweed.

VELVET SWIMMING CRAB *(Macropipus puber)* Sometimes known as the fiddler crab, its 5" (12cm) shell is covered in a dense velvety flock, and it is an adept swimmer. It will defend itself aggressively against trespassers in the kelp forests where it lives.

MASKED CRAB *(Corystes cassivelaunus)* A nocturnal forager for worms and shrimps, this crab spends the day buried in clean sand with its antennae protruding like a snorkel. At 1½" (4cm) long, it is prey to many birds and fishes. Males have long pincers.

PEA CRAB *(Pinnotheres pisum)* A tiny ¼" (5mm) crab, cohabiting mussel shells with their owners, and feeding on their waste products, the pea crab is almost globular. The male is yellowish, the female translucent with a yellow spot and tail. Scarce in the north.

Lesser Black-backed Gull

Common Tern

Arctic Tern

COMMON TERN *(Sterna hirundo)* A slim 14″ (36cm) bird with a glossy black cap in summer. Inhabits noisy nesting colonies in the summer on shingle banks and islands. It lays 2-4 dappled eggs in an unlined scrape. Feeds on a variety of sea creatures.

LESSER BLACK-BACKED GULL *(Larus fuscus)* Smaller, at 22″ (55cm), and greyer than the great black-back, this gull is widespread in summer, and winters inland. It breeds in colonies on islands and moors, laying 2-3 mottled eggs in a grassy nest amongst vegetation.

ARCTIC TERN *(Sterna paradisaea)* A summer visitor to northern shores and islands, this has shorter legs than the common tern, darker underparts and an all deep-red bill. Nests among rocks or on shingle, laying 2-4 mottled brown eggs. Dives for fish.

Herring Gull

Great Black-backed Gull

Sanderling

HERRING GULL *(Larus argentatus)* The typical seagull of resorts and fish quays, this is a large (23", 57cm) and noisy bird congregating in great breeding colonies, and laying 2-3 eggs on a grassy pad on a cliff-ledge. Eats anything including rubbish.

SANDERLING *(Calidris alba)* Sanderlings gather to paddle in sandy shallows in a busy quest for food. Winter visitors from the Arctic, they assume brown colouring in the summer. Small 8" (20cm) birds, they have a conspicuous white wingbar in flight.

GREAT BLACK-BACKED GULL *(Larus marinus)* At 26" (66cm) long this is the largest gull, and is aggressively predatory, eating anything from weak lambs down to worms. It is widespread but commonest in the north, laying 2-3 mottled eggs in a clifftop nest.

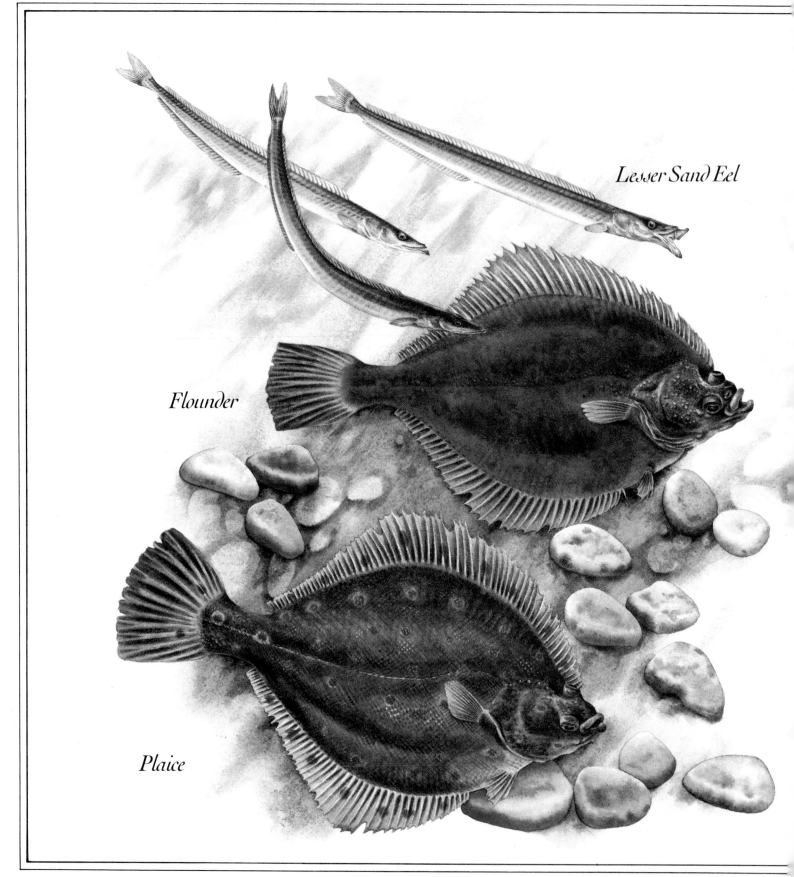

Lesser Sand Eel

Flounder

Plaice

PLAICE *(Pleuronectes platessa)* Common on all shores, 5″ (12cm) long on the shore and four times as big out to sea, the plaice is camouflaged to blend with the seabed. The left eye migrates after one month, and the fish may live up to 20 years.

FLOUNDER *(Platichthys flesus)* Adapted for life on the seabed, the flounder can grow to 20″ (50cm) long, and usually lies on its left side, its left eye migrating when the fish is 1″ (25mm) long. Common in muddy or sandy creeks or estuaries on all coasts.

LESSER SAND-EEL *(Ammodytes tobianus)* Common and widely distributed, a slim 6″ (20cm) eel-like edible fish, which swims in silvery shoals in shallow water, this is used as bait by anglers and is prey to many fish and seabirds. It likes to burrow in sand.

Fish of Coastal Waters

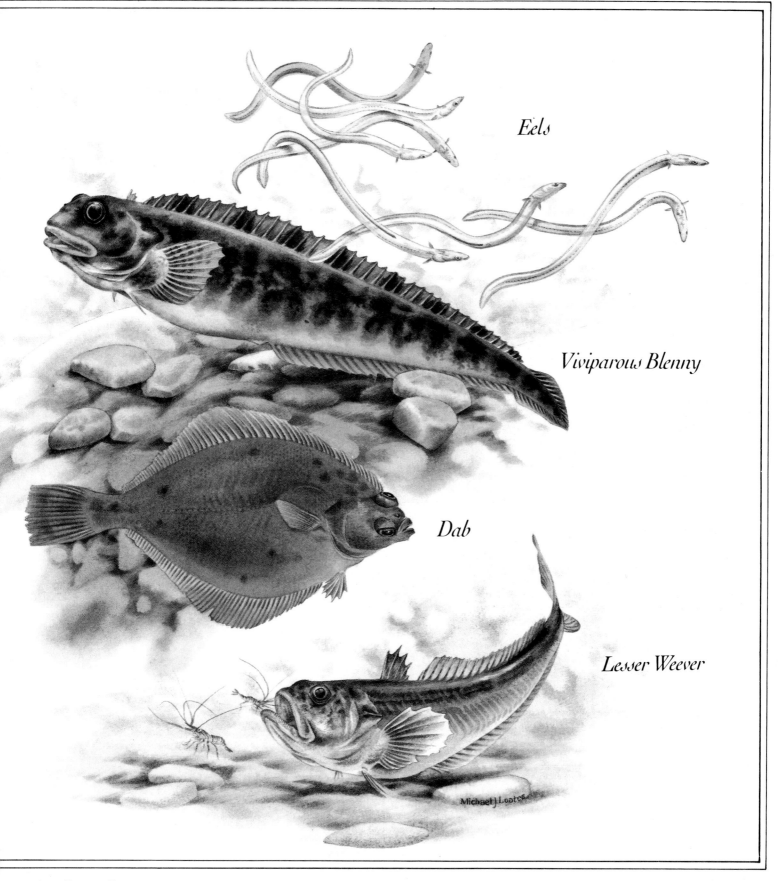

Eels

Viviparous Blenny

Dab

Lesser Weever

Michael J Loates

EEL *(Anguilla anguilla)* In spring young eels (known as elvers) start to swim upriver following a three year journey from their spawning ground in the Sargasso Sea. At 3-6″ (7-15cm) they are like miniature versions of their parents with long slippery bodies.

VIVIPAROUS BLENNY *(Zoarces viviparous)* Common on the north and east coasts, but not elsewhere, this 12″ (30cm) edible fish has an unusual continuous fin along back and belly, with a notch out of the rear part. The young are born fully formed.

DAB *(Limanda limanda)* Hidden beneath the sand or gravel of the seabed, the dab is a voracious feeder on any small creature or plant that comes within range. It grows to 15″ (38cm) long, and has a kinked lateral line. Commonly found near sandy or muddy shores.

LESSER WEEVER *(Echiichthys vipera)* Scarce around all coasts except the south west, this 5″ (12cm) fish has a tuft of spines above its gills, which inject poison into the unwary trespasser. It lies buried in the sand, feeding on small crustaceans and fish with its upturned mouth.

Pollack

Bass

Lesser-spotted Dogfish

BASS *(Dicentrarchus labrax)* A strong and fiercely predatory fish up to 40″ (100cm) and up to 20lbs (9½ kg) found chiefly in the south. It feeds on small crustaceans. It has a sharply spined front dorsal fin, and a dark blotch on the gill covers. It spawns between May and June.

LESSER-SPOTTED DOGFISH *(Scyliorhinus caniculus)* Related to sharks, these 30″ (76cm) dogfish feed on molluscs and crustaceans on the sea bed. They are abundant all round the coast. 18-20 egg capsules – mermaid's purses – are laid tangled in seaweed during winter and spring.

POLLACK *(Pollachius pollachius)* One of the cod family, this fish is most common in the south in waters off rocky headlands, coming into harbours at night to feed on planktonic animals and small fish. It spawns in March or April. Grows to 50″ (130cm) and 20lbs (9½ kg).

Thick-lipped Grey Mullet

Mackerel

Codling

THICK-LIPPED GREY MULLET *(Chelon labrosus)* Seen in the summer in harbours and estuaries, cruising near the surface, mullet feed on the organic material present in mud, gradually reaching 24″ (60cm) and about 14lb (6½kg). They spawn in early summer.

MACKEREL *(Scomber scombrus)* Usually found in bays and harbours in small shoals from July to November. Powerful swimmers, mackerel collect in huge shoals in spring to spawn off the south-west coast. They weigh up to 1lb (½kg).

CODLING *(Gadus morhua)* Young cod frequent shallow coastal waters. They are bottom feeders, eating fish and crustaceans. At about two years and 14″ (36cm), they move out into open sea. Though prolific, cod take over five years to mature but may reach 70lbs (32kg).

ON *THE* ROCKS

The plants and animals of the rocky shore are remarkably adapted for a life in two elements: they are based on land but rely for food on the regular return of the sea.

As the waves chop on the rocks the gulls scream overhead, alert for fish or crabs moving in the newly created pools. Driven by the spring tide, once each month, the sea rises much higher (and falls lower) up the beach, swamping the locks of dry seaweed scattered over the topmost rocks of the shore. Channel wrack, a brown seaweed, is best seen at this time, for then its fronds are plumpish and yellow brown in colour. But after only a few hours exposure to the sun and breeze it dries and turns almost black, until the next proper dousing revives it.

In the crannies of the rocks nearby lurk sea slaters, looking like overgrown woodlice. They emerge to feed at night, though bright moonlight deters them. Colonies of bristletails – primitive wingless insects – shelter, too, in the crevices. Small winkles – sharp pointed sea snails – also cluster here. They can survive weeks, even months, out of water, though they are marine animals and need the sea to carry away their larvae.

Both the winkle and the channel wrack benefit from the frequent storms and the veils of windblown spray that rain on the rocks far above the high tide mark. This 'splash zone' of storm spray also enables the barnacles to occupy noticeably higher rock faces on windy, exposed shores than they can on calmer coasts.

The barnacles coat rocks at the top of the shore in hundreds, sometimes thousands, to the square yard. Unlike the winkles they remain fixed in one place, and strain the seawater for particles of food. Although at first glance they resemble small sea snails, they are crustaceans, related to shrimps and lobsters.

FLOATING SEAWEEDS

Further down, in the middle zone of the shore which the tides regularly cover twice a day, lusher growths of brown seaweed are found. One of them is bladder wrack; its fronds carry 'poppers', air sacs which help them float even in the shallows of the tide. Serrated wrack which is found at the third, bottom zone of the shore, has no poppers, for the water there is usually deep and the fronds float free.

Seaweeds are plants and, like land plants, create their own food with the help of sunlight.

GREY SEALS
(left) Grey seals are mammals of northern seas, and the bulk of the European population is centred on the British Isles. They are commonest around the Hebrides and Orkney – the main breeding areas – but can, from time to time, be seen all around our coasts. Although numbers are small – about 50,000 around the British Isles – the population has increased over the last 60 years.

WILDLIFE ON THE ROCKY SHORE

Coastal rocks, washed by the food-rich sea, provide a firm home base for both animals and plants. The wracks generally grow in well defined zones down the shore: channel wrack near the highest tide mark, then flat wrack, bladder and/or knotted wrack and, near the lowest tide mark, serrated wrack. Green seaweeds often grow where there is freshwater run-off, while oarweed and other kelps grow below the lowest tide mark. Tube worms encrust serrated wrack while winkles graze on the fronds. Limpets and topshells are both grazers of algae but dog whelks feed on barnacles and mussels. Sea slaters and paddleworms are scavengers but beadlet anemones, when covered by the tide, catch shrimps and fish. The birds of the shore feed mainly on crustaceans and molluscs.

KEY TO THE SPECIES

 1 Puffins
 2 Lichen Xanthoria
 3 Various grey lichens
 4 Herring gull
 5 Lichen Caloplaca
 6 Tar spot lichen
 7 Channel wrack
 8 Flat wrack
 9 Basking shark
10 Shag
11 Great black-backed gull
12 Breadcrumb sponge

13 Bladder wrack
14 Grey seals
15 Rock pipit
16 Common mussels
17 Green seaweeds
18 Turnstone
19 Common limpet
20 Dog whelk
21 Purple topshell
22 Paddleworm
23 Shore crab
24 Beadlet anemone
25 Sea slaters
26 Serrated wrack
27 Oarweed

28 Thong weed
29 Red seaweed Gigartina stellata
30 Barnacles
31 Coiled tube worm
32 Keel worm
33 Flat winkle
34 Dulse

With wracks the green colour is masked by brown pigments, but bright green seaweeds can be found, usually on the upper shore for they do best in bright light. Seaweeds carrying red pigment, on the other hand, are suited to cope with the gloom of deep water and are found more on the lower shore, or growing on the holdfasts of the wracks.

Holdfasts may look like roots, but only attach the seaweed to the rock. There is no nourishment to be gained from rocks, so seaweeds obtain their nutrients from the sea water which bathes them.

GRAZING LIMPETS

Limpets are the 'sheep' of the upper half of the shores, with thick shells that allow them to withstand the heaviest waves. Seemingly immobile, they nevertheless do move around, scouring the rock when it is submerged and at night. Where they graze in large numbers they scrape the surface bare, and the only weed left may be out of their reach, growing atop their shells. After grazing, limpets return to their home site. Here the edge of the shell makes a

ROCKY COAST SEAWEEDS
(left) Among the seaweeds on this Devon shore can be seen the thin strands of thong weed, mushy green sea lettuce, purplish carragheen and, in the foreground, serrated wrack.

EDIBLE CRAB
(above) This young crab tones in well with the coral weed surrounding it. White spirals on the weed are tube worms. The pimply yellow encrustations are breadcrumb sponges.

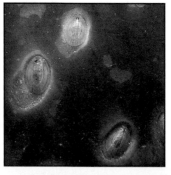

watertight seal and a groove may be worn in softer rock. This close fit defeats even hungry gulls that try to pry them off.

Often seen among the limpets and barnacles is another tough shell, that of the dog whelk. This is a carnivore, feeding on the barnacles or invading the mussel banks which can cover more sheltered rocks. Its shell colour reveals its diet: white shows that it has preyed on barnacles, while a dark shell indicates that it has fed on mussels.

At low tide, the wracks coat the rocks with a moist blanket under which many animals seek shelter. In fact, most of the life of the rocky shore hides itself away. Here thinner shelled snails can survive. They, too, zone themselves down the shore: flat winkles, which can be coloured bright yellow, orange or greenish brown (the cause remains a mystery), are found on the middle shore on bladder wrack, but edible winkles can be found in rock pools and among the weed of the lower shore. The gaudy topshells also zone themselves down the sea shore.

The scuttle of the shore crab is often a surprise; it is hard to outwit its eager senses and catch it unawares, before it hurries to the cover of a crack or below a rock. It is one of the most successful of all shore animals, aggressive and tough enough to withstand long exposure. But

BLUE-RAYED LIMPETS
(centre) These brightly coloured limpets are grazing on a frond of kelp. Young limpets are found more commonly on the fronds – adults usually graze the kelp's rock-clinging holdfast – and tend to be more brightly hued.

OYSTERCATCHER FLOCK
(right) As the tide covers their feeding grounds, a neat wader squadron roosts on a rocky shoreline.

POLYCERA QUADRILINEATA

ARCHIDORIS
PSEUDOARGUS
(SEA LEMON)

ONCHIDORIS BILAMELLATA

SEA SLUGS
(left) These extraordinary creatures come in a wide variety of shapes, sizes and colours. They are generally found below the low tide mark so are not often seen. Crawling slowly over rocks and seaweed, they feed on encrusting barnacles and sea mats. The feathery, snowflake-like structures on their backs are external gills. Their colours often come from pigments in the food they eat.

SEA SLATER
(left) The sea slater is at home both in and out of the water. Here it is seen crawling in the splash zone over a rock covered with channel wrack. This seaweed gets its name from a groove on one side of the frond.

KEEL WORMS FEEDING
(centre) Housed in limy shells fixed to the rock, these tube worms extend their feathery tentacles to feed only when covered by the tide.

SHORELINE TURNSTONE
(below) Turnstones are a common sight on coasts around the British Isles. Non-breeders can be seen at any time and breeding birds arrive in strength from Arctic regions to overwinter.

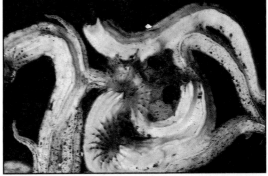

Colourful in black, white and chestnut, turnstones tread the exposed rocks, picking over stones and seaweed in search of sandhoppers and other titbits. A flock of them often marks a dead animal yielded by the waves. The purple sandpiper, another wader, also prefers rocky shores.

Oystercatchers, too, may scavenge on the rocky shore, while the gulls stand proudly on an exposed rock, supervising their domain. Their heavy beak and belligerent eye betray their piratical tendencies and they are not slow to take food from other birds, and thus exploit the amazing productivity of the shore to the full.

like many other hard skinned animals, the shore crab has to moult to grow, so empty shells are a common sight littering the strand line.

Stranger creatures inhabit the dark fissures where the sun never reaches and the air remains damp. Here dwells the inert-seeming sponge. It looks like a lower plant of some kind, but is actually an animal that gains food by straining the seawater. Even stranger is the fact that an apparently single sponge is, in fact, a colony of separate individuals, sharing the pore openings that can be seen on its surface.

Here, too, are found the more familiar sea anemones. The beadlet anemone can live out of water; but others of the clan cannot and are restricted to rock pools which never empty. Much larger animals may also be seen on or near the rocky shore. Apart from the grey seals, which haul themselves out on shelving rocks, there are large predatory fish, such as the conger. Conger eels often lurk under boulders near low tide mark and can reach more than 6 feet in length when full grown. Porbeagles and other sharks sometimes approach at low water to scratch themselves on the rocks.

Birds are frequent visitors, though they treat the rocky shore only as a feeding ground, nesting and roosting on the cliffs or other sites out of reach of the spray.

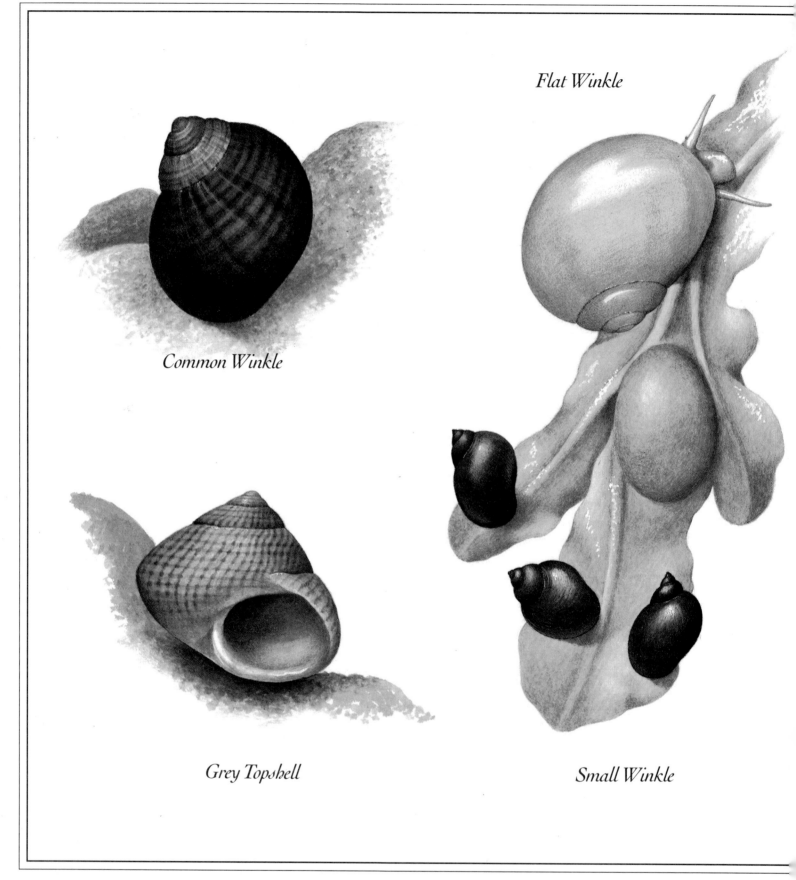

Flat Winkle

Common Winkle

Grey Topshell

Small Winkle

COMMON WINKLE *(Littorina littorea)* A large, edible winkle with a 1″ (25 mm) high shell, tough enough to withstand buffeting. Abundant on the mid-shore and in estuaries, it browses on algae and organic debris. It lays floating egg-sacs and breathes with gills.

GREY TOPSHELL *(Gibbula cineraria)* Found beneath stones and seaweed on the lower shore, this is a widespread, ½″ (13 mm) shell. The dark patterning on the 7 flattish whorls is often faded and worn. These molluscs have a fringed foot and feathery gill.

FLAT WINKLE *(Littorina littoralis)* Though of variable colour and sometimes striped, the compressed spiral of its 0.4″ (10 mm) shell makes it easy to identify. Widespread and abundant, grazing on mid-shore wracks, it breathes with gills. Eggs are laid on seaweeds.

SMALL WINKLE *(Littorina neritoides)* Widespread all round the coast on exposed rocky shores, this tiny 0.2″ (5 mm) mollusc is found in crevices high up the beach – even in the splash zone. It feeds on lichens which encrust the rocks, and is lung-breathing.

Painted Topshell

Thick Topshell

Purple Topshell

Rough Winkle

PAINTED TOPSHELL (*Calliostoma zizyphinum*) Widespread on the lower shore and some way out to sea, on rocks and among kelps, this is a straight-sided conical shell, 1″ (25 mm) high and 1″ wide at the base. Attractively marked, pearly inside, it has a 'lid' to close the opening.

ROUGH WINKLE (*Littorina saxatilis*) An air-breathing winkle with a 'lung', the 0.3″ (8 mm) shell has 6-9 whorls, ridged and rough to touch. Widespread, it lives on the upper shore in rock crevices and among Channel wrack from which it grazes algae. Live young are born.

THICK TOPSHELL (*Monodonta lineata*) These conical 1″ (25 mm) high shells are pearly inside – and outside when worn. Found on Welsh and Irish coasts among the wracks on mid-shore rocks, browsing on algae. Identified from other Top-shells by a 'peg' in the opening.

PURPLE TOPSHELL (*Gibbula umbilicalis*) Locally abundant on west and south-west coasts, it browses amongst low-mid shore seaweeds. The ½″ (13 mm) shell is a flattish cone, with distinct stripes – appearing pearly as the top layer wears. It has a feathery gill.

Grey Seal

Male

Female

Pup

GREY (ATLANTIC) SEAL
(Halichoerus grypus) These large, heavy seals, males 126″ (320 cm), females 98″ (250 cm), live in herds. Both sexes are strongly territorial in the September to December breeding season, when noisy colonies amass on exposed rocks. The aggressive bull guards his cows, mating with them soon after birth of the pup. After suckling 2-3 weeks, the pups are deserted – and go to sea at 2 months. In profile, this seal has a straight muzzle. Seen round most of Britain, except the south coast, where they dive for quite large fish.

Mammals

Common Seal

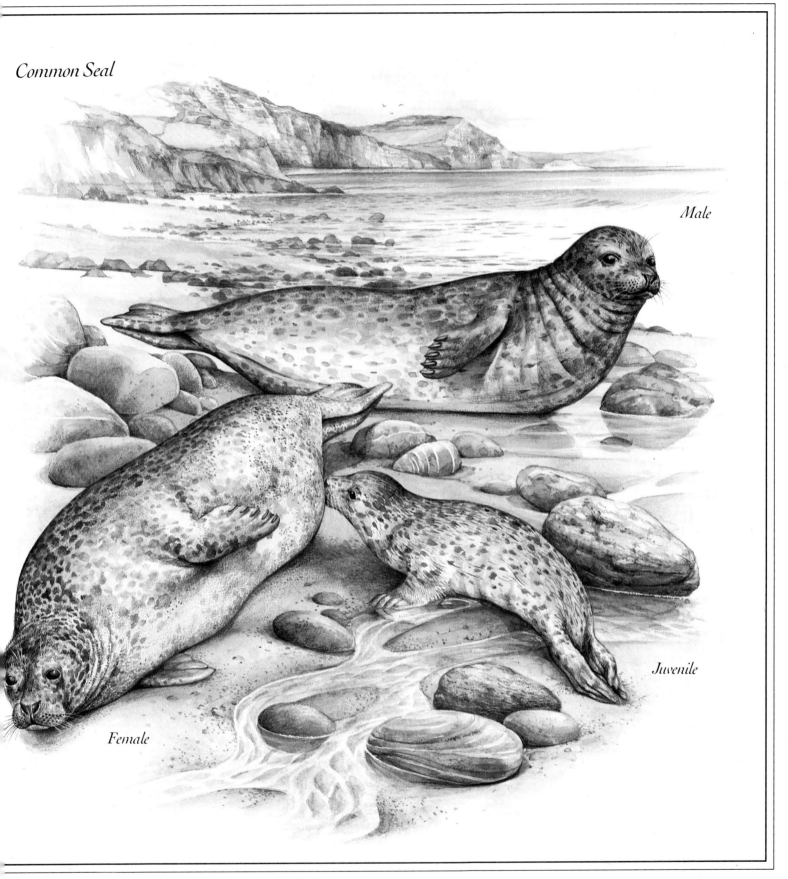

Male

Juvenile

Female

COMMON SEAL *(Phoca vitulina)* Seen off the east and north-west coasts in shallow water, these quiet, placid animals bask on sand banks as well as more sheltered rocks. At about 68″ (170 cm), they are much smaller than Grey seals and have short, upturned muzzles. Mating in autumn, the single pup is born the next summer. They breed on tide-covered rocks where no territories are held. Pups go to sea almost immediately, suckling on land and in water for 1 month. They live for up to 30 years, feeding on fish, crustaceans and molluscs.

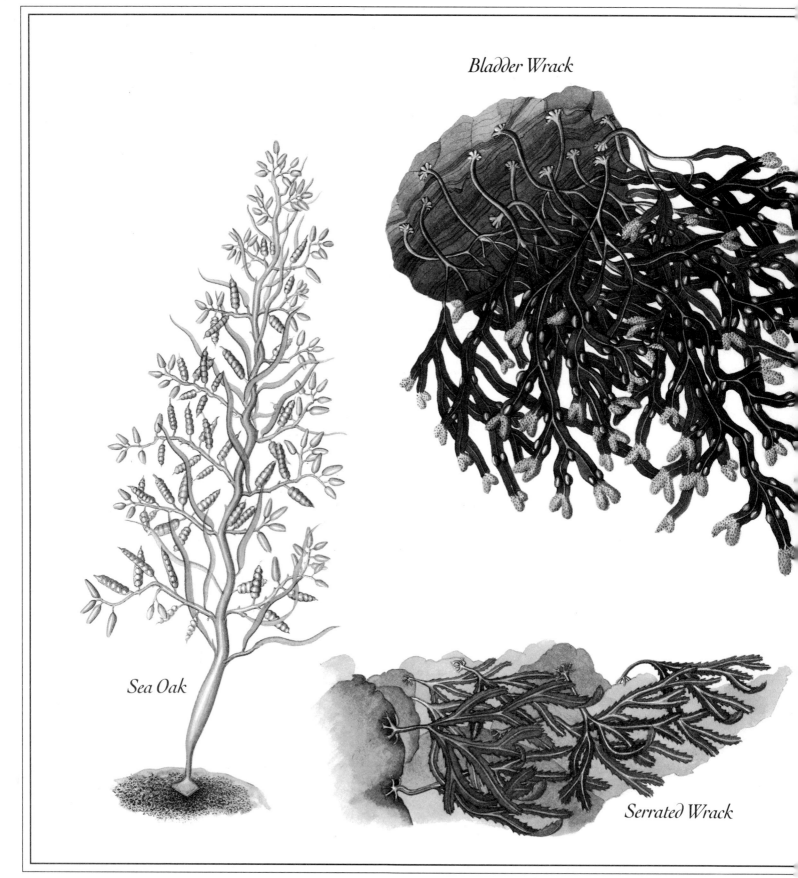

Bladder Wrack

Sea Oak

Serrated Wrack

SEA OAK (*Halidrys siliquosa***)**
A stiff, much branched seaweed usually 8-16″ (20-41 cm), sometimes more. Growing in rock pools on the lower shore, it is widespread, but not very common. Many of the short, alternately arranged branches end in pointed air bladders.

BLADDER WRACK (*Fucus vesiculosus***)** Growing mid-shore in all but very exposed conditions, this is a tough, branched wrack, reaching 40″ (100 cm). Air-bladders in pairs or threes each side of the mid-rib float fronds to the surface. Fruiting bodies grow on branch tips.

SERRATED WRACK (*Fucus serratus***)** Clothing rocks near low tide level, a slippery wrack up to 24″ (61 cm). Fronds are flat, with toothed edges and a distinct midrib. The fruiting bodies are slightly thickened granular patches found on branch tips in autumn and winter.

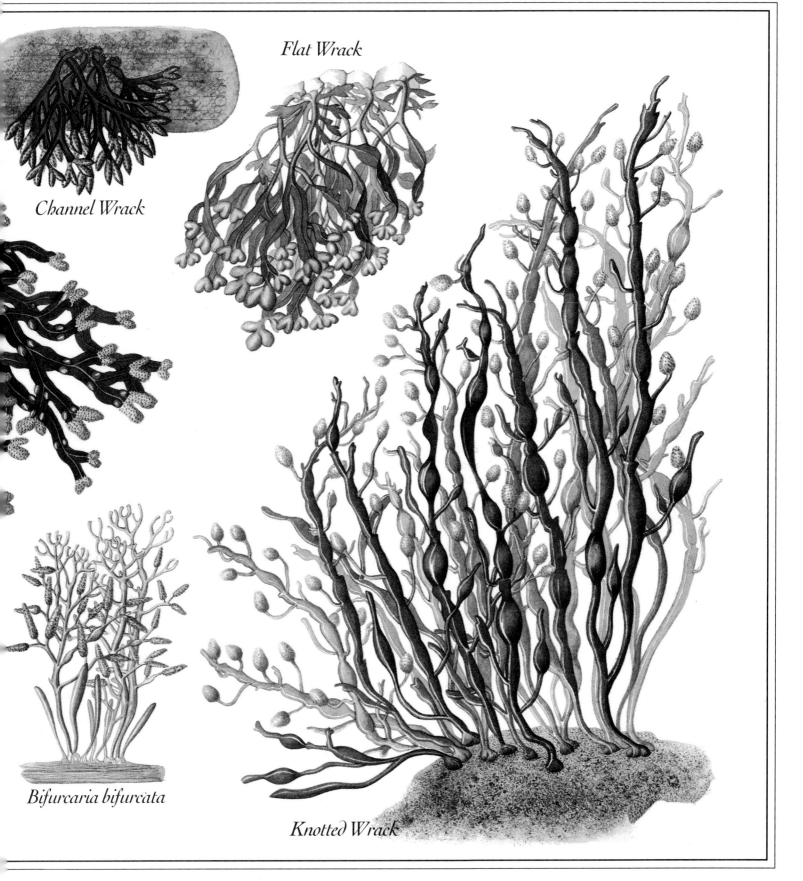

Channel Wrack

Flat Wrack

Bifurcaria bifurcata

Knotted Wrack

CHANNEL WRACK (*Pelvetia canaliculata*) Tolerant of exposure and drying, branched clumps grow on rocks at high water mark, even in the splash zone. Flat fronds 2-6″ (5-15 cm) long lack midribs and curl inwards to conserve water – swollen tips contain reproductive bodies.

BIFURCARIA BIFURCATA Attached to rocks, always below the water line, this brownish 12-20″ (30-50 cm) seaweed has a rounded main stem, branching irregularly. Fruiting bodies may develop at branch tips, while air bladders occur along the stems.

FLAT WRACK (*Fucus spiralis*) Tough and leathery, this wrack is found on rocks high up the shore in all but very exposed places. Smooth branched fronds 6-16″ (15-40 cm) have distinct midribs and are twisted near the reproductive tips which are granular and swollen.

KNOTTED WRACK (*Ascophyllum nodosum*) Only growing on sheltered rocky coasts where long strands may reach 10′ (3 m) often covering large areas mid-shore. Oval air bladders are spaced singly along midrib-less fronds. Fruiting bodies are borne on short lateral stalks in spring.

Ling

Pouting

Lumpsucker

POUTING, BIB *(Trisopterus luscus)* A deep-bodied coppery fish found in shoals off rocky shores particularly in South and West. Large pout can be 16″ (40 cm) and weigh 5 lb (2 kg) – but usually less. They feed on bottom-dwelling invertebrates, spawning March-April.

LING *(Molva molva)* Older ling are caught commercially out at sea but they spend their first few years in shallower waters off rocky coasts. The long tapering body may reach 80″ (2 m) and they are fierce predators of smaller fish. Spawning occurs April-June.

LUMPSUCKER *(Cyclopterus lumpus)* Scaleless, this bulky fish has many bony 'lumps' and a ventral sucker. Fairly common all round the coast, moving inshore to breed in spring. 24″ (60 cm) females swim to sea after spawning. Smaller, red-tinged males guard the eggs.

Rocky Shore Fish

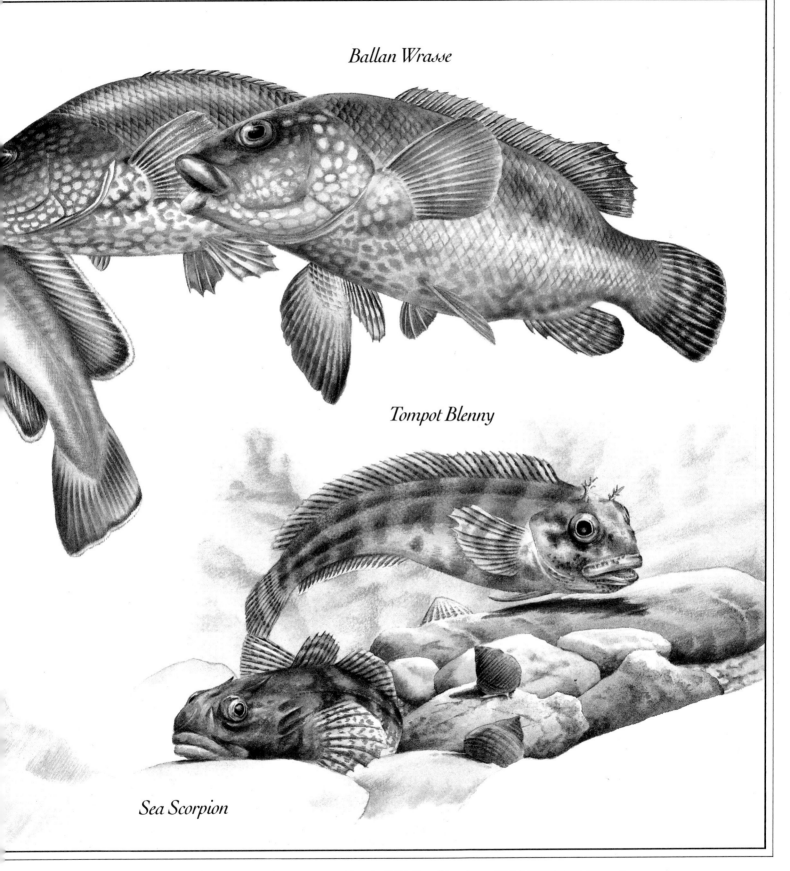

Ballan Wrasse

Tompot Blenny

Sea Scorpion

BALLAN WRASSE *(Labrus bergylta)* All ballan wrasse are born female, some turning male after about 10 years. The young are green, but when full-grown, 10-13" (25-33 cm), they turn brown. Common off rocky shores, they have mollusc-crushing teeth and sharp spines on their fins.

TOMPOT BLENNY *(Parablennius gattorugine)* Dark bars identify this 10" (25 cm) scaleless blenny. With 2 branched tentacles above the eyes, and spiny dorsal fin, it is a strange, uncommon denizen of rock pools and waters below low-tide mark, hiding among seaweeds.

SEA SCORPION *(Taurulus bubalis)* Thickset, with spiny gill covers, this fish reaches 7" (18 cm) and is common on rocky shores in seaweedy pools. The courting male displays coloured fins and guards the yolky eggs – spawned in spring – until they hatch.

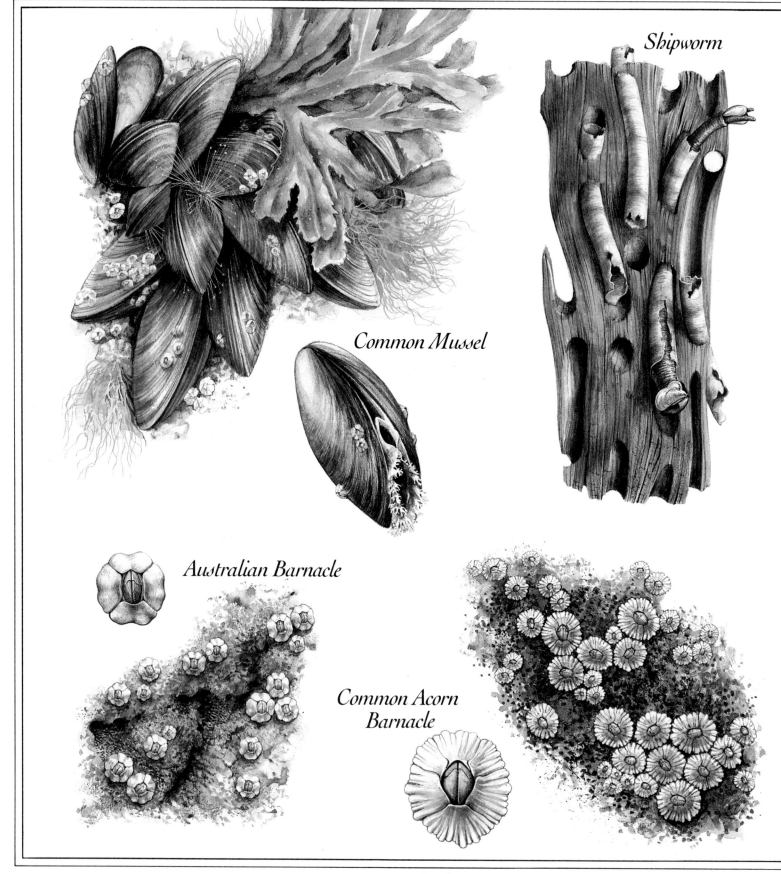

Shipworm

Common Mussel

Australian Barnacle

Common Acorn Barnacle

AUSTRALIAN BARNACLE
(Elminius modestus) Brought to
British shores from Australia on the
hulls of ships, this ½″ (1.5cm)
barnacle is now very widespread. It
breeds throughout the summer,
lodging on mid-shore rocks in
sheltered estuaries near freshwater.

COMMON MUSSEL *(Mytilus
edulis)* Very common on rocky
shores, harbour walls and piers,
where they cluster in large numbers
midway between the tides. Anchored
to the rocks by byssal threads,
mussels grow to 4″ (10cm) and
spawn in spring, feeding on plankton.

COMMON ACORN BARNACLE
(Semibalanus balanoides) These tiny
crustaceans are abundant all round
the coast, especially in exposed
positions. The free-swimming larvae
settle firmly on rocks from the high
water mark downwards. They reach
½″ (1.5cm) and breed in winter.

SHIPWORM *(Teredo navalis)*
Using a small three-lobed shell to
bore into submerged or floating
wood, this mollusc causes great
damage to structural timbers. As it
grows, it builds up a hard tube up to
8″ (20cm) long to protect its body.
It feeds on wood and organic matter.

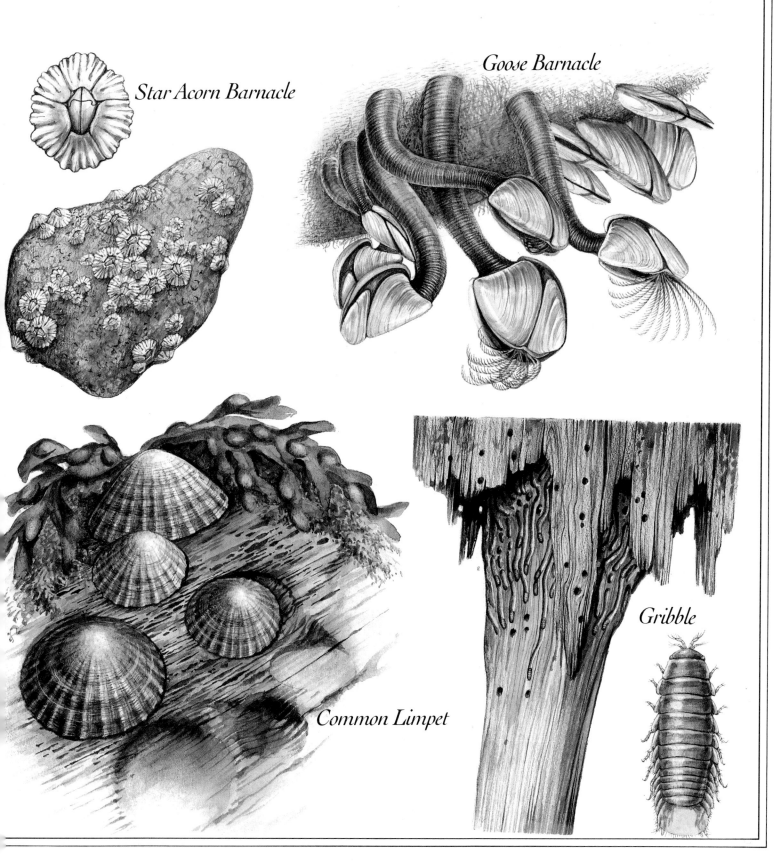

Star Acorn Barnacle

Goose Barnacle

Common Limpet

Gribble

STAR ACORN BARNACLE (Chthamalus stellatus) Occurring only on the south and west coasts, where it replaces the common acorn from the high water zone, this mollusc breeds in summer, and feeds by trapping organic debris with its legs extended through the opening.

COMMON LIMPET (Patella vulgata) These molluscs are found on rocks or harbour walls between the mid and upper shores. The strong 'foot' holds fast by means of suction, but they can move to graze on algae. The radially ribbed shell reaches 2½″ (6cm).

GOOSE BARNACLE (Lepas anatifera) Enclosed in a 2″ (5cm) shell of five translucent plates, this barnacle attaches itself to submerged surfaces by an extending stalk 4-8″ (10-20cm) long. A fan of filaments traps minute animals, quickly pulling them into the shell.

GRIBBLE (Limnoria lignorum) A tiny pin-head sized crustacean, the gribble is a pest of submerged structural timbers and boats. It bores into wood in large numbers, making tunnels which soon coalesce, causing decay and then collapse. It is common everywhere.

OUT TO SEA

Out beyond the sight of land, shearwaters, petrels and fulmars hunt for fish rising to graze the surface plankton – visible proof of the life which teems below the waves.

Far from land, waves crash over the ship's decks, scattering foaming water and silvery sand eels. A flying fulmar engrossed in the chase is momentarily stranded on board. In the teeth of the storm the ship ploughs through a sea littered with thousands upon thousands of Manx shearwaters, razorbills, puffins and gannets, all frantically plunge-diving for food.

When rough weather concentrates plankton at the surface, bringing shoals of sprats and sand eels to feed on it, a great number of seabirds may be concentrated in relatively small areas. At other times they are scattered more widely but are nevertheless the most obvious of marine creatures, even in mid-Atlantic over a thousand miles from land.

Most seabirds only come ashore to breed. Gannets spend their winters in inshore waters, seldom more than a couple of miles from land. Razorbills and guillemots move south to the coasts of Biscay in autumn, while terns follow the Atlantic coast as far south as West Africa. Manx shearwaters and great skuas undertake awesome journeys, crossing the Equator to winter off the coast of Brazil, but puffins and kittiwakes ride out the winter storms in mid Atlantic, alongside little auks and Brunnich's guillemots from the high Arctic, enduring some of the worst sea conditions imaginable.

FLYING SKILLS

To survive in the trackless oceans requires special skills. The tiny storm petrel, no bigger than a greenfinch, comes ashore only intermittently during the breeding season, and often spends the winter as far south as the Cape seas off South Africa. With a weak, fluttering flight it lives through the severe storms by feeding sheltered in the lee of huge waves, apparently oblivious to the turmoil all around as it daintily picks plankton from the surface.

The stiff-winged, zig-zagging flight of shearwaters, fulmars and even the black-browed albatross, which occurs off the coast of Scotland in most years, is another adaptation to conditions at sea. By soaring into the wind coming up from the crest of a wave the bird gains height and then turns down wind to glide along the

RAFT OF GUILLEMOTS
Only coming to land to nest, guillemots spend many months at sea, wintering from Norway to Biscay. Food – mainly fish – is caught in a shallow hunting dive from the surface. Because the birds gather in large flocks, or 'rafts', at sea they are particularly prone to oil pollution. Large oil slicks can wipe out thousands of birds.

PREDATORS AND PREY IN THE OPEN SEA

In the sea, the smaller a creature is, the more predators it is likely to have. Plankton – too small to be shown here – is the food on which all sea life ultimately depends. It is eaten by sprats, squid, jack-sail-by-the-wind, Portuguese men-of-war, storm petrels and the huge basking sharks. Sprats and other small fish fall prey to squid, Portuguese men-of-war, and to medium sized fish such as herring and mackerel. Porpoises and most seabirds feed primarily on small and medium sized fish. The skuas, however, rather than catching their own, generally force other seabirds to disgorge their catch. At the top of the predatory chain, the killer whale hunts anything that's large enough to be worthwhile – big fish, seabirds, porpoises, other large whales and even – in Arctic seas – polar bears.

KEY TO THE SPECIES

1 Sooty shearwater	11 Portuguese man-of-war
2 Razorbill	12 Guillemots
3 Arctic skua	13 Puffin
4 Great skua	14 Storm petrel
5 Manx shearwater	15 Sprats
6 Gannet	16 Squid
7 Killer whale	17 Herring
8 Cormorants	18 Mackerel
9 Common porpoise	19 Basking sharks
10 Jack-sail-by-the-wind	

SCHOOL OF KILLER WHALES
*(above) Growing up to 30ft
long, these toothed whales
are found in all oceans and
are fairly common in British
waters. They are finely
tuned hunters, able to swim
at over 30 mph in pursuit of
seals, dolphins, seabirds
and large fish. Despite
their fearsome reputation
there is no record of an
unprovoked attack on man.
Schools or 'pods' of 5-20
whales swim together and,
being intelligent mammals,
sometimes co-operate in
hunting down prey.*

HERMIT CRAB LARVA
*(above right) This much
enlarged view shows the
head of a crab larva. These
minute larvae hatch from
eggs carried on the female
hermit crab's abdomen.
Floating to the surface
they swim with other
animal plankton, moulting
several times over a period
of weeks before taking on
adult form.*

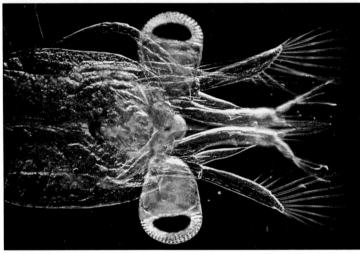

line of the wave trough, before turning and soaring into the wind once more. This zig-zagging manoeuvre is repeated again and again, for it is a very efficient way of covering large distances without expending too much energy — an important consideration when opportunities to feed may be a hundred miles apart.

Migrating land birds cross the open sea, generally at night, and bad weather can lead staggering numbers to seek shelter on ships, lighthouses and oil rigs. Jostling starlings and thrushes throng every perch, while finches and warblers flutter at windows and lights. Many thousands may be involved and dawn can reveal hundreds of dead and dying birds with many more corpses dotting the sea for miles around.

Plankton is a very important part of marine life. Myriad tiny creatures are grouped together under this name, and it includes the larval stages of familiar sea creatures such as crabs, shrimps, shellfish and jellyfish, as well as fish fry, young squid and cuttlefish, and millions of tiny single-celled plants. Plankton is directly eaten by many sea creatures and provides, indirectly, for the needs of practically every other species in the sea.

One plankton eater, the basking shark, is the largest fish in British waters. It grows to thirty

feet and a weight of three tons on a diet of chiefly microscopic organisms.

Eight other shark species occur in the seas off southern and western Britain in summer. Of these the blue, porbeagle and mako are considered dangerous in other parts of the world but there has never been an authenticated attack on humans in British waters.

MAMMALS AT SEA

There are relatively few mammals in the open sea. Common porpoises, though, are frequently encountered offshore, particularly in late summer, while bottle-nosed dolphins and pilot whales pass through British waters on their southerly migration from the Arctic seas to wintering grounds off western Britain and northern Spain, often coming within sight of land.

Ten species of dolphin and fifteen species of whale occur in British waters, although many are extremely rare. Fin whales move south in autumn from their Arctic breeding grounds and once supported a whaling industry based in the Outer Hebrides. Species like killer whales, Risso's dolphin and the huge Rorquals are not often seen, but provide an experience without equal if observed at close quarters.

Less glamorous but equally interesting are

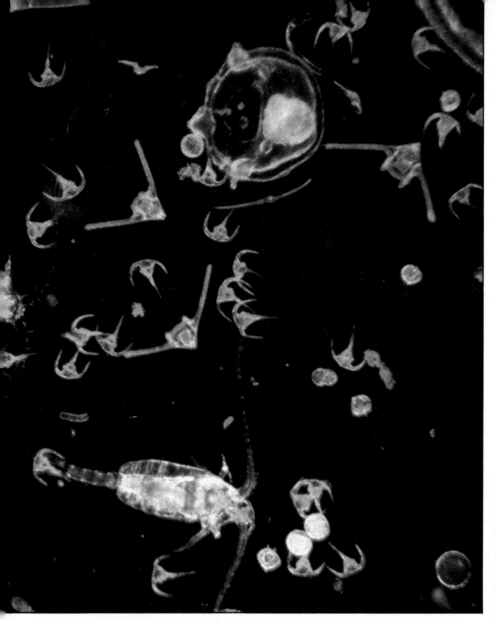

GANNETS ON A FISHING FLIGHT
(above) Locating shoals of herring, mackerel or whiting from the air, gannets dive from a height after their prey. Birds winter offshore in the Channel, the Bay of Biscay and as far south as West African waters.

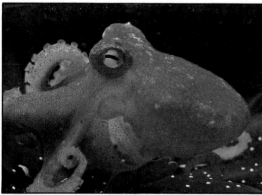

the invertebrates, particularly jellyfish and squid. On calm summer days jellyfish are easy to watch as they pulsate through the warm surface water trailing their tentacles. The common jellyfish, which is largely colourless, is the species most frequently seen. Rarer forms include the brown compass jellyfish – it has dark compasslike markings – and the greeny-grey Rhizostoma which grows to three feet in diameter.

The Gulf Stream brings a warm current across the North Atlantic from the Caribbean and drifting in its surface waters are several creatures which occasionally turn up off western Britain. The Portuguese man-of-war appears to be a jellyfish but is actually a hydrozoan, a complex colony of different individual animals each adapted to carry out specific functions: feeding, attack, defence, movement or reproduction.

Another hydrozoan is Jack-sail-by-the-wind, which resembles an oval of dark blue flattened plastic with a diagonal fin on top. It drifts under the influence of the wind, using its fin as a sail, and may be attacked by the violet sea snail. This snail is an unlikely surface-drifter but it manages the feat by expelling a mucus bag from its shell and trapping air bubbles in it to create a float.

Squids have a complex communal breeding cycle which results in certain areas of the sea

DENIZENS OF INNER SPACE
(above) Marine plankton comes in an extraordinary and dramatic variety of shapes and has been the inspiration for space aliens in countless films. The microscopic plankton shown here includes the larvae of jellyfish and a mollusc, along with numerous copepods – microscopic free-living crustaceans which are important as fish food.

LESSER OCTOPUS
(above right) Slightly smaller than the common octopus, the lesser octopus shares the ability to quickly change colour to match its background. It is found all around British coasts, and feeds mainly on crabs.

swarming with countless thousands of squid during mating and egg-laying. As with shoaling fish these congregations attract vast numbers of seabirds, sharks and porpoises, as well as commercial fishermen. When egg-laying is complete most of the squid die, the future of the population depending on the survival of sufficient of the eggs that lie in great clusters on the sea floor.

Oceanic fish like the herring live in vast shoals, sometimes containing several thousand tons of fish. The North Sea herring population falls into two main groups, one which spawns off the north-east coast of Scotland and winters in the Skagerrak, between Denmark and Norway, the other spawning in the southern North Sea and wintering in the Straits of Dover. Wherever they occur herring are an important source of food for birds, mammals and larger predatory fish.

The oceans are wonderfully rich in species, many of them dramatic, but they are threatened by overfishing, pollution and numerous other hazards. The continuing existence of so many exciting species will depend on man's determination to conserve them.

Female Winter

Grey Phalarope

Female Summer

Little Auk

GREY PHALAROPE *(Phalaropus fulicarius)* A tiny 8" (20cm) wader, which actually spends most of its life swimming and feeding on plankton. Both sexes undergo a seasonal change of plumage. It nests in the Arctic and the duller male incubates the 4 olive eggs.

LITTLE AUK *(Alle alle)* The smallest diving seabird at 8" (20cm) long, it is only seen close to land following gales submerging frequently for small fish. It nests in vast colonies amongst boulders on arctic islands, where it lays a single pale green egg in May or June.

POMARINE SKUA *(Stercorarius pomarinus)* A large 20" (51cm) gull-like bird with twisted tail feathers. It harries other seabirds to steal their food. Seen around the coastline during spring and autumn it breeds on the ground on arctic tundra, and lays 2-3 olive-brown eggs.

Wintering Seabirds

Long-tailed Skua

Brünnich's Guillemot

Female Winter

Female Summer

Red-necked Phalarope

Pomarine Skua

LONG-TAILED SKUA (*Stercorarius longicaudus*) 20″ (51cm) long, this elegant, aggressive seabird is seen off the west coast during its spring and autumn migration. Spending the winter at sea it breeds on the arctic tundra, feeding on lemmings, and lays 2 green eggs.

BRÜNNICH'S GUILLEMOT (*Uria lomvia*) An extremely rare winter visitor, this 16½″ (42cm) bird dives for fish well out to sea. It breeds in the high Arctic, laying a single greenish-brown egg on bare rock. It is very similar to the common guillemot, but has a larger bill.

RED-NECKED PHALAROPE (*Phalaropus lobatus*) Like the grey phalarope this rare 7″ (18cm) wader spins on the water to stir up food. It breeds beside arctic pools and (rarely) in the Scottish Isles. The drabber male incubates 4 olive eggs laid in a cup-shaped nest.

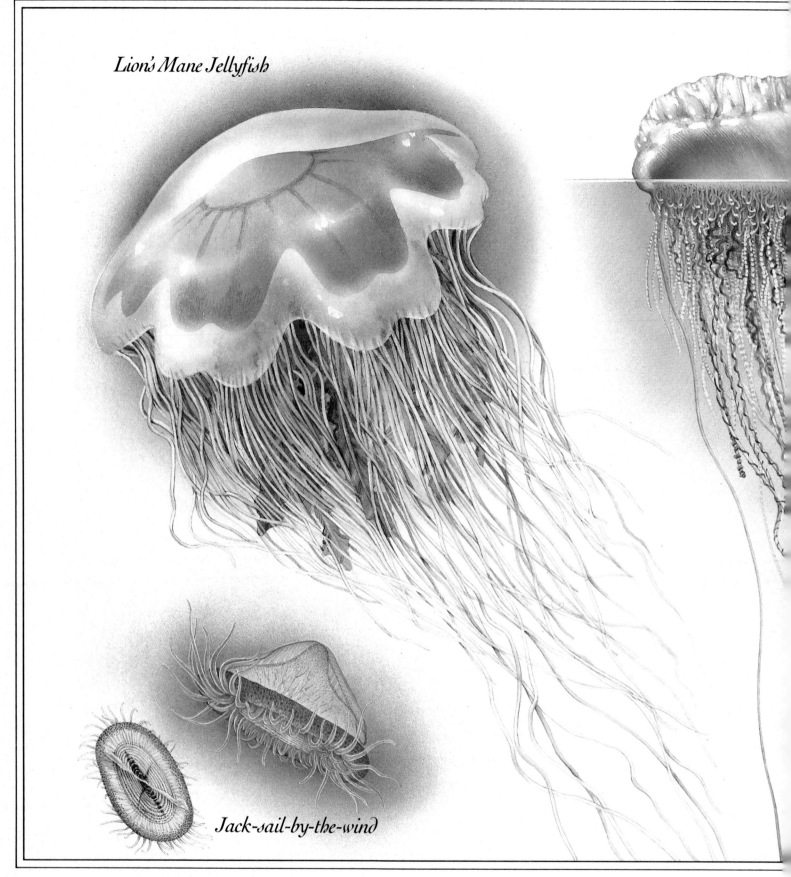

Lion's Mane Jellyfish

Jack-sail-by-the-wind

LION'S MANE JELLYFISH
(*Cyanea capillata*) So called because of its frilly tentacles, this widespread jellyfish, over 20″ (50cm) in diameter, can enter coastal waters. It may be accompanied by whiting, which seem to be immune to the stinging tentacles.

JACK-SAIL-BY-THE-WIND
(*Velella velella*) A colonial relative of the jellyfish, 3″ (8cm) in diameter, with a raised sail to catch the wind. A ring of tentacles captures prey and special cells release free-swimming, jellyfish-like medusae which develop into new colonies.

PORTUGUESE MAN-OF-WAR
(*Physalia physalis*) Not strictly a jellyfish but a colony of animals or polyps supported by a gas-filled float 12″ (30cm) long. Stinging tentacles up to 66′ (20m) long paralyse prey such as small fish, and are painful to humans.

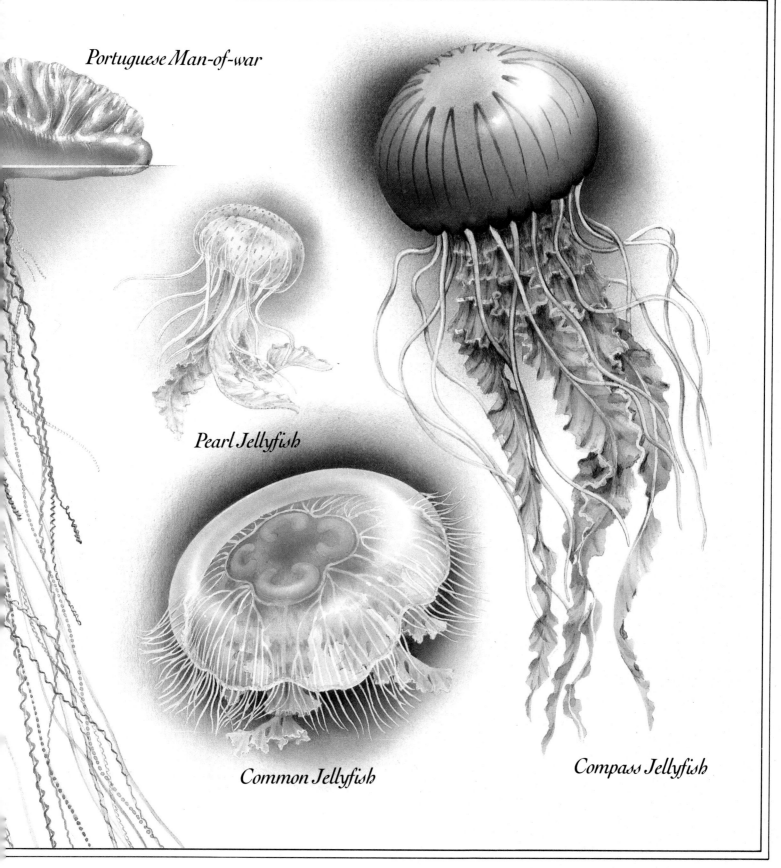

Portuguese Man-of-war

Pearl Jellyfish

Common Jellyfish

Compass Jellyfish

PEARL JELLYFISH (*Pelagia noctiluca*) A hazard to fishermen, the 12 tentacles of this small uncommon jellyfish, 4″ (10cm) in diameter, can inflict a very painful sting. If disturbed at night it 'lights up' and leaves a phosphorescent slime on anything it touches.

COMMON JELLYFISH (*Aurelia aurita*) Up to 10″ (25cm) in diameter this jellyfish swims gently but is easily carried by currents. Eggs released by four violet-pink reproductive organs produce larvae which attach themselves to rocks, and develop into tiny new jellyfish.

COMPASS JELLYFISH (*Chrysaora hyoscella*) Radiating streaks divide the edge of the body into 32 lobes and gives this 12″ (30cm) jellyfish its name. Four long mouth arms extend beyond the 24 tentacles to attract and catch fish, crustaceans and even other small jellyfish.

Herring

Skate

Witch

HERRING *(Clupea harengus)*
A wide-ranging, free-swimming fish, up to 16″ (40cm) long, found in vast shoals where the cold arctic waters meet the gulf stream. It moves to the surface at night to feed on small marine creatures, and lays up to 50,000 eggs.

SKATE *(Raja batis)* A large 5′ (1½m) member of the shark family, sometimes weighing 220lb (100kg), with a pointed snout and spines on its tail. It feeds in deep water on bottom-living fish. Its familiar 'mermaid's purse' egg-cases are sometimes washed ashore.

WITCH *(Glyptocephalus cynoglossus)* A small, elongated 20″ (50cm) deepwater flatfish whose tiny mouth restricts it to feeding on small invertebrates. It has a rough upper surface and a sharp spine near the anal fin and is fished for commercially.

Pelagic Fish

Cod

Halibut

Haddock

HALIBUT *(Hippoglossus hippoglossus)* The largest flatfish – on average about 3′ 6″ (1m) – it may reach 6cwt (300kg) and measure 12′ (4m). It lives at the bottom of deep water and hunts fish. The larvae turn into flatfish when 1½″ (4cm) long and adults can live 50 years.

COD *(Gadus morrhua)* A large fish with big eyes, an extended upper jaw and single barbel. It prefers deep water where it feeds on invertebrates, and produces up to 5 million eggs. Weighing about 30lb (14kg) it can measure 3′ 6″ (1m) at 20 years.

HADDOCK *(Melanogrammus aeglefinus)* Living close to the sea bed at depths of up to 650′ (200m), the haddock feeds on small fish and invertebrates. The female lays up to 1 million eggs, which float to the surface. Can reach 3′ (1m) and weigh 26lb (12kg) but is usually 12″ (30cm).

Saggital Squid

Common Squid

Lesser
Octopus

SAGGITAL SQUID (*Ptodarodes saggitatus*) An arrow-shaped squid with side fins joined at the tip of a 24″ (60cm) body. The longest tentacles cannot be withdrawn. Mainly confined to the South and West, it feeds on fish and is often found near the surface at night.

LESSER OCTOPUS (*Eledone cirrhosa*) A small octopus up to 20″ (50cm) long, with a single row of suckers. Found in rocky crevices at low tide during the summer, it feeds on crabs which it kills with its venomous bite. Females lay up to 150,000 eggs, which they guard until hatching.

COMMON SQUID (*Loligo forbesi*) Widespread but uncommon inshore, it is recognized by triangular side fins on a pink, red or brown 24″ (60cm) torpedo-shaped body. The horny internal shell is sometimes found on the strand-line. Eggs are laid in deep-water spawning grounds.

Cephalopods

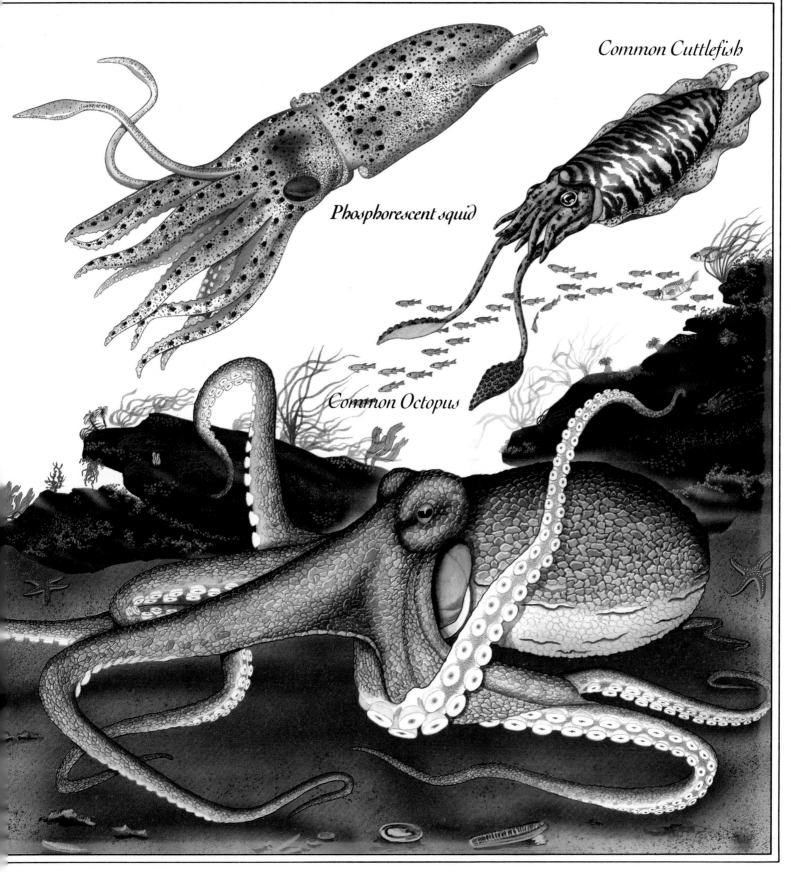

Common Cuttlefish

Phosphorescent squid

Common Octopus

PHOSPHORESCENT SQUID (*Histioteuthis bonelliana*) A strange deep water species, 5½″ (14cm) long, with one eye much larger than the other. Its body is covered in light-producing organs, which cause it to glow in the dark depths and may also attract small invertebrates.

COMMON OCTOPUS (*Octopus vulgaris*) Sometimes reaching 40″ (100cm), the tentacles bear a double row of suckers, and change colour to match the background. Found in crevices or a constructed lair, it feeds on crabs, and squirts ink to confuse predators. Eggs are laid in strings.

COMMON CUTTLEFISH (*Sepia officinalis*) A relative of the squid, the cuttlefish has 10 tentacles, and side fins running the length of its flattened 12″ (30cm) body. It is capable of rapid colour change. The internal shell or cuttlebone is often found on the shore.

Pilot Whale

Killer Whale

PILOT WHALE *(Globicephala melaena)* These toothed whales can grow to nearly 30ft (9m) and may live for 50 years. They breed during the winter and spring and live in large schools of up to 500 individuals. They breathe, as do all whales, by means of a blow hole on their heads. As they surface, a distinctive spume of air and water vapour marks their position. They dive down with a sinking motion to depths of over 3300ft (1000m) and can stay submerged for up to two hours. Normal feeding dives, however, only last 5-10 minutes.

Whales

Bottle-nosed Whale

KILLER WHALE *(Orcinus orca)*
A ferocious hunter and a strong and powerful swimmer, the killer whale is the world's fastest marine mammal over short distances, achieving speeds of almost 35 mph (56km/h). Its diet consists of most warm-blooded sea creatures, such as seals, penguins, porpoises and other whales – it has even been known to attack sharks and polar bears. Old males grow to 30ft (9m) and may weigh up to 8 tons. Females reach 15ft (4m). Killer whales live in groups of 5-20 members and hunt in 'packs'.

BOTTLENOSE WHALE
(Hyperoodon ampullatus) This fast-moving toothed whale migrates north to the Arctic in summer, returning in the autumn through British waters. Males reach 30ft (9m) and females 22ft (7m); at birth calves are 10ft (3m). They swim in small schools of up to 10 animals feeding on small fish and squid, in coastal waters. Like all toothed whales they have pronounced bulbous foreheads. Attracted by the noise of ships' engines and generators they fall easy prey to hunters.

INDEX

Picture credits

Aquila: 12(c) Michael Leach, 30(t) Abraham Cardwell, 30(b) Richard T. Miles, 52(t) E. A. Janes, 53(bl) M & V Lane, 71(t) M & V Lane, 98(c) R. Glover, 106(b) A. I. Bond, 144 M. C. Wilkes, 166 Mike Mockler, 169(br) Premaphotos, 180(tl) M. C. Wilkes, 180 (c) M. Leach, 180(b) M. C. Wilkes, 192 R. H. Fisher, 194 Sawford Castle, 195(c) R. T. Mills, 230(bl) J V & G R Harrison, 230(br) D. I. McEwan.

Ardea: 18, 40(t) Jack A. Bailey, 41(b) J B & S Bottomley, 63 (l) Liz & Tony Bomford, 68 K. W. Fink, 70(b) Ian Beames, 83(tr) J. A. Bailey, 83(bl) Avon, 114(bl) C & J Knight, 190/1, 252(tl) R. J. Blewitt, 304(b) P. Morris.

Biophotos/Heather Angel: 52/3, 98(b), 112(bl), 169(bl), 265(l, r), 276 (inset), 277(b), 291(t, c), 304(t) Soames Summerhays.

David Boag: 157(b).

Bruce Coleman Ltd: 40(c) Andy Purcell, 41(tr) M. Dakin, 52(bl) Jane Burton, 60(t) P. A. Hinchliffe, 62(t) Kim Taylor, 63(r) Jane Burton, 80 Duscher, 81(tl) P. A. Hinchliffe, 83(tl) Hans Reinhard, 83(br) Jane Burton, 105 Gordon Lansbury, 106(tl) Jane Burton, 144/5 Hans Reinhard, 145(br) Jane Burton, 156(tl) Leonard Le Rue, 157(c) Roger Wilmhurst, 168(b) Gordon Lansbury, 181(t) Jane Burton, 195(t) G. Downey, 206/7 R. K. Murton, 228 Gordon Lansbury, 240(b) Gordon Lansbury, 242(inset) O. Langrand, 242/3 © WWF/Eric Dragesco, 243(tl), 243(b) Pekka Helo, 253(t) Neville Fox Davies, 253(b) Hans Reinhard, 264/5 G. Lansbury, 290(c) John F. Taylor.

John Glover: 13(tl, b).

Brian Hawkes: 13(tr), 277(t).

Eric and David Hosking: 20/1, 180(tr), 288, 290(tr) Dr P. Wilson, 305(t) Dr P. Wilson.

Frank Lane Picture Agency: 30(c), 31(t) Peggy Heard, 40(b) D. Grewcock, 51(t) Silvestris, 71(bl) W. Broadhurst, 82(b) A. J. Roberts, 230(t) M. J. Thomas, 276/7 Roger Tidman.

Natural History Photographic Agency: 12(t) Stephen Dalton, 21(b) Michael Leach, 70(tl) John Shaw, 70/1 Stephen Dalton, 81(tr) Stephen Dalton, 82(t) J & M Bain, 98(t) Manfred Danegger, 106(tr) Stephen Dalton, 107(c) Manfred Daneger, 144(t) Stephen Dalton, 115(b) Stephen Dalton, 124 Manfred Danegger, 126(tl) John Buckingham, 154 L. Campbell, 168(t) G. J. Cambridge, 194(t) Melvin Grey, 204 G. J. Cambridge, 206(t) D. N. Dalton, 216 Joe B. Blossom, 218(cr) Stephen Dalton, 231(tr) Stephen Dalton, 250 Stephen Dalton, 252(tr) Stephen Dalton, 260/1 J. & M. Bain, 291(b) L. Campbell, 305 A. E. Janes.

Natural Image: 41(tr) Robin Fletcher, 206(b) Robin Fletcher, 219(bl) Peter Wilson.

Natural Science Photos: 20(t) O. C. Rourke, 31(br) P H & S L Ward, 71(bl) P. Kemp, 142 W. Cane, 145(bl) P H & S L Ward, 168/9 J. Bingley, 169(tr) J. A. Grant, 207(c) Geoffrey Kinns, 207(b) R. Revels, 218(tl) R. Revels, 218(b) C. Kinns, 219(br) J. F. Young, 276 C. A. Walker, 290(b) J. F. Young.

Natural Selection: 13(c), 53(t) Leo Maynes, 243(cr) Geoffrey Kinns.

Nature Photographers: 10 E. A. Janes, 20(b) E. A. Janes, 21(t) Paul Sterry, 21(c) D. Yendall, 38 Martyn Goldbeck, 50(t) Derick Bonsall, 53(br) Derick Bonsall, 62(c) Anthony Wharton, 62(b) Christopher Grey-Wilson, 94/5 Andrew Cleave, 99(b) T. Andrewartha, 101 Christopher Grey-Wilson, 107(t) Michael Leach, 126(t) Andrew Cleave, 126(cr) Paul Sterry, 126(bl) Hugh Clarke, 126(br) Derick Bonsall, 127(tl) T. Andrewartha, 127(tc) Keri Williams, 156(b) Hugh Miles, 178 Paul Sterry, 194(bl) J. Hyett, 195(b) Paul Sterry, 218(tr) Frank V. Blackburn, 240(t) Paul Sterry, 243(tr) Michael Gore, 252 Brinsley Burbidge, 262 Colin Carver, 276(tl) Andrew Cleave, 276(bl) Paul Sterry, 302 Michael Gore.

Oxford Scientific Films: 112(br) G. Bernard, 113 K. Moreton, 114(br) R. Blythe, 115(c) G. Bernard, 157(tr) G. Bernard, 242(b) G. Bernard.

Planet Earth Pictures: 27 John & Gillian Lythgoe, 290(tl) John & Gillian Lythgoe, 305 David Maitland.

Spectrum Colour Library: 9.

Swift Picture Library: 154 M. King, 179(t).

Iain Thornber: 231(b).

Artwork credits

Elaine Anderson: 277(r).

Russell Barnett: 219(t).

Joyce Bee: 63(b), 148/9.

Dick Bonson: 10/1, 18/9, 60/1, 74/5, 172/3, 198/9, 280/1, 294/5, 300/1, 308/9.

Zane Carey: 76/7.

Jim Channell: 127(r).

Jean Colville: 152/3, 200/1, 272/3, 291.

Fiona Currie: 14/5, 24/5, 42/3, 64/5, 88/9, 100/1, 108/9, 122/3, 128/9, 136/7, 158/9, 170/1, 184/5, 226/7, 236/7, 244/5, 258/9, 278/9, 296/7.

John Davis: 31(bl), 118/9, 124/5, 176/7, 210/1.

Brian Delf: 110/1, 182/3, 241.

Jill Dow: 99, 115(t).

Wayne Ford: 214/5.

The Garden Studio: 22/3 Cheryl Wilbraham, 44/5 Craig Austin, 78/9 Craig Austin, 86/7 Craig Austin, 92/3 Lyn Chadwick, 146/7 Liz Peppereli, 188/9 Lyn Chadwick, 196/7 Lyn Chadwick, 208/9 Lyn Chadwick, 220/1 Craig Austin, 254/5 Lyn Chadwick, 292/3 Richard Lewington.

Peter Hayman: 130/1.

Rosalind Hewitt: 134/5, 162/3, 181(b).

Ian Jackson: 186/7.

Karen Johnson: 34/5.

Martin Knowles: 256/7.

Terence Lambert: 120/1, 150/1, 164/5, 174/5, 268/9, 306/7.

Ken Lilly: 102/3.

Linden Artists: 54/5 Tim Hayward, 68/9 Tim Hayward, 80/1 Tim Hayward, 82(c) Mick Loates, 90/1 Mick Loates, 96/7 Tim Hayward, 104/5 Tim Hayward, 112/3 Tim Hayward, 138/9 Trevor Boyer, 142/3 Tim Hayward, 154/5 Graham Allen, 160/1 Mick Loates, 228/9 Tim Hayward, 238/9 Mick Loates, 248/9 Jim Channel, 250/1 Tim Hayward, 270/1 Mick Loates, 275 Tim Hayward, 284/5 Mick Loates, 286/7 Mick Loates, 298/9 Mick Loates, 302/3 Tim Hayward, 310/1 Mick Loates.

Steve Lings: 156(tr).

Dave Mead: 32/3, 66/7, 84/5, 282/3.

Peter Moreton: 56/7.

Tricia Newall: 132/3.

Denys Ovenden: 38/9, 50/1, 166/7, 204/5, 216/7, 288/9.

Virgil Pomfret Agency/Andrew Robinson: 26/7, 36/7, 48/9, 58/9, 224/5.

Chris Rose: 107(b), 242(t).

Mark Russell: 16/7.

Alan Suttie: 312/3, 314/5.

Eric Tenney/The Gallery: 222/3.

David Thompson: 116/7, 266/7.

Gill Tomblin: 140/1.

Barbara Walker: 192/3, 207(t), 232/3, 262/3.

Phil Weare: 88/9.

Mark Woods: 202.

Dep. Leg. B-41861-87